THE MONETARY PROCESS:
ESSENTIALS OF MONEY AND BANKING

Second Edition

ROBERT H. MARSHALL *University of Arizona*

RODNEY B. SWANSON *Security Pacific National Bank*

HOUGHTON MIFFLIN COMPANY   BOSTON
DALLAS   GENEVA, ILLINOIS   HOPEWELL, NEW JERSEY
PALO ALTO   LONDON

COVER: *Calligraphy by Jean Evans*

Printed in the U.S.A.

Library of Congress Catalog Card Number: 79-87857

ISBN: 0-395-26530-4

CONTENTS

PREFACE

A text's revision provides an opportunity for both renewal and reappraisal. Renewal emerges from retaining those distinctive features and strengths found in the first edition. At the same time, reappraisal occurs in light of operating results from the classroom and from the monetary sector's changing nature. The decade of the 1980s reflects the ongoing monetary developments and forces of the late 1970s. Thus this revision continues the first edition's emphasis on the *monetary process,* which includes the different evolving monetary institutions that elicit new (or at least modified) theoretical explanations of monetary phenomena. In turn, this institutional and theoretical background facilitates a careful study of monetary policy—society's actions affecting the monetary sector for the economy's welfare.

The basic objective of the book is to impart an integrated understanding of the monetary process within the modern economy, with particular reference to the United States. As such, the text is designed primarily for use in one-term college courses in money and banking, where the emphasis is on general knowledge that can be related to other courses. For those few courses extending over an academic year (or at least two academic quarters), the book may well be supplemented by any one of several published readings in money and banking.

Many tables and figures in the text as well as the suggested readings at the end of each chapter draw heavily on various publications of the Federal Reserve System. This emphasis is intentional. Especially in recent years, the Federal Reserve has been a key source of timely, lucid writing on various monetary topics. Furthermore, this material has good professional polish, is readily available or can be freely duplicated, and affords a real sense of the living drama in the monetary process.

In addition to Federal Reserve publications, we make frequent reference to other sources of information—both statistical and analytical—that afford general background for the professional business and economic decision maker. Generally these references are only illustrative, since the monetary process undergoes constant change. Knowing where to seek information is a vital aspect of the learning experience. Knowledgeable understanding of the monetary process requires an awareness of some of the major outlets for economic intelligence data.

The book consists of six parts. Major changes have been introduced throughout the text with considerable culling and compressing of material, especially in Parts Two and Three.

Part One provides an overview of the economy and the monetary process, and it discusses monetary standards, both past and present. Ongoing financial innovations and regulatory changes necessitated a new chapter (Chapter 3) on credit markets and financial institutions.

Part Two retains and augments a distinctive feature of the first edition: an industrial organization approach to commercial banking (especially Chapters 5 and 6).

Part Three provides an expanded, updated coverage of monetary policy variables, including monetary and reserve aggregates as well as interest rates (Chapters 9 and 10).

Part Four presents the core material on international economics. Chapters 12 and 13 offer a more analytical approach to understanding the basis for trade, U.S. international transactions, and various exchange rate mechanisms. Although the fixed and flexible exchange rate systems are emphasized, alternative suggestions for revising the world international monetary system are included as well as a discussion of special drawing rights (SDRs). Many traditional texts relegate the analysis of international monetary phenomena to the very end of the book. As a result, the student receives a truncated understanding of the international monetary process. Inclusion of the international monetary sector in an earlier part of the book permits a better balanced and integrated rendering of the theoretical and policy aspects of the monetary process.

Part Five covers the main aspects of monetary theory, with reasonable emphasis on the theory of income determination (Chapter 15). Various multipliers have been added in this edition for a more complete presentation. The theory chapters have been substantially revised for a better presentation of the monetarist model and a clearer comparison of the Keynesian and mone-tarist positions on monetary and fiscal policy (Chapters 16–20). Furthermore, Chapter 20 includes a separate section on the crowding-out effect.

Part Six includes a discussion of the lags in monetary and fiscal policy and their importance in formulating monetary and fiscal policy, together with relevant empirical data (Chapter 21). It also contains a discussion of the difficulty of using monetary and fiscal policy to achieve the macroeconomic goals of society: high-level employment, price level stability, international equilibrium, and a desirable economic growth rate (Chapter 22). The Phillips curve model is presented as well as a comparison of actual versus potential real GNP growth paths.

The book is written with the recognition that the study of the monetary process not only is socially significant but also can be a fascinating and intellectually rewarding experience. If this volume contributes in any measur-able way to this view, the authors will feel amply rewarded.

Like any such undertaking, this project reflects the assistance and encour-agement of many individuals. Over the years, Professor Marshall's many classes in money and banking at the University of Arizona have provided effective battle-testing of topical coverage and presentation for the revision. We are indebted to John David Ferguson of Miami University, Dale R. Funderburk of East Texas State University, Charles Lieberman of the Federal Reserve Bank of New York, and Stephen Miller of the University of Connect-icut for reviewing the manuscript and offering many helpful suggestions. Several graduate assistants from the Department of Economics, University of Arizona, rendered valuable service: John Cardwell, David Eagleton, Robert Furgerson, Mounir Rached, and Steven H. Wade. We offer sincere thanks to Loretta Unterkofler, who did the greatest part of the typing, to Margaret Robinson of Perth, Western Australia, and to Marylou Eslava and Kay Hattori in Los Angeles. Our deep appreciation goes also to the staff at Houghton Mifflin for their part in the undertaking. The authors accept responsibility for any errors of omission and commission.

R. H. M.

R. B. S.

Part One

MONEY, FINANCE, AND
THE ECONOMY

Chapter One

THE ECONOMY AND THE
MONETARY PROCESS

All modern economies are highly complex and interrelated. The complex mechanism of the modern economy is directed toward solving several basic economic problems: (1) What goods and services will be produced and in what way? (2) How much of each good and service will be produced? (3) How will the goods and services be distributed among users? (4) How will the future growth and productivity of the economy be assured? Answers to these and other related questions must be developed continuously if the economic system is to provide for the economic welfare of its citizens.

In meeting these needs the modern economy necessarily includes the basic economic processes of production, distribution, consumption, saving-investment, and financing the government. In turn, essential economic organizational units coordinate the economic decision making of many millions of individuals through the operations of firms, households, and government. These organizational units perform the basic economic processes in the market. The market affords a mechanism through which economic activity and decision making can be coordinated and performed.

THE STUDY OF ECONOMICS
DEFINED

This oversimplified description of the modern economy indicates the orientation of economics as a study area. In general terms, the study of *economics* is concerned with how society administers and uses scarce resources to satisfy the relatively limitless wants and needs of its members. Stated another way, the study of economics examines how society adapts to the ever-present problem of scarcity in the world. To deal with scarcity, society develops various economic processes and organizational units that work through the market to allocate scarce resources among various wants and needs of varying importance. Thus we can develop answers to the basic economic questions mentioned earlier. Essentially, then, economics is a social science, since it studies those aspects of human behavior relating to the scarcity condition.

It should be recognized that we are not completely economic beings. An individual is a "many-splendored thing" who exhibits simultaneously other kinds of behavior such as love, religious expression, political activity, and so on that interact with and modify economic behavior. But the economist, while acknowledging the complexity of human behavior, must nevertheless concentrate primarily on economic behavior (responses to the scarcity condition) in order to make the field of study manageable.

In making decisions affecting the use of scarce resources, society develops certain institutional arrangements that facilitate the economizing process. Broadly defined, economic institutional arrangements include all the customs, habits, laws, and devices that facilitate economizing behavior. One important set of economic institutional arrangements, among many others, is to be found in the monetary sector.

THE STUDY OF MONETARY
ECONOMICS DEFINED

Stated simply, the study of monetary economics examines the role of money in the economy's administration and use of scarce resources. The emphasis is on the monetary process, which includes the development of various monetary institutions and arrangements, the formulation of monetary theory, and policy alternatives for influencing money to stabilize the economy. A study of the monetary process in its various facets of institutions, theory, and policy permits an understanding of how the monetary sector affects the overall allocation of resources and the aggregate performance of the economy. Aggregate performance encompasses the determination of total levels of output, income, employment, and prices in the economy.

Note particularly that the study of monetary economics is not directed toward bank management or financial management considerations. Although the study of monetary economics is important to financial managers, this text is not oriented toward the daily financial management problems either of general institutions or of financial ones. Many bank management and corporate finance textbooks focus on the internal operations of the firm and the formulation of internal decision making that bears on the technical management of the firm. In contrast, monetary economics studies how the monetary sector affects the overall working of the economy. This aggregative approach entails primarily (though not exclusively) the use of *macroeconomic analysis*. This analysis involves the study of how broad aggregates—in this case the monetary sector—influence total economic performance.

A balanced knowledge of the monetary process requires an understanding of the internal organization and operation of monetary institutions such as the commercial banking system, the central banking system, and the national Treasury. Thus some use is made of *microeconomic analysis,* that is, the study of individual parts within the economy. The theory of the banking firm and the determination of the individual price called the interest rate also require the use of microeconomic analysis. Microeconomic analysis enhances knowledge of the monetary process within the economy.

THE IMPORTANCE OF STUDY: THEORY AND POLICY

The study of the monetary process is worthwhile. First, an integrated understanding of the monetary process within a modern economy, with particular reference to the United States economy, should appeal to the intellectual curiosity of any student. The monetary process is a vital force bearing upon the performance of the economic society. And it is within this society that individuals conduct the many activities necessary for making a living and enjoying the fruits of responsible citizenship.

Second, professional business and economic decision makers must consider the monetary process a major factor in the broad context of a given decision-making situation. Here the knowledge has some degree of relevance to the economic position of the decision maker.

Viewed from this general background, monetary economics involves the development of a body of knowledge for understanding not only *how* the monetary process works within the modern economy but also *how well* it facilitates the achievement of various economic goals of the society. These latter facets of the monetary process comprise the development of knowledge for knowledge's sake, strictly speaking. Beyond this purely intellectual exercise an additional compelling reason exists for gaining knowledge of the monetary process—to improve the effectiveness of the monetary process in the economy. Therefore, we examine alternative lines of action for modifying the monetary process so that it can best encourage the attainment of economic welfare. The specific definition of economic welfare will vary from society to society and will also change over time in a given society. Nevertheless, informed students must consider the area of policy alternatives. The examination of policy actions is tied closely to such important general considerations as price inflation or price deflation, economic growth, employment, the distribution of income, economic efficiency, and economic freedom. Thus a major thrust of the study of the monetary process is directed to the question of monetary policy in the economy. It is in the policy sphere that the power of knowledge can be applied to the attainment of a more effective working of the monetary process.

MONEY DEFINED: THE COMMODITY AND LEGAL APPROACHES

A starting point in the study of the monetary process is to establish a definition of money. A definition of money enables us to distinguish monetary phenomena from other kinds of phenomena in the economy and provides a definite scope or orientation to the study of the monetary process.

On first glance, defining money appears to be ridiculously easy. Is not money used almost daily by most people in a modern economy? Do not most individuals want more money? Is there not a glamor or romance connected with the very idea of money? Is not money so basic and commonplace that we take it for granted, much like breathing? Indeed; but very often the most familiar thing is the most misunderstood thing.

Consider some possible approaches to arriving at a definition of money. Should money be defined in terms of the commodity or material of which it consists? A moment's reflection reminds us that, over the centuries and in the various societies in which money has been used, many things have served as money. Starting with such crude commodities as grain, cattle, salt, spices, and wampum (a jewelry money of North American Indian fame), money later evolved to such relatively sophisticated items as pieces of precious metals, coins, and circulating notes.[1] Today a major type of money consists of demand deposits in commercial banks. These demand deposits are monetary liabilities of commercial banks and have little physical embodiment other than the bank drafts or checks used to make transfers of ownership of demand deposits. Obviously no suitable general definition of money can be established on the basis of the material of which it consists.

Another possible approach is to define money in legal terms. Here the emphasis is on the various laws and powers of the different governments that have issued money. Might not money be defined in terms of the legal stamp (figuratively or literally) of the authority creating it?[2] Here again, a general working definition is difficult to achieve. Many different nations and states have issued money at various times, and very often these issues subsequently did not perform effectively as money.

For example, the history of the United States provides instances wherein government-issued money ceased to serve as money. During the American Revolution large amounts of currency were issued by the Continental Congress to finance the American war of independence from England. In time, this currency ceased to serve as money despite the insistence of the Continental Congress that it was legally money. To this day, the phrase "not worth a Continental" is used to denote worthlessness. Similar results eventually ensued for the currency issued by the Confederate States of America during the Civil War in the United States.

The twentieth century provides many examples of the demise of various monies issued by governments that became defunct, including the Weimar Republic of post–World War I Germany (1919–1933), Hitler's Third Reich (1933–1945), the Hungarian government prior to the Communist takeover, and the Nationalist Chinese government on the mainland of China, which fell after World War II.

---

1. For a fascinating and informative account of the almost limitless ingenuity evident in the development of different kinds of money at different times and in various societies, see Paul Einzig, *Primitive Money, in Its Ethnological, Historical, and Economic Aspects* (London: Eyre & Spottiswoode, 1949).

2. Some writers have stressed legality aspects in defining money. The most notable statement of this position, which most observers still find lacking, is by G. F. Knapp in *The State Theory of Money*, trans. from German by H. M. Lucas and J. Bonar (London: Macmillan & Co., 1924).

The Weimar Republic's fate is especially well documented by historians. The astronomical price inflation experienced by the struggling infant republic underlines the shortcomings of a legal approach to defining money. By late 1919, the wholesale price index for Germany was more than eight times the 1914 level. A year later, the index was fourteen times higher, and by year-end 1921, it was thirty-five times greater. Then the index really took off. In late 1922 it zoomed to almost five hundred times the pre–World War I level. By the time the republic collapsed in late 1923, prices were more than one *trillion* times the 1914 average. This almost mind-boggling inflation brought out more than just the wheelbarrows in which to transport the paper currency. The resourceful Germans redid some of the smaller denominations of Reichsbank notes. For instance, the original one-thousand-mark notes were overprinted in red ink and transformed into billion- (milliarde) mark notes (see Figure 1.1).

Figure 1.1   REICHSBANK NOTE ISSUED BY THE WEIMAR REPUBLIC
IN EARLY 1920s

One-thousand-mark note overprinted as one-milliard-(billion-) mark note

MONEY DEFINED: THE
FUNCTIONAL APPROACH

A more satisfactory means of defining money emphasizes the *functional* or operational characteristics of money. Economists cannot use the approach of the chemist, who can define chemical elements and compounds on the basis of their chemical properties. To the chemist, for example, the compound known as water is defined chemically as anything that has a molecular structure consisting of two atoms of hydrogen and one atom of oxygen. In symbolic language, the chemist writes water as the familiar H_2O. Thus any substance that has this composition would be labeled water by the chemist. The essential point is that the chemist defines chemical substances on the basis of precise molecular composition. As has been shown earlier, the economist cannot define money on the basis of its composition given the historical development of money.

Devising an effective definition of money is a much more difficult task. Unable to define with the same precision as a physical scientist, the economist is compelled to develop a functional definition of *money* by saying "Money is as money does." A functional definition requires an examination of the essential features or characteristics of money, features that can stand the test of time or place. Anything that has the basic characteristics of money would be defined as money, regardless of its specific physical or legal attributes.

In functional terms, money is defined as anything that exhibits simultaneously the following two properties: (1) fixity of price stated in terms of a basic measuring unit, and (2) general acceptability in payment for goods and services or in payment of debt. Each of these two basic features of money will now be examined and explained.

Fixity of Price

Money is the only asset whose price is fixed in terms of the basic monetary unit of measurement. The price fixity of money arises as soon as the basic monetary unit of measurement is established in a given society or place. The monetary unit of measurement can be set in an explicit, formal fashion, such as when a government declares the basic unit. In its early years the United States of America established the dollar as the basic monetary unit through specific legislation. Thus, as soon as the dollar was declared to be the unit of measurement, the price of a dollar was fixed. Paraphrasing the familiar line "A rose is a rose is a rose," one can say, "A dollar is a dollar is a dollar." Stated in different words, the price fixity of money implies that the price of a dollar is a dollar. Money's price fixity does *not* mean fixed real value or purchasing power, however. Purchasing power, as we shall see later, refers to command over real goods and services. Many of us know first hand the dollar's shrinking purchasing power as the general price level rises.

Once the basic monetary unit is established, then all monetary quantities can be expressed as either multiple units or fractional units of the monetary unit of measurement. To illustrate, the price of one hundred dollars is one hundred dollars; the price of a dime is one tenth of a dollar; the price of a cent is one hundredth of a dollar, and so on.

Even in those instances where no formal monetary unit of measurement is established, a basic unit of measurement is implied. An excellent example is the emergence of the cigarette as the basic monetary unit of measurement among Allied soldiers and airmen in German prisoner-of-war camps during World War II. The cigarette money of Stalag 17 fame had the essential property of price fixity, much as the dollar does in the United States, or the pound sterling in Great Britain, or the franc in France.[3] In essence, once the cigarette was used as money, the price of the money was implicitly fixed. Indeed, in the prison camp the price of a cigarette was a cigarette.

General Acceptability

The second essential feature of money is its general acceptability in exchange for goods and services or in payment of debt. Money becomes a device by which one can rid oneself of debt—debt arising either from current purchases of goods and services or from obligations incurred in an earlier period. As long as whatever is used as money commands general and willing acceptance by the members of a given society, then it is money, functionally speaking. On the other hand, as soon as the general acceptance property is seriously eroded or questioned, then the money ceases to be money.

---

3. See Richard A. Radford, "The Economic Organization of a Prison Camp," *Economica* 12 (November 1945): 189–201, for an interesting, well-documented account by a former POW of the use of cigarette money in a German prison camp. This study details the use of cigarette money in facilitating the various economic processes within the "camp economy."

Viewed in this light, it is clear why the Continental Congress currency or the currency issued by the Confederate States of America or, in recent memory, the Reichsmarks of Hitler's Germany ceased to be money despite official pronouncements by the governments concerned. People refused to accept these currencies because they considered them worthless; consequently, the currencies were worthless, notwithstanding contrary governmental opinions.

THE FUNCTIONS OF MONEY

Once money is defined as anything that has fixity of price (in terms of the monetary unit of measurement) and general acceptability in payments transactions, it acquires various uses. Recall the example of water in chemistry. When the chemical properties of water are detected, the chemist can determine chemical uses or functions for water that emerge from its inherent chemical properties.

So, too, the basic properties of money determine its use. People are basically functional beings who have learned, often by trial and error, how to use resources for their own beneficial purposes. Money becomes an institutional arrangement or device from which people obtain certain functions. These functions, which are derived from the essential characteristics of money, enable people to satisfy various needs and wants in society. Let us examine briefly some of the more obvious uses or functions of money.

Medium of Exchange

Money's function as a *medium of exchange* emerges from its general acceptability in payments transactions. In our society money serves as a medium of exchange through which transfers of goods and services can be conveniently and efficiently made. The use of money enables people to avoid the cumbersome and inefficient workings of a direct barter system, which requires a coincidence of wants of the parties to the transaction. In simple words, each party in the direct barter transaction must want what the other party has to offer. For example, a butcher who needs shoes must deal with a shoemaker who at the same time wants or needs beefsteaks. At the very least, the butcher must barter with someone who will accept beefsteaks in exchange for shoes.

Little imagination is required to recognize the importance of money as a medium of exchange in a modern economic system. For example, in a barter system involving one hundred goods, a total of 4,950 exchange ratios or prices would exist. The total number of exchange ratios under a barter arrangement is computed from the formula $n(n-1)/2$, where n equals the total number of goods to be exchanged. In contrast, in a system using money, only ninety-nine exchange ratios would exist, because all the prices would be expressed in terms of the commonly accepted means of payment.

The modern economy is a highly specialized, interdependent exchange economy, wherein much of production is indirect; the goods and services are not produced to satisfy directly the wants of the producers. Production is for exchange or sale in the market, and money performs the vital function of facilitating the exchange process between the millions of producers and consumers. Money, in its function as a medium of payment, is the lifeblood of the modern exchange economy.

Unit of Account

The price fixity feature of money provides the essential function whereby a set standard exists for expressing economic values in the market. Money acts as a measuring rod, or *unit of account,* in the economy. The countless decisions involved in conducting the basic economic processes are facilitated by the monetary unit of measurement. The statement of prices, costs, and incomes in monetary units is at the very core of the economizing activity of society. Any efficient accounting system requires a monetary unit of account, whether it be at the level of the individual producer or consumer, or in the form of the National Income and Product Accounts that are estimated by the United States Department of Commerce in its publication *Survey of Current Business.* These accounts provide a systematic approach for measuring the level and composition of total economic activity.

The measuring-rod function of money derives from the price fixity characteristic of money. The basic monetary unit provides a fundamental unit of measurement in which economic values can be expressed. In this aspect money is similar to any unit of measurement; for example, in the United States the unit of length is the foot; the unit of weight is the pound; the unit of electrical energy is the watt. Many examples of physical measurement units can be found in the physical and natural sciences.

Though in its use money is similar to a standard measure, it is at the same time different from the usual standard measure. The basic feature of price fixity of money does not imply fixity in real value or purchasing power. *Purchasing power of money* relates to the ability of a unit of money to command real goods and services in the marketplace. A rising average price for all of the goods and services for which money can be exchanged reflects a declining real value of money, and vice versa. The familiar phenomenon of price inflation (a general rise in the prices of goods and services) illustrates the commonplace observation that the dollar can "shrink."

In its function as a unit of account, money is used to express the payment of obligations that are deferred until some time in the future. People perceive a time horizon, and thus many transactions in the modern economy give rise to payments that will be made only at some subsequent date. The satisfactory expression of these future payments requires a device in which the obligations can be stated with certainty and precision.

Deferred payments arise in any *credit transaction*, in which one party receives current consideration in exchange for a promise to pay the other party in the future. "Going it on the cuff" is an earmark of the modern economy, wherein human ingenuity is reflected in the development of various credit instruments and credit institutions that facilitate countless credit transactions. The importance of credit in the modern economy is illustrated in Table 1.1, which details at the year-end 1976 the outstanding credit extended to various public and private groups in the United States.

We are well on our way to over 3.5 trillion dollars ($3,500,000,000,000) of credit outstanding. Since a credit transaction implies a future debt to be paid, the words *credit* and *debt* are used to refer to the same thing. Two faces to any credit (or debt) transaction exist: the amount owed by the debtor—the debt—is simultaneously the amount due to the creditor—the credit. Credit or debt transactions are a necessary feature of the modern economy. If money can be called the lifeblood of the modern economy, then credit may be viewed as the lubricant of the basic economic processes carried on within the economic system.

Store of Economic Value

A third major function of money arises when money is held as a *store of economic value*, that is, a particular asset from which certain utility (or want-satisfying power) is derived. Here the emphasis is on the use of money as a

Table 1.1   NET PUBLIC AND PRIVATE DEBT, UNITED STATES—
YEAR-END 1976
(billions of dollars)

Public			833.4
Federal government		515.8	
Federal financial agencies		81.4	
State and local governments		236.3	
Private			2,521.5
Corporate		1,414.7	
Individual and noncorporate		1,106.8	
Farm	108.5		
Nonfarm	998.5		
Mortgage	684.1		
Commercial and financial	96.4		
Consumer	217.8		
Total			3,354.9

Source: Adapted from *Economic Report of the President,* January 1978, p. 337.

convenient and special means to hold command over goods and services. Money is only one asset among many by which people can hold command over goods and services. Direct command over goods and services occurs when real tangible assets are held, such as furniture, automobiles, food, drink, housing, real estate, and so on. Assets can also be held in the form of property claims, such as common stocks, bonds, and other types of financial assets.

Any spending unit would hold various kinds of assets, and the relative proportions of the different assets held would change over time depending upon several factors, including expectations, personal preferences, habits and customs, and so forth. Money is a unique asset, because a person holding or owning money holds a special kind of option—that person can exchange the money for any goods or services available in the market. This option exists because money is 100 percent liquid.

All assets have some degree of *liquidity,* which is the characteristic of being convertible into money quickly with little or no loss from fair market value. Since by definition money is already money, it is an asset with complete liquidity. The degree of liquidity of all other assets would range over a broad spectrum from such highly liquid assets as savings deposits in commercial banks and shares in savings and loan associations to such extremely nonliquid assets as specialized machinery or equipment.

The liquidity of money enables people to satisfy a liquidity preference. *Liquidity preference* is the inclination to hold a part of one's assets in the form of money. The concept of liquidity preference can be applied to a single individual, a group of individuals, or an economic system as a whole. Various psychological motives underlie the phenomenon of liquidity preference. As these underlying motives wax and wane, liquidity preference gets stronger or weaker. Liquidity preference is a key concept in the monetary process. The brilliant British economist John Maynard Keynes (1883–1946) ascribed an important role to liquidity preference in affecting the aggregate performance of the economy.

Liquidity preference, according to Keynes, reflects the simultaneous influence of the transactions, precautionary, and speculative motives for holding money. The transactions motive derives from the payment and expenditure patterns that exist in the economy. Expenditures of money income are made on a fairly continuous day-to-day basis, while the receipt of money income occurs intermittently. Thus asset holdings include cash to bridge the gap between the receipt of money income and the relatively continuous expenditure of that income. The strength of the transactions motive for holding cash will be influenced by various factors, including among others the frequency and regularity of income receipts and income disbursements (or payments); the prevailing level of prices for goods and services; the tastes or customs bearing on the relative affluence of the economy; and the availability and use of credit. Many economists focus on the transactions motive by insisting that the essential function of money is not so much as a means of payment, but as a "temporary abode of purchasing power." Here money is viewed basically as a reservoir bridging the gap between the receipt and disbursement of payments.

The precautionary motive in liquidity preference arises from the fact that we are mortals living in an uncertain world in which various unexpected events can and do occur. Precautionary cash holdings provide utility by minimizing the adverse consequences of these events. Once again, various factors affect the intensity of the precautionary motive for holding money, including the availability and use of credit; the development of the institution of insurance; and the costs and other frictional elements affecting the liquidation of both financial and real assets. Some analysts, taking note of the precautionary motive, emphasize money's role as a store of value held to meet *unexpected* transactions. These observers also regard precautionary money holdings as necessary to balance illiquid assets such as long-term securities and nonfinancial assets owned by households and business firms.

The speculative motive for holding money is much more volatile than the transactions and precautionary motives. Its sensitivity derives from the expectations held by people about future prices. Speculative cash holdings reflect people's desire to profit from *expected* price change. Expectations reflect people's ability to extend the time horizon and to act on their conceptions of this time horizon. Expectations are not always realized; nevertheless people base many decisions—economic and otherwise—on the strength of these expectations. Witness the role of expectational analysis as it is used by the businessperson or entrepreneur (who is essentially a bearer of economic risk) in making decisions relating to costs, outputs, and prices. Judgments about these crucial data often contain an expectational element.

This expectational stance imparts a particularly dynamic aspect to liquidity preference. The speculative holding of money generally becomes attractive when there are mounting expectations that the general level of prices will fall and a gloomy or "bearish" outlook about short-term economic conditions. On the other hand, money becomes a relatively unattractive store of economic value when there is a strong or continued expectation of price inflation, that is, a general rise in the level of prices. In this case various nonmonetary assets—such as real estate, plant and equipment, inventories of various kinds, or property claims in the form of common stocks—are more attractive stores of economic value than money. The reverse is true during a period of contraction or depression. These adjustments to a changed liquidity preference affect the monetary process and have implications for the aggregate performance of the modern economy.

THE MONETARY PROCESS AND
ECONOMIC ACTIVITY

The precise definition of money and the examination of the specific uses of money emphasize the significance of the monetary process in the overall

---

Figure 1.2 THE CIRCULAR FLOW OF INCOME

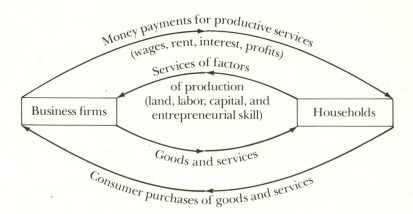

performance of the modern economy. The monetary process is related to the real flow of goods and services in the economy. In effect, the modern economy includes a monetary process and a real process, the latter consisting of the real income of goods and services produced in the economy. The relation between the monetary process and the real process can be illustrated by reference to the *circular flow of income*—both money income and real income (goods and services). Figure 1.2 represents a simplified economy consisting solely of business firms and households (assuming the absence of government and the foreign trade sector) and the resulting money income and real income flows. The inner circle represents the flow of real income, and the outer circle represents the flow of money income. In the upper portion of the diagram the households provide the business firms with the real services of the factors of production (land, labor, capital, and entrepreneurial ability) and receive in return money income in the form of payments for the services of the factors of production (wages, rent, interest, and profits). In the lower portion of the diagram the households make money expenditures to the business firms to purchase the goods and services produced by these firms. The diagram shows the continuous flow of both money income and real income within the simplified economy. Underlying the flow of money income (outer circle) is the flow of real income (inner circle).

Households need not spend all their money income; they can save by postponing the expenditure of part of their money income. Figure 1.3 illus-

Figure 1.3   THE CIRCULAR FLOW OF INCOME WITH SAVING AND
INVESTMENT

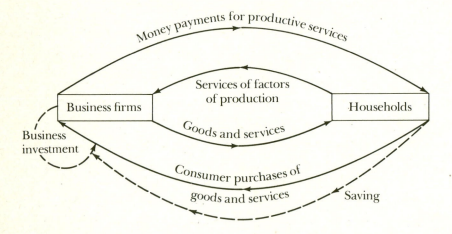

trates saving as a leakage from the spending stream. The greater the saving
the lower the money income of business firms and therefore the less they can
pay to income recipients in the next period. If saving can be channeled into
investment (the purchase and production of capital goods), then the circular
flow of income need not be disturbed. Figure 1.3 shows the return of saving
via investment spending by firms. In this sense, investment can be viewed as
an injection or addition to the spending stream. A later chapter will cover the
significance of the saving-investment process within the economy. At this
point it is sufficient to recognize the general influence of the monetary process
on saving-investment activity. The saving-investment process, in turn, affects
the level of total activity through its impact on the flow of income.

KEY TERMS

Economics	Money
Monetary economics	Medium of exchange
Macroeconomic analysis	Unit of account
Microeconomic analysis	Purchasing power of money

Credit transaction   Liquidity preference
Store of economic value   Circular flow of income
Liquidity

REVIEW QUESTIONS

1. What basic economic problems arise within a modern economy?

2. Define and explain the nature of the study of economics.

3. Give a specific definition of monetary economics.

4. Contrast the use of macroeconomic and microeconomic analysis within the study of monetary economics.

5. List and evaluate briefly some possible approaches to defining money.

6. Discuss briefly, in functional terms, the two basic features or characteristics of money.

7. In the light of its basic features, examine briefly the functions of money.

8. How does money enable a person to satisfy a liquidity preference?

9. With reference to the circular flow of income within a simplified economy, illustrate and explain briefly the relationship between the monetary process and the real process.

SUGGESTED READINGS

Broaddus, Alfred. "Aggregating the Monetary Aggregates: Concepts and Issues." Federal Reserve Bank of Richmond, *Economic Review* (November/December 1975): 3–12.

Einzig, Paul. *Primitive Money, in Its Ethnological, Historical, and Economic Aspects.* London: Eyre & Spottiswoode, 1949.

Friedman, Milton, and Anna Schwartz. *A Monetary History of the United States, 1867–1960.* Princeton, N.J.: Princeton University Press, 1963.

Quiggin, A. Hingston. *A Survey of Primitive Money.* London: Methuen, 1949.

Robertson, Dennis H. *Money.* Rev. ed. New York: Pitman Publishing Corp., 1948.

Wagge, Thomas O. *Money: Master or Servant.* Federal Reserve Bank of New York, 1971.

Yeager, Leland B. "Essential Properties of the Medium of Exchange." *Kyklos* 21 (1968), fasc. 1, pp. 45–69.

Chapter Two

MONETARY STANDARDS:
PAST AND PRESENT

Now that we have discussed what money is and some of its main functions, a next logical step is to see how society attempts to control the quantity and quality or types of money for its own welfare. Actions bearing on the quantity and quality of money are expressed in the particular monetary standard established within a given society. In effect, this specific monetary standard establishes formal guidelines or rules of the game that affect the monetary process.

MONETARY STANDARD DEFINED

Precisely defined, a *monetary standard* includes the overall set of laws, practices, and customs that influence the quantity and quality of money within a given monetary system. It encompasses the various institutional arrangements that determine the quantity and different forms of money within a system.

In general, monetary standards can be classified into two broad types, each with several subtypes: (1) a commodity standard, generally metallic, and (2) an inconvertible "managed" paper standard. Let us examine the distinguishing characteristics of each of these general types of monetary standards.

The Metallic Monetary Standard

The metallic standard is the more common monetary standard historically, dating from early antiquity.[1] A *metallic monetary standard* has three essential

---

1. For example, the Egyptians used gold as money as early as 3400 B.C. In the Western world

characteristics: (1) the definition of the basic monetary unit as a certain weight or quantity of one or more precious metals; (2) complete and unlimited convertibility of metal into money at the official fixed rate of exchange, and vice versa; (3) unrestricted right to import and export the precious metal at the official fixed rate of exchange of money for metal. These three features tie the quantity of circulating money to precious metals, and reflect the automatic discipline exerted by the moneyholders' right to demand redemption in the precious metals.

The Inconvertible "Managed" Paper Standard

The inconvertible "managed" paper standard dates from more recent times. The many nations under a metallic monetary standard were to learn through painful experience that money will not always automatically manage itself in a satisfactory manner. Thus a monetary standard of the inconvertible managed type evolved. Stated briefly, the pure managed paper standard is the diametric opposite of the metallic standard; it is cut off from any formal or set dependence on metal.

The three essential features of the *inconvertible monetary standard* are (1) the definition of the basic monetary unit by simple declaration (or fiat), without any reference to precious metal; (2) absolute inconvertibility of circulating money into precious metal at an official fixed rate; (3) the absence of any connection between the import and export of the precious metal and the formal operation of the monetary standard.

THE EVOLUTION OF MONETARY STANDARDS

As mentioned in the previous section, historical experience with different monetary standards shows a definite evolutionary pattern. This evolution has been away from reliance on a metallic standard, which is typically tied to gold or silver, and toward a managed inconvertible standard. This experience may

---

some of the earliest known coins were the gold and silver coins issued by Croesus, a famous king and merchant of Lydia. The Greeks and the Romans also made wide use of gold coins. During the Middle Ages, Byzantine and Arab gold coins were important for international trade and for hoarding purposes.

be illustrated by a brief examination of the development of the United States monetary system.

In the late eighteenth century the United States emerged as an infant republic from the Revolutionary War. The newly adopted Constitution, which replaced the weak and ineffective Articles of Confederation, reserved to the Congress the "power to coin money, regulate the value thereof, and of foreign coin . . ." and stipulated that "No State shall . . . coin money, emit bills of credit, make anything but gold and silver coin a tender in payment of debt."

The Bimetallic Standard

The Coinage Act of 1792 provided for the establishment of the United States Mint and a bimetallic monetary standard. The dollar, which became the basic monetary unit, was defined as being equal to 371.25 fine grains of silver or 24.75 fine grains of gold, for a mint ratio of 15 to 1.[2] All coins were *full-bodied coins* (metallic commodity value equivalent to face or monetary value), with foreign coins continuing to circulate up through the mid-1800s because of the scarcity of domestic coins.

The bimetallic standard soon encountered difficulty in its operation. Until 1834 gold flowed from the country, partly because it carried a higher value in France, with a mint ratio of 15.5 to 1, and because England adopted a gold standard in 1821. In an attempt to stem the gold outflow the United States changed the mint ratio in 1834 to 16 to 1, which overvalued gold and thus undervalued silver in its monetary use. Consequently, silver coins moved out of circulation. The loss of silver coins handicapped business transactions. Shinplasters (paper currency issued by commercial banks) and other private *token money* (money whose face value exceeds its commodity value) were unsatisfactory in facilitating monetary transactions. Then, in 1853, Congress passed legislation converting fractional silver coins (coins in denominations less than a dollar) into token coins. Even these coins disappeared from circulation during the height of the Civil War inflation.

---

2. The dollar was made the monetary unit of account because of the prevailing use of the Spanish milled dollar (worth eight *reals,* the famed "pieces of eight"), which was more uniform in quality than the variety of shillings issued by the individual states. This foreign coin, along with its fractional parts, continued to circulate as legal tender in the United States until 1857. To this day, the term "two bits" refers to a quarter-dollar.

The experience of various nations using a bimetallic monetary system verifies the operation of a simple phenomenon known as Gresham's law. *Gresham's law* refers to the tendency for overvalued money to remain in circulation while the undervalued money is taken out of circulation and used as a commodity rather than money. The law is named after Sir Thomas Gresham (1519?–1579), a finance minister during the reign of Queen Elizabeth I (1533–1603). Sir Thomas observed that the lighter-weight or worn coins freely circulated as money, whereas the full-weight coins were driven from circulation. As usually stated, the law says that "bad money drives out good money." More precisely, the "bad" money (overvalued in its monetary use) drives out the "good" money (undervalued in its monetary use). The undervalued money is not used as a means of payment, but is removed from circulation and held as a store of value.

The Impact of the Civil War

During the Civil War, and for fourteen years afterward, the United States was in fact on an inconvertible paper standard. The principal circulating media consisted of state and national bank notes, Treasury greenbacks (United States notes), and bank-created demand deposits, since the metallic value of coins rose above their official mint prices.

The Act of 1878 returned the dollar to its pre–Civil War silver-gold parity of 16 ounces of silver to 1 ounce of gold, thus precipitating a sharp deflation in an economy burdened by an inflated price-cost structure arising from the Civil War. An inconvertible paper standard prevailed for some fourteen years after the end of the war largely because no general agreement existed on defining the dollar's metallic content, since United States prices were double prewar levels. Several monetary acts had paved the way for the re-establishment of the prewar standard. Congress ended the free and unlimited coinage of silver dollars in 1873, an action subsequently referred to by "cheap money" proponents as the "Crime of '73." The return to a gold-based dollar was specified in the Gold Resumption Act of 1875. Finally, in 1879, gold convertibility was restored; at that time greenbacks became redeemable in gold.

The Act of 1879 established a de facto gold standard, although legally the country was still on a bimetallic standard. At this same time most of the major

Western European countries had already adopted a gold monetary standard.[3] Following these events silver's position in the United States monetary system declined rapidly. Silver legislation in 1878 and 1890 permitted the Treasury to purchase silver for monetary use, but legally this silver money was not standard money, that is, money in which the Treasury monetary authority could meet its obligations.

In the political arena the money issue loomed large. Generally, the eastern seaboard city dwellers favored "sound money" policies, whereas the debtor rural frontier groups opposed limitations on the money supply, which they attributed to Wall Street manipulation. The defeat of William Jennings Bryan in the presidential election of 1896 largely disheartened the silver supporters, although it left unresolved the more basic issue of "cheap" versus "sound" money. The finale to this eventful period was the Gold Standard Act of March 14, 1900, officially placing the United States on a gold standard.

World War I Developments

World War I brought the suspension of the gold standard by most Western nations. Gold accumulated in the hands of the national monetary authorities as nations eliminated convertibility and the free exporting of gold. At the end of the war in 1919 the United States removed these restrictions, thereby returning to a full-fledged gold coin standard, with no change in the dollar's pre-war gold content. Other countries, recovering slowly from the inflationary effects of war financing, delayed the return to a gold standard: Great Britain adopted it in 1925 and France in 1928. Typically, the Western European nations returning to gold adopted a gold bullion standard, under which coinage of gold was abolished and other types of money were not necessarily redeemable in gold. In addition, the national government bought and sold gold in unlimited quantities at a fixed price, with gold serving as a monetary reserve and as a means of international payment.

---

3. For example, the Peel Act of 1844 reconstituted the monetary authority of the Bank of England by specifically limiting its fiduciary note issue (notes backed by government bonds) and requiring any additional amounts of notes to be fully backed by gold. Similarly, in 1871 the German Reichsbank's notes required a gold cover when the German Empire changed from a silver to a gold standard.

At this time some countries established a gold exchange standard, whereby the monetary unit is defined not in gold but in the currency of the particular country that is on either a gold coin or gold bullion standard. The movement away from a gold coin standard reduced gold's role as a domestic medium of exchange and tended again to concentrate gold in the hands of national monetary authorities, thus strengthening their discretionary monetary powers.

The post–World War I international gold standard differed markedly from the prewar model. Its environmental and institutional setting had changed significantly. Prewar foreign exchange relations were disturbed, as was the very efficient and centralized international banking system. The crash in the United States stock market in 1929, linked with spreading bank failures here and abroad, upended the very shaky international monetary balance that had been achieved. The Great Depression brought about the abandonment of the gold standard by various countries attempting to insulate their economies from external deflationary pressures.

The demise of the international gold standard that began in 1929 is by no means attributable solely to the Great Depression, however. For example, a major contributing factor was the deep-rooted change in international trade patterns and practices from those operative before the war. High and rising trade barriers, as exemplified in the United States by the passage of the Smoot-Hawley tariff in 1931, restricted multilateral trade and stimulated retaliatory measures by other nations. Another significant element was the abdication by the United States and Great Briatin of their important roles as international lenders. War debts and reparations also added to the burden on international trade and finance relations.

Following Britain's abandonment of the gold standard in September 1931, the United States, severely racked by a depressed economy, officially went off the gold coin standard in March 1933 and established a highly modified gold bullion standard with the passage of the Gold Reserve Act in January 1934. This legislation inaugurated for the domestic economy of the United States a monetary standard leaning heavily toward inconvertible managed paper. Abandonment of the classical gold standard (a "cruel and barbarous relic," as John Maynard Keynes called it) reflected the desire of the United States to control more effectively the quantity and quality of domestic money in its own self-interest.

THE PRESENT UNITED STATES
MONETARY STANDARD

The present United States monetary standard dates essentially from the Gold Reserve Act of 1934. With this act the United States "turned the corner," going from a metallic monetary standard to a managed paper (or fiat) standard. Specifically, the 1934 action ended domestic convertibility of dollars for gold at a fixed, official price and prohibited gold ownership for all U.S. citizens, who had been required earlier to turn in all gold to the national government. The Treasury became the sole official buyer and seller of gold at the new official price of $35 per ounce. Dollars held by foreign official agencies such as central banks and treasuries were still convertible into gold, and minimum gold reserve requirements were maintained against note and deposit liabilities of the Federal Reserve, the U.S. central bank.

In the post–World War II period, a steady march of events cut the remaining strands tying gold to the formal domestic and international monetary standards. For instance, the minimum gold reserve requirements of 25 percent against Federal Reserve note and deposit liabilities were removed in two stages in March 1965 and March 1968. The removal of minimum gold cover provisions for the central bank is evidence of legislative recognition that the domestic monetary system is highly managed and that effective and responsible monetary management requires a reasonable area of discretion, free from artificial constraints.

Furthermore, the establishment in March 1968 of the two-tier gold market by the United States and major European governments indicated abandonment of official efforts to stabilize the private gold market. The two-tier system, which ended in late 1973, strictly separated the official price of gold for transactions among central banks from the market-determined price. In August 1971 President Nixon announced an indefinite "closing of the gold window" to foreign official holders of dollars, who up to that time had enjoyed convertibility of dollars into gold. Then, a few months later, in December 1971 at the Smithsonian Institution in Washington, D.C., major nations agreed to a restructuring of foreign exchange rates (rates at which different nations' currencies exchange for one another) initiated by an increase in the official price of gold to $38 an ounce. This cut in the dollar's defined gold content, or *devaluation,* as it is called, was followed by an additional 10 percent devaluation in February 1973, when gold's official price was raised to $42.22

an ounce. Finally, the fixed–exchange-rate system ended in March 1973, when most nations adopted a regime of fairly flexible or fluctuating foreign exchange rates.

These actions downgraded gold's place in the international monetary arena and served as a prelude to a new phase in the monetary history of the United States. Without much fanfare, and almost like a belated holiday gift to its citizens, on the last day of December 1974 the United States legalized private gold ownership. A week later, on January 6, 1975, and then again in June 1975, the U.S. government auctioned portions of its gold stock on the open market. Interestingly, these auctions were conducted by the General Services Administration, a housekeeping arm of the federal government, rather than by the Treasury, a monetary agency. Symbolically, the demonetization of gold within the U.S. monetary system is made complete when gold is handled in much the same way as peace surplus and war surplus materials.

In early 1978 the Treasury unveiled plans for a series of regular monthly gold sales, starting in May 1978. The first six sales each involved 300,000 ounces of gold. By December 1978, Treasury gold offerings had increased greatly to a monthly volume of 1.5 million ounces. Furthermore, in that same year, Congress mandated the Treasury to sell a million ounces of gold medallions in each of five years starting in 1980.

Finally, even gold's formal role within the international monetary scene seems largely foredoomed. The August 1975 meeting of the Interim Committee of the Governors of the International Monetary Fund (IMF) made the following recommendations, which are already being implemented: (1) abolition of the $42.22 official price of gold; (2) removal of all formal IMF procedures requiring the use of gold between member nations and the IMF; and (3) the return by the IMF of one-sixth of its some 150 million ounces of gold to member nations and the sale over a four-year period of another one-sixth at market prices, with profits used to establish a fund to benefit needy developing nations.

THE ROLE OF SILVER IN THE UNITED STATES MONETARY SYSTEM

The considerable decline in the importance of gold in the United States monetary system has been accompanied by the elimination in the later 1960s

Figure 2.1   SILVER'S PRICE CHRONOLOGY 1870–1968

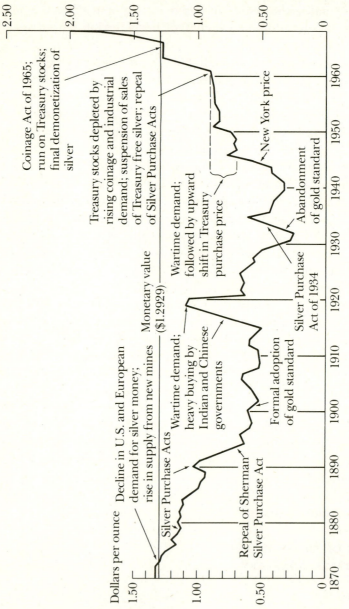

Source: William Burke and Yvonne Levy, *Silver: End of an Era*, rev. ed. Federal Reserve Bank of San Francisco, *Monthly Review* Supplement, 1969, pp. 16–17.

of the role of silver as money. The events leading up to the final demonetization of silver in June 1968 need not be given in great detail here. Figure 2.1
shows the chronology of silver's price over the period 1870 to 1968 along with
the major incidents affecting its price behavior. The reference line indicating
silver's monetary value of $1.2929 per ounce is obtained by dividing the
number of grains in an ounce (480) by the number of grains of pure silver in
the silver dollar (371.25).[4]

Some general observations emerge from an examination of the chronology
depicted in Figure 2.1. In the period prior to the United States abandonment
of the gold standard in 1933 the market price of silver coursed downward
with but two exceptions: the silver-purchase period around 1890 and during
World War I. At the end of 1933, with silver's market price at 44 cents an
ounce, the Treasury made unlimited purchases of newly mined silver at
$0.6464 per ounce under authority of the Thomas amendment to the Ag-
ricultural Adjustment Act of 1933.[5]

The clamor of monetary inflationists (including the not disinterested silver
mining interests) brought enactment of the Silver Purchase Act of 1934. This
act gave carte blanche to the secretary of the Treasury to purchase domestic
and foreign silver until its market price rose to its monetary value (or mint
price) of $1.2929 per ounce or until the monetary value of the Treasury's
silver stock attained one-third of the monetary value of its gold stock. The set
price at which Treasury purchases were made was changed several times over
the next dozen years, from the original $0.6464 in 1934 to $0.9050 in 1946.

Until the mid-1950s the Treasury's set price for newly mined domestic
silver exceeded the market price. Thus Treasury domestic purchases were
made at the higher price, while domestic silver-using industries bought the
lower-priced foreign metal. Increasing slowly in the late 1950s and soaring in
the 1960s, silver's market price reflected the upsurge in world demand.[6] The
widening gap between silver purchases and new silver production brought

4. Recall that the Coinage Act of 1792 defined the silver dollar as equivalent to 371.25 grains of
pure silver. See the section in this chapter entitled "The Evolution of Monetary Standards."

5. Of even greater interest to students of monetary affairs is that this amendment authorized,
among other things, a reduction in the gold content of the dollar, which became an accomplished
fact with the passage of the Gold Reserve Act of 1934.

6. By late 1961, for example, worldwide demand for silver for both industrial and coinage
purposes was about 300 million ounces annually, with the United States accounting for half of this
amount. Worldwide silver production, on the other hand, approached 235 million ounces
annually, with about one-sixth produced by American mines.

mounting sales from the Treasury's stocks of free silver (stocks not tied to currency backing or coinage).[7]

The Demonetization of Silver

Against this background, several steps led to the eventual demonetization of silver in 1968: (1) a presidential order suspended temporarily sales of Treasury free silver in November 1961; (2) the Act of June 1963 repealed the Silver Purchase Act of 1934 and authorized the issuance of paper currency by the Federal Reserve to replace Treasury silver certificates, thus releasing silver reserves to free silver status; (3) the Coinage Act of 1965 provided, among other things, for the issuance of copper-clad dimes and quarters, reduced the silver content of newly minted half dollars to 40 percent from the original 90 percent, specified that no silver dollars be minted for five years, and authorized the secretary of the Treasury to ban the melting, treating, or export of coins; (4) the Act of June 24, 1967, to meet the threat posed by the mounting redemption of silver certificates for silver dollars or bullion, limited the period for such redemption to one year from the date of the act; (5) in July 1967 the Treasury announced it would thereafter sell each week specified amounts of silver at the going market price through the facilities of the General Services Administration. These weekly sales continued until early November of 1970, when all available stocks were sold, exclusive of strategic stockpile requirements.

With the demonetization of silver completed, the Treasury rescinded in 1969 its prohibition against the melting and exporting of coin. For planning long-range coinage policy in the postsilver era, a Joint Commission on the Coinage was established under authorization of the Coinage Act of 1965. This twenty-four–member group, representing the legislative and executive branches as well as the general public, makes recommendations on such matters as projected coinage needs, technological advances in metallurgy and coin selector devices, supply factors in metal markets, the future of the silver dollar, and the future role of the government in the silver market. The

7. The Treasury's free silver stocks peaked at 222 million ounces in early 1959. By year-end 1960 half of this was depleted, and by late 1961 only 22 million ounces remained. At the latter date almost 1.7 billion ounces of silver bullion were held as reserves behind paper silver certificates, primarily in denominations of one and two dollars.

government is now completely out of the silver market with but one small exception: an obscure clause of the Coinage Act of 1965 requires the Treasury to buy newly mined domestic silver, when offered, at $1.25 an ounce.

This review of the changing role of silver within the United States monetary system gives a basic insight: it is not necessary for coin and currency (or, for that matter, money of any kind) to have the backing of a precious metal. Coin and other money derive their value from what they can command in the way of goods and services and not from their physical embodiment. Ultimately, the worth of money depends on the productive ability of the economy, which produces the things for which money is exchanged. A stable, viable economy assures this fundamental backing for money.

MONEY SUPPLY DEFINED

The examination of the monetary standard of the United States provided information on the various factors affecting the evolution of the monetary system. With this background, we can now examine the specific makeup and dimensions of the money supply in the United States.

In precise terms, the *money supply* can be defined as all those assets owned by the general public (or nonbank private sector) that have two essential features: (1) fixity of price in terms of the monetary unit of account, and (2) general acceptability in payment for goods and services or in payment of debt. Note that this definition of the money supply is the functional definition of money presented in Chapter 1.

The general public's money supply (sometimes termed the private money supply) excludes money owned by the Treasury, the Federal Reserve, and the commercial banking system. Thus defined, the money supply consists of two broad components: (1) coin and paper currency outside the Treasury, Federal Reserve, and vaults of commercial banks; and (2) demand deposits (adjusted for some items), transferable by means of checks. Table 2.1 indicates that the currency component averages 20 to 25 percent, and the demand deposit component 75 to 80 percent, of the general public's total money supply.[8]

Currency, which is referred to as hand-to-hand money, pocket money, hard

---

8. The generic term *currency* includes both coin and paper currency. Thus a reference to *currency* implies both coin and paper currency.

Table 2.1   THE GENERAL PUBLIC'S MONEY SUPPLY IN THE UNITED
STATES
(data seasonally adjusted, billions of dollars)

		Money Supply	
Period*	Total	Currency Component	Demand Deposit Component
December 1974	282.8	67.8	215.0
December 1975	294.5	73.7	220.8
December 1976	312.6	80.7	231.9
December 1977	336.7	88.5	248.2
March 1978	340.1	90.6	249.5

*Averages of daily figures for given period.

Source: *Federal Reserve Bulletin*, May 1978, p. A14.

cash, or legal tender money, is issued by the Treasury and the Federal Reserve under monetary authority granted by the Congress in monetary legislation. The largest part of currency in circulation (outside the Treasury and Federal Reserve banks) consists of Federal Reserve notes issues by the central banking system. Some seven-eighths of the dollar amount of circulating currency consists of Federal Reserve notes, with the remaining one-eighth consisting of Treasury currency, which is mostly coin. In effect, the Treasury is a comparative "piker," issuing currency primarily in the form of small change, or fractional coin, which is coin under one dollar denomination. Overall, currency in circulation is determined by the money-using habits and practices of the general public. The changing amount and composition of currency in circulation reflects such institutional features as the growing use of vending machines, imposition of state sales taxes, and so on.

The demand deposit component of the money supply is adjusted to exclude from gross demand deposits those amounts on which the general public cannot draw checks: (1) interbank deposits, that is, demand deposits owned by commercial banks; (2) United States government demand deposits; and (3) cash items in the process of collection and Federal Reserve float, that is, checks drawn on demand deposits that have not yet been cleared and collected. Table

Table 2.2   METHOD OF DERIVING THE OFFICIAL UNITED STATES
MONEY STOCK (M_1)

Demand Deposits Adjusted

1.		Gross demand deposits at commercial banks
2.	Less:	Deposits due to U.S. commercial banks
3.	Equals:	Gross demand deposits at commercial banks, excluding interbank deposits
4.	Less:	Gross demand deposits held by U.S. government
5.	Equals:	Gross demand deposits of the nonbank public at commercial banks
6.	Less:	Cash items in process of collection
7.	Less:	Federal Reserve float
8.	Plus:	Foreign deposits held at Federal Reserve banks
9.	Equals:	Demand deposits adjusted (demand deposit component of the money stock)

Currency in Circulation

10.		Total currency issued
11.	Less:	Currency held in vaults of commercial banks
12.	Equals:	Currency in circulation (currency component of the money stock)
9.		Demand deposits adjusted
12.	Plus:	Currency in circulation
13.	Equals:	Total money stock (M_1)

Source: Federal Reserve Bank of Dallas, *Business Review*, September 1972, p. 5.

2.2 summarizes these various demand deposit adjustments required for deriving a measure of the general public's money supply (M_1).

Technically, demand deposits of the general public are not classified as *legal tender money;* that is, they are not viewed by the courts as lawful consideration for the payment of debt, both public and private. Then why include these deposits in the money supply? Although in a statutory sense they are not legal tender, demand deposits are money according to the functional definition. Demand deposits have the two features of price fixity and general acceptability. In the modern economy the largest part of total money transactions is accomplished by transfers of ownership of demand deposits. These transfers are made largely through the drawing of checks on demand deposit accounts.[9] Checks in themselves are not money; they provide a device by which transfers in ownership of demand deposits are made.

Demand deposits, which comprise the largest part of the money supply, are monetary liabilities of the commercial banking system. In a subsequent chapter we will examine the process by which commercial banks, operating on fractional reserves, create demand deposits for the general public by extending loans and purchasing securities. Changes in demand deposits reflect primarily the lending and investing activities of these privately owned commercial banking firms. The demand deposit component of the money supply is the source from which changes in the overall money supply arise. Thus in any modern monetary system the major money-creating sector is the commercial banking system, with lesser money-issuing roles played by the Treasury and the central banking system.

KEY TERMS

Monetary standard	Gresham's law
Metallic monetary standard	Devaluation
Inconvertible monetary standard	Money supply
Full-bodied coins	Currency
Token money	Legal tender money

REVIEW QUESTIONS

1. What is meant by a monetary standard?
2. Indicate the two basic types of monetary standards and the essential features of each type.
3. State and explain the meaning of Gresham's law.
4. What was the significance of the Gold Reserve Act of 1934?
5. Outline briefly the principal features of the present United States monetary standard.

9. The growing use of sophisticated electronic data-processing equipment accounts for a rising portion of money transfers, so that some observers foresee an emerging "less-check" society, if not a "checkless" society.

6. What steps taken in the 1960s brought about silver's demonetization in 1968?

7. What two broad components comprise the general public's money supply?

8. Why are demand deposits of the general public regarded as money, even though they are not legal tender?

SUGGESTED READINGS

Cox, William N., III. "Measuring the Money Stock." Federal Reserve Bank of Atlanta, *Monthly Review* (July 1974): 94–99.

Burke, William. "The Semiprecious Metal." Federal Reserve Bank of San Francisco, *Monthly Review* (December 1971): 205–211.

Knight, Robert E. "The Changing Payments Mechanism: Electronic Funds Transfer Arrangements." Federal Reserve Bank of Kansas City, *Monthly Review* (July-August 1974): 10–20.

Kvasnicka, Joseph G. "Gold—Part I: An Historical Perspective." Federal Reserve Bank of Chicago, *Business Conditions* (November 1971): 12–19.

Salley, Charles D. "The Georgia Tech Findings: Checks and the Payments Mechanism." Federal Reserve Bank of Atlanta, *Monthly Review* (February 1972): 18–22.

"Special Issue: Gold." Federal Reserve Bank of San Francisco, *Business Review* (Winter 1974–1975): 2–31.

Throop, Adrian W. "Bicentennial Perspective—Decline and Fall of the Gold Standard." Federal Reserve Bank of Dallas, *Review* (January 1976): 1–11.

Chapter Three

CREDIT MARKETS AND FINANCIAL INSTITUTIONS

The previous chapter showed how a monetary standard affects the quantity and quality of money in a given society. As defined earlier, money is a special asset in that it has 100 percent liquidity. Liquidity relates to an asset's convertibility into money without loss. Various assets in the economy approach the perfect liquidity of money. These other highly liquid assets are created by financial institutions operating in credit markets of the economy.

In this chapter, we will initially trace the *general* nature and significance of financial institutions within the setting of credit markets. Then we will cover the operations and activities of the major *individual* types of financial institutions found within the United States. We will emphasize privately owned financial institutions, although we will refer briefly to important credit programs operated by the federal government.

NEAR-MONIES AND CREDIT MARKETS

Assets that exhibit to a somewhat lesser degree the two essential features of money—price fixity and general acceptability in exchange for goods and services—are called *near-monies*. Although they are not money in a strict definitional sense, near-monies come very close to being money. Some examples of important near-monies include time and savings deposits in commercial banks and in mutual savings banks, share accounts in savings and loan associations and in credit unions, United States savings bonds, Treasury bills, and the cash surrender value of life insurance policies. Near-monies, along with money, represent different types of financial claims to wealth, which may be defined as ownership of immediate or potential spending power.

Near-monies, which represent the liabilities or promises to pay of the various groups and institutions issuing them, occupy an important place in credit markets. *Credit markets* are markets wherein lenders and borrowers exchange funds. Credit markets deal in credit, which essentially involves the exchange of current goods or services or money in return for future purchasing power. Lenders (or *creditors*) transfer present goods or purchasing power, and in turn receive claims to certain sums of money in the future. Those receiving credit are called borrowers (or *debtors*), and they incur obligations (or debts) to pay money sometime in the future. Thus credit markets include borrower-lender relationships that arise from the exchange of current consideration for promises to pay in the future.

Widespread use of credit and debt is a distinguishing feature of any modern economy. Those spending units who desire to spend more than they are currently receiving must borrow purchasing power from those spending units who prefer to spend less than they are currently receiving. Credit links these two groups together. In this transfer of purchasing power, the borrowers (or debtors) promise to repay the lenders (or creditors) sometime in the future. In addition to the funds borrowed, the borrowers pay a premium, known as interest.

Modern society derives some very important services from credit (or debt). Credit allows individuals to space their consumption over time effectively; otherwise, how many would be able to purchase and enjoy such high-ticket items as automobiles, household durables, homes, and so on? Credit also enables individuals to hold convenient stores of purchasing power that earn a premium or interest—consider the great variety of financial claims emerging from credit transactions. Even more basic, credit use enhances an economy's growth by facilitating the production and purchase of plant and equipment needed for modern productive processes. It allows firms to use "round-about" methods of production that give society the benefits of highly productive, specialized industry. Additionally, credit is a strong force widening markets for goods and services, thus promoting large-scale, low-cost production.

The Role of Financial Intermediaries

An important role in modern credit markets is played by a group of specialized institutions known as financial intermediaries. *Financial intermediaries* serve as middlemen between ultimate borrowers and ultimate lenders by issuing near-monies to savers and, in turn, allocating these savings to borrowers. The growth and development of such privately owned nonbank financial institutions as savings and loan associations, mutual savings banks, credit unions, and insurance companies, as well as the expansion of commercial bank time and savings deposit business, have institutionalized a large part of savings funds in the United States.

The operation of financial intermediaries in credit markets may be depicted by means of a simplified diagram (see Figure 3.1). Credit flows between nonfinancial lenders (left side) and nonfinancial borrowers (right side). Credit originates when a spending unit (business or household, for example) decides to lend part of its income rather than spend it on goods and services. The loanable funds move through the financial system to another nonfinancial unit that wishes to borrow within the credit markets. Financial intermediaries, including commercial bank savings departments, facilitate the flow of credit by receiving the funds of nonfinancial lenders and allocating these funds to nonfinancial borrowers seeking funds in the credit markets.

We are using the term credit markets in a conceptual or analytical sense rather than in a geographical or physical sense. In Figure 3.1, credit markets are represented by the box at the extreme right. This figurative rendering of credit markets thus includes all markets in which nonfinancial borrowers obtain funds.

When a household deposits its funds in a savings and loan association, for example, it lends *indirectly* to the recipient of the association's credit. In Figure 3.1, the household's funds follow the middle channel of indirect credit flow. Direct lending to borrowers can also occur in credit markets. For example, when a household purchases a new U.S. Treasury bill, funds are lent *directly* to the government. This is depicted in Figure 3.1 by the lower channel of direct credit flow.

Should a direct credit flow be substituted for an indirect credit flow, then *disintermediation* occurs, as was the case in the United States in the late sixties (see Table 3.1). In 1969, an appreciable rise in market interest rates brought an increase in direct lending by nonfinancial lenders, since financial intermediaries were unable to match these rate increases, largely because of regulatory interest rate ceilings. *Reintermediation*, the opposite of disintermediation, occurs when an indirect credit flow is substituted for a direct credit flow.

For simplified illustration, the Federal Reserve System's place in the flow of credit is represented by the box at the upper left of Figure 3.1. Depending on

Figure 3.1 SIMPLIFIED REPRESENTATION OF FLOW OF CREDIT IN ECONOMY

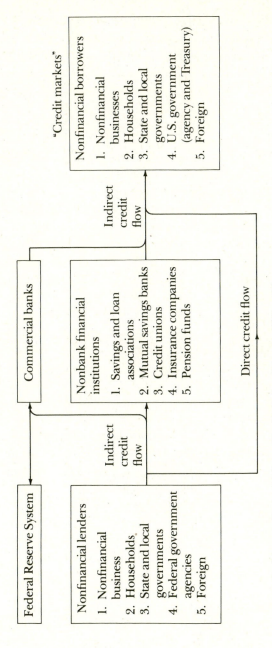

Source: Federal Reserve Bank of Atlanta, *Monthly Review,* February 1970, p. 25.

Table 3.1   FLOW OF FUNDS IN 1973, 1972, 1969: DISTRIBUTION
OF LENDING IN CREDIT MARKETS
(billions of dollars; percentage of total lending in parentheses)

Indirect Lending by
Commercial Banks

1973: 76.0 (42.2%)
1972: 65.4 (41.9%)
1969: 9.2 (10.7%)

Indirect Lending by
Financial Institutions

1973: 127.2 (70.6%)
1972: 130.0 (83.3%)
1969: 39.3 (45.9%)

Indirect
Lending by Nonbank
Financial Institutions*

1973: 51.2 (28.4%)
1972: 64.6 (41.4%)
1969: 31.3 (35.2%)

Total Lending
in Credit Markets

1973: 180.1 (100%)
1972: 156.1 (100%)
1969: 85.7 (100%)

Direct Lending
by Households

1973: 29.7 (16.5%)
1972: 8.9 (5.7%)
1969: 21.0 (24.5%)

Direct Lending
by Businesses

1973: 9.1 (5.1%)
1972: 4.6 (2.9%)
1969: 10.9 (12.7%)

Direct Lending from
Nonfinancial Lenders

1973: 52.9 (29.4%)
1972: 26.1 (16.7%)
1969: 46.4 (54.1%)

Direct Lending
by Other
Nonfinancial
Lenders†

1973: 14.1 (7.8%)
1972: 12.6 (8.1%)
1969: 14.5 (16.9%)

*Savings and loan associations, mutual savings banks, credit unions, mutual funds, insurance companies.
†United States government agencies, Federal Reserve System, state and local governments, foreign.

Source: Flow of Funds Accounts, Board of Governors of the Federal Reserve System.

its policy objectives, the Federal Reserve either supplies funds (reserves) to commercial banks or absorbs funds (reserves) from them. This representation is overly simplistic on at least two counts. First, since commercial banks operate with fractional cash reserves, one dollar of additional commercial bank reserves can support several dollars of bank lending in credit markets. Second, the central bank (Federal Reserve) supplies (or absorbs) reserves by buying (or selling) federal government securities in credit markets. Later chapters will explain these technical factors in considerable detail. The diagram portrayed in Figure 3.1 has been simplified to aid general understanding of credit flows.

Flow of Funds Accounts

There are various ways of examining the credit that flows through credit markets. A detailed source of information on the nation's credit flows is found in the *flow of funds accounts,* published quarterly by the Federal Reserve System and printed in the monthly *Federal Reserve Bulletin.*

First developed in 1947, the flow of funds accounts constitute a macroeconomic accounting system just as do the national income and product accounts. Essentially, these accounts tie together statistically the many financial activities of the United States economy, and in turn directly relate these activities to data based on nonfinancial activities that generate income and production in the economy. The flow of funds accounts provide a data base for examining such areas as the sensitivity of borrowing to interest rates as compared with other influences, the responsiveness of the demand for real capital to changing credit conditions, the place of money holdings in the public's structure of assets and liabilities, and the relation of financial positions to demands for goods and services, for credit, and for investment in financial claims.[1]

Tables 3.1 and 3.2, which are derived from the flow of funds accounts, present two different breakdowns of the total volume of credit in the United States in recent years. Table 3.1 shows the origination of funds from the indirect sources of commercial banks and nonbank financial institutions and

---

1. For a lucid and more detailed explanation of the general composition and analytical uses of the flow of funds accounts, see Board of Governors of the Federal Reserve System, *Introduction to Flow of Funds* (February 1975), especially pp. 1–13.

Table 3.2   FLOW OF FUNDS IN 1973, 1972, 1969: DISTRIBUTION
OF BORROWING IN CREDIT MARKETS
(billions of dollars; percentage of total borrowing in parentheses)

	1973	1972	1969
Borrowing by			
U.S. government	9.7 (5.4%)	17.3 (11.1%)	−5.4 (−6.3%)*
State and local governments	12.3 (6.8%)	12.3 (7.9%)	9.2 (10.7%)
Households	72.7 (40.4%)	63.2 (40.5%)	30.9 (36.1%)
Corporate businesses	59.7 (33.1%)	44.2 (28.3%)	37.3 (43.5%)
Other businesses (including farms)	17.9 (9.9%)	15.3 (9.8%)	10.1 (11.8%)
Foreigners	7.7 (4.3%)	3.8 (2.4%)	3.6 (4.2%)
Total borrowing in credit markets	180.1 (100.0%)	156.1 (100.0%)	85.7 (100.0%)

*Indicates federal government (exclusive of nonbudget financial agencies) was a net redeemer of debt in 1969.

Source: Flow of Funds Accounts, Board of Governors of the Federal Reserve System.

---

from the direct sources of nonfinancial lenders. Table 3.2 looks at these same credit flows, but from the opposite direction of how the total flows of credit have been allocated among nonfinancial borrowers: government, households, business, and foreigners.

**FINANCIAL INTERMEDIARIES:
THEIR SIGNIFICANCE IN CREDIT
FLOWS**

In general terms, financial intermediaries borrow for the purpose of lending rather than for spending on goods and services. As an activity, intermediation is usually associated with financial business, such as commercial banks, savings institutions of various types, insurance companies, and investment companies. The distinction between intermediaries and nonintermediaries within credit markets is a matter more of degree and of operational differences than a precisely defined theoretical concept.

Furthermore, although financial intermediaries have different operating features, they perform the same basic function. Essentially, intermediaries create liquidity by selling short-term liquid claims against themselves (deposit accounts, savings accounts, insurance policies, and so on) that are convertible into money without loss. In turn, they use the proceeds from these sales to buy long-term illiquid assets (stocks, bonds, home mortgages, and so on). As a group, financial intermediaries borrow short term and lend long term. They provide a useful service by creating liquidity and by bearing risk through the acquisition of illiquid long-term assets. Basically, these institutions fill the gap between the types of financial claims the nonfinancial public wants to *hold* as assets, such as bank deposits and insurance reserves, and the quite different types of financial claims the public wants to *owe* as debts, such as bank loans, consumer credit, and mortgages.

Even in the absence of financial intermediaries, the *total* of claims held as assets by members of the nonfinancial public is about equal to the *total* of their liabilities, or debts, because they hold one another's IOUs. How, then, does intermediation fit into the picture? Intermediation allows the composition of the public's assets to differ greatly from the composition of its debts. In effect, financial intermediaries serve as transformers within credit markets. They conduct a transformation process between the asset and liability sides of the nonfinancial public's balance sheet by changing debt into credit. Specifically, intermediaries create liabilities against themselves to satisfy the asset preferences of surplus spending units. Simultaneously, these intermediaries acquire the debt of deficit spending units as earning assets.

Financial intermediaries generate important effects within credit markets and, in turn, within the overall economy. For one thing, their operations give the public more options in terms of forms of financial investment and borrowing. In their role as transformers within credit markets, financial intermediaries decrease risk exposure for ultimate lenders. Specialized expertise and knowledge enable intermediaries to pool funds from many sources and to achieve large-scale, risk-diversified asset holdings. Additionally, creation of near-monies by financial intermediaries permits the community to hold less money and therefore to spend money faster than it otherwise would have. An increase in money's spending velocity affects the sale of goods and services, and ultimately the economy's production, employment, and price level.

As indicated in Table 3.1, these institutions channel a major portion of credit in the United States economy. With their ability to mobilize savings, the intermediaries affect the pattern of credit flows by meeting demands for various specialized forms of credit. Legal factors relating to rate structures, lending practices, and borrowing activities can impede adjustments to changing market conditions, thus causing disintermediation and reintermediation effects. The composition or structure of total credit changes as intermediaries develop new practices and techniques. Certainly these innovative influences, along with existing legal constraints, shape the role that financial institutions play in the economy's growth and development.

CREDIT MARKETS AND INTEREST RATES

All operating markets, including credit markets, generate prices. Credit markets are markets wherein lenders and borrowers exchange funds at a price. The price (or premium) paid for credit is called the *interest rate*. Like any price, the interest rate focalizes all factors affecting the supply of and demand for credit.

As explained earlier, the demand for credit emerges from borrowers' desires to change the time pattern of their purchasing power. Borrowers increase their current purchasing power and promise to repay lenders with future purchasing power. On the other hand, lenders supplying credit forgo present purchasing power in exchange for additions to future purchasing power. Given their different preferences, both borrowers and lenders alike benefit from this transfer of purchasing power.

At any given time, a pattern of interest rates exists in credit markets. These different interest rates reflect the interplay of various factors in credit transactions: default risk of borrowers, maturity period, collateral (or backing) pledged against credit, tax considerations, and any factor affecting expected future purchasing power. Generally, interest rates tend to move together. Simultaneously, the varying rates at which different interest rates move reflect changing credit market evaluations of the characteristics of various loans. For example, these adjustments tend to occur if relative interest rates deviate from the pattern dictated by factors affecting expected returns. Equilibrium would be restored by shifts in the demand and supply of funds in credit markets.

Furthermore, various factors can change the level of interest rates over time. These influencing factors fall into two groups: (1) variables that affect anticipated future returns from additional current purchasing power, and (2) spending units' preferences for present or future purchasing power. Although it is difficult to observe changes in these factors, economic research specifies various determinants underlying these two sets of factors. Some of these determinants in turn affect interest rates, especially price-level expectations, fluctuations in economic activity, and monetary policy actions. Subsequent chapters, mainly in Part Five, examine these key determinants of interest rate movements in credit markets.

PRIVATE FINANCIAL
INTERMEDIARIES: MAJOR TYPES

Credit markets, which have many aspects, can be viewed in several ways— according to types of financial instruments used, for example, or to geographic scope. Another approach focuses on the different types of participating financial institutions. These institutions interact with other market participants such as nonfinancial business, households, and governments. Financial intermediaries tend to specialize in the forms of debt claims or IOUs they offer, and in the forms of credit they extend. Basically, the operating differences among financial intermediaries are more of degree than of kind. For instance, insurance companies secure funds largely through policy premiums but lend diversely in credit markets, while finance companies narrow their lending scope but not their borrowing forms. Savings and loan associations specialize on both sides of the market: borrowing through the issuance of highly liquid claims in the form of savings accounts, and lending primarily for residential mortgage purposes. In their different specialized ways, financial intermediaries create utility (that is, satisfy wants and needs) within credit markets. This section describes the activities and operations of the major types of privately owned noncommercial bank financial intermediaries found within the United States.

On the basis of asset size and amounts and types of credit they create, commercial banks constitute the most important type of privately owned intermediary. Commercial banks also hold a special place among financial intermediaries in that bank demand deposit liabilities are used as money.

Generally, nonbank financial intermediaries do not create means of payment that can be spent directly.[2] Just like private individuals, nonbank intermediaries have demand deposits (checking accounts) in commercial banks for making money payments and for giving borrowers their loan proceeds. Given its crucial role in credit markets, the commercial banking system receives detailed study in subsequent chapters, especially in Part Two.

All told, the discussion covers different types of nonbank financial intermediaries. These intermediaries include a varied group of institutions. For instance, the deposit institutions, such as mutual savings banks, savings and loan associations, and credit unions, afford a high degree of liquidity along with interest yield. Then there are those institutions that provide primarily risk protection and security plus limited liquidity, such as life insurance companies, property-casualty insurance companies, and private pension plans. And finally, specialized types include finance companies, investment companies, and real estate investment trusts. Each type of institution has characteristic sources and uses of funds. Furthermore, factors underlying the different composition of assets can be examined, as well as the response of these different institutions to changing credit conditions. Let us turn to a brief examination of each type of institution starting first with the deposit institutions.

Mutual Savings Banks

A total of some five hundred mutual savings banks (MSBs) operate primarily in states along the eastern seaboard. *Mutual savings banks* are major thrift institutions, and they obtain most of their funds in the form of deposits of small individual savers. They are permitted to pay interest on savings deposits one-quarter percentage point higher than similar accounts at commercial banks. Since these banks are mutuals, they have no stockholders, with net earnings either paid as interest to depositors or retained.

Solely state chartered, savings banks are subject to state laws and appro-

---

2. For several years, commercial banks, mutual savings banks, and savings and loan associations in New England have offered "negotiable order of withdrawal" (NOW) accounts. Functionally, NOWs are interest-bearing checking accounts. Most likely Congress eventually will allow NOWs for all depository institutions in the country. Credit union use of share drafts is another example of "checklike" instruments offered by intermediaries.

Table 3.3 CONSOLIDATED BALANCE SHEET, ALL MUTUAL SAVINGS
BANKS, UNITED STATES, YEAR-END 1976

Assets	Amount (Billions of Dollars)	Percent	Liabilities and Net Worth	Amount (Billions of Dollars)	Percent
Cash assets	2.4	1.78	Deposits	122.9	91.20
Mortgage loans	81.7	60.61	Other liabilities	2.9	2.15
Other loans	5.2	2.61	General reserve		
Securities:			accounts	9.0	6.65
U.S. government	14.9	11.05			
State and local	2.4	1.78			
Corporate and other	24.7	18.32			
Other assets	3.5	3.85			
Total	134.8	100.00	Total	134.8	100.00

Source: Board of Governors of the Federal Reserve System, *Flow of Funds Outstanding, 1965–76,* December 1977, p. 11.

priate state regulatory authorities. Those mutual savings banks holding voluntary membership in the Federal Home Loan Bank (FHLB) system follow regulations imposed by the Federal Home Loan Bank board, and savings banks carrying Federal Deposit Insurance Corporation (FDIC) coverage must also meet that agency's requirements. Typically, state authorities establish so-called legal lists regulating the lending-investing activities of savings banks by stipulating the types of loans and investments that may be held as assets. Frequently, ceilings expressed as percentages of total assets or total deposits for each particular bank apply to specific types of loans and investments.

Over the years mutual savings banks have obtained broad and flexible investment powers. These investment powers are broader than those of savings and loan associations but more restricted than those of commercial banks and life insurance companies. The principal assets of mutual savings banks include mortgage loans (both conventional and federally underwritten), United States government securities, federal government agency obligations, state and local government securities, and various high-grade corporate securities (see Table 3.3).

Mutual savings banks had large holdings of United States government securities at the end of World War II, reflecting heavy wartime financing.

Peacetime brought a shift of funds into mortgages, corporate securities, and state and local government bonds. The most significant post–World War II change in asset composition of savings banks is the appreciable growth in mortgage loans from one-quarter of total assets at year-end 1945 to some three-fifths of total assets in the 1970s. Various elements contributed to the increase in mortgages in savings bank portfolios: an appreciable increase in housing demand, legislation permitting acquisition of out-of-state mortgages, and relatively attractive mortgage yields.

Mutual savings banks hold a larger proportion of assets in mortgages than do commercial banks or life insurance companies but a smaller share than do savings and loan associations. Important lenders in the nonfarm residential mortgage market, savings banks have been more attracted to federally un- derwritten mortgages than have the other types of financial institutions.

Both the inflow of funds to mutual savings banks and their asset structure react to changing monetary conditions. For example, during the credit crunch of 1966 and the tight money period of 1969–1970 their share of assets held as corporate bonds grew relative to the share held as mortgage loans. This shift in assets occurred as yields on other types of financial assets outpaced mortgage interest rates. Under eased credit conditions, mortgages carry rela- tively more attractive yields and thus are acquired at a faster rate than corporate bonds. In these cases, corporate bonds may be liquidated to provide additional funds for mortgage lending. Their flexible investment policy in response to changing credit conditions enables savings banks to remain com- petitive with other financial institutions and to achieve adequate earnings performance.

Savings and Loan Associations

Predominantly of the mutual type, a total of over five thousand *savings and loan associations* (S and Ls) mobilize the savings of many individuals by issuing shares rather than savings deposits to customers. Technically these shares are not contractual liabilities, but operationally they are treated as highly liquid claims against the associations. When they are compared with mutual savings banks, savings and loan asset structures reflect differences in regulatory framework and in investment policies (see Table 3.4).

Associations are chartered by both federal and state authorities. Federal chartering requires membership in the FHLB system and regulation by the

Table 3.4 CONSOLIDATED BALANCE SHEET, ALL SAVINGS AND
LOAN ASSOCIATIONS, UNITED STATES, YEAR-END 1976

Assets	Amount (Billions of Dollars)	Percent	Liabilities and Net Worth	Amount (Billions of Dollars)	Percent
Cash assets	7.6	1.94	Savings capital	336.0	85.71
Mortgages	323.1	82.42	Reserves and undivided		
Investment securities*	42.2	10.77	profits	25.5	6.51
Other assets†	19.1	4.87	Borrowed money‡	15.9	4.06
			Loans in process	6.8	1.73
			Other	7.8	1.99
Total	392.0	100.00	Total	392.0	100.00

*Includes United States government obligations, federal agency securities, state and local government securities, time deposits at banks, and miscellaneous securities, except Federal Home Loan Bank Board (FHLBB) stock.
†Includes other loans, stock in the Federal Home Loan Banks, other investments, real estate owned and sold on contract, and office buildings and fixtures.
‡Consists of loans from FHLBB and other borrowing.

Source: Board of Governors of the Federal Reserve System, *Flow of Funds Outstanding, 1965–76,* December 1977, p. 11.

FHLB board. Voluntary membership in the FHLB system is open to state-chartered associations, who are also subject to state regulatory authorities. In the same way as the FDIC insures deposits for commercial banks, the Federal Savings and Loan Insurance Corporation (FSLIC) insures individual accounts in savings and loan associations up to $40,000, with most associations carrying this insurance coverage.

The FHLB board requires member associations to maintain minimum liquidity reserves, in the range of 4 to 10 percent, that relate to a stipulated percentage of total savings and short-term borrowings of the association. Liquidity reserves include cash items, United States government securities, government agency obligations, banker acceptances, and certificates of deposit.

More restricted in their investment powers than some other types of financial institutions, savings and loan associations have various permissible investment outlets. In addition to such investment possibilities as cash, residential mortgages, government securities, and passbook loans, other alternatives

include loans for higher education, home improvement loans, general obligations (rather than revenue bonds) of state and local governments, stock of
corporations wholly owned by savings and loan associations (maximum of 1
percent of total assets), real property investments for urban renewal
(maximum of 2 percent of total assets). In addition, member associations must
purchase specified amounts of stock in their respective Federal Home Loan
Banks.

Largely oriented toward mortgage lending, savings and loan associations, in
contrast to mutual savings banks, typically favor conventional mortgages. In
the 1960s and 1970s conventional mortgages comprised over 90 percent of
total mortgage lending by associations. Effective development of markets for
conventional home mortgages made federally underwritten loans less attractive to savings and loan associations.

Although heavily weighted by mortgage loans, the associations' asset structures show responsiveness to varying credit conditions. In periods of restrictive monetary conditions, savings and loan associations encounter strong
disintermediation effects and are compelled to liquidate certain assets to
obtain funds for mortgage loans. In such periods asset shifts occur—generally
out of United States government securities, cash, bank deposits, and real
estate into mortgage loans.

The differing maturity composition of assets and liabilities of savings and
loan associations generates wide swings in earnings under varying monetary
conditions. In effect, associations borrow at short term and lend at long term.
The cost of funds obtained short term varies with the general level of interest
rates, while long-term mortgage loans carry fixed interest rates. This varying
spread between cost of funds and return on assets can produce sharp fluctuations in earnings. Factors that might reduce the problem of cash flows for
associations include possibly liberalized lending by the Federal Home Loan
Bank System, widespread use of variable-rate mortgages, and greater development of secondary markets for conventional home mortgages.

Credit Unions

Credit unions (CUs) are cooperative savings groups consisting of members with
a common interest such as the same employer; affiliation with a labor union, a
church, a fraternal order; or residence in a specific geographic area. Members
pool their savings by buying ownership shares that resemble savings accounts.

Table 3.5   SELECTED ASSETS AND LIABILITIES, FEDERAL AND
STATE-CHARTERED CREDIT UNIONS, UNITED STATES,
YEAR-END 1976

Account	Amount (Millions of Dollars)	Percent
Total assets/liabilities and capital	45,225	100.00
Federal credit unions	24,396	100.00
State credit unions	20,829	100.00
Loans outstanding	34,384	76.03
Federal credit unions	18,311	75.06
State credit unions	16,073	77.17
Savings	39,173	86.62
Federal (shares)	21,130	86.62
State (shares and deposits)	18,043	86.62

Source: Federal Reserve Bulletin, May 1978, p. A29.

Members in turn may borrow from the association, and receive dividends on their share holdings.

In the United States a total of 23,000 credit unions operate under either federal or state charter and are exempt from payment of federal income taxes. Generally, state-chartered credit unions are regulated by the same state authorities that supervise banks and savings and loan associations. The National Credit Union Administration (NCUA) regulates federally chartered credit unions. In the late 1970s almost 60 percent of all credit unions had federal charters. The NCUA provides share insurance up to $40,000 per account for all federally chartered credit unions and those state-chartered groups that qualify for insurance coverage. By the mid-1970s 30 percent of all state-chartered credit unions carried federal insurance, and these institutions owned half the total assets of state credit unions.

The pooled savings shares of members provide the major source of credit union funds. Minor other sources include reserves, retained earnings, and borrowings from other credit unions and from commercial banks. The principal earning assets are loans, which account for over 75 percent of total assets (see Table 3.5). The rapid growth of credit unions in recent years makes them an important source of consumer credit, accounting for about 15 percent of total consumer credit outstanding in the United States. Credit unions are now the third largest consumer installment lender, trailing commercial banks and finance companies. Beyond loans to members, credit union investments are restricted mainly to such assets as government securities and accounts in other thrift institutions.

Deposit Institutions: Their Growing Similarity

Deposit institutions perform essentially the same basic function: they mobilize the savings of economic units and allocate them to borrowers. Since 1970 these institutions show growing similarity in various specific ways. Reacting to high and variable interest rates, these institutions have broadened and diversified the composition of their asset holdings. For example, in recent years savings and loan associations have emphasized shorter-term assets in their portfolios through acquisitions of U.S. government and agency securities and state-local government securities. Such securities typically have shorter maturities than mortgages, and still meet regulatory guidelines.

Furthermore, mutual savings banks and state-chartered savings and loan associations in several eastern states now have authority for wider consumer lending operations. The mid-1970s saw a major bank credit card service extend membership to mutual savings banks, savings and loan associations, and credit unions, thus providing the potential for more diversified consumer lending operations. Greater credit union participation in mortgage lending is likely to result from congressional legislation enacted in 1977 that widens the scope of credit union mortgage lending by authorizing thirty-year home mortgages and up to fifteen-year home improvement or mobile home loans.

During the 1970s major changes have also heightened competition for deposits among institutions. Mutual savings banks, savings and loan associations, and commercial banks in all New England states may offer *negotiable order of withdrawal (NOW) accounts,* which are interest-yielding saving accounts on which checks may be written. Expanded authority for NOW accounts most likely will include all states by the early 1980s. Similarly, *share draft* accounts at credit unions permit the making of checklike payments. Share drafts are drawn on members' interest-bearing share accounts and are processed through the credit union's commercial bank.

Deposit institutions also offer other substitutes for commercial bank checking accounts. Off-premise electronic terminals, called remote service units (RSUs), are for making deposits and withdrawals from savings accounts at sites off the institutions' premises. In some cases, RSUs enable consumers to make direct transfers from their own to merchants' accounts. Bill-paying services allow the payment of bills by direct transfer of funds from savings accounts. In its preauthorized version, bills are paid automatically on a regular basis after initial authorization by consumers. The telephone version requires consumers to telephone each time a third-party payment is desired. These changing roles of deposit institutions support the observation that the more these institutions change, the more similar they become.

Having examined briefly the principal deposit institutions, we will now describe other, more specialized, private financial intermediaries, starting first with life insurance companies.

Life Insurance Companies

Life insurance companies enjoy a relatively great latitude in their investment activities. These companies, of course, are subject to state regulation by both the chartering states and the states in which insuring operations are conducted. Regulatory officials are concerned particularly about the adequacy of a company's policy reserves, which are held to ensure fulfillment of a company's policy commitments. Companies must hold "admitted assets" at least equivalent to policy reserves. Since admitted assets are those assets that meet specified investment standards, the loans and investments of insurance companies are subject to regulatory evaluation.

In their investment activities, life insurance companies balance the need for meeting future commitments to policyholders against the objective of earning an adequate rate of return. Compared with other types of financial institutions, life insurance companies have an important advantage in planning investment. The cash inflows of life insurance companies are more stable than those of other types of financial institutions, and thus long-term investment planning can proceed more smoothly and accurately. The determination of premium rates for life insurance assumes a minimum rate of return on investments, based partly on past experience.

Such relatively high yielding investments as conventional mortgages and corporate securities take a large place in the asset portfolios of life insurance companies. The steady post–World War II decline in the proportion of their

Table 3.6   PRINCIPAL ASSETS OF ALL LIFE INSURANCE COMPANIES,
UNITED STATES, YEAR-END 1976

Assets		Amount (Billions of Dollars)		Percent
Government securities		13.3		4.28
United States	7.7		2.48	
State and local	5.6		1.80	
Business securities		156.7		50.40
Bonds	122.4		39.37	
Stocks	34.3		11.03	
Mortgages		91.6		29.46
Real estate		9.8		3.15
Policy loans		25.8		8.30
Other assets		13.7		4.41
Total assets		310.9		100.00

Source: **Board of Governors of the Federal Reserve System,** *Flow of Funds Outstanding, 1965–76,* **December 1977, p. 12.**

assets held as United States government securities accompanied the greater reliance on mortgages and corporate stocks and bonds. During most of the 1960s and 1970s, policy loans of insurance companies showed appreciable growth. These loans, which are extended to policyholders on the collateral of the policies' cash surrender values, increased especially during periods of high interest rates, when fixed rates on policy loans became extremely attractive.

Although life insurance company portfolios are more diversified than those of some other financial intermediaries, mortgages and corporate bonds are the biggest part of asset holdings (see Table 3.6). Of lesser importance are policy loans, corporate stocks, and government securities. Given their long-range investment stance, life insurance companies show less sensitivity to short-run swings in monetary conditions than do other financial groups. Nevertheless, some responsiveness occurs, particularly during periods of restrictive monetary policy, when policy loans tend to outpace the growth in mortgage loans.

Property-Casualty Insurance Companies

Typically, *property-casualty insurance companies* are diversified in the various lines of insurance offered, ranging from property coverage and casualty insurance to surety bonds and health-accident insurance. Property-casualty insurers follow different forms of legal organization: stock companies, mutual companies, reciprocals, and domestic Lloyds. Stock companies are owned and controlled by their stockholders, while mutuals are owned and controlled by policyholders. Policyholders in mutuals may receive dividends on their paid-in premiums. Most companies are either stock types or mutual types. Reciprocals are essentially nonprofit insurance cooperatives whereby subscribers share losses of fellow members and the costs of operation. Domestic Lloyds, fashioned after the famous Lloyds of London, are associations of unincorporated individual underwriters who share to varying degrees risks accepted by the associations.

The investment objectives of property-casualty insurance companies resemble only partly those of life insurance companies, since basic differences in claims structure enable life insurers to invest in longer-term, more illiquid assets than do property-casualty insurers. In the mid-1970s, property-casualty companies held some three-quarters of their assets in governmental bonds (federal, state, and local) and in common stocks. Life insurance companies, in contrast, held some two-thirds of assets in mortgage loans and corporate bonds.

As is the case with life insurers, property-casualty insurers obtain funds mainly from premiums and from investment income. With premiums usually collected in advance and with the investment of available funds, the property-casualty underwriters amass sizable assets and liabilities. Liabilities consist largely of unearned premiums, claim reserves, and policyholders' surplus (or net worth). As a group, property-casualty companies are still fairly small when compared with the other types of nonbank financial intermediaries, exceeding only investment companies, credit unions, and real estate investment trusts in total asset holdings at year-end 1973. Their total asset growth in the post–World War II period responds partly to business cycle swings, but more especially to stock market fluctuations since common stocks are important investment holdings.

Investment Companies

By pooling and investing the funds of a number of investors, *investment companies* provide financial diversification and economical management for shareholders. Investment companies are of two types: *open end* and *closed end.* Often called *mutual funds,* open-end companies are willing to repurchase their own shares from investors at market price and usually issue as many new shares as the public wants to buy. Closed-end companies issue only a fixed number of shares, and investors must acquire shares from other investors rather than from the investment company. Some closed-end companies issue preferred stocks and bonds.

Investment companies are a mixed bag in terms of their asset holdings. The typical company is a "stock fund" that channels most assets into common stocks. "Balanced funds" acquire common stocks, preferred stocks, and bonds. Some companies restrict themselves to preferred stocks or to bonds. For working liquidity needs, all companies hold a small percentage of total assets in liquid form, including cash, bank balances, and U.S. Treasury securities.

Investment companies have had their share of ups and downs, reflecting the changing conditions in securities markets and in the economy. Along with pension funds, they are major holders of common and preferred stocks owned by the various financial intermediaries (see Table 3.7).

Finance Companies

Finance companies lend to households and business firms for various purposes. Based on their major, specialized lending operations, there are three general categories of finance companies. *Sales finance* companies provide financing for the purchase of automobiles and other consumer durables, primarily by buying consumer installment loan paper from dealers. Frequently, sales finance companies are "captive companies" controlled either by the dealers or by the manufacturers of the durable goods. For example, General Motors Acceptance Corporation is a sales finance company that is wholly owned by General Motors.

Consumer finance companies make mainly personal loans to individuals, either on signature or with collateral backing the loans. *Commercial finance* companies provide loans to businesses, largely on the basis of their accounts

Table 3.7   DISTRIBUTION OF STOCKS OWNED BY PRINCIPAL
NONBANK FINANCIAL INSTITUTIONS, UNITED STATES,
YEAR-END 1976

Type of Institution	Amount (Billions of Dollars)	Percent
Private noninsured pension funds	109.7	46.35
Open-end investment companies	37.3	15.75
Life insurance companies	34.3	14.49
State and local government investment funds	30.1	12.72
Property-casualty insurance companies	17.1	7.22
Mutual savings banks	4.4	1.86
Security brokers and dealers	3.8	1.61
Total	236.7	100.00

Source: Board of Governors of the Federal Reserve System, *Flow of Funds Outstanding, 1965–76,* December 1977, pp. 12 and 13.

receivable. The finance companies either accept accounts receivable as collateral for loans or purchase the accounts receivable outright.

Finance companies obtain funds from three main sources: commercial bank loans, short- and long-term IOUs (securities) sold in financial markets, and stockholders. Being active lenders, finance companies hold few assets in cash or in securities. The major portion of total assets consists of consumer and business receivables, with some small holdings of other loans and investments.

Private Pension Funds

Private pension funds facilitate saving for retirement by collecting contributions from the employee and/or employer during the employee's working life. Upon retirement the employee receives monthly payments. Many employers, including both business and government, have established pension plans. Perhaps the best known (as well as the biggest) pension fund is operated by the federal government—the Federal Old Age and Survivors' Insurance Trust Fund, usually called Social Security.

Private noninsured pension funds, which include all private retirement funds *not* managed by life insurance companies, are directed frequently by bank or nonbank trustees. The two main sources of funds are employer contributions and income earned from investments. Employee contributions and realized capital gains are relatively small sources of funds. In recent years, employers contributed more than half of all receipts of these funds, while employees contributed less than a tenth.

Private pension funds have something in common with life insurance companies: regular, long-term cash inflows and fairly predictable cash outflows. Having less need for short-term liquid investments, these pension funds hold large amounts of corporate equities. When the stock market loses some of its allure, pension funds tend to reduce net purchases of common stocks and to increase their bond buying.

Real Estate Investment Trusts

The latest additions to the ranks of the major financial intermediaries are the *real estate investment trusts,* REITS for short (pronounced REETS). REITS resemble closed-end investment companies by offering initially a fixed number of shares that are not redeemable on request to the issuing companies but must be sold in the securities market.

These trusts confine activities to the real estate sector and constitute a source of financing for real estate development and use. Basically, these institutions pool funds from various sources to make mortgage loans and acquire "income" properties. The three main sources of funds are commercial bank borrowings, sales of short-term marketable IOUs (commercial paper), and additions to shareholders' equity. Depending on existing credit and market conditions, the relative importance of these three sources varies. For instance, in 1973 commercial bank loans and lines of credit supplied 59 percent of new funds acquired by REITS, while commercial paper sales and shares sales each contributed about 12 percent.

Real estate mortgage loans with different maturities constitute the major type of asset holding. Income properties, including apartment and office buildings and shopping centers, are important assets, as shown in Table 3.8. Holdings other than realty investments comprise only a small part of assets. These nonrealty types of assets must be limited for the REITS to qualify for special tax status.

Table 3.8 CONSOLIDATED BALANCE SHEET, ALL REAL ESTATE
INVESTMENT TRUSTS, UNITED STATES, YEAR-END 1976

Assets	Amount (Billions of Dollars)	Percent	Liabilities and Net Worth	Amount (Billions of Dollars)	Percent
Physical assets	8.9	47.3	Multifamily residential		
Home mortgages	1.1	5.9	mortgages	0.8	4.3
Commercial mortgages	5.2	27.7	Commercial mortgages	1.6	8.5
Multifamily mortgages	3.1	16.5	Corporate bonds	1.9	10.1
Miscellaneous assets	0.5	2.6	Bank loans	8.9	47.3
			Open market paper	0.6	3.2
			Shareholders' equity	4.8	26.6
Total	18.8	100.0	Total	18.8	100.0

Source: Board of Governors of the Federal Reserve System, *Flow of Funds Outstanding, 1965–76,* December 1977, p. 13.

In the mid-1970s, many of these trusts, especially those heavily involved in construction and development projects, experienced stormy financial weather. Several factors generated mounting liquidity pressures: rising interest rates, tighter credit availability, rising construction costs aggravated by materials shortages, and a generally depressed housing market.

FEDERAL CREDIT PROGRAMS

Beyond the operation of private financial intermediaries, United States credit markets also include the increasing activity of various federal government credit programs. Generally, *federal credit programs* assume three forms: (1) direct lending by agencies owned by the United States government; (2) direct lending by privately owned agencies that are sponsored by the federal government to serve a public interest; and (3) the insuring or guaranteeing of loans extended directly by private lenders to private borrowers. Since the loan-insuring operations do not entail use of government agency funds except when loan defaults occur, the analysis focuses on those federally owned or sponsored credit agencies that channel funds into particular sectors of the economy. Federal insurance of or guarantee of loans via such agencies as the

Federal Housing Administration and the Veterans Administration provides risk protection to private lenders and thus tends to stimulate a greater flow of private funds into particular areas than would otherwise occur.

Essentially, the immediate function of federal credit agencies is to provide credit accommodation for borrowers who are generally considered marginal or at least subject to relatively high risk arising from cyclical fluctuations or other special factors. In a more fundamental sense, these agencies are oriented toward redistributing economic resources for achieving greater economic stability for certain sectors of the economy. Credit assistance programs are concentrated in two main sectors: agriculture, which has been chronically beset with special credit problems; and housing, where availability of private mortgage credit is reduced appreciably during periods of credit restriction. In recent years, these assistance programs have been extended to other sectors of the economy. For example, an increasing amount of federal lending is directed toward stimulating exports, promoting community development, encouraging small businesses, and assisting higher learning.

Lending by federal credit agencies depends primarily on the sale of agency debt issues in the private securities markets. Currently, at least nine major federal agencies have outstanding debt obligations (see Table 3.9). Of these nine organizations, five are privately owned, government-sponsored agencies and four are agencies owned directly by the federal government. The federally sponsored agencies are especially large borrowers in financial markets and have considerable operating independence. As a group, these sponsored agencies have become major financial intermediaries in recent years. Their pronounced growth occurred especially when financial markets experienced high interest rates and generally restricted total credit availability. A few years after the close of World War II, the Federal Land Banks and the Federal Home Loan Bank system went over to full private ownership. The Federal Land Banks (FLB) provide long-term real estate loans to farmers and ranchers through 643 local Land Bank Associations. The twelve Federal Home Loan Banks affect mortgage credit not by dealing in mortgages directly, but by offering credit assistance to their member savings and loan associations and mutual savings banks. Lending efforts by the Home Loan Banks tend to smooth and expand the operations of private financial intermediaries specializing in mortage credit.

The other three government-sponsored agencies had mixed federal and private ownership until late 1968. In October 1968 the secondary mortgage

Table 3.9   FEDERAL AND FEDERALLY SPONSORED CREDIT
AGENCIES DEBT OUTSTANDING, YEAR-END, 1973–1977
(millions of dollars)

Agency	1973	1974	1975	1976	1977
U.S. government-sponsored					
Federal Home Loan Banks	15,362	21,890	18,900	16,811	18,345
Banks for Cooperatives	2,695	3,655	4,023	4,330	4,434
Federal Intermediate Credit					
Banks	6,932	8,589	9,254	10,494	11,174
Federal Land Banks	10,062	12,653	15,000	17,127	19,118
Federal National Mortgage					
Association	23,002	28,167	29,963	30,565	31,890
U.S. government owned					
Export-Import Bank	2,625	2,893	7,188	8,574	9,156
Federal Housing Administration	415	440	564	575	581
Government National					
Mortgage Association	4,390	4,280	4,200	4,120	3,743
Tennessee Valley Authority	2,435	3,070	3,915	4,935	6,015

Source: Federal Reserve Bulletin, June 1977 and May 1978, p. A35.

market operations of the Federal National Mortgage Association (FNMA),
involving purchases and sales of government-guaranteed mortgages, were
shifted to full private ownership. The remaining functions of the original
FNMA were transferred to a newly created federally owned agency called the
Government National Mortgage Association. At the end of 1968 both the
Federal Intermediate Credit Banks (FICB) and the Banks for Cooperatives
(COOP) achieved full private ownership when all remaining federal holdings
in these agencies were removed. The twelve Federal Intermediate Credit
Banks supply essentially working capital to agriculture. These banks discount
agriculture and livestock loan paper and extend loans to local financing institutions, including production credit associations, agricultural credit corporations, livestock loan companies, and commercial banks. The thirteen Banks
for Cooperatives specialize in short-term loans to farmers' cooperatives.

Thus three government-sponsored agencies provide credit to the agricultural sector: the Banks for Cooperatives, the Federal Land Banks, and Federal Intermediate Credit Banks.[3] Housing receives credit assistance from two federally sponsored agencies, the Federal National Mortgage Association (FNMA, sometimes called "Fannie Mae") and the Federal Home Loan Banks (FHLB), and from two federally owned agencies, the Government National Mortgage Association (GNMA, also known as "Ginnie Mae") and the Federal Housing Administration (FHA). Of the remaining two government-owned agencies, the Export-Import Bank (Eximbank) provides credit assistance in foreign trade transactions, and the Tennessee Valley Authority (TVA) finances facilities for electric power production and flood control purposes.

Recognizing the significant borrowing activities of various federal agencies, including the government-owned credit agencies, Congress created the Federal Financing Bank (FFB) in late 1973. The FFB's major purpose is to coordinate and consolidate the borrowing activities of some twenty federal agencies. Effectively, it serves as an intermediary between credit markets and the frequent but varied borrowing needs of a growing number of individual federal agencies. These agencies are quite diverse, ranging from Amtrak and the Environmental Financing Authority to the Tennessee Valley Authority and U.S. Postal Service.

The FFB provides a central source of financing for federal agencies wholly or partially owned by the U.S. government. Homogeneous FFB debt issues will replace variegated federal agency debt issues, thus making the financing of these agencies' needs more efficient and less expensive. Since the bank's activities are directed by the secretary of the Treasury, its financings are coordinated with direct Treasury debt management operations. However, government-sponsored agencies are excluded from use of the FFB because they are privately owned.

KEY TERMS

Near-monies	Creditors
Credit markets	Debtors

3. The government owned Commodity Credit Corporation deals with agricultural lending, but the corporation has issued no securities since August 1969. Formed in 1933, the agency performs a wide range of activities related to agricultural price support programs as well as to farm export programs.

Financial intermediaries
Disintermediation
Reintermediation
Flow of funds accounts
Interest rate
Mutual savings banks
Savings and loan associations
Credit unions
NOW accounts

Share drafts
Life insurance companies
Property-casualty insurance companies
Investment companies
Finance companies
Private pension funds
Real estate investment trusts
Federal credit programs

REVIEW QUESTIONS

1. What are near-monies? Give examples.
2. Briefly describe the general nature of credit markets.
3. What important services does a modern society derive from credit (or debt)?
4. Define the meaning of financial intermediaries, and discuss briefly their role in modern credit markets.
5. As a data source, describe flow of funds accounts.
6. Explain briefly the nature of interest rates in credit markets.
7. "Financial intermediaries serve as transformers within credit markets." Explain briefly.
8. Give three broad groupings for classifying the major types of private financial intermediaries in the United States.
9. Summarize briefly the basic operating features of the major deposit non-bank financial institutions in the United States.
10. How have deposit institutions in the United States shown growing similarity in recent years?
11. Outline briefly the characteristics of those major private financial institutions that provide risk protection and security in the United States.
12. Describe briefly the main features of each of the following specialized types of private financial institutions found in the United States: (a) finance companies, (b) investment companies, (c) real estate investment trusts.
13. What general forms do U.S. federal credit programs assume?

14. What is the immediate function of the various federal credit agencies?
15. Briefly trace the development and operation of the major federal credit agencies in the United States.

SUGGESTED READINGS

Board of Governors of the Federal Reserve System. *Introduction to Flow of Funds.* Washington, D.C.: Board of Governors, 1975.

Brockschmidt, Peggy. "Credit Union Growth in Perspective." Federal Reserve Bank of Kansas City, *Monthly Review* (February 1977): 3–13.

Burgess, B. Gayle. "Federal Agency Issues." Federal Reserve Bank of Richmond, *Monthly Review* (January 1972): 15–20.

Debs, Richard A. "Our Changing Financial System." Federal Reserve Bank of New York, *Monthly Review* (May 1976): 119–123.

Dobson, Steven W. "Bicentennial Perspective—Development of Capital Markets in the United States." Federal Reserve Bank of Dallas, *Business Review* (April 1976): 1–11.

Francis, Jack C. "Helping Americans Get Mortgages." Federal Reserve Bank of Philadelphia, *Business Review* (January 1974): 14–21.

Harless, Doris E. *Nonbank Financial Institutions.* 4th ed. Federal Reserve Bank of Richmond, 1975.

Light, Jack S. "Increasing Competition Between Financial Institutions." Federal Reserve Bank of Chicago, *Economic Perspective* (May-June 1977): 23–31.

Lovati, Jean M. "The Changing Competition Between Commercial Banks and Thrift Institutions for Deposits." Federal Reserve Bank of St. Louis, *Review* (July 1975): 2–8.

———. "The Growing Similarity Among Financial Institutions." Federal Reserve Bank of St. Louis, *Review* (October 1977): 2–11.

"Nonbank Thrift Institutions in 1975 and 1976." *Federal Reserve Bulletin* 62 (December 1976): 980–985.

Smaistrla, Charles J. "The Payments Mechanism—Current Issues in Electronic Funds Transfer." Federal Reserve Bank of Dallas, *Review* (February 1977): 1–7.

Part Two

THE COMMERCIAL BANKING SYSTEM

Chapter Four

THE STRUCTURE OF THE
COMMERCIAL BANKING SYSTEM

Part One traced the role of the monetary process in the economy and the main aspects of the modern monetary system. Our next task is to examine in some detail each of the three major levels (commercial banking, Federal Reserve, and the federal government) that comprise the modern monetary system. Part Two covers the commercial banking system. A modern monetary system contains a commercial banking sector that affects the monetary process mainly by the creation of demand deposit money. The particular ways in which a given commercial banking system functions reflect the laws and institutional arrangements of the country in which it operates. This chapter examines the structure of the commercial banking system in the United States. The structural features of other nations' commercial banking systems will vary, but all commercial banking systems have the common characteristic of creating money in the form of demand deposits.

FACTORS AFFECTING THE
BANKING STRUCTURE

The *commercial banking structure* refers to the number, organization, and relative size of banking firms operating within a given market or markets. Many factors can affect the structure of commercial banking. Some of the more significant elements shaping the commercial banking structure in the United States are described in the following sections.

The Dual Banking System

A distinguishing feature of the commercial banking structure in the United States is the existence of a dual authority governing the chartering of new commercial banks. According to this *dual banking system,* the federal and the state governments grant national and state charters, respectively, for the operation of new commercial banking firms. State governments have long been in the business of chartering commercial banks, dating from the time the republic of the United States was founded.

National (or federal) charters for commercial banks began with the passage of the National Banking Acts of the 1860s. The Office of the Comptroller of the Currency, which is a part of the United States Department of the Treasury, administers provisions of the federal legislation relating to the chartering of national banks. In general, these federal requirements are more stringent than those of the individual state governments. Recommendations for the establishment of more uniform bank chartering requirements at the federal and state levels unfortunately remain unheeded. The divergence of standards partly reflects the question of states' rights in the area of banking regulation.

At the time the initial National Banking Act was passed by Congress in 1863, informed observers anticipated that eventually all operating commercial banks would have national charters. Under the pressure of a 10 percent federal tax levied in 1865 on their outstanding note issues, state banks ended their lending activities in the form of the issuance of state bank notes. At the same time, the rise of deposit banking sustained these existing state banks. To this day some two-thirds of all commercial banking firms in the United States carry state charters. On the other hand, the remaining one-third, those banks with national charters, account for the majority of commercial banking resources in the United States.

This same dual authority also regulates the issuance of permits to establish branch offices of banks. State-chartered banks are subject to state authorities in applying for branch permits, while federally chartered banks apply to the Comptroller of the Currency for branch permits. In a 1976 ruling, the Supreme Court held that even commercial bank electronic terminals (nicknamed "twenty-four-hour tellers") are branches within the meaning of the national bank laws and thereby subject to state laws limiting commercial bank branching activity. Under terms of the McFadden Act of 1927, national

Figure 4.1 THE STRUCTURE OF COMMERCIAL BANKING

Statewide branch banking predominates in the West and on the East Coast; unit banking prevails in the Midwest.

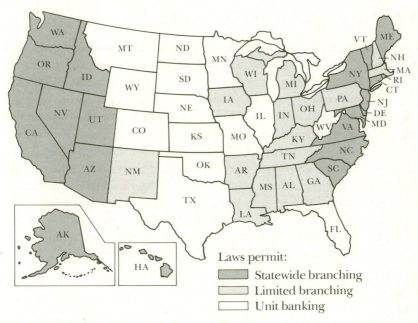

Laws permit:
- ▨ Statewide branching
- ▨ Limited branching
- ☐ Unit banking

Source: Board of Governors of the Federal Reserve System.

banks may branch only to the same extent that state law permits branching for state-chartered banks.

Currently, legal factors partly limit the extent of branch banking in the United States. State branching laws (which are followed by the federal authorities for national banks) vary and may be classified into three groups: (1) states permitting *statewide branching* (twenty states and the District of Columbia); (2) states permitting *limited branching,* usually in head-office county (sixteen states); and (3) states that allow only *unit banking* (fourteen states).

Figure 4.1 shows the prevalence of statewide branching in the far West and on the East Coast; limited branching is predominant in states between the East Coast and the Mississippi River; and unit banking is found mainly in the midwestern states. Interstate branching by banks is not permitted, while the establishment of foreign branches abroad is subject to federal regulation, primarily by the Edge Act.

Number of Banks

One feature of commercial banking in the United States evident even to a casual observer is the presence of a large number of commercial banks throughout the country. While each of the major Western countries has one or two dozen commercial banks, the United States numbers its commercial banks in the thousands. At the end of 1977, for instance, the total number of commercial banks in the United States exceeded 14,700. By way of comparison, the United States's northern neighbor, Canada, has about a dozen commercial banks. Similar results occur when the United States is compared with Latin American and European nations. With such a large number of commercial banks in the United States, it is not surprising that a majority of these banks are "small fry," that is, banks with total deposits of $25 million or less (see Table 4.1). As shown in Table 4.1, the relatively few "big" commercial banks are those with more than a billion dollars of deposits each.

Unit Banking

The large number of commercial banks in the United States reflects the dominance of *unit banking,* that is, individual banking firms operating single offices. At the beginning of 1975, for example, a total of 9,334 commercial banks operated single (unit) offices, while the remaining 5,123 commercial banks operated multiple offices (two or more banking offices). These additional offices and branches numbered over 28,000.

Although the number of commercial banking firms has declined since World War II, there has been an appreciable expansion of banking *offices,* reflecting the large growth in branch banking. The sustained growth in branch banking keeps alive a continuing debate regarding the advantages and disadvantages associated with this form of banking organization. Many of the presumed benefits of branching relate to efficiency and safety in mobilizing funds, especially by providing banking facilities in small towns. A branch banking system provides flexible mobilization of funds by shifting excess reserves for lending among various offices of the system. As a result, branch

Table 4.1 NUMBER AND DEPOSITS OF ALL COMMERCIAL BANKS,
UNITED STATES, YEAR-END 1976

Asset Size (Millions of Dollars)	Number of Banks	Percentage Distribution	Amount of Deposits (Millions of Dollars)	Percentage Distribution
Less than 5	1686	11.47	4,780	0.57
5–10	2879	19.59	19,035	2.26
10–25	5004	34.05	74,250	8.82
25–50	2655	18.06	82,663	9.82
50–100	1322	8.99	80,571	9.57
100–300	743	5.06	104,616	12.43
300–500	159	1.08	50,560	6.00
500–1,000	120	.82	68,032	8.08
1,000–5,000	112	.76	162,377	19.29
5,000–or more	18	.12	195,005	23.16
Total	14,698	100.00	841,889	100.00

Source: Federal Deposit Insurance Corporation, *Annual Report*, 1976, p. 228.

offices can be established in localities that generate a fairly unbalanced banking business. Also, in initiating operations, a new branch often draws on the pool of experienced management personnel within a large branch system.

A criticism frequently raised against branch banking is its adverse effects on banking competition and concentration. No firm consensus exists on this issue, but there is emerging skepticism regarding the impact on banking competition of expanded branch banking. This view is reflected in the following comment by a former Federal Reserve official:

Our thinking needs reorienting about our banking structure. What kind of a banking system can best serve the U.S. economy as it is evolving? The kind of banking structure we have now seems to be singularly inappropriate; it is time to put more emphasis on scale and services and less on locally protected market areas.[1]

1. George W. Mitchell, "What Can We Do About Bank Structure," *Proceedings of a Conference on Bank Structure and Competition* (Federal Reserve Bank of Chicago, 1969), p. 114.

Membership in the Central Banking System

All nationally chartered commercial banks must be *member banks,* that is, they must hold membership in the central banking system of the United States (Federal Reserve System). State-chartered banks may join the Federal Reserve System provided they meet certain requirements. Most state banks have not chosen to join the Federal Reserve, particularly in light of the system's generally more stringent legal reserve and capital requirements. Although a minority of all commercial banks have Federal Reserve membership, these member banks hold over 70 percent of all commercial banking deposits in the United States.

Since World War II the Federal Reserve has faced a continuing problem relating to membership. Between 1947 and 1978 the proportion of all commercial banks that were members dropped from 48.8 percent to 38.5 percent, and the fraction of all deposits held by member banks decreased from 85.0 percent to 72.3 percent.

In the decade ending in 1977, 551 banks withdrew from Federal Reserve membership. Although many of these "dropout" banks were small, there is an emerging trend among larger member banks to become nonmembers. For instance, of the 69 banks that left the Federal Reserve in 1977, 15 each had deposits exceeding $100 million.

Some observers, including the Commission on Money and Credit (whose report was published in 1961) and the President's Commission on Financial Structure and Regulation (report given in 1971), suggest a broadening of membership in the Federal Reserve System through passage of federal legislation in order to improve the span of monetary control. It is unlikely that this change will be made, if one judges from the attitudes of many commercial banks that prefer the existing arrangement. In effect, these bankers favor the escape hatch provided by the voluntary nature of Federal Reserve membership for state-chartered banks.

Bank Deposit Insurance

The Federal Deposit Insurance Corporation (FDIC), established in 1934, provides deposit insurance to over 98 percent of all U.S. commercial banks.

Technically, all Federal Reserve member banks must be *insured banks,* that is, have deposits insured by the FDIC; however, most nonmember commercial banks also carry the federal insurance.

If a federally insured commercial bank is closed and liquidated, the FDIC will pay insured depositors up to the maximum of $40,000 per account within ten days after the closing. Interestingly, at the start of 1977, the FDIC's liquidation division was, in terms of assets, the largest real estate investment trust in the country. At various times, this division had owned or operated a flotilla of shrimp and tuna boats, a taxicab fleet, vineyards, abandoned churches, and a copy of the *Koran* valued at several million dollars. In cases where the deposit liabilities of a failed bank are assumed by another, sound, bank with financial assistance from the FDIC, depositors have the full and unrestricted use of all their funds.

The widely publicized failure of certain large commercial banks in the mid-1970s raises the question of bank deposit safety. The record, however, indicates the low incidence of commercial bank failures in the United States. In the difficult period from 1973 through 1976, only thirty-nine banks failed, and most were relatively small. In 1977, six banks failed. Generally, the authorities are able to arrange takeovers of the failed institutions by healthy banks. Few failed banks are liquidated, thus permitting uninterrupted services to bank customers and minimizing depositors' losses on uninsured balances (see Table 4.2).

The FDIC has always met its deposit insurance commitment. The federal insurance fund of more than $6 billion at year end 1974 reflects insurance premiums paid by insured banks and the investment income on such premiums. This fund, which is growing yearly by about $400 million, is supplemented by a $3 billion line of credit with the United States Treasury. The FDIC has never had to borrow from the Treasury, however. Although the federal deposit insurance fund totals about 1 percent of all insured deposits in the country, the FDIC has had to use only a small portion of the fund at any one time, even when big banks have failed.

The largest commercial bank failure in United States history was the Franklin National Bank of New York in October 1974. The second largest bank failure involved the United States National Bank of San Diego a year earlier. Even including these two bank failures, the FDIC's *net loss* in 506 bank failures between 1934 and 1974 was only about $225 million.

Table 4.2 ESTIMATED LOSSES FROM COMMERCIAL BANK
FAILURES, UNITED STATES, 1970–1976

Year	Number of Failures	Disposition		Estimated Losses to Creditors (thousands)				
		Deposit Payoff	Purchase and Assumption	Depositors	Debtholders	Stockholders	FDIC	Total
1970	7	4	3	$ 585	$ 0	$ 8,572	$ 825	$ 9,982
1971	6	5	1	3,541	0	31,124	1,215	35,880
1972	1	1	0	713	0	1,863	4,000	6,576
1973	6	3	3	0	15,000	56,097	150,269	221,366
1974	4	0	4	0	29,600	167,243	4,100	200,951
1975	13	3	10	1,138	2,600	49,103	35,045	87,886
1976	16	3	13	649	7,038	88,191	15,308	111,186
Total	53	19	34	$6,626	$54,246	$402,193	$210,762	$673,827

Source: Chayim Herzig-Marx, "Bank Failures," Federal Reserve Bank of Chicago, *Economic Perspectives*, March-April 1978, p. 30.

International Influences

In recent years, international factors increasingly affect the structure of U.S. commercial banking. These international influences have a two-way effect. Not only have a rising number of domestic commercial banks tended to establish operations overseas, but foreign banks have made a major entry into banking operations in the United States.

United States commercial banks have expanded their foreign operations over the years so that by year end 1973 some 140 U.S. banks had opened either branches or subsidiaries in 150 foreign countries. Furthermore, at the start of 1975, 125 Federal Reserve member banks operated a total of 732 overseas branches, with estimated total assets of over $150 billion. Several factors attracted U.S. banks abroad: the dollar's role in international finance, continued expansion of international activities of U.S. corporations, strong growth of world trade, and the increasing internationalization of financial markets throughout the world.

In addition to being subject to the laws of their host countries, U.S. member commercial banks operating abroad are subject to Federal Reserve regulations relating to the establishment of foreign branches of member banks, investment in foreign subsidiaries and affiliates, and the chartering of so-called Edge Act corporations, which are domestic companies that engage in international banking business. In addition, state authorities retain jurisdiction over the foreign branching activity of state-chartered banks that are not members of the Federal Reserve System.

At the same time that U.S. commercial banks have gone abroad, foreign banks have been attracted to the United States. By April 1978 there were 122 foreign banks operating in the United States with total assets of $90 billion and more than $26 billion in commercial and industrial loans. European, Japanese, and Canadian banks accounted for most of these assets. Motivated largely by a desire to participate in foreign trade financing and also to gain access to United States financial markets, these foreign banks have located mainly along the east and west coasts, with some banks operating in Chicago.

Until recently, foreign banks operating in the United States were primarily subject to state, rather than federal, regulation. Unlike U.S. commercial banks, which are forbidden by the McFadden Act to engage in interstate banking, foreign banks have been able to open interstate offices. Prior to September 1978, foreign banks could have branches in several states, assuming permission was granted by the states concerned. This situation reflected the fact that branches of foreign banks operated under individual state charters and thus came under state banking laws. Thus an individual foreign bank can maintain branches, for example, in New York and in California, and offer full-scale domestic banking business in each branch.

In September 1978 the International Banking Act was signed into law. This act established for the first time a national policy regulating foreign banks' activities in the United States. A key feature of the law is that it places foreign banks essentially under the same limitations that prohibit domestic banks from opening a branch in more than one state. Existing interstate branches of foreign banks were exempted from the new legal restrictions.

Bank Merger Activity

Bank merger activity has been a major factor in the decline in the number of commercial banking firms since World War II. Merger activity reached its peak in the 1950s, when 1,503 banks with combined assets of more than $25 billion were absorbed through mergers. During the 1960s mergers continued at a slightly lower rate.

Although it is difficult to weigh the specific factors operating in a particular bank merger, some of the more important economic factors contributing to bank mergers include (1) moves by banks to strengthen market positions through diversified operations, particularly in the growing area of "retail banking" for households and small businesses; (2) adaptation to appreciable population shifts into outlying suburban areas through the acquisition of readymade banking facilities, often more legally accessible than newly established offices; (3) adjustment to the enhanced role of commercial lending, which has prompted banks to merge so that they can counteract lagging growth in deposits and business, expand stipulated loan limits, meet rising competitive pressure of nonbank lenders, and forestall officer shortages; and (4) attempts to offset the undervaluation of bank shares and to augment financial prestige.

The heightened merger activity of the 1950s, linked with the absence of clear-cut standards for appraising proposed mergers, prompted congressional passage of the Bank Merger Act of 1960. This act stipulated, among other things, several criteria for evaluating bank mergers, and it provided for prior written approval by a federal bank supervisory agency of all mergers involving banks insured by the Federal Deposit Insurance Corporation. This legislation covers virtually all commercial banks, since fewer than 2 percent of all banks are not insured by the corporation.

During the 1960s the antitrust division of the Department of Justice and the courts effected bank merger regulation by extending the antitrust laws to banking. Confusion about the application of antitrust laws to bank mergers induced Congress to amend the Bank Merger Act in 1966. Essentially, the amendment incorporates pertinent sections of the Sherman Act and Clayton Act into the Bank Merger Act.

Bank Holding Companies

A further feature of the banking structure is the prevalence of bank holding companies. Stated simply, *bank holding companies* are companies that own or control, directly or indirectly, one or more commercial banks. Frequently, the holding company relation arises through a corporation obtaining control of banks, whether by the direct purchase of stock or by the exchange of holding company stock for the stock of individual independent banks.

In general, two types of bank holding companies can be distinguished: multibank and one-bank companies. Multibank holding companies are often established as alternatives to bank branching systems in those states prohibiting branching. The Bank Holding Company Act of 1956 required registration with the Board of Governors of the Federal Reserve System of all multibank companies holding 25 percent or more control in the stock of each of two or more banks. Congress did not extend regulation to one-bank holding companies either in 1956 or when the act was amended in 1966 because these companies were typically small concerns controlling small banks, located largely in unit-banking states.

One-bank holding companies can be nonbank-originated or bank-originated. A bank-originated company, sometimes called a financial con-generic, occurs when an operating bank forms a holding company in which the bank ultimately becomes a subsidiary. In this case, the bank is the main part of the holding company organization and the other parts of the holding company engage in financial or bank-related activities.

In the late 1960s the number of single-bank holding companies grew rapidly: in the five years between 1966 and 1970 some 890 such companies were started as compared with a net increase of 344 in the previous

Table 4.3   GROWTH OF BANK HOLDING COMPANIES IN THE
UNITED STATES, 1971–1976

Year-end	Number of Companies	Number of Offices		Total Deposits (Millions of Dollars)	Percent of Total U.S. Deposits
		Banks	Branches		
1971	1,567	2,420	10,832	297,011	55.3
1972	1,607	2,720	13,441	379,355	61.5
1973	1,677	3,097	15,374	446,567	65.4
1974	1,752	3,462	17,131	509,737	68.1
1975	1,821	3,674	18,382	527,515	67.1
1976	1,802	3,791	19,199	553,649	66.1

Source: Board of Governors of Federal Reserve System, *Annual Statistical Digest,* 1971–1975, pp. 279–80; Federal Reserve Bank of Richmond, *Economic Review,* March-April 1978, p. 4.

decade. The upsurge in the number of one-bank holding companies during this period reflected the banks' use of a legal loophole to diversify operations beyond limits set by state and federal banking laws. In fact, at year end 1968, thirty-four of the largest one hundred commercial banks in the United States either had formed or had announced they would form one-bank holding companies. One-bank holding companies, which account for most bank holding company activity in the United States, held over one-third of the nation's deposits at commercial banks in 1970.

Table 4.3 gives recent data for bank holding companies (both multibank and one-bank types) that report to the Federal Reserve as required by the amended Federal Bank Holding Company Act. At the beginning of 1977, more than 1,800 holding companies existed, and these companies accounted for two-thirds of total commercial bank deposits in the United States (see Table 4.3). At that time, more than four out of every five holding companies were one-bank holding companies.

Concentration in Banking

A significant aspect of commercial banking structure is the degree of concentration existing in banking resources. Generally, the extent of *banking concen-*

tration is measured by the proportion of either total deposits or total assets held by a given number of the largest commercial banks within a specified market area. In local (urban and metropolitan areas) banking markets the concentration ratio is typically the proportion of total commercial bank deposits in the area accounted for by the three biggest commercial banks. For states, concentration ratios frequently relate to the five top banks; for the nation as a whole, the coverage usually includes the one hundred largest banks.

There are certain limitations in the use of concentration ratios for gauging market structure. Determination of the number of banks to be used in computing the concentration ratio is highly arbitrary. Should the magic number include the top two, three, five, or some other number of banking firms? A meaningful concentration ratio requires the determination of the boundaries of the relevant market. This involves many difficulties and assumptions that are open to dispute, as evidenced by the various judicial interpretations over the years. In addition, concentration ratios computed on the basis of total magnitudes (deposits or assets) ignore the explicit product line—for example, demand deposits or business loans—to be examined. The overall ratios may differ markedly from the actual degree of concentration in a given product line.

Furthermore, the concentration ratio does not allow for the number and size distribution of all banking firms in a given market. What is the disparity in size, if any, among the individual banks, and what is the total number of banks involved? This question bears heavily on the measurement of the banking structure.[2]

In assessing banking concentration, failure to allow for the role of nonbank financial institutions can overstate the position of commercial banks in various markets. Beyond demand deposit services, most of the product lines offered by commercial banks have close substitutes supplied by other financial institutions. For example, mutual savings banks, savings and loan associations, and credit unions all offer services similar to commercial banks' time and savings deposit services.

As of late 1978, commercial banks and savings institutions competed di-

---

2. The Herfindahl index attempts to lessen these shortcomings by taking account of the size of all banks in a market. The index is computed by taking the sum of the squares of the market shares of the firms in the given market. The Herfindahl index is evaluated much like the concentration ratio: higher magnitudes of the index reflect more concentrated markets.

rectly with checking services in the six New England states and in New York, where negotiable orders of withdrawal (NOW) accounts were authorized by Congress. These accounts pay interest and allow holders to write checklike negotiable orders of withdrawal. Thus, functionally, NOWs are interest-bearing checking accounts. Proposals have been submitted in Congress to legalize NOWs nationwide.

Competitive forces arise from another development. Under amended federal banking regulations effective November 1, 1978, commercial banks may make preauthorized transfers of funds between savings and demand deposit accounts of customers. The use of automatic funds transfer (AFT) services effectively enables banks to mix savings and checking accounts.

With this background in mind, we can examine some of the factors affecting United States banking concentration during the 1970s. On a nationwide basis, the percentage of total domestic deposits held by the largest one hundred banking organizations actually declined from 49 to 47 percent in the five years between 1968 and 1973. Banking organizations consist of holding company groups and independent commercial banks. All commercial banks affiliated with a bank holding company would constitute a single banking organization. This decline in concentration occurred even though the holding companies included among those top one hundred banking organizations had acquired banks over that five-year period that held almost $17 billion total deposits in 1973. In the absence of these holding company acquisitions, overall banking concentration would have dropped another 2.3 percentage points over the period.

On an individual state level, banking concentration varies greatly. Generally, concentration is highest in states with statewide branching, and lowest in unit-banking states. For our purposes, banking concentration is measured by the percentage of total domestic deposits held by the five largest banking organizations in an individual state. Between 1968 and 1973, banking concentration increased in twenty-eight states, declined in twenty-two states, and was unchanged in one state. If the changes in statewide concentration for the fifty states and the District of Columbia are taken together, both the *mean* and *median* changes in concentration for the group amounted to less than one percentage point over the five-year period. Acquisitions by holding companies raised concentration ratios in twenty-four states, but only six of these states recorded increases greater than ten percentage points. None of these six states is in the group of states considered to have high levels of banking concentration. Furthermore, in those states with high banking concentration, holding company acquisitions had no effect on concentration levels during the period from 1968 to 1973.

THE BANKING STRUCTURE AND REGULATION

A review of the major elements affecting the banking structure shows that commercial banking is heavily regulated and supervised. Commercial banking is regulated because its operations greatly affect the public interest. Since demand deposits comprise the major part of the general public's money supply, the failure or other malfunctioning of a commercial bank can have adverse effects on the community beyond the loss accruing to the bank's stockholders. In addition, commercial banks have liabilities that are very great relative to their capital (or owner's equity), and thus opportunities arise for highly speculative lending activity by reckless bankers.

The development of banking regulation also reflects an attempt to avoid the disturbing effects of past events affecting commercial banking in the United States. A sensitive reading of banking history reveals several incidents that tended to support government intervention: the turbulent and chaotic conditions during the period of "free banking" between 1837 and 1863, when newly enacted state laws granted open access to bank charters; the many bank failures of the 1920s; and the widespread economic depression of the early 1930s with its shattering effect on commercial banking. The apparent need for government intervention in the operations of the industry brought an intricate and widespread system of commercial bank regulation at the federal and state levels: specific restrictions on lending and borrowing, usury laws, interest rate ceilings on time and savings deposits, prohibition of paying interest on demand deposits, minimum capital and management requirements for establishing new banks, limitations on bank branching, stipulations for periodic publication of financial condition, and bank examinations by supervisory groups.

At the same time that commercial banking is subject to many specific regulations, there is considerable leeway for banking firms to engage in various forms of price and nonprice competition. For example, banks have reasonable discretion regarding the choice of particular kinds of lending and interest rates charged. Nonprice competition affords even more alternatives for keeping old customers and attracting new ones. In recent years banking regulation has become concerned with promoting a constructive role for competition in banking. Here the emphasis is on improving efficiency, that is, on achieving a banking system that provides the maximum in banking services to customers at the lowest possible cost. In effect, the economic theory of competition provides a rough benchmark for appraising banking structure and for orienting the operations of regulatory authorities. However, the competitive model offers limited operational guidance, because it is difficult to quantify the various factors that bear on banking competition.

ANTITRUST POLICY AND BANKING COMPETITION

The regulatory approach to banking competition is shown in the evolution of antitrust policy relating to commercial banking. The Sherman Act of 1890 is the basic legislation for antitrust policy in the United States. A brief and vaguely worded statute, the Sherman Act prohibits the illegal restraint of trade and monopolization of commerce. Failure of Congress to specify what constitutes unlawful restraint of trade, plus a lack of common-law precedents, brought about the gradual evolution of antitrust jurisprudence on a case-by-case basis for some sixty years. In the six-decade period following its enactment, the Sherman Act was supplemented by varied legislation that defined specific types of illegal practices. One of the earliest and most significant of these was the Clayton Act of 1914, which covered especially price discrimination, tying contracts, full-line forcing, corporate stock acquisitions, and interlocking directorates.[3] Not surprisingly, judicial interpretation and application of antitrust law provide the basis for determining the substance of illegal conduct under the law.

Generally, it was not until the 1960s that the gradually evolved body of national antitrust law was applied to commercial banking. A major factor

---

3. Other legislation enacted after the Clayton Act included the Robinson-Patman Act of 1936, which replaced the weak price discrimination coverage of the Clayton Act with detailed provisions relating to differential pricing and other discriminatory marketing practices; and the Celler-Kefauver Act of 1950, which amended the Clayton Act by forestalling corporate mergers, consolidations, and acquisitions of assets that promote undue economic concentration.

responsible for this delay was the Supreme Court's justification of federal antitrust legislation under the commerce clause of the Constitution, while several decisions of the Court made in the nineteenth century held that money transactions did not constitute "trade or commerce." At the same time, federal regulation of banking and currency was upheld on the basis that Congress had power to "coin money and regulate the value thereof." This background supported the judicial view that Congress intended commercial banking to be exempt from antitrust law. Further support for this view arose from the explicit legislation affecting commercial banks, for example, the National Banking Acts, the Federal Reserve Act, and existing state laws.

However, in 1944 the Supreme Court's ruling in the *South-Eastern Under-writers Association* case made the Sherman Act applicable to commercial banking by concluding that ". . . the transmission of great quantities of money, documents and communications across . . . state lines" is interstate commerce for antitrust purposes.[4] Subsequently, in the *Transamerica* case of 1948, the Federal Reserve instituted under the Clayton Act the first antitrust proceeding against corporate acquisitions of stock in commercial banks. The complaint held that the large diversified bank holding company's bank stock acquisitions imparted unlawful control of a large proportion of commercial banking business in a five-state western area (Arizona, California, Oregon, Nevada, and Washington). Although the Federal Reserve eventually lost the case, the circuit court's opinion in 1953 held that commercial banking was interstate commerce and subject to antitrust regulation.

REGULATION OF BANK HOLDING
COMPANIES AND MERGERS

The *Transamerica* case anticipated the passage of the Bank Holding Company Act of 1956, the first comprehensive legislation controlling the formation and expansion of registered bank holding companies (legally defined as controlling 25 percent or more of the stock of each of two or more banks) and requiring the disposal of their nonbanking interests. The act listed three groups of factors to be considered by the Board of Governors of the Federal

---

4. *United States* v. *South-Eastern Underwriters Association*, 322 U. S. 533 (1944).

Reserve in evaluating a proposed acquisition of a bank: (1) "banking factors" relating to solvency, earnings prospects, and management capabilities; (2) factors affecting community convenience; and (3) factors affecting banking competition. The first group reflected traditional regulatory concern for safety of bank deposits by stressing liquidity and solvency considerations. The last two groups evidenced for the first time legislative concern for nonsafety-oriented elements such as competitive results for banking and the probable service benefits for the community.

In response to the postwar upsurge in bank merger activity, Congress enacted the Bank Merger Act of 1960. Prior to 1960 bank mergers had been subject to a loose combination of capital requirements and branching restrictions. The act required every bank merger involving an insured bank to have the prior written approval of one of the three federal bank supervisory agencies (Comptroller of Currency, Federal Reserve, and Federal Deposit Insurance Corporation). Furthermore, the act gave specific regulatory standards for evaluating mergers. These were similar to those included in the Bank Holding Company Act of 1956, but both acts were unclear regarding the relative importance to be accorded to each of the three groups of factors. In addition, the act required the Department of Justice and the two federal banking agencies not having jurisdiction to submit advisory reports assessing the competitive implications of the proposed bank merger. The legislation made no stipulation about the applicability of the antitrust laws to bank mergers.

The question surrounding the applicability of the antitrust laws was answered by two significant Supreme Court decisions that permitted antitrust challenges to bank mergers approved by federal banking agencies. In the *Philadelphia Bank* case (1963), the Court held that the proposed merger of two Philadelphia banks would violate section 7 of the Clayton Act.[5] Basically, section 7 prohibits a corporation engaged in commerce from acquiring the stock or assets of another corporation if the merger would substantially lessen competition or tend to create a monopoly. The Court also asserted that a merger cannot be saved by some reckoning of social benefits to the community if it violates antitrust laws. The *Lexington Bank* case (1964) established the

5. *United States* v. *Philadelphia National Bank, et al.*, 201 F. Supp. 348 (1962) 83 S. Ct. 1715 (1963).

position that if a merger eliminates a substantial competitor in banking, the merger violates the Sherman Act.[6]

These two Supreme Court decisions stressed the judicial emphasis on competitive factors in evaluating bank mergers, while the federal bank regulatory agencies gave relatively greater weight to the banking, convenience, and needs factors. Attempting to reconcile these differences, Congress in 1966 enacted legislation amending the Bank Merger Act of 1960. The amendment accorded greater significance to the competitive factors than the original act by incorporating essentially section 2 of the Sherman Act and section 7 of the Clayton Act. Under the 1966 act, the responsible federal banking agency would not approve any merger proposal that would result in a monopoly or that would attempt to monopolize banking in any section of the country. However, a proposed merger likely to bring about reduction of competition of substantial but not monopolistic proportions could be approved under certain conditions. Approval would be justified if the adverse competitive effects were "clearly outweighed in the public interest by the probable effect of the transaction in meeting the convenience and needs of the community to be served." Bank merger proposals involving less than a substantial reduction in competition could be approved only if the community benefits (convenience and needs) exceeded any anticompetitive effects. In all merger cases, regulatory agencies were directed to continue to consider "banking factors."

A similar revision of the Bank Holding Company Act of 1956 was made in 1966. In both amending acts Congress asserted the applicability of antitrust laws to bank mergers, but at the same time provided for possible (and probably rare) exceptions. In addition, under the Merger Act amendment a mandatory thirty-day waiting period enables the Department of Justice to bring suit to stop the proposed merger or acquisition approved by the responsible banking agency.

Until year end 1970 the Bank Holding Company Act covered only multibank holding companies, that is, companies controlling at least 25 percent of the stock in each of two or more banks. Generally, these bank holding companies were prohibited from engaging in any business other than banking

---

6. *United States* v. *First National Bank and Trust Company of Lexington, et al.*, 208 F. Supp. 457 (1962); 84 S. Ct. 1033 (1964). The provisions of the Sherman Act are more stringent than those of the Clayton Act, since the Sherman Act prohibits any tendency toward monopolization or restraint of trade by contract, combination in the form of trust, or otherwise.

and managing banks. The great increase in the number of one-bank holding companies originated by commercial banks during the late 1960s brought legislation at the end of 1970 amending the Bank Holding Company Act of 1956 to include holding companies owning 25 percent or more of one bank.

The 1970 amendments established broad standards to be used by the Federal Reserve in determining those nonbank activities that would be permitted to regulated bank holding companies. The interpretation of these standards will determine the extent to which bank holding companies can diversify, both in services offered and in geographical expansion. In making its determination, the Federal Reserve applies two related standards. First of all, it must decide if an activity is "so closely related to banking or managing or controlling banks as to be a proper incident thereto." In addition, it must determine whether the offering of a particular activity "can reasonably be expected to produce benefits to the public, such as greater convenience, increased competition, or gains in efficiency, that outweigh possible adverse effects such as undue concentration of resources, decreased or unfair competition, conflicts of interests, or unsound banking practices."

Early in 1971 the Federal Reserve authorities offered a "laundry list" of activities acceptable for bank holding company acquisitions. A bank holding company could apply for permission to obtain an interest in a company engaged solely in one of ten "permissible" activities, including, for example, an industrial bank, a concern servicing loans, or a firm making loans for its own account or for the account of others. By the mid-1970s this approved list had increased to twenty-one activities. At that same time several activities were specifically denied to bank holding companies, while five pending activities were under consideration by the Federal Reserve Board.

SUPREME COURT DECISIONS AND
THE BANK MERGER ACT OF 1966

Supreme Court decisions relating to the interpretation of the Bank Merger Act of 1966 indicate a melding of the Bank Merger Act with the Clayton Act. The first cases heard under the amended act were in 1967: the *Provident Bank* case and *First City Bank* case.[7]

7. *United States* v. *Provident National Bank, et al.,* 262 F. Supp. 397 (1966); 87 S. Ct. 1088 (1967) and *United States* v. *First City National Bank of Houston, et al.,* 87 S. Ct. 1088 (1967).

In a single opinion covering these two cases the Supreme Court held that the Department of Justice need contest a bank merger only on grounds of violation of antitrust laws rather than on violation of the Bank Merger Act. Although the two bank mergers had been approved by the Comptroller of the Currency, the Court upheld the Department of Justice's contention that decisions of bank regulatory agencies are not binding on the courts. Another procedural matter involved the Court's placing on defendant banks the burden of proof to establish that the anticompetitive effects of a merger were outweighed by convenience and needs considerations.

In the *Third National Bank* case (1968), involving a merger between the second and fourth largest commercial banks in Nashville, Tennessee, the Court reaffirmed and clarified its earlier decisions in the *Provident Bank* case and *First City Bank* case.[8] Specifically, the Court ruled that a valid defense of an anticompetitive bank merger on the basis of public interest required an explicit description and definition of the value of the merger's benefits. More importantly, the defendants would have to show that the gains expected from the merger could not reasonably be attained other than through merger.

The first major bank merger decision of the Supreme Court in the 1970s was given in the *Phillipsburg National Bank* case (1970).[9] The merger proposal involved the third and fifth largest banks located in the two-city area of Phillipsburg, New Jersey, and Easton, Pennsylvania, the cities being directly opposite each other on the Delaware River. The main thrust of the Court's decision was that antitrust laws could be applied to mergers involving two directly competing banks, regardless of the absolute size of the banks involved. Each of the two banks had deposits under $30 million. In reaching its decision, the Court adopted the Department of Justice's relatively narrow definition of the geographic and product market and reasoned that consumers and small businesses are generally likely to establish banking connections on the basis of convenience. Rejecting the lower court's position that banking competition should be viewed from the various submarkets in which a bank competed, the Supreme Court held that commercial banks are unique through their offering of diversified financial products and services and that

---

8. *United States* v. *Third National Bank of Nashville, et al.,* 260 F. Supp. 869 (1966); 88 S. Ct. 882 (1968).

9. *United States* v. *Phillipsburg National Bank and Trust Company, et al.,* 306 F. Supp. 645 (1969); 90 S. Ct. 2035 (1970).

therefore only commercial banks can be included in an analysis of market competition.

These Supreme Court decisions in bank merger cases following the enactment of the Bank Merger Act of 1966 suggest no great change in judicial interpretation of bank mergers. Although the 1966 legislation was to fill in the gaps of the original merger act of 1960, it still left several important questions unanswered. For example, there was no stipulation of specific factors involved in evaluating competitive effects of bank mergers or of the validity of the use of changes in concentration ratios for determining results for banking competition.

Furthermore, the law overlooks the task of determining the overall market effects of a merger by not providing standards for evaluating a bank's standing in various product and service markets. Likewise, the law is silent on the extent to which a merger's estimated benefits must exceed potentially adverse competitive effects to justify an approval.

In its bank merger decisions the Supreme Court has stressed Clayton Act benchmarks of competition and has used orthodox quantitative measures such as concentration ratios and number of market participants to assess anticompetitive results. Nonbank financial institutions are excluded from market structure analysis because the Court has held that commercial banking is the only relevant line of commerce or product market for evaluating bank mergers. At the same time, the Court has expressed willingness to accept a public interest defense of a contested bank merger if positive net benefits can be shown and if no other feasible alternative exists for achieving these benefits.

KEY TERMS

Commercial banking structure

Dual banking system

Statewide branching

Limited branching

Unit banking

Member banks

Insured banks

Bank holding companies

Banking concentration

REVIEW QUESTIONS

1. Give the meaning of commercial banking structure.
2. Describe briefly the nature of the dual banking system in the United States.
3. Comment on the amount and extent of unit banking in the United States.
4. What elements influence commercial bank membership in the Federal Reserve System?
5. Briefly explain the Federal Deposit Insurance Corporation's role in providing safety for bank deposits.
6. Assess the international influences on the structure of U.S. commercial banking.
7. What forces have influenced the bank merger movement in the United States since World War II?
8. Describe the general nature and extent of bank holding company activity in the United States.
9. Explain and evaluate various criteria for measuring the extent of banking concentration in the United States.
10. How do you justify government regulation and supervision of commercial banking?
11. Describe briefly the evolution of United States antitrust policy relating to commercial banking.
12. Summarize the main features of the Bank Holding Company Act of 1956 and its amendments in 1966 and 1970.

SUGGESTED READINGS

Broaddus, Alfred. "The Banking Structure: What It Means and Why It Matters." Federal Reserve Bank of Richmond, *Monthly Review* (November 1971): 2–7f.

Drum, Dale S. "MBHCs: Evidence After Two Decades of Regulation." Federal Reserve Bank of Chicago, *Business Conditions* (December 1976): 3–15.

Gambs, Carl M. "Bank Failures—An Historical Perspective." Federal Reserve Bank of Kansas City, *Monthly Review* (June 1977): 10–20.

Knight, Robert E. "Comparative Burdens of Federal Reserve Member and Nonmember Banks." Federal Reserve Bank of Kansas City, *Monthly Review* (March 1977): 13–28.

Lawrence, Robert J., and Samuel H. Talley. "Staff Economic Study: An Assessment of Bank Holding Companies." *Federal Reserve Bulletin* 62 (January 1976): 15–21.

"Recent Growth in Activities of U.S. Offices of Foreign Banks." *Federal Reserve Bulletin* 62 (October 1976): 815–823.

Salley, Charles D. "Concentration in Banking Markets: Regulatory Numerology or Useful Merger Guidelines." Federal Reserve Bank of Atlanta, *Monthly Review* (November 1972): 186–190.

Scott, John Troy. "Public Policy Toward Competition in Banking." Federal Reserve Bank of Boston, *New England Economic Review* (July-August 1977): 44–50.

Upshaw, William F. "Antitrust and the New Bank Holding Company Act." Federal Reserve Bank of Richmond, *Monthly Review* (February 1971): 2–7; (March 1971): 3–10; (April 1971): 3–8.

Varvel, Walter A. "FDIC Policy Toward Bank Failures." Federal Reserve Bank of Richmond, *Economic Review* (September–October 1976): 3–12.

Weiss, Steven J. "Factors Affecting Bank Structure Change: The New England Experience 1963–74." *New England Economic Review* (July-August 1975): 16–25.

Chapter Five

THE COMMERCIAL BANKING SYSTEM:
OPERATIONS AND PERFORMANCE

In Chapter 4 we examined some of the main aspects of the structure of commercial banking in the United States. Banking structure establishes the context in which commercial banks operate. The present chapter describes in general terms the operations and performance of the United States commercial banking industry. It also refers to broad trends and developments affecting commercial banking in the post-World War II period, particularly the 1960s and 1970s. Finally, the concluding section examines some of the public policy and regulatory implications of the increase in bank failures, as well as other recent developments affecting bank performance.

THE BALANCE SHEET OF
COMMERCIAL BANKING

A convenient and illuminating approach to the study of the operations of the commercial banking industry is to examine the principal items that make up the industry's balance sheet (or "statement of condition," as it is sometimes called). The *balance sheet* is an accounting information device that presents for a certain date or point in time the dollar amounts and types of assets owned by a given person or institution. It also shows the dollar amounts and types of claims upon these assets. These claims may be classified in various ways, but traditionally they are divided into two broad groupings: liabilities and net worth (or capital accounts). The *liabilities* represent contractual claims that have precedence over the claims of the ownership group. The *net worth* (or capital accounts) represents the residual claims of the owners after the contractual claims of the liabilities-holders have been met. The balance sheet, based on a double entry system of bookkeeping, requires that the total value of assets must equal the total value of liabilities plus net worth. Stated differently, the total of all claims upon the value of assets (both contractual liabilites and equity) cannot exceed the total value of these assets at any given time.

The balance sheet for the commercial banking system shows the summation of all the individual commercial banks' balance sheets. The amounts indicate the principal asset, liability, and net worth accounts for all commercial banks taken together as a group.

Table 5.1 gives the balance sheet for all commercial banks in the United States at mid-1976. Only the main assets, liabilities, and capital accounts are shown. On the assets side of the balance sheet the items range from the highly liquid "cash" assets to the less liquid earning assets in the form of loans and investments. On the liabilities side the principal items are the demand and time deposits. Note that the totals on each side of the balance sheet include certain items that are not shown separately. Some comments are helpful in analyzing the significance of these principal balance sheet accounts.

Cash Assets

These assets represent funds that are either immediately available or in the process of being made available to commercial banks. Cash assets, which are nonearning assets, are sometimes called primary reserves. *Primary reserves* include vault or till cash, balances due from other banks (including both Federal Reserve banks and commercial banks), and cash items in process of collection. Primary reserves are held for working purposes and for required reserve purposes. Vault cash serves largely as a working reserve for meeting day-to-day deposit withdrawals.[1] Cash due from other banks is used both for required reserve purposes and for working purposes in conducting various banking transactions with outlying correspondent banks.[2] Cash items in pro-

---

1. Since late November 1960 member banks of the Federal Reserve System are allowed to count all vault cash as legal reserves. Therefore, vault cash serves both working and required reserve purposes for member banks. Those commercial banks that are nonmembers of the Federal Reserve System could generally include vault cash as legal reserves under state stipulations. The November 1960 change in Federal Reserve regulations eliminated disparity in the treatment of vault cash between member and nonmember banks.

2. Member banks of the Federal Reserve System count as legal reserves only vault cash and their deposits in the Federal Reserve. Member banks' deposits in other commercial banks, though not allowed as legal reserves under Federal Reserve rules, are used to conduct various correspondent banking transactions. Correspondent banks hold deposits of other commercial banks and perform various banking services for these bank customers.

Table 5.1   BALANCE SHEET, ALL COMMERCIAL BANKS,
UNITED STATES, MID-1976
(millions of dollars)

Assets			Liabilities and Capital Accounts		
Cash assets—total		128,299	Deposits—total		794,987
Vault cash	12,062		Demand deposits	312,959	
Balances with Federal			Individuals, part-		
Reserve banks and			nerships, and		
domestic commer-			corporations	237,703	
cial banks	72,875		United States		
Other cash items	43,362		government	4,659	
			Other	70,597	
Loans and discounts—					
total		557,691	Time deposits	482,028	
Commercial and			Individuals, part-		
industrial	176,584		nerships, and		
Agricultural	22,182		corporations	350,138	
For purchasing or			United States		
carrying securities	11,776		government	734	
To financial			Other	131,156	
institutions	41,835				
Real estate	143,699				
Other loans to			Borrowings		84,699
individuals	111,275				
Federal funds sold	36,219				
Miscellaneous loans	14,122		Other liabilities		23,219
Securities or					
"investments"—					
total		238,748			
United States					
Treasury securities	88,231				
State and local					
government					
securities	102,850				
Other securities	47,667				
			Capital accounts		69,889
Other assets		48,056			
			Total liabilities and		
Total assets*		972,794	capital accounts*		972,794

*Items may not add to totals because of rounding.

Source: Federal Deposit Insurance Corporation, *Annual Report,* 1976, pp. 235–237.

cess of collection reflect largely checks presented for deposit by bank customers. As these items are collected via check clearing, they are added to balances due from other banks, either commercial banks or regional Federal Reserve banks.

Loans

The next broad group of assets is composed of loans, which are earning assets for the commercial banking system. Interestingly, the designation *commercial* is applied to the banking system to indicate the system's traditional role in providing short-term working capital loans to commercial (business) borrowers. Commercial banks deal in a variety of loans, reflecting their diversified lending operations, which respond to changing needs for finance from different sectors. In fact, they have been aptly called "department stores of finance" to emphasize their varied lending activities. These activities can be classified according to the different types of borrowers. Major types include commercial and industrial, real estate, agricultural, financial, and consumer borrowing. Table 5.1 presents such a breakdown for loans of commercial banks at mid-1976. Each of these categories can in turn be classified according to either the maturity of the loan or the purpose for which the loan proceeds are used, for example, short-term working capital loans versus long-term loans to finance capital expenditures on plant and equipment.

However they are classified, the total loans reflect the commercial banking system's "monetization of private debt." The process of monetizing private debt implies that the commercial banking system exchanges its IOU, or promise to pay, in the form of demand deposits for the private borrower's promise to pay in the form of the loan instrument. These promises to pay are quite different in qualitative terms. The banking system's IOU is money, according to our functional definition, while the borrower's IOU, which does not have price fixity and general acceptability, is not money.

Securities

Another major category of earning assets consists of securities or "investments" held by commercial banks. In large part, these securities are of the fixed-interest or debt type rather than the equity type, because generally commercial banks are prohibited from purchasing the equity type of securities.[3]

Most of the securities holdings of commercial banks reflect the "monetization of public (governmental) debt." In this case, just as in monetization of private debt, the commercial banking system's monetary liability in the form of demand deposits is exchanged for the nonmonetary liability of a level of government in the form of a security.

Securities or "investment" holdings of commercial banks are classified according to the issuer of the securities: United States government, state and local governments, and all other issues (including corporate stock and securities issued by federally sponsored credit agencies). United States government securities held by commercial banks are direct marketable public issues, that is, the securities are direct obligations of the United States Treasury. They are available for general purchase and may be sold before maturity to other buyers. These marketable issues are of various maturity types: Treasury bills, certificates, notes, or bonds. *Treasury bills,* which include tax anticipation bills (TABs), carry maturities that run in multiples of three months but not in excess of one year. The bills, sold at a discount at auction, are highly liquid low-earning assets that banks hold as *secondary reserves,* that is, earning assets that can be quickly and safely converted into money.[4] Treasury certificates have one-year maturities, while Treasury notes range from two to seven and a half years and bonds typically have maturities exceeding ten years at time of issue.

Debt obligations of state and local governments and of other governmental subdivisions are called *municipals.* These securities, sometimes called *tax-exempts,* are attractive earning assets for commercial banks because their interest income is exempt from federal income taxation. Note that in mid-1976 the dollar volume of municipals held by commercial banks exceeded that for United States Treasury securities (see Table 5.1), reflecting the increased

3. There are a few exceptions here. For example, membership for commercial banks in the Federal Reserve System requires the purchase of a certain amount of capital stock in the regional Federal Reserve bank. Commercial banks may gain temporary ownership of equity issues that have served as collateral on defaulted loans.

4. The largest dollar amount of new Treasury bill offerings consist of three-month and six-month bills that are sold at weekly auctions. At these auctions commercial banks offer bids for their own account and/or for their customers.

importance of these securities in the earning assets portfolio of the commercial banking system in the post–World War II period.

Other securities include miscellaneous "investments" composed mainly of debt obligations of federally sponsored credit agencies such as the Federal Home Loan Banks, Federal National Mortgage Association, and Federal Intermediate Credit Banks. These securities issues are not direct obligations of the United States Treasury; therefore, the amounts held by commercial banks are listed under "other securities."

Deposit Liabilities

The principal liabilites of the commercial banking system consist of deposits: demand deposits and time deposits. As discussed earlier, the demand deposits arise primarily from the monetization of debt by commercial banks. Total demand deposits adjusted for certain excluded items, namely, United States government demand deposits and interbank demand deposits and cash items in process of collection, comprise the largest part of the money supply of the general public.

United States government demand deposits in commercial banks, called *tax and loan accounts* (T and L's), are a major part of the federal government's cash position. These government deposit accounts are so named because the proceeds obtained from tax collections and the sale of new Treasury security issues are initially deposited in these accounts. T and L's are receiving accounts in that federal government disbursements are made by drawing on the general accounts of the United States treasurer in the Federal Reserve banks. They are used by the federal government to minimize any disruptive effects its taxing and borrowing activities may have on the monetary system.

Under new legislation signed by President Carter in October 1977, the U.S. Treasury is authorized to collect interest on its tax and loan accounts at commercial banks. Initially implemented in the summer of 1978, this legislation also allows nonbank financial institutions (mutual savings banks, savings and loan associations, credit unions) to handle U.S. Treasury accounts. For many years, the Treasury's demand deposits at commercial banks have been available for bank use interest free. Use of these funds presumably compensated commercial banks for various services rendered the Treasury. Mounting criticism of the practice brought congressional legislation whereby the Treasury receives interest on balances held longer than one day. At the same time, the Treasury will reimburse banks, on a per-item basis, for the various transaction services provided.

Time deposits, which exceed the dollar amount of demand deposit liabilities, are an important type of near-money in the financial system. Time deposits activity, especially in the growth of negotiable certificates of deposit since 1961, represents the role of the commercial banking system as a financial intermediary that brings together savers and investors, thus contributing to capital formation in the economy. The interest rates offered on time deposits are subject to ceiling regulations of banking regulatory agencies (Regulation Q of the Federal Reserve, as an example). These ceilings, along with adjustments in their levels, affect the position of the commercial banking system relative to other types of financial institutions.

Liquidity considerations are particularly important for commercial banks since most of the liabilities of the commercial banking system consist of demand and time deposits, which are payable in currency either upon demand or after notice is given. All individuals and business firms have varying liquidity needs, and the lack of adequate liquidity can create major problems, as shown by the great pressures created on the financial system by the Penn Central Railroad bankruptcy petition in midsummer 1970.[5] Commercial banks are especially sensitive to liquidity needs, simply because a major part of liabilities are monetary liabilities payable upon demand.

Borrowings

Liabilities in the form of borrowings include primarily federal funds transactions, Eurodollar borrowings, and borrowings from the Federal Reserve. *Federal funds* are reserve balances at the Federal Reserve that have been lent for short periods, usually one day. A major part of the federal funds market consists of temporary loans by member banks with excess reserves to those member banks having reserve deficiencies. *Eurodollars* include dollar-denominated deposits held in commercial banks outside the United States as

---

5. Essentially, the Penn Central's petition for bankruptcy had wide repercussions because the company had issued large amounts of *commercial paper* (marketable short-term promissory notes issued by well-known firms with top credit ratings), which had been purchased by various groups, including commercial banks. The company's precarious condition cast a pall over the commercial paper market, thus making it difficult for other businesses to meet their financial obligations as a result of the loss of confidence in commercial paper generally.

well as dollars that commercial banks abroad obtain with their own or foreign currencies. Eurodollar borrowings by commercial banks increased greatly in the late 1960s, particularly during times of highly restrictive monetary conditions, marked by sharply rising interest rates and slower money growth rates.

Capital Accounts

Capital accounts represent the residual claims of the owners of the commercial banks upon the value of the banking system's assets. Since the equity group's claims are subordinated to the claims of the liabilities-holders, the capital accounts provide a cushion or protection to the solvency of the banking system. Technically, *solvency* exists when the total value of the assets exceeds the total claims of the contractual liabilities-holders. Any decline or deterioration in the values of assets is necessarily written off against the equity claims. Thus, if capital accounts comprise 10 percent of the total book value of assets, then the total book value of these assets can decline up to 10 percent without endangering the solvency of the system. Accordingly, bank regulatory groups have used the ratio of total capital accounts to total assets (capital-assets ratio) as a rough guideline in appraising the capital adequacy of the commercial banking system.[6] This crude ratio has been replaced, or at least supplemented, by the use of a capital-risk-assets ratio where risk assets are defined as total assets less cash assets and United States government securities. This ratio helps to measure the adequacy of the owners' equity to absorb declines in the values of those assets that are presumably subject to considerable risk. At best these broad ratios are approximate or preliminary measures of capital adequacy, whether for the entire commercial banking system or for individual commercial banking firms. Judging capital adequacy entails a consideration of various quantitative and qualitative factors that are not encompassed within these deceptively simple ratios.

---

6. The federal bank regulatory agencies now allow commercial banks to count long-term debt that is subordinated to deposit liabilities as part of their capital. In the event of bank liquidation, holders of subordinated debt are paid only after all depositors are paid in full. In recent years banks have issued more long-term debt, but in the mid-1970s, long-term debt outstanding for all U.S. commercial banks amounted to less than 7 percent of total capital accounts and less than half a percent of total assets.

SOME TRENDS IN COMMERCIAL
BANK ASSET MANAGEMENT

The review of the principal asset and liability accounts in the balance sheet of commercial banking underlines the importance to commercial banks of conducting their operations so as to provide adequate liquidity for continued performance. Sufficient liquidity is needed to absorb possible deposit withdrawals and to provide reasonable accommodation of customers' demands for loans. At the same time, considerations of liquidity must be tempered by the opposing concern for adequate income to ensure the continued provision of productive resources in banking. In effect, the liquidity objective conflicts with the objective of profitability in the conduct of commercial bank management of assets.

Commercial Loan Theory of Bank Credit

Methods for attaining sufficient liquidity in a profit-oriented commercial banking system have varied greatly over the past several decades. One traditional view of the liquidity question, widely held until the depression of the 1930s, was the real-bills doctrine, or commercial loan theory of credit. The *real-bills' doctrine* held that a balanced approach to liquidity is achieved through commercial banks acquiring primarily short-term self-liquidating loan assets. The earning asset stressed was the short-term working capital loan secured by real goods in production, marketing, or shipment. Sale of these goods would provide the means for repaying the loan. Understandably, long-term loans for purchase of plant or equipment or real estate were regarded as inappropriate.

Basically, the real-bills doctrine emphasized the need for balancing the maturity structure of assets against those of deposit liabilities. Deposit liabilities, payable on demand or on short notice, require lending of the short-term self-liquidating type, particularly in loans for working capital purposes. Although full adherence to the dictates of the real-bills doctrine was virtually impossible because of the changing loan needs of customers (for example, term loans for capital purposes or for purchasing real estate), the theory guided banking practice until the Great Depression worked its havoc. A bitter lesson learned by commercial bankers and others was that many loans, self-liquidating in periods of high employment and growing income, become nonliquid and in default in periods of low employment and falling income. The demise of the real-bills doctrine, which also was to have deep implications for central banking, occurred at this time. Adherence to the doctrine did not provide liquidity for the commercial banking system at the very time when liquidity was needed most desperately.

Shiftability Theory

During the 1920s and 1930s increased holdings by commercial banks of debt-type securities elicited a *shiftability theory* of asset management, according to which liquidity needs could be met by "shifting" or selling bank-held securities to other buyers in the secondary securities' market. Protection against large deposit withdrawals supposedly resulted for banks monetizing securities traded in highly organized financial markets.

The World War II deficit-financing needs of the federal government gave added impetus to the shiftability theory, especially since the commercial banking system monetized a sizable proportion of the more than fivefold increase in federal government securities outstanding. The Treasury, concerned that huge wartime deficits would bring a sharp rise in interest rates and in the cost of financing its debt, obtained a Federal Reserve commitment to peg the prices (and hence, interest rates) of federal government securities. Accordingly, commercial banks could sell government securities readily without loss of principal whenever they experienced rising liquidity needs.

In much of the post–World War II period the commercial banking system continued to depend on its holding of United States government securities for liquidity. At the end of World War II more than one-half of commercial banking assets were in Treasury securities, with one-quarter of these being short term (maturing in one year or less). Although the Federal Reserve ended its support policy in March 1951, the market for Treasury securities continued basically strong and resilient, reflecting the large volume of securities outstanding and the participation of a large number of different types of investors. Treasury bills, readily marketable and subject to relatively minor changes in price, serve as the principal type of secondary reserve. Long-term securities (those maturing in over five years) are readily shiftable, but are less liquid than Treasury bills. During periods of monetary stringency marked by slower money growth, long-term bond prices decline as interest rates rise; thus, sales of bond holdings at these times could bring capital losses to banks.

Nevertheless, commercial bank holdings of United States government securities tended to change in a direction opposite to that for loan demand. Increasing demand for loans brought bank sales of Treasury securities; subsiding loan demand and repayment of loans saw banks acquiring securities.

Adjustments in bank holdings of government securities are only one avenue, though an important one, for providing liquidity. Policies governing the monetization of private debt can also provide access to liquidity. However, the amount of liquidity available from different lending practices is relatively limited. Loan repayments on short-term loans may provide less liquidity because of the practice of loan renewals.

Call loans (loans repayable upon demand by the lender) to brokers and consumer finance companies, although quite liquid, are a small part of the loan portfolio for commercial banks. Sensitive to maintaining good customer relations, banks are reluctant to call in other types of loans or to refuse new loans to old-line customers.

Another liquidity source is generated by the amortization and maturing of consumer and real estate loans as well as by an increasing proportion of amortized commercial and industrial loans. On the surface, loan repayments can provide appreciable liquidity for commercial banks, although this liquidity channel becomes more uncertain during a period of declining economic activity or one of increased deposit withdrawals.

Bank Liquidity

A major trend affecting commercial banking in the post–World War II period is the marked decline in liquidity, as measured by certain traditional liquidity ratios. Two commonly used liquidity ratios include the loan-deposits ratio and the ratio of United States government securities maturing within five years to total deposits. Given that certain loans cannot be liquidated readily, a rising loan-deposit ratio suggests a deterioration in banks' ability to meet withdrawals by depositors. On the other hand, a fall in the ratio of Treasury securities maturing within five years to total deposits implies a decline in banks' liquidity. Figure 5.1 traces the levels of these ratios over the postwar period. The huge growth in bank loans is reflected in the fact that the loan-deposits ratio rose to over 50 percent in the 1960s from a 1946 low of 20 percent. The secular rise in this ratio was halted temporarily during the recession periods (shown by shaded areas in the figure) and during the mini-recession of 1967.

Figure 5.1 LIQUIDITY RATIOS FOR ALL INSURED COMMERCIAL
BANKS

*Shaded areas represent periods of business cycle contractions as designated by the
National Bureau of Economic Research.*

Percent

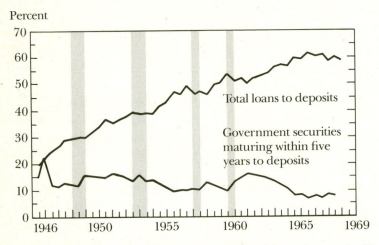

Source: Federal Reserve System, National Bureau of Economic Research, as presented in Robert E. Knight, "An Alternative Approach to Liquidity: Part 1," Federal Reserve Bank of Kansas City, *Monthly Review*, December 1969, p. 13.

Not surprisingly, the ratio of securities to deposits shows a secular decline over this period.

On first glance, the long-term results for these two liquidity indicators suggest a marked deterioration in the banking system's liquidity during the postwar period. Since these ratios are only crude measures of liquidity, certain limitations affect their analytical use. The loan-deposit ratio makes no allowance for factors influencing liquidity, such as the maturity structure and quality of loans, the cash flow arising from loan repayments, or the overall behavior and composition of the deposit base. Similarly, the ratio of United States government securities maturing in five years to total deposits overlooks certain elements: the holding of securities for meeting reserve requirements set by states for nonmember banks or for pledging behind United States government deposits in commercial banks; the nature of the secondary market for securities; and banks' ownership of other short-term liquid assets, for example, top-rated municipals, short-term federal government agency securities, and directly placed prime finance company paper.

In addition to these shortcomings inherent in the use of traditional ratios for appraising the liquidity of the banking system, we must recognize the dramatic change in banks' money management techniques that occurred in the 1960s. These new methods, largely reflecting an innovative response by commercial banking to the restrictive monetary policies of the late 1960s, suggest the need for a cautious interpretation and analysis of simple liquidity ratios.

INNOVATIONS IN MONEY MANAGEMENT

During the 1960s, an increasing number of commercial banks (particularly the larger, metropolitan-area banks) resorted to new money management techniques that utilized liability management rather than asset management. *Liability management* involves the purchase of reserves, primarily for meeting reserve requirements and commitments arising from outstanding lines of credit, through the issuance of various types of liabilities. Under the concept of liability management, changing liquidity needs tend to induce commercial banks to change the rates of interest offered on various liabilities used to borrow or acquire reserves. Asset management involves adjusting the volume, cost, and availability of bank credit in response to changes in bank reserves and deposits. This approach implies, for example, that a decline in deposits and reserves induces the commercial bank to sell securities, increase lending rates, and ration available funds by applying more stringent credit standards.

Liability management and asset management are not mutually exclusive approaches for banks. Banks are concerned with both of these aspects in order to enhance earnings and maintain liquidity. The new features of liability management arise from (1) the use of nondeposit types of liabilities; (2) bank competition for funds on a price basis; and (3) the acquiring of reserves by the sale of liabilities rather than of liquid assets, such as Treasury bills.

The specific techniques of liability management used by the larger commercial banks include use of federal funds, issuance of negotiable certificates of deposit (CDs), borrowing of Eurodollars, loan and security repurchase agreements, and the issuance of bank-related commercial paper.

Federal Funds Transactions

Traditionally, in federal funds transactions, commercial banks borrow and lend excess reserve balances held at Federal Reserve banks, hence the term federal funds. Today this description is incomplete because the federal funds market includes many other active participants that do not hold deposit balances at the Federal Reserve. Operationally, *federal funds* are overnight loans that are settled in immediately available funds. Only commercial banks and some other financial institutions can effectively borrow in this manner. The federal funds rate is the rate of interest charged for these overnight borrowings, and is a very sensitive indicator in the market for highly liquid, short-term financial claims.

The market for federal funds, which first started among New York City banks in the 1920s, has grown in its scope and operations. Today, many large banks borrow federal funds on a regular basis, while many smaller banks, attracted by high rates, regularly lend federal funds as an alternative to holding short-term government securities. Figure 5.2 shows federal funds transactions of forty-six large banks during recent years. As shown in Figure 5.2, these transactions include borrowings from those institutions (other than domestic commercial banks) from which Federal Reserve member banks may borrow free of reserve requirements. Under Federal Reserve regulations, member banks may borrow reserve-free funds not only from other commercial banks, but also from federal agencies, savings and loan associations, mutual savings banks, and government securities dealers. The two lower segments of Figure 5.2 indicate that growth in net purchases of federal funds by large commercial banks has been sporadic. Bursts of rapid growth in this market have occurred generally during periods when short-term interest rates were either rising rapidly or at high levels.

Certificates of Deposit

Just as the market for federal funds provides larger banks with discretionary access to the liquidity of the banking system, negotiable certificates of deposit provide these banks with discretionary access to the liquidity of the nonbank sector (corporations, insurance companies, individuals, federal agencies, and state and local governments). Essentially, a *certificate of deposit* (CD) is a time deposit that the buyer agrees to maintain in a commercial bank for a specified

Figure 5.2 FEDERAL FUNDS AND REPURCHASE AGREEMENTS
(RPS) HELD BY FORTY-SIX LARGE COMMERCIAL
BANKS

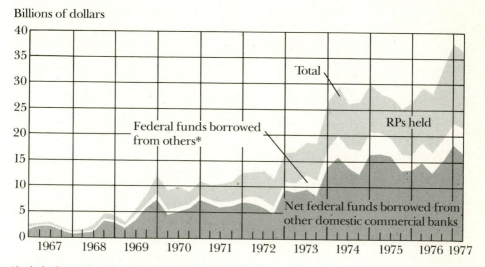

Billions of dollars

*Includes borrowings from those institutions other than domestic commercial banks from which member banks may borrow free of reserve requirements.

Source: Charles M. Lucas, et al., "Federal Funds and Repurchase Agreements," Federal Reserve Bank of New York, *Quarterly Review*, 2, Summer 1977, p. 40.

period. Negotiability means the certificate can be sold in the secondary market if the holder of the CD requires the money before it matures.

With relatively small amounts outstanding in the early 1960s, large denomination CDs ($100,000 or more) increased greatly in volume, thus becoming a major type of short-term financial claim in the money market. The *money market* is the overall market dealing in short-term financial claims.[7] The issuing banks quickly recognized that the demand for CDs reacted sensitively to changes in interest rates paid on the CDs and that their actions affecting

7. The dramatic growth of large denomination CDs occurred after a secondary market for CDs was organized in February 1961 by a United States government securities dealer and a New York City bank. Only the large commercial banks issue CDs in denominations of $100,000 or more. For example, most of the trading in the secondary market for these CDs involves certificates issued by some thirty to thirty-five large commercial banks.

Figure 5.3   NEGOTIABLE CERTIFICATES OF DEPOSIT
OUTSTANDING AT LARGE COMMERCIAL BANKS

*Shaded areas in chart represent periods when commercial
paper rates exceeded maximum rates on CDs.*

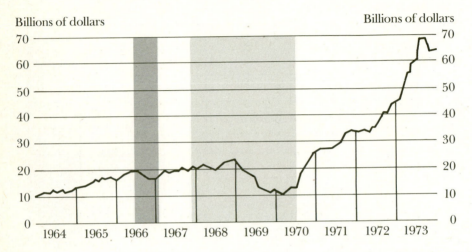

Source: Federal Reserve System, as presented in Federal Reserve Bank of Philadelphia, *Business Review*,
December 1974, p. 14.

flows of time deposits could provide a major source of liquidity. If funds were
needed to meet loan commitments or deposit withdrawals, offering rates on
CDs could be raised; if liquidity requirements eased, offering rates could be
lowered.

Interest rate ceilings limit banks' access to liquid funds via the issuance of
CDs.[8] Thus, when short-term market interest rates exceed the ceiling rates,
CDs become relatively unattractive as earning assets, and holders of CDs
switch to higher-yielding assets. Such "runoffs" of CDs at commercial banks
were especially prevalent in 1966 and 1969, two periods of credit stringency
marked by rising interest rates (see Figure 5.3). An easing of monetary
restraint can bring an upward revision in ceiling rates by authorities, as

8. Under banking legislation passed in 1933 the Board of Governors of the Federal Reserve
System regulates by Regulation Q the maximum rates payable by member banks on time and
savings deposits, and similar regulation by the Federal Deposit Insurance Corporation covers all
insured banks.

occurred in early 1970. By mid-1970, regulators removed ceilings on certificates with maturities of less than ninety days. This change enhanced commercial banks' competition for liquid funds and facilitated the reintermediation of funds from the commercial paper market to banks, following the announcement of the Penn Central Railroad's petition for bankruptcy. Later, in May 1973, the authorities eliminated the maximum rates payable on all maturities of large denomination CDs.

Eurodollar Borrowing

The large runoffs of CDs in 1966 and 1969, combined with mounting pressure for bank loans at rising interest rates, prompted large commercial banks to seek alternative liability sources of liquidity. An imaginative new source of bank funds emerged with banks' borrowing of Eurodollars. As mentioned earlier, Eurodollars are basically dollar deposits in commercial banks outside the United States. Foreign branches of domestic banks receive deposit claims on United States banks through the conduct of banking transactions for customers and through competitive bidding for dollar balances. When these deposit claims are entered in the foreign branch's account at the head office of the domestic bank, the head office increases its "liabilities to foreign branches" and also receives reserves from other domestic banks on whom the deposit claims are drawn.

Most Eurodollar borrowing in the United States is conducted between head-office banks in New York City and their foreign branches. Domestic banks not operating foreign branches borrow Eurodollars by dealing directly, or indirectly through brokers and dealers, with foreign banks and individuals. Head-office banks, hampered by interest rate ceilings and maturity minimums applying to domestic CDs, used their foreign branches to openly bid for Eurodollar deposits in 1966 and 1969. In effect, Eurodollar borrowing provides a discretionary source for head-office domestic banks to buy reserves through a foreign branch.

Repurchase Agreements

Continued strong loan demands in 1969, along with official restrictions on CDs and Eurodollar borrowing, stimulated the use of repurchase agreements by large commercial banks.[9] A *repurchase agreement* (RP) is basically a "sale–buy back" arrangement. Specifically, the seller of the financial asset (in this case, the commercial bank selling a loan asset or security asset) formally agrees to repurchase the asset on a specified date at a stipulated price or yield. Repurchase agreements, heavily used by U.S. government security dealers for financing purposes, provide a flexible low-risk means for mobilizing temporarily idle funds in the money market. Furthermore, their maturities can be adapted to needs of buyer or seller.

For the overall banking system, the RP produces excess reserves when liabilities are transferred from demand deposits (subject to reserve requirements) to nondeposit liabilities (not subject to reserve requirements). The sharp growth in *loan* RPs stopped in August 1969, when the Federal Reserve declared them deposit liabilities and therefore subject to interest rate ceilings and legal reserve requirements. *Security* RPs, on the other hand, are free from these regulatory restrictions and provide a regular source of funds for the larger commercial banks in financial centers.

In recent years the market for RPs involving U.S. government and federal agency securities has expanded considerably. In addition to commercial banks and other financial institutions, this market includes large nonfinancial corporations, state and local governments, and dealers in U.S. government and federal agency securities. Typically, RP market transactions are for one business day, and are settled in immediately available funds.

Commercial banks acquired especially large amounts of RPs in the mid-1970s (see Figure 5.2). Various factors operated here. A major factor involved a change in the U.S. Treasury's management of its tax and loan accounts at commercial banks. Starting in August 1974, most of these cash balances were transferred to Treasury accounts in Federal Reserve banks. These transfers released a large volume of U.S. government and federal agency securities, which commercial banks had to hold as pledged collateral against Treasury T and L's. Thus commercial banks could readily use these securities for transacting repurchase agreements.

---

9. At this time of restrictive monetary policy, the authorities precipitated a runoff of CDs by not raising interest rate ceilings. Officials viewed Eurodollar borrowing as a means for partially offsetting monetary restraint and for large banks to avoid the strictures of interest rate ceilings. Thus, in August 1969, the cost of Eurodollar borrowing was raised by the initial imposition of a 10 percent reserve requirement on any borrowing exceeding a specified base amount. In December 1970 this was raised to 20 percent.

Bank-related Commercial Paper

Large banks' innovations in liability management techniques, dampened by regulatory restrictions on Eurodollar borrowing and loan RPs, produced still another approach for obtaining liquid funds: *bank-related commercial paper*. Commercial paper is a marketable short-term promise to pay that is issued by a firm and sold at a discount. Bank-related commercial paper is issued by organizations connected with large commercial banks: bank holding companies, affiliates, and subsidiaries. The sale of bank-related commercial paper provides funds for buying loans from the related bank. Because these transactions created a shift from deposit liabilities (subject to reserve requirements) to commercial paper liabilities (free of reserve requirements), their net effect on the commercial banking system was to generate excess reserves.

Some sixty large banks tapped this source of funds, with total bank-related commercial paper growing to almost $8 billion by July 1970. Many banks were able to replace CD losses by selling commercial paper to owners of maturing CDs. Not only was commercial paper free of reserve requirements, but maturities could be less than thirty days.

Regulatory authorities reacted to this method of liability management by proposing restrictions in late October 1969, at a time when banks were making extensive use of this technique. Almost a year later, in October 1970, the regulatory definition of bank deposits was modified to include bank-related commercial paper where the proceeds are used to purchase assets from the related bank.

IMPLICATIONS OF LIABILITY MANAGEMENT

Liability management techniques have several results. Aggressive and flexible use of these techiques permit large money market commercial banks to mobilize liquid funds, thus enhancing their ability to meet lending commitments and to avoid reserve deficiencies. The provision of competitive offering rates enables these banks to market an appreciable volume of their liabilities. The newness of these activities and the lack of complete statistical series make precise measurement difficult; however, initial estimates indicate the significant role of nondeposit sources of funds in affecting the liquidity of large banks (see Table 5.2).

Table 5.2   DEPOSIT AND NONDEPOSIT LIABILITIES OF LARGE
COMMERCIAL BANKS, UNITED STATES, YEAR-END 1974

Type*	Reserve Required (Percent)	Interest Rate Constraint (Percent)	Maturity
Demand deposits	7½–16½	Prohibited	On demand
Savings deposits	3	5	Can require 30 days' notice
Time deposits less than $100,000	3–6	5½–7½	3 mos.–6 years
Negotiable CDs over $100,000	3–6	Suspended	Min. 30 days
Other time deposits over $100,000	3–6	Suspended	Min. 30 days
Eurodollar borrowing	4	None	No limit
Federal funds purchased and borrowing from banks	None	None	Federal funds, 1 day; other, no limit
Repurchase agreements on Treasury and U.S. agency securities	None	None	No limit, 1 day or more
Capital notes and debentures	None	None	Min. 7 years

*Deposits insured to $40,000; other liabilities not insured.

Source: Federal Reserve Bank of Chicago, *Business Conditions,* June 1975, p. 4.

Table 5.2 (cont.)

Type*	Other Factors Affecting Use	Outstanding† Dec. 31, 1974 (*Billions of Dollars*)
Demand deposits	Serve as holders' working balances and as compensation to bank for services.	$185.2
Savings deposits	No minimum amount; no specific maturity; ownership restricted.	58.5
Time deposits less than $100,000	$1,000 minimum required for rates over 6½ percent; banks may set more restrictive conditions.	42.7
Negotiable CDs over $100,000	Well-developed secondary market.	93.0
Other time deposits over $100,000	May be converted to negotiable form at option of holder.	33.9
Eurodollar borrowing	Cost related to foreign interest rates.	3.6‡
Federal funds purchased and borrowing from banks	May be purchased only from banks (and S&Ls) and U.S. agencies.	44.3
Repurchase agreements on Treasury and U.S. agency securities	Bank must own securities; interest payable for periods less than 30 days.	
Capital notes and debentures	$500 minimum; included in capital for some purposes; subject to borrowing limits.	n.a.§

†Liabilities of major U.S. banks totaled $490 billion on December 31, 1974, including liabilities for outstanding bankers' acceptances, mortgage indebtedness, and other liabilities not shown separately.

‡Gross amounts due to own foreign branches; does not include Eurodollars borrowed directly or other reservable Eurodollar borrowings.

§Included in capital accounts of $34 billion.

The use of open price competition (through offering rates) has also attracted some liquid funds to commercial banks away from nonbank groups. Since consumers and small businesses do not have direct access to the nonbank sector of the money market, these small borrowers probably benefit from this shift. The imaginative tailoring of liabilities provides strong incentives for economizing in holdings of excess reserves and in demand deposits, thus expanding somewhat the total availability of credit.

Finally, regulatory authorities have shown a willingness to influence the methods of liability management for stabilization purposes. During periods of monetary restraint, higher reserve requirements were placed on CDs, and interest rate ceilings were left unchanged in the face of rising market rates. Such stringency induced large banks to develop various nondeposit types of liabilities for borrowing reserves. Subsequently, reserve requirements were placed on these liabilities. Periods of monetary expansion brought regulatory actions promoting the growth of CDs and less interference in the development of nondeposit liabilities.

RECENT DEVELOPMENTS
AFFECTING BANK PERFORMANCE

In the early 1970s, the financial system in the United States sustained several severe shocks. These dramatic disturbances raised questions regarding the stability and security of the financial system in general and of the commercial banking system in particular.

As mentioned earlier, the Penn Central crisis of 1970 was a bombshell for the commercial banks. In 1973 the United States National Bank of San Diego failed. Shortly thereafter, the Beverly Hills National Bank was forced into merger. The case of the Beverly Hills bank illustrates possible risks for a commercial bank affiliated with a bank holding company. Specifically, through selling its own commercial paper, the parent holding company made, via an affiliated nonbank subsidiary, large loans to a real estate developer. When these real estate developments soured, the holding company had trouble refinancing its commercial paper debt. In the meantime, the affiliated Beverly Hills bank suffered a run on its deposits as the financial position of the holding company became more widely known. Later, in order to pay off its debts, the holding company sold its interest in the Beverly Hills bank to another commercial bank.

The failure in October 1974 of the giant Franklin National Bank of New York (total assets of $3.6 billion) further shook the financial system. Around this same time, the failure of the Herstatt Bank in West Germany spotlighted the international aspects of banking difficulties. Meanwhile, the $20 billion United States real estate investment trust (REIT) industry, heavily indebted to commercial banks, tottered on the brink of collapse. To this depressing list of disturbances must be added the sharp upsurge in oil prices in 1973–1974, threatening adverse economic and financial repercussions throughout the world.

As these turbulent events were taking place, the United States economy was also being rocked by mounting price inflation combined with a recession. Increases in production costs and surging interest rates hit many borrowers, especially those in real estate. The quality of bank credit eroded and the New York municipal financial crisis of 1975–1976 also erupted.

Within this setting a growing concern emerged regarding the increased potential for commercial bank failures. A stable, secure financial system that facilitates productive activity has wide appeal throughout the community. But the ironclad protection against risk of bank failure from illiquidity that would exist if commercial banks held 100 percent reserves against their liabilities would make loan markets much less competitive, thus imposing certain economic costs on the public. Most observers agree that 100 percent reserves are not needed for banks to compete effectively and still maintain a sound, viable banking system. The real crux of the problem is to determine the optimum amount of liquidity for the individual commercial bank.

In social welfare terms, the ideal amount of bank liquidity is that which generates maximum net benefits for society. Operationally, identifying and measuring society's costs and benefits are extremely difficult, if not impossible. Generally, commercial banks respond to costs that affect their stockholders' profits, and these costs may not include all aspects of social costs.

A commercial bank's failure implies loss of stockholders' investment in the bank; however, the general public may lose the uninsured portion of its deposits, as well as other bank debt owed to the public. Furthermore, the bank failure may seriously shake the public's confidence in other commercial banks. This is where bank regulation becomes important. The role of bank regulators is to balance the interests of society and of the banks, making sure that commercial banks consider both public (social) and private factors in their operations.

One approach to achieving adequate liquidity in commercial bank operations emphasizes strict application of formal regulatory standards. Even assuming that regulatory standards could be enforced effectively, the basic question relates to what these standards should be. In simple words, what is the optimum liquidity ratio to be required of a bank? What tradeoff should be allowed between liquidity and bank earnings? These vexing, complex questions suggest that faulty regulatory standards might well be established—thus burdening society with considerable economic costs. The pitfalls inherent in an ironclad regulatory approach have shifted attention to approaches that rely mainly on the market mechanism.

One such approach involves providing the public with more detailed, meaningful information regarding the financial condition of commercial banks. Information now available to the general public is frequently thin and sketchy; thus investors are hampered in making rational choices in their selection of commercial banks. National banks are now examined about every eight months, and state authorities examine state-chartered banks about once a year. These arrangements do not lend themselves to early detection of major changes in a bank's financial condition.

Quarterly bank examinations, for example, would provide a timely summary of an individual bank's capital, asset, and management quality. Public access to such current information should make the financial market less susceptible to disturbing rumors. If such a plan were instituted, commercial banks would be given a profit incentive to maintain financial soundness. Banks with shaky financial standing could attract customers and investors only by offering premium interest rates, which would give them the incentive to reduce their risk exposure and enhance their liquidity.

Operationally, the closing of the financial information gap for banks would require certain changes. The statute prohibiting the release of bank examiners' ratings would have to be changed. Bank regulators would require time and other resources to develop an effective system involving more frequent bank examinations. Commercial banks, too, would need an adjustment (or transition) period to adapt to the new procedures. Once these operational difficulties were resolved, however, the new scheme should not only generate beneficial competitive results, but also reduce the danger of bank failures.

Interestingly, in November 1974, the Comptroller of the Currency unveiled new procedures for periodically updating that office's information on national bank loan quality and liquidity. Specifically, all national banks were required to submit regular reports of past-due loans. The two hundred largest national banks were also required to furnish the comptroller with quarterly reports on asset and liability maturities. Along with these efforts, the regulatory authorities directed attention to development of an effective "early warning" system to detect initial signs of serious weakness in a bank's financial condition.

KEY TERMS

Balance sheet	Solvency
Liabilities	Real-bills doctrine
Net worth	Shiftability theory
Primary reserves	Call loans
Treasury bills	Liability management
Secondary reserves	Certificates of deposit
Municipals	Money market
Tax and loan accounts	Repurchase agreements
Federal funds	Bank-related commercial paper
Eurodollars	

REVIEW QUESTIONS

1. In general terms, what does a balance sheet show?
2. Define primary reserves of commercial banks and indicate the components of primary reserves.
3. Why are commercial banks sometimes called "department stores of finance"?
4. What is the general nature of securities (or "investments") held by commercial banks?
5. Indicate the principal types of bank-held securities.
6. List the major types of deposit liabilities of commercial banks.

7. What purpose do capital accounts serve for banks, and how may banks' capital adequacy be measured?

8. Why do liquidity requirements have special meaning for commercial banks?

9. Compare the real bills doctrine with the shiftability theory of bank credit.

10. What rough guides are used to gauge the overall liquidity of the commercial banking system?

11. Distinguish between liability management and asset management as approaches to the management of bank funds.

12. Why did liability management emerge so prominently in the late 1960s?

13. What specific techniques of liability management were developed by United States commercial banks?

14. Recount briefly the major disturbances that hit the U.S. financial system in the first half of the 1970s.

15. In light of these disturbances, what general alternatives exist for ensuring the safe, stable operation of the commercial banking system in the United States?

SUGGESTED READINGS

Burns, Arthur F. "Maintaining the Soundness of Our Banking System." Federal Reserve Bank of New York, *Monthly Review* (November 1974): 263–267.

Friedman, Milton. "The Euro-Dollar Market: Some First Principles." *Morgan Guaranty Survey* (October 1968). Reprinted in the Federal Reserve Bank of St. Louis, *Review* (July 1971): 16–24.

Korobow, Leon, and David P. Stuhr. "Toward Early Warning of Changes in Banks' Financial Condition: A Progress Report." Federal Reserve Bank of New York, *Monthly Review* (July 1975): 157–165.

Little, Jane Sneddon. "The Impact of the Euro-Dollar Market on the Effectiveness of Monetary Policy in the United States and Abroad." Federal Reserve Bank of Boston, *New England Economic Review* (March-April 1975): 3–19.

Lucas, Charles M., Marcos T. Jones, and Thom B. Thurston. "Federal Funds and Repurchase Agreements." Federal Reserve Bank of New York, *Quarterly Review* (Summer 1977): 33–48.

Schweitzer, Stuart A. "Bank Liability Management: For Better or for Worse?" Federal Reserve Bank of Philadelphia, *Business Review* (December 1974): 3–11.

Smaistrla, Charles J. "Bank Liquidity—Is the Level Adequate For Future Loan Expansion?" Federal Reserve Bank of Dallas, *Business Review* (May 1976): 7–10.

Summers, Bruce J. "Bank Capital Adequacy: Perspectives and Prospects." Federal Reserve Bank of Richmond, *Economic Review* (July-August 1977): 3–8.

Summers, Bruce J. "Loan Commitments to Business in United States Banking History." Federal Reserve Bank of Richmond, *Economic Review* (September-October 1975): 15–23.

Valerius, Jean L. "Liabilities That Banks Manage." Federal Reserve Bank of Chicago, *Business Conditions* (June 1975): 3–9.

Veazey, Edward E. "Federal Funds—Market Expansion Aids Mobilization of Funds." Federal Reserve Bank of Dallas, *Business Review* (January 1975): 1–6.

Watson, Ronald D. "Insuring Some Progress in the Bank Capital Hassle." Federal Reserve Bank of Philadelphia, *Business Review* (July-August 1974): 3–18.

Woodworth, G. Walter. "Theories of Cyclical Liquidity Management of Commercial Banks." *National Banking Review* 4 (June 1967): 377–395.

Chapter Six

A THEORY OF THE BANKING FIRM

Construction of a simple theory or model of the banking firm requires a microeconomic analytical approach similar to that used in studying a firm's behavior in various types of economic markets ranging from pure competition to pure monopoly. Chapters 4 and 5 examined in general terms the structure and operations of commercial banking in the United States. This background helps us develop a systematic understanding of the decisions made by the individual banking firm and of the implications of the firm's behavior for market results.

The theoretical model should provide an analytical blueprint for assessing and understanding results in the complex, actual market setting. The intent in using theory is not to photograph the real world but to fashion a conceptual device for bringing to light meaningful insights and questions about the real world. In effect, a theory of the banking firm attempts to present a formalized, reasonable explanation of various kinds of banking behavior. Furthermore, it should illuminate some of the aspects of public policy affecting commercial banking. The theory's explanation of banking firm behavior complements other, more traditional, descriptive explanations of banks' operations.

PURE COMPETITION AND
FEATURES OF BANKING
MARKETS

In economic analysis, a *purely competitive market* has four essential features: (1) many sellers of output, (2) no influence by any individual seller upon market price, (3) an identical or homogeneous product for all sellers, and (4) completely free entry and exit of sellers in the market. These four conditions provide a point of departure for analyzing in general terms the nature of banking markets in the United States. Basically, the purely competitive market serves as a benchmark for judging the performance of banking markets because pure competition generates economically efficient (or optimal) price-output results.

The Number of Sellers

Although there are thousands of commercial banks in the United States, it is clear that not all of them actively compete with one another. Given the wide geographic dispersion of these thousands of banking firms in various localities across the nation, the pattern of banking market structure consists essentially of a large number of fairly small groupings of competing banks. For example, in the 1960s estimates indicated that almost one-half of all local banking markets had between two and four separate banks, with a little less than one-half of the total population residing in these two-to-four-bank towns.[1]

On the other hand, it should be noted that both financial cost and travel time required to transact business effectively limit the geographic area within which bank customers shop for services. Since travel costs are not influenced by the size of a given banking transaction, the per-dollar travel cost of a service declines as the size of the transaction increases. Thus, the geographic market of the customer expands with the increased size of the banking transaction. Several surveys indicate that households and small firms choose a bank primarily on the basis of convenience to home or place of work.[2]

1. See Clifton H. Kreps, Jr., "Characteristics of Local Banking Competition," in *Banking and Monetary Studies,* ed. Deane Carson (Homewood, Ill.: Richard D. Irwin, 1963), p. 330. Professor Kreps estimated that about 5 percent of the nation's population resided in "bankless towns" and about one-fifth of the populace lived in one-bank towns.

2. For example, see the two studies by George Kaufman, *Business Firms and Households View Commercial Banks* and *Customers View Bank Markets and Services: A Survey of Elkhart, Indiana* (Federal Reserve Bank of Chicago, 1967). In his 1965 study for the Board of Governors of the Federal Reserve System, entitled *Banking Market Structure and Performance in Metropolitan Areas,* Theodore G. Flechsig found that 90 percent of business loans under $100,000 were from banks within the metropolitan area where the firm was located. A survey of business loans in the St. Louis area found that 77 percent of loans to firms with net worth under $750,000 were made to firms located within fifteen miles of the bank, while only 48 percent of loans to larger corporations were made within this distance. See Clifton B. Luttrell and William E. Pettigrew, "Banking Markets for

Table 6.1 AN APPROXIMATE CLASSIFICATION OF COMMERCIAL BANKING MARKETS IN THE UNITED STATES TODAY

Geographic Scope of Banking Market	Average Number of Bank Firms in Typical Market	Percentage of Total Banking Industry Operating on Given Geographic Level
National	Many (100–150)	Nil
Regional (or state)	Some (under 100)	Minor
Local	Few (under 15)	Major

Source: Estimated by authors.

Local economic factors are more important for smaller banks than for large banks. Small banks deal mostly with neighborhood customers, since legal restrictions and concern for risk diversification limit the size of loans by these banks. Large banks, however, provide loans to distant firms who draw on banking services over a wide geographic area. Large banks, less dependent on local banking markets, may have customers throughout the nation and even in foreign countries.

A stylized device such as Table 6.1 summarizes some general insights relating to the number of sellers found in U.S. banking markets today. This table shows the approximate relationship between banking markets of differing geographic scope and the average number of bank firms (sellers) found in the *typical* market at each of these geographic levels. It also gives rough estimates of the percentage of the total commercial banking industry's firms operating on a given geographic market level. Note that Table 6.1 conveys generalized and descriptive information rather than quantitatively precise results; it simply presents the authors' qualitative impressions derived from casual observation of operating commercial banking markets in the United States.

In the first column of Table 6.1 the geographic scope of banking markets is

Business Firms in the St. Louis Area," Federal Reserve Bank of St. Louis, *Review* (September 1966): 9–12.

classified according to three levels: national, regional (or state), and local. While only one national geographic market exists, there are at most a few dozen separate markets covering a region or at least an entire state. Finally, there are several thousand separate banking markets confined to individual cities, towns, or localities.

As the geographic scope of the banking market narrows, the *average number* of bank firms found in the *typical* market at that given geographic level declines. For example, most likely only the 100 to 150 largest commercial banks (or banking organizations, if allowance is made for the existence of bank holding companies) compete across the length and breadth of the nation for customers, especially those key customers that require large-scale banking services. These giant banks operating in national (even international markets) constitute a nil percentage (1 percent or less) of the total industry's firms, as shown in the third column of Table 6.1.

A banking market that covers a geographic area such as a region (for example, the Southwest region may be defined arbitrarily to include southern California, the entire states of Arizona and New Mexico, and the southwestern portion of Texas) or at least one entire state typically averages fewer than one hundred bank firms in any *one* such regional or state market. Fewer than half the firms operate on a geographic level as large as a state.

In contrast, almost all firms in the banking industry operate on at least the local level. However, the typical local banking market has only a few sellers. Thus, if we zero in on the most active level of banking, that is, the one with the most bank customers, we can best describe U.S. banking markets as localized, with few sellers. Interestingly, in determinations relating to banking competition, the courts have held generally that the relevant geographic market area is smaller than an entire state. For example, in the *Philadelphia Bank* case of 1963, mentioned in a previous chapter, the U.S. Supreme Court clearly stressed the local nature of banking markets.

Furthermore, the Federal Reserve authorities typically use the local market as a benchmark in assessing the competitive impact of a bank merger, a proposed holding company formation, or a proposed acquisition of a bank by a holding company. This regulatory approach recognizes that local markets offer the fewest alternatives to bank customers. Defining the relevant geographic market is one of the toughest chores of such a competitive analysis. Information on prices, banking service lines, commuting and trade patterns, and the geographic coverage of local news media is used to determine market boundaries. For the most part, local banking markets are approximated by counties or metropolitan areas.

Pricing Practices: Seller Influence on Price

In many banking markets certain banking practices or conventions reflect the influence of banking firms on the pricing and quality of service attached to specific product lines. Local and regional clearing-house associations can serve as channels for achieving uniform banking practices, affecting such things as rates of interest and other credit terms on particular kinds of loans, banking service charges, interest rates paid on time and savings deposits, and banking office hours. The "ritual" related to setting the prime rate on loans to top-rated large business borrowers as well as practices governing compensating balances on business loans reflect the interdependence of banking firms in given markets.[3]

Some events of the mid-1970s illustrate the interdependence among banking firms, even for the giant banks who compete in the national market. For example, in 1973 and 1974 the extremely high interest rates gave business corporations extra incentive to become even more sophisticated in the management of their cash balances. Not only the large national business firms, but also the intermediate-sized and small-sized firms, devised ways to economize on their checking account balances beyond whatever minimum compensating balances commercial banks required against credit extensions to these firms. Regional banks as well as major money-center banks such as in New York City, Chicago, and San Francisco felt this tightening up by business firms. After interest rates retreated from 1974 peak levels in 1975, the 1973–1975 recession's effects on corporate profits pressed business to maintain tight control of cash positions. In this setting, national firms tended to concentrate their

---

3. Compensating deposit balances connected with business loans represent compulsory tie-in sales by banking firms. In effect, the credit-granting service is tied to the sale of a specified amount of deposit-holding service. For an examination of this convention and its relation to the multiproduct features of bank output, see David A. Alhadeff, "Monopolistic Competition and Banking Markets," in *Monopolistic Competition Theory: Studies in Impact,* ed. Robert E. Kuenne (New York: Wiley, 1967), p. 365.

deposit balances in a few banks rather than scatter them in small amounts among a number of competing institutions.

During this period, compensating balance requirements against corporate loan extensions or other bank-provided services also tended to decline. This reflected the eagerness of the banks to provide self-contained packages of banking services. Some of these package deals emphasized specific fees (prices) instead of compensating balances, especially for noncredit services. These service packages have become more common as businesses have needed more operating funds, partly due to price inflationary forces. This phenomenon was clearly evident in 1973 and 1974: in each of these two years business loans by banks spurted a record $27 billion, making it tough for banks to enforce their usual compensating-balance requirements.

The Nature of Output

Commercial banks provide *multiproduct* (or multiservice) *lines* to customers: in addition to deposit-holding services for demand and time depositors and credit-granting services for consumer, business, and government borrowers, a commercial banking firm may afford many other services, such as credit collections and information, trust activities, safekeeping facilities, and so on. A banking firm also tries to differentiate its product lines from those of its competitors by the use of nonprice competitive tactics and by stressing convenience factors and the importance to customers of established "banking connections." Competitive groups of banks will vary in number and composition for different product lines, because not all banking firms offer the same set of product lines. Certain product lines will face considerable competition from nonbank financial firms, and the geographic scope of competition will differ for various product lines.

For example, the market for term loans to large national corporations is nationwide, with only the largest commercial banks as sellers. Nonbank sources would include life insurance companies, trust and pension funds, and private placements. In contrast, personal checking services are offered in a basically local market in which only local commercial banks, large and small, operate as suppliers. Thus depending on the particular product line selected, competition can range in scope from the national level to a regional level to the local level. Most banking firms deal primarily in local markets.

Market Entry

The structure of banking markets is influenced not only by the operations of existing banking firms but also by the barriers confronting new entrants into these markets. The threat of new entry may moderate the prices charged by existing banks in a given market. Thus, easy entry generates a strong potential competition in the market, even though actual entry is negligible.

Market entry barriers may be classified into two broad groups: those involving economic factors and those arising from regulatory policy and procedure. Economic barriers develop from such things as the use of product differentiation, absolute cost advantages enjoyed by existing firms, and the presence of appreciable economies of large-scale operation.

Differentiation of product, often reinforced by legal regulatory practices, is achieved by firms already operating in markets by means of long-established, expensive advertising efforts. Though product differentiation is a significant barrier to entry in certain manufacturing industries, it is not as important in banking markets. Generally, borrowers do not prefer loans from old established banks to those from new banks. Most depositors (particularly small depositors) are not too sensitive about the record of operating experience for their banks, since most banks have deposit insurance. Similarly, convenient banking office locations may give some banks an advantage in certain product lines, but this factor is not decisive, particularly in light of population shifts and growth in many communities.

Established firms in an industry can enjoy certain absolute cost advantages because of superior methods of production or the ability to obtain needed factors of production (land, labor, capital, and entrepreneurial ability) on more favorable terms than can new firms. It is true that many banks (both established and new) find it difficult to obtain competent management personnel, but there is no reason to assume that this problem is significantly greater for new banks.

The impact of capital requirements on bank entry is difficult to assess. Capital accounts of banks serve as protective cushions guarding depositors against declines in the values of bank assets, and minimum capital requirements are imposed by law and by bank supervisory agencies. Assuming these minimum capital requirements are not imposed, it is estimated that a bank of reasonable size could be started with total capital of less than $500,000.[4] This figure compares favorably with the minimum operating capital required for new entrants into many other industries, particularly manufacturing. These comparisons suggest that absolute cost advantages are not appreciable barriers to entry into banking markets.

The extent of economies of scale in banking has still not been completely determined. In theoretical terms, the concept of *economies of scale* may be stated quite simply: given a production situation in which the inputs of all of the productive factors are increased by the same proportion, total output tends to increase at a faster rate than the rate of increase in inputs. In effect, the concept considers the long-run tendency for average unit costs to decline as the scale (size) of a firm's productive capacity increases.

Economies of scale are easier to measure in a single-product firm than in a multiproduct firm, making it difficult to measure their precise nature in banking. As indicated, commercial banking is a service industry producing multiple products, and the product mix will vary among individual banks. For example, relatively small banks are limited in their lending operations, while large banks offer both small and large loans. Thus, cost data relating to loans by various-sized banks will not always be comparable.

Further difficulties arise when analyzing costs for branch and unit banks. Generally, branch banks concentrate more on retail banking than unit banks of similar size. High-income, high-cost installment loans as well as mortgage loans account for a higher proportion of branch banks' loan portfolios than for unit banks of similar size. Then, too, branch banks frequently hold a higher proportion of time deposits.

In measuring the effect of scale, a basic distinction arises from the two possible methods for expanding the banking firm. A unit-banking firm or a branch-banking firm with a fixed number of branches (plants) may expand its total output. An alternative for banking firm expansion is the addition of more branches. The input-output relation implied in economies of scale requires that firm expansion be accomplished through an increase in plant size for a unit bank or through enlargement of the already existing system of branches for a branch bank.

4. Bernard Shull and Paul M. Horvitz, "Branch Banking and the Structure of Competition," *National Banking Review* (March 1964): 309.

Although no definitive conclusions can be made about economies of scale in banking, recent empirical studies of bank costs suggest that such economies exist for both branch and unit banks. These investigations, which make use of different stratified samples of commercial banks, indicate among other things that average cost tends to decrease as bank size increases. The decline in average cost is relatively great for the very small banks; however, for banks with deposits exceeding $5 million, average costs decline very slowly as the bank's size increases.[5] Furthermore, a reasonable inference from these studies is that an alert commercial bank with deposits of $5 million can compete fairly effectively with banks of much greater size. In fact, there are many actual instances where both large and small banks compete in the same market for a banking service. It would appear, then, that economies of scale do not constitute a major barrier to entry into banking markets.

REGULATORY POLICY AND
BANK ENTRY

Although economic barriers do not greatly hinder entry into banking, major barriers are found in the area of regulatory policy and procedure. Commercial banking is a heavily regulated industry, and this regulatory framework affects entry into banking markets. Essentially, banking regulation aims at promoting a banking structure that is compatible with such broad and partly conflicting goals as depositor safety, technological efficiency in banking, efficient allocation of financial resources, and the avoidance of undue concentration of economic power.

Before a commercial bank can be established, it is necessary to obtain a charter. State banks are chartered by the authorities in the individual states,

5. The literature on economies of scale in banking has grown in recent years. A representative listing of some important contributions to the analysis of scale economies in banking includes Lyle Gramley, *A Study of Scale Economies in Banking* (Federal Reserve Bank of Kansas City, 1962); George Benston, "Branch Banking and Economies of Scale," *Journal of Finance* 20 (May 1965): 312–332; Stuart Greenbaum, *Banking Structure and Costs: A Statistical Study of the Cost-Output Relationship in Commercial Banking,* unpublished Ph.D. dissertation, Johns Hopkins University, 1964; F. W. Bell and N. B. Murphy, "Economies of Scale and Division of Labor in Commercial Banking," *Southern Economic Journal* 35 (October 1968): 131–139; John A. Powers, "Branch Versus Unit Banking: Bank Output and Cost Economies," *Southern Economic Journal* 36 (October 1969): 153–164.

while national banks are chartered by the Comptroller of the Currency. These same agencies are also empowered to grant or withhold branch office certificates.

An application for a new national bank charter requires the Comptroller to investigate and determine such factors as the background and financial position of the group organizing the proposed bank, the current availability of banking facilities to customers in the area of the proposed bank, and the likely need for and acceptance of the proposed banking facility in the area. An especially important factor is the overall competitive nature of the market in which the proposed bank will be located.

State chartering authorities follow procedures similar to those of the Comptroller. In most cases, however, state officials utilize a less complex procedure. Weight given to various factors in assessing applications will vary among individual state chartering authorities.

Banking regulatory legislation emphasizes the community's need and convenience in appraising chartering and branching applications. A sensitive weighing of the need factor by supervisory officials can be a major obstacle to bank entry, particularly since this criterion is not defined or measured in any precise fashion in existing banking legislation.

Assessment of the need factor can have implications for the competitive tone of certain banking markets. Relatively few charter applications are denied specifically on the basis of potential detriment to another bank in a given locality. It is likely that a judgment of "insufficient need" implies lack of sufficient business to support existing banks plus a new entrant. For most industries other than banking, considerations of need and extent of the given market are tied to the barrier arising from economies of scale. In banking, regulatory authorities have largely assumed the task of determining the extent of this barrier.

Some aspects of banking regulation can lower various economic barriers to entry in banking markets. The emergence of federal deposit insurance and the adoption of reasonably uniform federal-state bank supervisory standards tend to decrease differentiation of product lines among banks.

On the other hand, minimum capital requirements for new banks and branches may raise the entry barrier due to the absolute cost advantages enjoyed by banks already operating in certain markets. In actual practice, bank regulatory agencies usually insist on capital amounts exceeding those minimums specified in the statutes. It is conceivable that regulatory officials could impose capital requirements exceeding amounts considered optimal for profitable operation by newly entering banks. Under such conditions, regulatory policy governing capital requirements could be a real hindrance to bank entry.

Finally, in those areas in which branching is permitted, several factors make entry by a new branch of an existing bank generally easier than entry by a new bank. A branch banking system can provide flexible mobilization of funds by shifting excess reserves for lending among the various branches in the system. Thus, branch offices can be established in localities that generate a fairly unbalanced banking business. For example, in certain communities there may be a strong demand for agricultural loans and mortgage loans, while deposit volume is fairly skimpy. In initiating operations, a new branch may also draw on the pool of experienced management personnel within a large branch system.

Not only may economic factors make entry easier for branches than for new banks, but regulatory authorities are often more inclined to permit entry by branches of existing banks rather than by new banks. The branching alternative is particularly preferred when entry by a new bank could have adverse effects on local bank safety.

BANKING MARKETS AND PUBLIC POLICY

This brief examination of banking markets in the United States indicates some important deviations from the economist's theoretical view of purely competitive markets. Of particular significance is the varied, complex nature of bank product lines in actual markets. Not only do commercial banks offer multiple products in various geographic markets, but entry into these markets, especially at the local level, is hindered by significant regulatory obstacles. Anyone attempting to enhance competitive market results in banking must carefully consider the barriers arising from legal and regulatory sources. Banking law and regulation must be tempered by a realistic regard for the changing context in which commercial banks and other financial firms operate. Especially relevant is the need to avoid outdated or rigidly applied controls to banking.

Indeed, commercial banking is a field in which the completely unrestricted working of free market forces will not necessarily achieve the desired degree of competitiveness within banking markets. Unavoidably, the nature of banking competition is related to such factors as banking safety, financial history and condition of banks, adequacy of bank capital, prospects for future earnings, makeup of bank management, and the community's needs and convenience.

Much of the rationalization for supervisory agency restriction of entry into the banking industry rests on the need for maintaining a stable monetary system. Stated another way, it is generally held that the social costs of bank failures would exceed those costs incurred by restricting bank entry.

Some observers argue that the apparent dilemma of how to enhance banking competition without creating undue dangers rests on too sensitive a reading of banking history in the United States. Admittedly, the United States suffered numerous bank failures in the 1920s and especially in the early 1930s, partly as a consequence of the appreciable "overbanking" that developed during the initial two decades of the twentieth century.

In assessing this record of bank failures, we should remember that the economy in which the banking industry operates has changed significantly since the initial decades of this century. Today the United States is a highly industrialized, relatively mature economy characterized by a predominantly urban middle-income society. This society demands active participation by the national government in the essential task of maintaining a conscious policy of economic stabilization.

With these changes in the composition of the economy and in the financial community, a reasonable case can be made for greater application of the principles of the free market to banking to ensure the provision of adequate and sound banking facilities without adverse results for banking competition. Regulatory policy should enhance the present and future performance of banking and other financial institutions in the country. In this way, progress can be made toward promoting a more viable, responsive financial structure for the United States.

A MODEL OF THE BANKING FIRM

The operating features of banking markets indicate marked differences from the characteristics of pure competition. A meaningful theory of the banking firm must incorporate these aspects of imperfect competition. As an imperfectly competitive industry, some commercial banking markets would be monopolistic, others oligopolistic, and still others monopolistically competitive. For the individual banking firm, short-run decisions affecting price and output reflect an ability to practice price discrimination and to differentiate various product lines. *Price discrimination* means simply that buyers are treated differently in price, quality, and service when the difference is not attributable to any difference in costs. In effect, commercial banks can be viewed as multiple-product, price-discriminating firms.[6]

Assumptions of the Model

In constructing the model, we make several assumptions regarding the banking firm's operations, including the following:

1. The banking firm has mobility of resources, principally bank reserves, that can produce a variety of product lines.
2. The scale or size of the banking firm's plant is fixed; that is, the firm varies output within the fixed plant capacity.
3. Bank output is homogeneous with respect to costs, and marginal costs increase gradually over ordinary ranges of output, increasing sharply as full capacity is approached.
4. Price elasticities of demand differ for the bank's various product lines.
5. The demands for various products are not related; that is, the markets for the banking firm's product lines are separate and distinct.
6. The banking firm attempts to maximize profits.

These assumptions carry certain implications for the analysis of the banking firm. Assumptions 1 and 2 imply a short-run time period of adjustment within

---

6. The formulation of the banking firm as a combination of a price-discriminating monopolist and product-differentiating monopolistic competitor is found in Bernard Shull's essay "Commercial Banks as Multiple-Product Price-Discriminating Firms," in *Banking and Monetary Studies,* ed. Deane Carson (Homewood, Ill.: R. D. Irwin, 1963), pp. 351–368. Shull derives his analysis largely from Eli W. Clemens's work "Price Discrimination and the Multiple-Product Firm," *Review of Economic Studies* 19 (1950–1951): 1–11, reprinted with changes in Richard B. Heflebower and George W. Stocking, *Readings in Industrial Organization and Public Policy* (Homewood, Ill.: Richard D. Irwin, 1958), pp. 262–276.

the confines of fixed productive capacity. Assumption 3 suggests that units of output for all product lines have equal direct costs under ordinary conditions. In effect, the banking firm can direct excess plant capacity into any product line without significantly different increases in cost. This assumption departs from operating results in that different product lines of a bank actually carry different direct costs. For purposes of analysis, these cost differences are not considered significant in affecting the banking firm's output decisions. To illustrate, a banking firm considering a given dollar increase in output of either mortgage loans or business loans presumably will use the same dollar amount of funds drawn from its overall pool of funds. The cost of funds is unchanged by the particular use made of them. Furthermore, the Federal Reserve System's functional cost analysis of commercial banks assumes that the total cost of funds (demand deposits, time deposits, and capital funds) can be divided proportionately among the several types of a bank's earning assets in order to calculate net return on each type of asset. In effect, then, this functional cost approach views various kinds of bank assets (products) as homogeneous with respect to cost of funds.

Assumption 4 recognizes the differentiation of product lines among individual banking firms and, more importantly, the alternative sources of supply of banking services for various types of bank customers.[7]

Assumption 5 views banking markets as being compartmentalized or separate, with no opportunity for customers charged the low price to resell to customers charged the higher price. This assumption deviates partly from the actual situation existing in some banking markets. It is highly likely, for example, that demands for bank loans by consumers and by personal finance companies are pretty much interrelated. In the main, however, assumption 5 is reasonable in implying that demand interdependence is not generally prevalent in banking markets, at least in the short run. Furthermore, it should be noted that assumptions 4 and 5 provide the conditions whereby the practice of price discrimination by banking firms is made possible and profitable.

---

7. In loan transactions, for example, differentials in lending rates (prices) charged different customers cannot be fully explained by differences in risks, maturities, or costs of making the loans. Various studies stress these different alternatives open to bank customers and suggest the possibility of price discrimination in banking markets. See Lester V. Chandler, "Monopolistic Elements in Commercial Banking," *Journal of Political Economy* 46 (February 1938): 5f; David A. Alhadeff, "Bank Mergers: Competition Versus Banking Factors," *Southern Economic Journal* 29 (January 1963): 218; Shull and Horvitz, "Branch Banking and the Structure of Competition," p. 328.

Figure 6.1   EQUILIBRIUM ADJUSTMENT BY BANKING FIRM
Multiple-product discriminatory-pricing case.

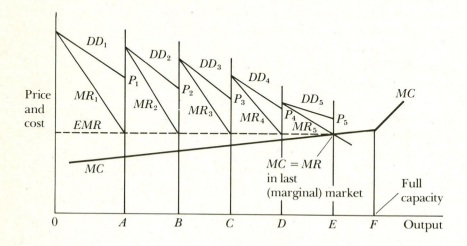

Finally, the profit-maximizing assumption, assumption 6, implies that equilibrium is reached when the banking firm maximizes profits. Depending on the extent of imperfect competition in a given market, the banking firm's equilibrium position can provide either a normal competitive return or excess (pure) profits.

Results of Model

Figure 6.1 helps explain the short-run adjustment by the banking firm in light of these assumptions. The figure indicates at least five separate markets in which the given banking firm operates. Potentially, the number of markets open to the firm could well be innumerable. Each of the five markets has its own demand (average revenue) curve (DD_1 to DD_5) and related marginal revenue curve (MR_1 to MR_5). The different markets are arranged from left to right in declining order of profitability and of chronological entry by the firm. A pattern of market entry emerges: the banking firm deals initially in the most profitable markets; with excess productive capacity, it expands into less profitable markets rather than reducing price in the initial markets. Entry into separate new markets occurs as long as there are accessible markets in which the demand price exceeds the marginal cost.

Output is expanded to that level at which marginal cost *MC* is equated to marginal revenue *MR* in the last (marginal) market entered. By adjusting output and prices in all other markets, the firm equalizes marginal revenue in all five markets. The *equal marginal revenue line EMR* shows the equating of marginal revenue in all markets. Equilibrium price and output levels for the individual markets are established where *equal marginal revenue* equals marginal revenue in each specific market. Market prices range from a high of P_1 in the first market to a low of P_5 in the fifth market. Total output is allocated among the various markets, ranging from OA in the first market to DE in the fifth (marginal) market.

The model depicted in Figure 6.1 affords several concluding observations that can be contrasted with actual behavior by banking firms:

1. Production is barely profitable in the marginal market, since marginal cost approximates demand price. Banking firms operate in marginal markets by producing up to the maximum permitted by reserve holdings. At times, purchases of certain types of government securities or governmentally guaranteed or insured loans, particularly during periods of monetary restraint, suggest marginal operations where sales margins would tend to vary in these different markets.

2. Entry into less profitable markets will tend to raise prices and restrict output in the more profitable (supramarginal) markets, given existing capacity. These results emerge from the equating of marginal revenue in all markets and from the gradual rise in marginal costs. At times, many banks that have acquired greater excess reserves have diversified into new markets with little or no change in prices charged in old markets. For instance, during a period of monetary expansion when lending capacity increases, many banks take on new lending and "investing" lines, with little or no change in prices for existing lines. Under more competitive market conditions, prices for these existing (old) product lines would tend to be lowered as bank firms gain increased capacity during a period of monetary ease.

3. The marginal market has a relatively elastic demand curve; therefore, the firm's market power varies in different markets. Separation or segmentation of the market into various submarkets permits more effective use of price

discrimination. Various studies referred to previously suggest differing elasticities of demand for banks' product lines, and therefore a rational basis exists for discriminatory pricing behavior by banking firms.

4. Since the model depicts the typical or representative firm, profit-maximizing behavior by a relatively large number of competing firms may provide only a normal competitive return. Generally, actual rates of return in banking appear reasonably moderate, as compared with other industries.

SOME USES OF THE MODEL

The model of the banking firm developed here seems to explain some aspects of banking behavior and performance. The banking firm's responses in various markets, as shown in the model, focus on multiple-product production and discriminatory pricing. The model is useful in analyzing the possible effects on banking firms of changes in fundamental forces affecting banking markets. A case in point is the impact of changes in monetary policy on the market behavior of banking firms.

A change in policy to monetary ease or to monetary restraint can be interpreted as affecting the shape of the banking firm's marginal cost curve by changing the point at which marginal costs increase greatly. Hence, central bank actions affect the productive capacity of individual banking firms. A period of monetary ease, for example, tends to shift the occurrence of sharply rising marginal costs to a higher level of output, so that the bend in the marginal cost curve would move to the right in Figure 6.1. Monetary restraint brings opposite effects by reducing the productive capacity of banks, or in relation to Figure 6.1, the point of steeply rising marginal costs would shift to the left to a lower level of output.

Monetary authorities can also affect the level of the firm's marginal cost curve, for example, by changing interest rate ceilings on time and savings deposits. Monetary restraint may increase the banking firm's schedule of marginal costs by increasing the costs of borrowed funds and by stimulating more intensive competition for funds. Under a policy of monetary restraint the entire marginal cost curve shifts upward and to the left.

Changes in the shape and level of the marginal cost curve will induce the profit-maximizing banking firm to adjust the amount and proportion of resources devoted to marginal markets. A move to monetary ease tends to increase the amount and share of a bank's output devoted to marginal markets, for instance, short-term Treasury bills. It also tends to increase output and to lower prices in the other markets. Reverse price-output effects occur when the monetary authorities pursue restrictive actions. Modifications in the firm's schedule of marginal costs induce these changes in pricing-output behavior, because the line of equal marginal revenue moves to a different level, thus indicating new equilibrium results.

The insights derived from the model aid in explaining bank behavior during periods marked by changes in monetary policy, for example, the restrictive impact of the "credit crunches" of 1966 and 1969 and the transition to monetary ease in 1970–1971. Additionally, the model affords a rationale for bank merger and bank holding company activity—two important forces affecting the structure of commercial banking in the United States.

Bank mergers and acquisitions by bank holding companies can be explained partly as devices for establishing banks in new markets. The new markets, though not necessarily more profitable than the old markets, attract entry as long as they are profitable. Entry into the new (marginal) market permits the banking firm not only to accrue profits in the new market but also to make more profitable use of resources in old markets by raising prices and restricting output in these markets. These advantages emerge in addition to any market power gained by the firm from the reduction in the number of competitors in the old markets.

THE VALIDITY OF THE MODEL

The theory of the banking firm is a reasonable and consistent explanation of certain types of banking behavior and performance. The model of the multiple-product, price-discriminating firm is presumably an analytical device that enhances understanding and the power of prediction relating to banking operations.

However, the model is only one of several approaches for explaining the behavior of banking firms. Other, more traditional, descriptive explanations rationalize bank diversification into different product lines on the basis of risk minimization (impelled partly by regulatory authorities) and liquidity needs.[8]

8. Many studies examine the management of bank portfolios from either a risk diversification

Furthermore, interest rate differentials for different classes of borrowers are explained by underlying differences in "credit worthiness." Indeed, a banking firm's entry into marginal markets can be partly explained by the factors of diversification and liquidity requirements. Then, too, credit worthiness sheds light on the different rates charged for the same type of loan. Entry into marginal banking markets when monetary policy eases is believed to improve bank liquidity, which may have deteriorated in the previous period of economic expansion. Restrictive monetary action, on the other hand, induces banks to sell government securities (thereby reducing their liquidity) in order to take advantage of increased profit opportunities for bank loans. In this case, the end result is a reduction in liquidity of the bank's earning assets.

These observable forms of banking behavior occur within a context of changing demands in various markets and of bank willingness to allocate resources to the most profitable lines. Our model of the banking firm incorporates these elements by indicating that profits are maximized for the banking firm that adheres closely to multiple-product, price-discriminating behavior. Both the traditional, descriptive approach and the model of the banking firm provide complementary explanations of banking behavior and performance. It is the mixture of competitive (or profit-maximizing) behavior with behavior stemming from regulation and traditional banking practice that makes it difficult to form workable public policies affecting banking competition.

KEY TERMS

Purely competitive market   Economies of scale
Multiproduct lines   Price discrimination
Market entry barriers

---

approach or a liquidity approach. For example, see R. C. Porter, "A Model of Bank Portfolio Selection," *Yale Economic Essays* 1 (Fall 1961): 323–359; D. R. Hodgman, *Commercial Bank Loan and Investment Policy* (Champaign, Ill.: University of Illinois, 1963); G. W. Woodworth, "Theories of Cyclical Liquidity Management of Commercial Banks," *National Banking Review* 4 (June 1967): 377–395; J. L. Pierce, "Commercial Bank Liquidity," *Federal Reserve Bulletin* 52 (August 1966): 1093–1101.

REVIEW QUESTIONS

1. Why is it important to develop a theory of the banking firm?
2. How do the operating features of commercial banking markets compare with the characteristics of a purely competitive market?
3. Using a geographic scope of market, how might the United States commercial banking markets be classified according to number of sellers?
4. Banking practices or conventions reflect the influence of banking firms upon price and nonprice aspects of product lines. Explain by means of some examples.
5. In general, what barriers limit entry into banking markets?
6. What broad implications for public policy emerge from the study of actual banking markets?
7. What basic assumptions are made in deriving a theory of the banking firm?
8. In light of the assumptions just mentioned, what equilibrating adjustments are made by the banking firm?
9. How do the theoretical results of the model of the banking firm compare with the actual behavior of banking firms?
10. What are some analytical uses for the theory of the banking firm?
11. What are other general approaches for explaining the behavior of banking firms?

SUGGESTED READINGS

Alhadeff, David A. "Monopolistic Competition and Banking Markets." In *Monopolistic Competition Theory: Studies in Impact,* ed. Robert E. Kuenne. New York: Wiley, 1967.

Benston, George J. "Economies of Scale and Marginal Costs in Banking Operations." *National Banking Review* 2 (June 1965): 507–549.

Broaddus, Alfred. "Linear Programming: A New Approach to Bank Portfolio Management." Federal Reserve Bank of Richmond, *Monthly Review* (November 1972): 3–11.

Darnell, Jerome C., and Howard Keen, Jr. "Small Bank Survival: Is the Wolf at the Door?" Federal Reserve Bank of Philadelphia, *Business Review* (November 1974): 16–23.

Elzinga, Kenneth G., and Thomas F. Hogarty. "The Problem of Geographic Market Delineation in Antimerger Suits." *The Antitrust Bulletin* 18 (Spring 1973): 45–81.

Erdevig, Eleanor. "Deposit Service—New Tool for Cash Management." Federal Reserve Bank of Chicago, *Business Conditions* (April 1976): 11–15.

Gallick, Edward C. "Bank Profitability and Bank Size." Federal Reserve Bank of Kansas City, *Monthly Review* (January 1976): 11–15.

Greenbaum, Stuart I. "Costs and Production in Commercial Banking." Federal Reserve Bank of Kansas City, *Monthly Review* (March-April 1966): 11–20.

Herzig-Marx, Chayim. "Advertising for Demand Deposits." Federal Reserve Bank of Chicago, *Business Conditions* (September 1975): 10–14.

Mackara, W.F. "The ABC's of the Prime Rate." Federal Reserve Bank of Atlanta, *Monthly Review* (July 1974): 100–105.

Mote, Larry R. "Competition in Banking: The Issues." Federal Reserve Bank of Chicago, *Business Conditions* (January 1967): 8–16.

Osborne, D.K. "Bank Structure and Performance—Survey of Empirical Findings on the Cost of Checking Accounts." Federal Reserve Bank of Dallas, *Review* (May 1977): 7.

Scott, John Troy. *Price and Nonprice Competition in Banking Markets: A Study of the Theoretical and Empirical Justification for Regulatory Attempts to Promote Competition in Banking Markets.* (Research Report No. 62) Boston: Federal Reserve Bank of Boston, 1977.

Stolz, Richard W. "Competition for Banking Services: Three Analyses: Philadelphia National Bank Case Revisited." Federal Reserve Bank of Minneapolis, *Ninth District Quarterly* (Winter 1977): 5–11.

Summers, Bruce J. "A Time Series Analysis of Business Loans at Large Commercial Banks." Federal Reserve Bank of Richmond, *Economic Review* (May-June 1975): 8–14.

Chapter Seven

THE PROCESS OF DEMAND
DEPOSIT CREATION

The study of the monetary process emphasizes the importance of demand deposits within commercial banks. Demand deposits, which comprise the largest part of the general public's money supply, arise from the process of debt monetization by the commercial banking system. They are closely related to the various credit-granting product lines of the commercial banking firm.

This chapter examines in some detail the process whereby commercial banks create (and extinguish or destroy) demand deposits. Just as in constructing a theory of the banking firm, an analytical model is developed to help us understand the process of demand deposit creation. This model, drawn simply at first, is then modified to permit a more realistic examination of the deposit-creating process. As with the theory of the banking firm, the intent is to provide a conceptual framework that will facilitate an understanding of the main aspects of demand deposit creation and make possible an assessment of some important implications arising from the deposit-creating process.

THE ANCIENT GOLDSMITH AND
BANKING PRINCIPLES

Before we examine the specifics relating to demand deposit creation, a quick journey back through time will provide some valuable analytical insights into our understanding of money creation. Specifically, let us return to the ancient goldsmith, who, while plying his trade, stumbled across the basic operating principles that underlie the operation of today's commercial banking system. In effect, through the evolving nature of the tasks he performed, the goldsmith was a forerunner of today's commercial banker.

Many of the long-established, venerable merchant banking houses of Europe began their operations as goldsmiths. The internationally famous House of Rothschild is one of the more outstanding examples. Then, too, Shakespeare uses a goldsmith, Shylock, as the central figure in *The Merchant of Venice*. In fact, the affluent thriving economies that were the city-states of Venice, Genoa, and Florence of the twelfth and thirteenth centuries created a favorable setting for the growing importance of the goldsmith.

Initially, the ancient goldsmith was a skilled artisan in the fabrication and manufacture of objects from precious metals, especially gold. Quite literally, the goldsmith was to gold what the blacksmith was to iron and other nonprecious metals. In the course of his work, the goldsmith performed assaying and safe-keeping services for his clientele. That is, he determined the gold content of full-weighted coins, many of which were left with him for safekeeping. In fact, the word *bank* is derived from the early Italian word *banca*, which means "bench": the workbench at which the goldsmith labored.

Upon leaving some of their assayed gold coins for safekeeping, customers received paper certificates of deposit from the goldsmith. These were made payable to depositors specifically named on the receipts. Coin withdrawals were made upon presentation of these paper receipts (sometimes called warehouse receipts) to the goldsmith. As his experience and business volume grew, the goldsmith observed that a fairly stable portion of the total number of gold coins left for safety deposit actually lay idle in his vault. Why not put these resources to work by lending out gold coins at interest? Thus the goldsmith became a financial lender, lending out the otherwise idle gold coins deposited by his customers. Note that the goldsmith did *not* expand the community's total (aggregate) stock of gold coins. He merely (but most significantly for the local economy) increased the average velocity or rate of turnover of gold coin. By getting more mileage from the existing stock of gold coins, the goldsmith anticipated in a simple way the varied, sophisticated operations of today's financial intermediaries.

As the goldsmith performed his safety deposit and coin-lending operations, the money-using habits and practices of the community were changing gradually. As the goldsmith's reputation for safe and honest dealing became widely known, the paper certificates of deposit he had issued to gold-coin depositors began to be endorsed and re-endorsed over to others in payment for goods and services. The negotiability of these receipts became even more convenient when the goldsmith, heeding his depositors' requests, issued gold certificates of deposit made payable simply to bearer upon demand, rather than to a specifically named depositor. Issuance of these paper certificates in various denominations (ones, fives, tens, etc.) further enhanced their convenience. These developments became widespread and recognized throughout the community—"institutionalized," as the sociologists say.

Not surprisingly, one day a perceptive loan customer requested his loan proceeds in the form of paper certificates rather than in the bulky and less convenient coin. At this point, the goldsmith's function evolved to a new level: that of money creator. The paper IOU issued to the borrowing customer was a form of paper money. It had fixed nominal value in gold coin, and was generally accepted throughout the community in exchange for goods and services or in payment of debt. By issuing paper certificates to borrowers, the goldsmith increased the community's total stock of money assets, which now included through general usage both gold coins and paper gold certificates.

In reaching this third plateau, the goldsmith was able to maintain his enviable position because he recognized, consciously or otherwise, three operating principles: (1) fractional reserves, (2) clearings, and (3) debt monetization. These three principles constitute important mainstays on which the modern commercial banker relies today.

Fractional Reserves

Fractional reserves, the first basic lesson or principle, emerged when the goldsmith's reserves (coins) were but a fraction of the *total* outstanding claims upon these reserves. These claims were the paper gold certificates issued to depositors and borrowers alike. Upon presentation to the goldsmith, each paper certificate was fully redeemable (payable) in gold coin. Effectively, how could the total outstanding claims continue to be greater than the goldsmith's coin reserves? Usually, the goldsmith could expect some withdrawals to occur from day to day, but over this same time some coins were deposited for safekeeping. Thus over a given period the goldsmith was able to economize on the use of his coin reserves, by balancing off coin deposits against coin withdrawals.

Clearings

In its simplest manifestation, the *clearings* principle involves the reciprocal matching of deposits against withdrawals in order to minimize use of coin (cash). In commercial banking, clearings involve exchanges among individual banks of checks and other items, and the settlement of net differences arising from these exchanges. The modern commercial banking system draws on this principle in its use of clearinghouses, both local and regional, which facilitate payments settlements among banks arising from customer checking account transactions.[1]

In this day of electronic funds transfer (EFT) systems, automated clearinghouses (ACHs) are functionally analogous to clearinghouses that process paper checks: both types clear funds transfers between banks. An ACH, however, transfers funds by electric impulses on magnetic computer tapes. Payments such as payroll deposits, preauthorized billings, and point-of-sale transactions can be settled through an ACH.

1. The following hypothetical example illustrates one day's activities for a local clearinghouse that handles settlements arising from checking account activities of four banks.

| | Dollar Amount of Checks Held Against Other Banks | | | | |
Individual Bank	A	B	C	D	Total
A	—	$6,000	$2,000	$4,000	$12,000
B	6,000	—	2,000	2,000	10,000
C	1,000	3,000	—	5,000	9,000
D	1,000	4,000	2,000	—	7,000
Total checks on given bank ($ amt.)	$8,000	$13,000	$6,000	$11,000	$38,000

Using the individual bank totals from the above table, a net settlement position can be calculated for each bank:

Individual Bank	(1) Claims Against Other Banks	(2) Due Other Banks	$(3) = (1) - (2)$ Net Settlement Position
A	$12,000	$8,000	$4,000
B	10,000	13,000	−3,000
C	9,000	6,000	3,000
D	7,000	11,000	−4,000
TOTAL	$38,000	$38,000	0

Note that banks A and C have positive (credit) balances of $4,000 and $3,000, respectively, while banks B and D have negative (deficit) balances of $3,000 and $4,000, respectively. The total volume of $38,000 of checks is settled by $7,000 of net payments among the four banks.

Debt Monetization

Our pragmatic goldsmith discovered yet a third lesson or principle, *debt monetization,* when he exchanged his promise to pay (IOU) in the form of a gold certificate for the promise to pay (IOU) of the borrower. The process of debt monetization involves the swapping of two *qualitatively* different kinds of debt. The borrower's IOU has *limited acceptability* when offered in exchange for goods and services. The goldsmith's IOU, on the other hand, has *general acceptability* throughout the community. In plain terms, the goldsmith's paper IOU represented a monetary liability that served effectively as money. As indicated briefly in an earlier chapter, the modern commercial banking system creates demand deposits money via debt monetization, namely through extending loans and buying securities. Let us now prepare to develop a simple, clear understanding of this demand deposit creation.

A SIMPLE MODEL OF DEMAND DEPOSIT CREATION

Partial equilibrium analysis is useful in constructing a simple analytical model of deposit creation. Partial equilibrium analysis is used, for example, in developing price theory for explaining the determination of prices of products, and of factors of production in various economic markets. For instance, chapter 6 presented the determination of short-run equilibrium price and output for the multiple-product, price-discriminating banking firm. This approach implies an examination of a given phenomenon, with all other factors considered to be unaffected. Similarly, an understanding of the process of demand deposit creation requires the use of simplifying assumptions from which logical conclusions about bank behavior can be drawn, other factors remaining unchanged.

Assumptions of the Simple Model

Several basic assumptions are made in constructing the model. These depart somewhat from reality, but help us to derive meaningful conclusions. They can be modified later to permit a closer approximation to conditions found in the real world. The simplifying assumptions include the following:

1. The central bank makes a $1,000 open market purchase of securities from commercial bank A, an individual bank in a commercial banking system consisting of many banks.

2. All commercial banks are member banks (MBs) in the central banking system, subject to a minimum required reserve ratio of 20 percent against demand deposits; reserves are MB deposits with the central bank.

3. No currency drain by the general public exists; that is, bank borrowers or individuals to whom bank checks are given have no desire to hold currency.

4. No vault or till cash is held by commercial banks; that is, commercial banks do not hold vault cash as a precaution against unexpected withdrawals of demand deposits.

5. No change in liquid asset preferences of the general public occurs; specifically, conversion by the general public of demand deposits into time deposits in commercial banks or into other types of highly liquid assets does not take place.

6. Commercial banks are fully willing to lend.

7. Bank customers are fully willing to borrow.

In deriving conclusions from these assumptions, a helpful device is the *T account,* which indicates the changes in the individual balance sheet items that result from a specified transaction. The T account is similar to the balance sheet in that it shows the particular balance sheet entries affected by a given transaction, with all other items on the balance sheet remaining unchanged. This simplified visual device is equivalent to a modified miniature balance sheet; therefore, the changes shown in the T account must always balance. For example, a decrease of $100 in a specific asset account must be offset either by an equivalent increase in another asset account or by an equal decrease in a liability account or by some combination of changes in asset and liability accounts.

Results of the Simple Model

The logical results of the simplifying assumptions are given in T accounts that depict transactions emerging from different phases of the deposit-creating process. The *first* transaction involves the central bank's $1,000 open market purchase of securities from member bank A (MB-A):

CENTRAL BANK		MB-A	
Securities +$1,000	Deposits for MB-A +$1,000	Deposits at central bank +$1,000	
		Securities −$1,000	

For the central bank, the open market purchase of $1,000 of securities is shown in the addition of this amount to its assets in the form of securities and balanced by an equivalent increase in MB deposits (reserves) in the central bank. Note that the initial increase in the reserves of the system of MBs is shown in the account of MB-A, the commercial bank that sold securities to the central bank. The central bank's T account shows the creation of new reserves for the commercial banking system by open market operations, one of the most important monetary controls used by a modern central bank. (A detailed description and analysis of the central banking system is presented in Part Three of this text.)

The open market transaction is reflected in MB-A's T account—securities assets decrease by $1,000 and are offset by an equivalent increase in another asset, namely deposits at the central bank. Since the acquisition of $1,000 of new reserves by MB-A is not accompanied by an increase in its deposit liabilities, this first transaction provides MB-A with $1,000 of excess reserves; that is, reserves over and above any required reserves. These excess reserves may be transferred to some other commercial bank, for example, by the clearing of checks, without causing MB-A to be deficient in meeting minimum reserve requirements. Since MB-A operates in a system of many individual commercial banks, MB-A recognizes that its customers can transfer ownership of demand deposits to persons who deal with other commercial banks.

In the *second* transaction MB-A monetizes its borrowing customer's debt by granting a loan of $1,000:

MB-A	
Loans +$1,000	Demand deposits +$1,000

Note that MB-A creates an amount of demand deposits *equal to* its *excess* reserve position of $1,000. In this way, when the borrower transfers ownership of these demand deposits by paying a check to a person who deals with another bank, MB-A will not be short in its required reserve position when this check clears through the central bank. In transaction *three,* the borrower from MB-A pays $1,000 to a person who deposits the check in MB-B, and the check clears through the central bank. The T accounts show this clearing operation:

CENTRAL BANK

	Deposits for
	MB-A −$1,000
	MB-B +$1,000

MB-A		MB-B	
Deposits at central bank −$1,000	Demand deposits −$1,000	Deposits at central bank +$1,000	Demand deposits +$1,000

The check clearing transfers reserves from MB-A to MB-B, but the clearing transaction does not change the total reserves of the *system* of member banks.

For MB-A, the *net* results of transactions one through three are an increase of $1,000 in loan assets and an equal decrease in its security assets. The $1,000 in demand deposits derived from the loan by MB-A to its customer now appears as demand deposits in MB-B. The increase in MB-B's deposit liabilities is offset by an equivalent increase in its deposits (reserves) at the central bank. The initial increase in demand deposits of MB-B occurs because MB-B's customer has presented a check for clearing and collection. A demand deposit that arises from the deposit of a check is referred to as a *primary demand deposit,* to distinguish it from a *derivative demand deposit,* which arises directly from a lending transaction. In effect, when the derivative demand deposit created for the borrower is transferred by the writing of a check to another person, it provides the basis for a primary demand deposit by this person. The distinction between derivative and primary demand deposits is for analytical use. The contrast is made in order to aid understanding of the deposit-creating process.

For MB-B, the primary deposit made by its customer provides an increase in its total reserves of $1,000. However, this increase is accompanied by an equal increase in MB-B's demand deposit liabilities. With the reserve requirement at 20 percent, the $1,000 increase in deposit liabilities necessitates minimum *required* reserves of $200, thereby leaving MB-B with $800 *excess* reserves.

In transaction *four,* MB-B monetizes the debt or IOU of its borrowing customer by creating derivative demand deposits in an amount equal to its *excess* reserve assets, as shown in the following T account:

MB-B	
Loan +$800	Demand deposits +$800

By limiting its demand deposit creation to $800, MB-B is prepared for the eventual loss of reserves that occurs when the check drawn by the borrower from MB-B clears through the central bank. In transaction *five,* the borrower from MB-B pays $800 to a person who is a depositor in MB-C, and this check also clears through the central bank, as the following T accounts indicate:

CENTRAL BANK	
	Deposits for
	MB-B −$800
	MB-C +$800

MB-B		MB-C	
Deposits at central bank −$800	Demand deposits −$800	Deposits at central bank +$800	Demand deposits +$800

The clearing of the check through the central bank decreases reserves of MB-B by $800 and increases reserves of MB-C by $800.[2] The *net* results of transactions three, four, and five for MB-B include a $200 change in total reserve holdings and an $800 increase in loan assets counterbalanced by the increase of $1,000 in demand deposit liabilities (representing the original

2. The check could, in fact, be deposited in the bank on which it was drawn, MB-B in this example, in which case the bank would not lose reserves. The *possible* loss of the reserves keeps the commercial bank, generally, from lending more than its excess reserves.

However, if the commercial bank knows from experience that some percentage of checks drawn on accounts created by loans will be redeposited with it, loans of an amount greater than excess reserves can be created, if so desired.

primary deposit of $1,000). Table 7.1 on pages 150–151 summarizes all the T accounts for the various transactions just described.

The process of deposit creation, under the given simplifying assumptions, continues within the commercial banking system until the original injection of new reserves (by the central bank's open market purchase) is now held as required reserves throughout the system of commercial banks. For every dollar of required reserves held by the commercial banking system, five dollars of demand deposit liabilities are outstanding, given the required reserve ratio of 20 percent. In general terms, for the overall commercial banking system, the *maximum* change in demand deposits that can occur with a given absolute change in total reserves is given in the following formula:

$$\Delta DD = \Delta R \times \frac{1}{r_D}$$

where

ΔDD = maximum change in demand deposits
ΔR = absolute change in total reserves for system
r_D = required reserve ratio for demand deposits

In the model, the assumed absolute change in total reserves was $1,000, arising from the central bank's purchase of securities, and the required reserve ratio was 20 percent. Therefore, the calculation is as follows:

$$\Delta DD = \$1,000 \times \frac{1}{0.20} = \$5,000$$

Since the system of commercial banks consists of many individual banks, any one commercial bank creates demand deposits in an amount equal to the individual bank's *excess* reserve holdings. The individual bank within the system limits its deposit creation in this way in order to absorb effectively the adverse clearing of checks drawn by the borrower from the individual bank. The individual bank within the system creates demand deposits, but to a considerably lesser extent than the commercial banking system as a whole. The threat of loss of reserves by the check-clearing process limits the individual commercial bank in its demand deposit creation through lending. For the *overall* commercial banking system, reserves are not lost through the clearing of checks, because the adverse clearings against one individual bank are offset by clearings in favor of another bank in the system. In effect, the clearings transactions for all the individual banks taken together cancel out, leaving the total reserves of the commercial banking system unchanged. It is only the distribution of the system's total reserves among the individual commercial banks that is changed by clearings transactions.

A MODIFIED MODEL OF DEMAND DEPOSIT CREATION

The results obtained from the simple model of deposit creation are determined by the specific assumptions made for this model. As indicated earlier, several of these assumptions depart greatly from real world conditions. However, these simplifying assumptions were made to sharpen our understanding of the process whereby commercial banks create money in the form of demand deposits. An even more meaningful model can be constructed by modifying some of these assumed conditions to allow for *reserve leakages.* As will be shown, these modifications will tend to reduce or dampen the process of deposit creation by the individual commercial bank and by the commercial banking system.

Several of the more important leakages include:

1. An allowance for currency withdrawals by demand depositors in commercial banks. As the general public's money supply increases, a fairly stable proportion of the change in money supply will be held in the form of currency. Stated another way, increased holdings of currency by the nonbank public drain away reserves from the commercial banking system, thus reducing the maximum amount of demand deposits that can be created given the existing required reserve ratio.

2. An allowance for commercial banks maintaining a cushion of excess reserves because of (a) unexpected future withdrawals of demand deposits in the form of currency, and (b) idle or unused lending capacity. In an uncertain world, commercial banks must be prepared to meet possible sudden demands for currency by depositors. Bank holdings of precautionary cash reserves will reflect various factors, including the general state of business confidence, seasonal influences arising from the observance of holidays (such as the

Table 7.1 SUMMARIZATION OF T ACCOUNT ENTRIES FOR A SIMPLE MODEL OF DEMAND DEPOSIT CREATION BY INDIVIDUAL COMMERCIAL BANKS

(through two expansion stages)

Transaction Number	Description of Transaction	Central Bank		Member Bank A	
		Assets	Liabilities	Assets	Liabilities
1	Central bank makes $1,000 open market purchase of securities from MB-A.	Securities +$1,000	Deposits for MB-A +$1,000	Deposits at central bank +$1,000 Securities -$1,000	
2	MB-A extends loan to borrowing customer.			Loans +$1,000	Demand deposits + $1,000
3	Borrower pays check to MB-B customer, who makes primary deposit in MB-B, and check clears through central bank.		Deposits for MB-A -$1,000 MB-B +$1,000	Deposits at central bank -$1,000	Demand deposits - $1,000
4	MB-B extends loan to borrowing customer.				
5	Borrower pays check to MB-C customer, who makes primary deposit in MB-C, and check clears through central bank.		Deposits for MB-B -$800 MB-C +$800		
	Net change in accounts.	Securities +$1,000	MB deposits +$1,000 (MB-B +$200) (MB-C +$800)	Loans +$1,000 Securities -$1,000	

Table 7.1 *(cont.)*

Trans-action Number	Description of Transaction	Member Bank B		Member Bank C	
		Assets	Liabilities	Assets	Liabilities
1	Central bank makes $1,000 open market purchase of securities from MB-A.				
2	MB-A extends loan to borrowing customer.				
3	Borrower pays check to MB-B customer, who makes primary deposit in MB-B, and check clears through central bank.	Deposits at central bank +$1,000 (Required +$200) (Excess +$800)	Demand deposits +$1,000		
4	MB-B extends loan to borrowing customer.	Loans +$800	Demand deposits +$800		
5	Borrower pays check to MB-C customer, who makes primary deposit in MB-C, and check clears through central bank.	Deposits at central bank -$800	Demand deposits -$800	Deposits at central bank +$800 (Required +$160) (Excess +$640)	Demand deposits +$800
	Net change in accounts.	Deposits at central bank +$200 Loans +$800	Demand deposits +$1,000	Deposits at central bank +$800	Demand deposits +$800

Christmas shopping season) and from weather conditions (such as those that affect harvesting and marketing conditions for agricultural products), the banking behavior of customers, the average size and number of bank deposit accounts, and so on. These precautionary cash reserves serve to reduce demand deposit creation by commercial banks, since the cash reserves represent bank decisions to hold additional reserves beyond those actually required by regulatory authorities.

Idle lending capacity arises from lack of effective demand for credit and/or bank unwillingness to utilize lending capacity fully. The granting of credit requires both a borrower and a lender who are willing and able to enter the credit transaction; if one of these parties is missing, the transaction is not completed. Idle lending capacity will increase in periods of political or economic uncertainty if borrowers and lenders "pull in their horns" until the clouded planning horizon improves. This situation occurred during periods marked by turning points in the level of economic activity, for example, during the worst years of the depression of the 1930s and, more recently, during the several post–World War II recessions.

3. An allowance for changes in liquid asset preferences of the general public, that is, the conversion by the general public of demand deposits into time deposits in commercial banks. Chapter 3 examined the role of near-monies and the general significance of financial intermediation within the economy. Decisions by the general public affecting its liquid asset holdings will affect the amount of reserves available to commercial banks for creation of demand deposits. The conversion from demand deposits to time deposits diverts reserves held against demand deposits to reserves required to be held against time deposits. Hence, the shift to time deposits (a near-money) reduces the amount of demand deposits that can be created against a given holding of total reserves by the commercial banking system.

All these leakages in the simple model of demand deposit creation tend to reduce the amount of demand deposits that could be created by either the individual commercial bank or the entire commercial banking system. For the individual commercial bank within the multibank system, the maximum amount of demand deposits created by debt monetization would be *less than* the dollar amount of excess reserves held by the individual bank. The individual bank's limiting the creation of demand deposits to an amount less than its excess reserve holdings reflects the operation of the modifying factors just discussed. In this case, the individual bank restricts its debt-monetizing activity in order to allow for the use of reserves by currency withdrawals, by precautionary holding of cash reserves, by the lack of effective demand for credit, and by changes in liquid asset preferences of its customers. To illustrate, an individual bank with $1,000 of excess reserves estimates that these four factors will use 30 percent of excess reserves. Therefore, this particular bank creates $700 of demand deposits via lending. In this way, it is able to stand the loss of $700 of reserves to other banks by the clearing of checks drawn by the borrower, plus the use of $300 of reserves by currency withdrawals, precautionary cash holdings by the bank, and the other uses discussed earlier.

The overall commercial banking system is also limited in its demand deposit creation by these various factors. The actual amount of demand deposits created by the system's lending will be less than the $5,000 derived for the simple model; that is, $1,000 change in total reserves multiplied by the reciprocal of the required reserve ratio (1/0.20). To compute the maximum change in demand deposits for the entire commercial banking system in the modified model, the following formula is used:

$$\Delta DD = \Delta R \times \frac{1}{r_D + c + x + (r_T \times t)}$$

where

ΔDD = maximum change in demand deposits
 ΔR = absolute change in total reserves for system
  r_D = required reserve ratio for demand deposits
   c = currency drain factor expressed as percentage of change in demand deposits
   x = idle lending capacity (excess lending capacity) expressed as percentage of change in demand deposits
  r_T = required reserve ratio for time deposits
   t = general public's liquid assets preference ratio, that is, the preferred ratio of time deposits to demand deposits

Given that the absolute change in total reserves for the system of commercial banks is $1,000; the required reserve ratio for demand deposits is 20 percent and for time deposits 10 percent; currency drain c is 5 percent and excess lending capacity x is 10 percent of any change in demand deposits; and the general public's liquid assets preference of time deposits to demand deposits is 1 to 2 (that is, $1 of time deposits is held for each $2 of demand deposit holdings), then the formula gives the following results for the maximum change in demand deposits (system of commercial banks):

$$\Delta DD = \$1,000 \times \frac{1}{0.20 + 0.05 + 0.10 + (0.10 \times \tfrac{1}{2})}$$

$$= \$1,000 \times \frac{1}{0.35 + 0.05}$$

$$= \$1,000 \times \frac{1}{0.40} = \$2,500$$

The creation of demand deposits in the modified model is limited to $2,500, as compared with $5,000 for the simple model.

To calculate the maximum change in the money supply, which includes both demand deposits and currency, multiply the absolute change in total reserves for the system by the following money multiplier:

$$\frac{1 + c}{r_D + c + x + (r_T \times t)}$$

with the various factors in the multiplier being defined in the same way as previously.

THE DESTRUCTION OF DEMAND DEPOSITS

Just as demand deposits are created by the lending and "investing" activities of the commercial banking system, they are destroyed or extinguished when loans and securities held by the commercial banks are repaid. The process of *demand deposit destruction* is simply the reverse of the process involved in deposit creation.

The process of deposit destruction can be described quite simply. Just as the purchase of securities by the central bank provides additional reserves to the commercial banking system, the central bank's *sale* of securities absorbs reserves from the commercial banking system. If the central bank's absorption of reserves creates a required reserve deficiency for the commercial banking system, then a process of deposit destruction or contraction is initiated. The contraction process occurs by reductions in commercial bank demand deposits and loans or securities in one stage after another, until total demand deposits are reduced to a level where commercial bank reserve holdings are adequate to meet existing reserve requirements.

As in the simple model of deposit creation, the multiple by which deposits are extinguished is determined by the required reserve ratio for demand deposits alone. Thus, a 20 percent required reserve ratio implies that demand deposits are reduced by five times the original reduction in reserve holdings for the commercial banking system.

Specifically, destruction of demand deposits arises when commercial banks either reduce their loans or sell some of their securities. Although both kinds of asset adjustments are used, the most likely response is for commercial banks to sell part of their government securities holdings. In addition, since most types of outstanding commercial bank loans cannot be called for payment before maturity, commercial banks may refuse to extend new loans or to renew existing loans so as not to replace loans currently maturing. In this way, demand deposits accumulated for purposes of loan retirement are extinguished when loans are repaid.

We have discussed these two processes of demand deposit creation and destruction separately for the sake of clarity. However, in the real world the process of deposit creation occurs simultaneously with the process of deposit destruction, since the commercial banking system consists of several thousand banking firms performing these activities. Thus, it is the net balance between deposit creation and deposit destruction that determines the overall movement in demand deposits for the commercial banking system.

SOME IMPLICATIONS OF
THE MODEL

Deposit creation and destruction are more than mechanical processes. The model of deposit creation outlines the various sectors that can affect the creation of demand deposit money and, in turn, can change the overall money supply. The equation for deposit expansion given in the modified model indicates that the monetary authority (or central bank), the general public, and commercial banks interact to determine money creation in the form of demand deposits. Since demand deposits comprise some three-fourths of the general public's money supply M_1, the monetary authority attempts to influence the money supply primarily by affecting the volume of bank reserves.

The central bank exerts appreciable control over the flow of bank reserves and determines the required reserve ratios applied to demand and time deposits. The other factors given in the formula are largely outside the immediate control of the monetary authority and reflect primarily the decisions of nonbank private individuals and commercial bankers. The general public's currency-holding motives and habits affect currency drain. The general public's liquid asset preferences influence their time deposit holdings relative to demand deposits. At times, the authorities try to modify asset preferences by changing the maximum rates of interest payable on time deposits.

Commercial bank holdings of excess reserves reflect the interplay of various factors, especially changes in interest rates and in the demand for bank credit. Furthermore, since differential reserve requirements actually exist among various commercial bank and deposit classifications, average reserve ratios for demand and time deposits will reflect shifts in deposits among these various groups. An awareness of the relations summarized in the model of deposit creation provides important background for the study of monetary policy, which is examined in later chapters.

KEY TERMS

Fractional reserves

Clearings

Debt monetization

T account

Primary demand deposit

Derivative demand deposit

Reserve leakages

Idle lending capacity

Demand deposit destruction

REVIEW QUESTIONS

1. Trace briefly the evolving functions of the ancient goldsmith.
2. What were the three banking principles discovered by the goldsmith as a money creator?
3. "The process of debt monetization involves the swapping of two qualitatively different kinds of debt." Explain, with particular reference to commercial banking today.
4. What simplifying assumptions are made in constructing a simple model of deposit creation?
5. What is a T account?
6. Distinguish between a primary demand deposit and a derivative demand deposit.
7. Given the simplifying assumptions, trace the various phases connected with the deposit-creating process.
8. Within the simple model, how long does the process of deposit creation continue?
9. Express in equation form for the simple model the maximum change that can occur in demand deposits for the overall system.
10. Within a multibank system, why does an individual commercial bank limit its demand deposit creation to an amount not exceeding excess reserve holdings?
11. In developing a modified model of deposit creation, what modifications are made in the simplifying assumptions?
12. Give the equation used in the modified model to (a) compute the maximum change in demand deposits for the commercial banking system, and (b) to compute the maximum change in the money supply.
13. Briefly, what is meant by demand deposit destruction?
14. "Deposit creation is more than a mechanical process." Explain briefly.

SUGGESTED READINGS

Burger, Albert E. "Explanation of the Growth of the Money Stock: 1974–Early 1975." Federal Reserve Bank of St. Louis, *Review* (September 1975): 5–10.

Cacy, J.A. "Commercial Bank Loans and The Money Supply." Federal Reserve Bank of Kansas City, *Monthly Review* (November 1976): 3–10.

Modern Money Mechanics: A Workbook, rev. ed. Federal Reserve Bank of Chicago, 1975.

Rutner, Jack L. "A Time Series Analysis of the Control of Money." Federal Reserve Bank of Kansas City, *Monthly Review* (January 1975): 3–9.

Tarshis, Lorie. "Money, the Commercial Banks, and the Federal Reserve." In *Money and Economic Activity: Readings in Money and Banking,* 3d ed., ed. Lawrence S. Ritter. Boston: Houghton Mifflin, 1967, pp. 13–31.

Timberlake, Richard H. "The Supply of Money in the United States. Part II: The Monetary Framework." Federal Reserve Bank of Richmond, *Monthly Review* (February 1971): 12–15.

Tobin, James. "Commercial Banks as Creators of Money." In *Banking and Monetary Studies,* ed. Deane Carson. Homewood, Ill.: Richard D. Irwin, 1963.

Towey, Richard E. "Money Creation and the Theory of the Banking Firm." *Journal of Finance* 29 (March 1974): 57–72.

Part Three

THE FEDERAL RESERVE SYSTEM
AND THE TREASURY

Chapter Eight

CENTRAL BANKING AND THE
FEDERAL RESERVE SYSTEM

A major sector of any modern monetary system is the *central bank,* which is important to the functioning of the private economy and the fiscal operations of the national government. Central banking is an activity separate from ordinary commercial banking, because a central bank usually has few transactions with private customers and deals primarily with commercial banks and with the national government. The roots of the central banking system go back more than two centuries.[1] Nevertheless, central banks as we know them today are a relatively recent development. Like electric power and the automobile, central banks are pretty much the products of the twentieth century. For example, at the turn of this century no central bank existed in the Western Hemisphere. The central banking system for the United States was established by passage of the Federal Reserve Act of 1913, with the Federal Reserve System starting operations in 1914. Our northern neighbor did not establish the Bank of Canada until 1934.

In this chapter we will first review the essential characteristics of a modern central bank. This background facilitates a brief summary of major events and developments affecting U.S. banking prior to enactment of the Federal Reserve Act in 1913. We will conclude with an examination of the structure and operations of the Federal Reserve System today.

1. It is generally considered that central banking first emerged with the creation of the Bank of England in 1694. However, it was not until 1833 that the Bank of England was given a monopoly of the note issue. Peel's Act of 1844 established the essential basis for the bank's modern-day operations and powers as a central bank.

THE CHARACTERISTICS OF THE
MODERN CENTRAL BANK

It is difficult to give a brief definition of a central bank that is both comprehensive and accurate. The nature of a central bank depends largely on its functions, which vary according to time and setting and the financial system of the country. Essentially, a modern central bank performs at least three functions: managing the nation's monetary system, serving as a bankers' bank, and acting as a bank for the national government.

Monetary Control

The most important characteristic of the modern central bank is that it controls the monetary system in order to facilitate the achievement of national economic goals. In exerting this control, the central bank regulates the supply, cost, and availability of money and credit. The central bank's monetary control is enhanced by its monopoly on the banknote issue and its ability to create and destroy monetary reserves by its lending and "investing" activities. Since monetary control is a prerogative of the sovereign government, the central bank is a public service organization that emphasizes the national interest rather than its own profit or welfare.

Bankers' Bank

Being a *bankers' bank* implies that the central bank provides services for the commercial banking system similar to those that the commercial banking system performs for individuals and business firms. Some of these services support the central bank's basic function of monetary control: holding the legal reserves of the commercial banking system, providing short-term loans or advances to commercial banks, and serving as a "lender of last resort." More commonplace services that nevertheless promote the smooth operation of the monetary and banking systems include clearing and collecting checks, distributing coin and paper currency to commercial banks, and providing some degree of supervision and regulation over the activities of commercial banks.

The bankers' bank function of central banking takes on added significance when we consider the growing international activities of many nations' commercial banks. As mentioned in Chapter 5, the turbulent forces affecting commercial banking in the mid-1970s were partly the adverse repercussions from the financial difficulties experienced by multinational commercial banks such as the Franklin National Bank of New York and the Herstatt Bank in West Germany.

These disturbances generated pressure on the central banks to expand their role as regulatory agencies and as lenders of last resort. An informal working consensus appeared to emerge on the appropriate pattern of action when a multinational commercial bank got into trouble abroad: the host country's central bank would alert the parent commercial bank and its home country's central bank. Presumably, the monetary authorities in the home country would take appropriate action to assist the distressed bank.

In this context, a thorny question emerges: how do you handle *consortia banks,* which are commercial banks whose ownership is shared among various other banks from different countries? In the case of a troubled consortium bank, a workable arrangement would require the banks to share responsibility in proportion to the nationality of ownership, for example, 20 percent American, 10 percent Dutch, and so on. An "early warning" communications network among central banks could provide early detection of possible trouble spots and minimize the amount of supportive action required by authorities.

Fiscal Agency Function

In its role as a *fiscal agent,* the central bank serves as a banker for the national government, receiving, holding, transferring, and disbursing government funds. Furthermore, the central bank provides technical services related to the public debt: it receives and allots subscriptions to new Treasury security issues, redeems interest coupons and maturing securities, and, under certain conditions, makes short-term advances to the government. Typically, the central bank is a major financial adviser to the national government, and in some nations it is responsible for managing the public debt.

Note that central banks ordinarily *do not* provide commercial banking services for the general public. Other than commercial banks and a small number of securities dealers, private individuals and business firms rarely deal directly with central banks. This lack of exposure may account for the general public's being unacquainted with central banking activities. Central and commercial banking functions involve widely differing objectives and methods, and therefore these functions are kept separate. The central bank orients its policy primarily toward the attainment of national economic objectives, whereas the commercial banking system is essentially profit motivated. Although central banks do not stress profit maximization, they accrue profits by acquiring earning assets through the conduct of credit policy, particularly by open market purchases and sales of securities.

Having reviewed the basic functions of a modern central bank, we will now briefly trace major developments affecting banking in the United States before the creation of the Federal Reserve System in 1913.

THE AMERICAN EXPERIENCE BEFORE 1913

Prior to the twentieth century the United States had no full-fledged central bank. In the period before 1913 the rise of the banking system paralleled the development of the United States monetary system. To facilitate the financing of the Revolutionary War, the first modern bank in the United States, the Bank of North America, was incorporated in Philadelphia in 1782, followed by the founding of similar institutions in Massachusetts and New York. The only other banks in existence at this time were unincorporated private banks.

First and Second Banks of the United States

In 1791 Congress chartered the First Bank of the United States. This bank, a majority of its stock owned privately, performed some central banking functions by providing fiscal agency services for the infant federal government and by exerting a kind of monetary discipline relating to the redemption of state bank note issues. However, this bank was not a central bank. The bank's conservative policies drew attack by "cheap money" agrarian-frontier groups, and the questioning of the constitutionality of Congress granting federal bank charters resulted in the bank's twenty-year charter lapsing in 1811. In the next five years the issuance of state bank notes increased, many of these note issues later becoming worthless.

To offset the mounting abuses in state banking, the Second Bank of the United States was federally chartered in 1816; but this bank met with much the same antipathy as its predecessor. Its central banking functions, especially its control over currency issues by state banks, were incompatible with its private ownership and commercial banking business. Again, the second bank was not a full-fledged central bank, for it exercised no control over the banking system. Frontier opposition, supported by President Andrew Jackson, led Congress to refuse to extend the bank's charter in 1836.

The demise of the Second Bank of the United States ushered in an era of state banking, or "wildcat" banking, as it was called, with state banks conducting most of the banking business. The passage of *"free" banking acts* by the state legislatures (led by Michigan's Free Banking Act of 1837) facilitated the growth in numbers of state banks by eliminating cumbersome granting of individual bank charters by specific legislative action. Most of these banks, subject to uneven and generally lax regulation, were poorly run, with few exceptions. The variety of state bank notes of varying quality offered no uniform paper currency for a nation that was entering the "takeoff" stage in its economic development.

National Banking Legislation

By 1863 chaotic conditions impelled the establishment of a national banking system to replace the unsound and unsafe state system and to aid financing of the Civil War. The National Banking Act required, among other things, federally chartered commercial banks to maintain adequate reserves against their outstanding national bank notes (until 1874) and against deposit liabilities. Noteholders were further protected by the fact that national banks maintained collateral in the form of government securities. After a prohibitive 10 percent federal tax was placed on the currency issue of state banks in 1865, a marked decrease occurred in the number of state banks over the next few years. However, state banking revived thereafter because of the growth in deposit banking and the attraction of the generally less restrictive state banking regulations.

At the same time, the national banking system had some serious shortcomings. Especially critical was the fact that issuance of national bank notes tended to be inflexible and unresponsive to seasonal and emergency needs, since their volume was tied to the supply of government bonds, which served as their collateral. Other weaknesses included rigid reserve requirements and the pyramiding of reserves via national banks holding interbank deposits in major cities. Frequent banking and financial panics—in 1873, 1884, 1893, and

1907—separated by intervening periods of severe credit shortages, attested to the system's defects. The racking experience of the 1907 panic precipitated congressional appointment of a National Monetary Commission to study and appraise the nation's banking and monetary system. The commission's work of several years provided essential information and recommendations leading to legislation establishing a central banking system for the United States in the form of the Federal Reserve System.

MONETARY AUTHORITY AND THE FEDERAL RESERVE

Just as the banking system of the United States developed in stages in the period before 1913, the structure and operations of the Federal Reserve System have evolved gradually in response to the changing needs of an increasingly complex economy. The new central banking system, established by legislation under the administration of President Woodrow Wilson in late December 1913, was organized initially along decentralized regional lines. Over the decades the Federal Reserve's structure has become more centralized, with greater power and influence accorded to the authorities in Washington, D. C. Furthermore, the system's structure has undergone deep-seated change as a result of the lessons gained from the Great Depression. Indeed, the experience of this depression wrought major modifications in the operations of the Federal Reserve that were to have important implications for monetary actions of later years.

The Constitution of the United States reserves to the Congress the "power to coin money, regulate the value thereof. . . ." Congress, then, is the ultimate *monetary authority,* that is, it holds the power to regulate the supply, cost, and availability of money. Congress has delegated part of its monetary authority in turn to the central banking system by legislating the Federal Reserve Act, and has also extended monetary authority to the Treasury Department and to various federal credit agencies. Thus the Federal Reserve shares monetary power with the Treasury and, to a lesser extent, with the different federal credit agencies. The Federal Reserve holds the major part of monetary authority delegated by the Congress. Its dominant position is reflected in its ability to create and destroy basic monetary reserves and to issue most of the paper currency within the monetary system.

Relative Independence Within Government

The Federal Reserve System is an independent agency established by Congress to conduct the major task of administering monetary policy in the United States. The Federal Reserve System is independent not *from* the government but rather *within* government. This relative independence within government derives from congressional delegation of monetary authority through the Federal Reserve Act. By this legislation, the Federal Reserve is free to conduct monetary policy within the limits of its authority. As an agency created by Congress, the Federal Reserve is responsible to the Congress. It submits an annual report to the Congress, and its top officials make periodic appearances before congressional committees on Capitol Hill. Technically, the Federal Reserve is a *quasi*-governmental agency, that is, the central banking system has a "split personality" involving public and private features. Congress, for example, does not control the Federal Reserve's purse strings; it operates on its own earnings rather than federal budget appropriations. Congress does oversee expenditures, however, and thus exerts reasonably effective control. The Federal Reserve need not seek prior approval from Congress for its actions and programs so long as they are within the legal scope of the Federal Reserve Act.

The Federal Reserve maintains close relations with the executive branch of the federal government in order to achieve a reasonably coordinated and generally unified national economic program. However, this close working liaison with the executive branch does not suggest the need for a physical merger of the central banking system with the executive branch.

The particular position that the central bank should have within government is a delicate and difficult question. Since the central bank has monetary authority, a major government power, and since it is responsible to the Congress, why not make the central bank a regular government bureau, presumably within the Treasury? Historical experience offers many warnings against this simple approach.

The national government exercises two major financial functions. The first is in the fiscal area: funds must be raised to cover various government expenditures. Taxation is a major source of government receipts, but taxes are generally unpleasant and can have political repercussions. The second major function entails provision of an effective and stable monetary system. Monetary power resides in the federal government. Should a single agency or department of the government control both the fiscal and monetary functions, there could arise strong temptation to finance current expenditures through money creation rather than through taxation. A shortsighted government subject to strong political pressures could rely heavily on the device of monetary inflation, with possible adverse effects for the economy.

Coordination of Policy

Nevertheless, economic stabilization policy requires reasonable coordination of monetary and fiscal operations. At various times, differences of opinion and orientation have arisen between the Treasury Department and the Federal Reserve. These differences need not compel the Congress to place the central bank within the executive branch in order to promote policy coordination. Congress, operating through specialized committees, periodically reviews Federal Reserve exercise of power delegated to it. Should Congress decide that relations between the Federal Reserve and the executive branch are unsatisfactory, legislative remedy is available. Amending legislation of Congress, for example, can define explicitly the nature of these relations.

A recent illustration shows the role that Congress plays in establishing the formal framework wherein the Federal Reserve operates. In March 1975, Congress passed a joint resolution, House Concurrent Resolution 133, that directed the Federal Reserve to report periodically on its plans for growth in the money supply over the year ahead. Quarterly hearings, alternating between the Senate and House banking committees, focus on targets for money growth rates and for interest rates as reported by the Chairman of the Federal Reserve Board.

In concluding a letter to the Joint Economic Committee of the Congress in 1952, Allan Sproul, at that time President of the Federal Reserve Bank of New York, stressed the adaptability of an independent central bank:

The Federal Reserve System is an expression of an adaptable creative government. The System is by no means perfect; it needs improvement. But it can provide a competent mechanism, and a continuity of able personnel, which will enable us to cope with the day-to-day intricacies of monetary policy, while remaining responsive to the general economic purposes of the Government.[2]

2. *Monetary Policy and the Management of the Public Debt*, Hearings Before the Subcommittee on General Credit Control and Debt Management, Joint Committee on the Economic Report, 82d

This adaptability of the Federal Reserve is reflected in its development of working relations with other agencies responsible for formulating economic stabilization policy. This interchange occurs via different avenues and is well illustrated in regular meetings of the "quadriad," representing four key participants in economic policy making: the chairman of the Federal Reserve Board, the Secretary of the Treasury, the director of the Office of Management and Budget (replacing the old Bureau of the Budget), and the chairman of the Council of Economic Advisors. The meetings of this group, along with their respective professional staffs, provide a common briefing ground and a working arrangement to channel information on matters of mutual interest. This pragmatic approach to coordinating policy actions has functioned reasonably well and affords flexibility and diversity of viewpoints in the consideration of complex, and frequently vexing, economic policy questions.

THE STRUCTURE OF THE
FEDERAL RESERVE SYSTEM

The Federal Reserve System today includes several constituent groups or bodies, each with particular responsibilities and duties. In some important respects the structure of the Federal Reserve resembles that of the national government. The separation of powers and the federal structure reflect the distrust of concentrated power. As in the case of the government, there has been a trend toward centralization of power and influence. A basic question arises as to how far this trend can continue without introducing serious weakening of the decision-making process. One source of strength for the Federal Reserve lies in the fact that many people from all sections of the country make contributions to policy. These diverse contributions will be even more meaningful as monetary policy making becomes more difficult and as the Federal Reserve is subject to even more demanding standards of performance, especially in additional activities outside the area of monetary policy. These participatory requirements involve, as one Federal Reserve official observed, "not just a matter of decentralization of work. . . . A truly federal

Congress, 2d Session, March 10–31, 1952 (Washington, D. C.: Government Printing Office, 1952), p. 985.

system requires that the sub-units contribute to the overall goal as a matter of right, not merely at the pleasure of the central unit."[3]

The operation of the Federal Reserve System involves at least five groups, each of which are described briefly here (see Figure 8.1).

The Board of Governors

The Board of Governors of the Federal Reserve System, informally called the Federal Reserve Board, is the top executive body in the system and consists of seven members appointed for fourteen-year terms by the President of the United States with the advice and consent of the Senate. Their terms are so arranged that one expires every two years. The length of the terms, which are not renewable, tends to insulate the board from the pressures of partisan politics. The president appoints the chairman and vice-chairman of the board from among the board members for a four-year term, which can be renewed. A united board possesses power to enforce its will by holding substantial authority over the instruments of monetary policy. These instruments include *general* (or indirect) controls—open market operations, changes in discount rates, and varying legal reserve ratios—and *selective* (or direct) controls— margin (cash downpayment) requirements for financing of securities traded on national security exchanges, and interest rate ceilings on time and savings deposits.

In addition, the board exercises general supervision over the twelve Federal Reserve banks and has the power to remove any officer or director of any Federal Reserve bank for good cause. It coordinates economic research and data collection within the system. Finally, in relations with commercial banks, the board must approve acquisitions by bank holding companies, some bank mergers, and other commercial bank actions.

In the mid-1970s, observers viewed with alarm the high turnover among members of the Board of Governors. Their concern centered on the fact that since the fall of 1974, five new governors had been named over a two-year period, with four of the five vacancies resulting from resignations before terms had been completed. At least three elements color this recent picture of high turnover: a salary squeeze, career aspirations, and job disenchantment.

3. David P. Eastburn, "The Federal Reserve as a Living Institution: A Prescription for the Future," Federal Reserve Bank of Philadelphia, *Business Review* (March 1970): 16.

Figure 8.1   THE FEDERAL RESERVE SYSTEM: ORGANIZATION

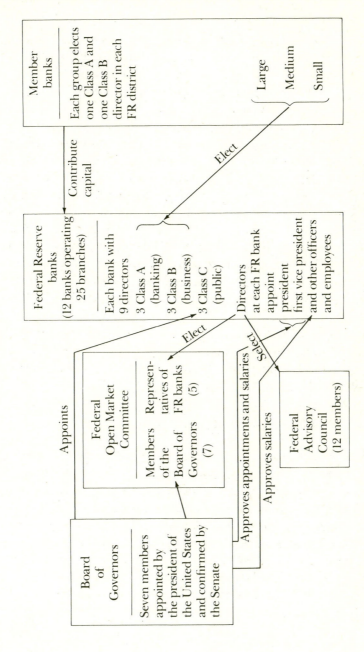

Source: Board of Governors of the Federal Reserve System, *The Federal Reserve System: Purposes and Functions*, 6th ed. Washington, D. C., 1974, p. 18.

A governor's annual salary looks pretty skimpy in the context of strong price inflation and raised salaries elsewhere. Some governors resign to take advantage of attractive career opportunities elsewhere. For example, after almost nine years as a governor, Andrew Brimmer resigned to take a university faculty position, citing creeping age as a major factor influencing his decision to follow the new career path.

The most sensitive factor in the high turnover rate is a sense of frustration among board members caused by their relative lack of power and influence. Part of this frustration reflects the dominant role maintained by the chairman of the Federal Reserve Board. Although each of the seven members of the Board of Governors has an equal vote, the chairman is "more equal than others," effectively speaking. Furthermore, for much of the Federal Reserve's history, the Board of Governors was headed by chairmen known for their strong, persuasive personalities: Marriner S. Eccles, William McChesney Martin, and Arthur F. Burns. One former board member, Sherman J. Maisel, who resigned to return to academe after some seven years' service, assigns the chairman a paramount role in framing monetary policy. In his fascinating book *Managing the Dollar,* Maisel estimates the "power distribution" in setting monetary policy as follows: 45 percent to the chairman, 25 percent to the technical staff of both the Board of Governors and the Federal Open Market Committee, 20 percent to the other six governors, and the remaining 10 percent to the district Federal Reserve banks.[4]

The Federal Open Market Committee

The most important policy-making agency in the structure of the system is the Federal Open Market Committee. This group is composed of the seven members of the Board of Governors and the presidents of five Federal Reserve banks, with permanent representation for the New York bank. The other four presidents are selected in rotation. Meetings are held usually every three or four weeks in Washington, with all Federal Reserve bank presidents attending and participating but only the formal committee members voting. The committee's main role is to formulate open market policy for the system, whereby general directives affecting the purchase or sale of government and

---

4. Sherman J. Maisel, *Managing the Dollar* (New York: W.W. Norton & Co., 1973), pp. 109–111.

other securities are issued to the manager of the open market account at the New York Federal Reserve bank. The committee also oversees Federal Reserve operations in foreign exchange markets, with the foreign department of the New York bank acting as its agent. Meetings of the committee provide a forum in which regional and national judgments are focused on national monetary policy. Analytical presentations by professional economists from the Board of Governors and the individual Reserve banks provide informational background and economic intelligence data for a wide-ranging discussion of monetary and general economic conditions, prior to formal voting on the committee's policy directives.

The Federal Advisory Council

The Federal Advisory Council, a twelve-member group of commercial bankers representing each of the Federal Reserve districts, provides a sounding board for views expressed directly to the Board of Governors. Elected annually by the boards of directors of the Reserve banks, the members meet in Washington four times a year. The council serves strictly an advisory function, and its recommendations may or may not be followed by the Board of Governors.

The Federal Reserve Banks

The United States is divided into twelve Federal Reserve districts, each containing a Federal Reserve bank. A total of twenty-five branches serve particular areas within the twelve districts (see Figure 8.2). Blending public and private influences, the corporate organization of the Federal Reserve banks resembles that of commercial banks. Each Reserve bank issues capital stock, is headed by a board of directors who select the top executive officers, and accrues earnings largely from loans and "investments." Basic differences from commercial banks include the absence of the usual privileges and powers held by stockholders in private corporations, and an orientation toward enhancing public welfare rather than maximizing profits, although profits are earned and paid mostly to the United States Treasury, ostensibly as interest on Federal Reserve notes.

The nine members of the board of directors serve three-year staggered terms; the board consists of equal numbers of three separate classes of direc-

Figure 8.2 THE FEDERAL RESERVE SYSTEM

Boundaries of Federal Reserve districts and their branch territories.

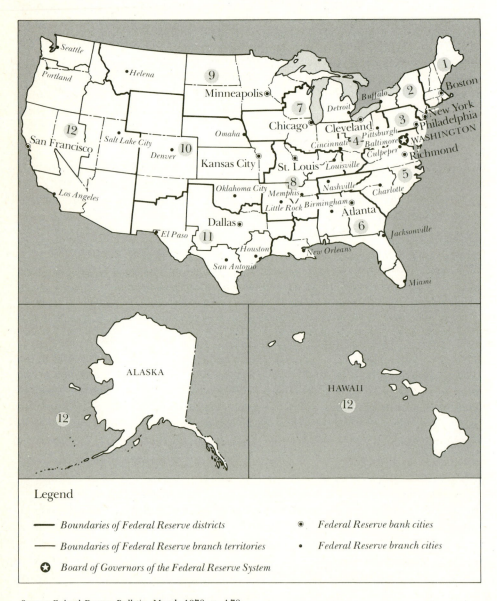

Legend

— Boundaries of Federal Reserve districts

— Boundaries of Federal Reserve branch territories

⊛ Board of Governors of the Federal Reserve System

⊙ Federal Reserve bank cities

• Federal Reserve branch cities

Source: Federal Reserve Bulletin, March 1978, p. A78.

tors. Class A and B directors, elected by the member banks in the district, represent banking and business-agricultural interests, respectively. For voting purposes, member banks are classified into three size-groups, each group selecting a class A and class B director. The Board of Governors, which appoints the three class C directors, designates one as chairman and another as deputy chairman of the board of directors.

Beyond supervising and controlling the operations of the Reserve banks, the boards of directors perform duties connected with monetary policy: establishing the discount rate, subject to review and determination by the Board of Governors; and electing the individual presidents of Federal Reserve banks, subject to the approval of the Board of Governors. In turn, these presidents provide five members of the Federal Open Market Committee.

Member Banks

Commercial banks holding Federal Reserve membership comprise less than half of the nation's commercial banks but account for almost three-fourths of total banking assets and deposits. Member banks are classified either as *reserve city banks* (if so designated by the Board of Governors) or as banks outside reserve cities (*country banks* was the technical designation used prior to November 9, 1972). Member commercial banks have several obligations: meeting minimum legal reserve requirements against deposits; subscribing to capital stock of the district Federal Reserve bank; adhering to stipulations of federal banking law; clearing checks at par; filing necessary reports with the system; and submitting to examination and supervision.

Member banks obtain various benefits from the system in addition to the prestige of membership: the privilege of borrowing, under specified conditions, from the district Federal Reserve banks; the use of check collection and wire transfer facilities; receipt of coin and paper currency shipments free of transportation charges; an annual cumulative 6 percent dividend on Federal Reserve bank stock; participation in the system's functional cost analysis program; access to safekeeping facilities of the Reserve banks; and the opportunity to receive consultative advice and assistance from the professional staff of the Federal Reserve.

SUGGESTED CHANGES IN
FEDERAL RESERVE STRUCTURE
AND OPERATIONS

The Federal Reserve has responded to changing, increasingly complex conditions by modifying its operating structure. A continuing evaluation of operating features is essential if the system is to remain viable and responsive in performing its many responsibilities. From time to time, congressional committees as well as other groups have examined the system with an eye toward making recommendations for improvement in its structure and operations, especially as related to the conduct of monetary policy. For example, in 1952 a subcommittee of the congressional Joint Economic Committee (known as the Patman subcommittee) conducted extensive hearings on monetary policy and management of the public debt. This investigation provided the basis for subsequent changes in system operations. Furthermore, in 1964 a congressional subcommittee held hearings examining the Federal Reserve's structure and operations after a half century's existence.

Commission on Money and Credit Recommendations

Under the auspices of the Committee for Economic Development, a nonpartisan, public interest group of leading businesspeople, financed by two major private foundations, the Commission on Money and Credit (CMC) was established in 1957 to conduct a wide-ranging study of the monetary system. The commission's membership of over two dozen prominent citizens was assisted in its study by a full-time professional research staff and an advisory board of some dozen well-known economists. The production of more than one hundred background papers by recognized experts provided the analytical foundation for the commission's report, published in 1961. The commission's recommendations on a large array of issues in financial policy included several suggestions for major modification of the Federal Reserve's operating structure. Although these recommendations are yet to be implemented, the commission's findings can be reviewed briefly, especially since they stirred considerable debate and discussion, which has continued to this day.

   With regard to member banks, which constitute the base of the system's structure, the commission recommended: (1) compulsory Federal Reserve membership for all FDIC insured commercial banks; (2) retirement of capital stock of member banks, to be replaced with nonearning certificates of membership; (3) uniform reserve requirements against demand deposits for all classes of member banks and elimination of reserve requirements for time and savings deposits; (4) the vesting of all powers of bank examination in the Federal Reserve.

Requiring Federal Reserve membership for all insured commercial banks would affect virtually all commercial banks, since fewer than 2 percent of all commercial banks are noninsured banks. The proposal would enlarge the base of the central banking system and close the "escape hatch" whereby banks forgo system membership to avoid requirements generally more stringent than those imposed by state authorities.

Attrition in Federal Reserve membership has been described by one system official as "a cancer eating at the morale of the system." Concerned about the system's community image, the official stressed the need for "strong, concerned grass-roots support" and for authorities "to move vigorously and decisively to deal with the inequities created by present requirements for membership."[5]

The commission's proposals concerning the Reserve banks would downgrade their role in determining central banking policy by giving the Board of Governors full discretionary power to establish a uniform discount rate for all Reserve banks. (Remember that the board of directors of each Reserve bank establishes the discount rate, subject to review and determination by the Board of Governors.) Furthermore, a reconstituted Federal Advisory Council, with members holding three-year terms and meeting twice a year, would be selected by the Board of Governors from a list of nominees presented by the Reserve banks.

A major recommendation of the commission entails the elimination of the Federal Open Market Committee, with open market powers centralized in the Board of Governors. This suggestion stirred much debate and comment, as evidenced in a statement by Allan Sproul, former president of the Federal Reserve Bank of New York, at Joint Economic Committee hearings on the commission's report: "The Federal Open Market Committee has become the heart of the Federal Reserve System; cut it out and you have a skeleton."[6]

5. Eastburn, "The Federal Reserve as a Living Institution," p. 13.
6. *Review of Report of the Commission on Money and Credit,* Hearings, Joint Economic Committee, 87th Congress, 1st Session, August 14–18, 1961 (Washington, D. C.: Government Printing Office, 1961), p. 482.

The commission directed attention to the apex of the Federal Reserve System by recommendations affecting the Board of Governors: (1) reducing board membership to five persons; (2) shortening the term of office to ten years, and eliminating specified occupational and geographical qualifications for board members; (3) synchronizing the four-year terms of office of chairman and vice-chairman of the board with that of the President of the United States; (4) formally recognizing the chairman as chief executive officer of the board.

The completion of the commission's work was followed in the next year (1962) by presidential appointment of a Committee on Financial Institutions. Examining many of the same problems as the Commission on Money and Credit, that committee published a report in 1963 that induced little change in legislation or policies.

Commission on Financial Structure and Regulation Recommendations

More recently, in late 1971, the presidential Commission on Financial Structure and Regulation (Hunt Commission) issued its report on the analysis and appraisal of the nation's financial system. Though concerned primarily with strengthening the future performance of financial institutions, the Hunt Commission's proposals had certain implications for monetary authorities.

A major recommendation involved compulsory membership in the Federal Reserve for all financial institutions holding demand deposits. Thus, mandatory Federal Reserve membership would be broadened to include all state-chartered commercial banks and all savings and loan associations and mutual savings banks providing third-party payment services (checking accounts, automatic bill paying, and credit cards). To the extent that required Federal Reserve membership would lessen the ability of nonmember commercial banks and nonbank financial institutions to thwart the operation of monetary policy, the effectiveness and efficiency of monetary controls would be strengthened.

FINE Study

Following the example of the Hunt Commission, the House Banking Committee of the Congress released in late 1975 its study of Financial Institutions and the Nation's Economy (FINE). The FINE study incorporated thirty-nine "discussion principles" oriented toward increasing competition among depository financial institutions. Concerned primarily with equity considerations and with more effective implementation of monetary policy, the FINE study also advocated that all federally insured depository institutions be subject to Federal Reserve legal reserve requirements on deposit liabilities. At the same time, all these institutions would have direct access to Federal Reserve services, including the discount window and wire-transfer system.

THE FEDERAL RESERVE'S BALANCE SHEET

We gain additional insight into the system's structure and operations by examining the consolidated balance sheet for the twelve Federal Reserve banks (see Table 8.1). Just as in the case of the commercial banking system's overall balance sheet (Table 5.1), this device shows the principal assets and liabilities accounts and capital accounts. Each of these accounts is described briefly, since this information will provide background for examining the Federal Reserve's influence on the reserve position of the commercial banking system.

Gold Certificates

The law prohibits Federal Reserve banks from owning gold. Although not available for circulation, gold certificates are issued by the Treasury to the Federal Reserve System. The system's gold certificate assets are increased whenever the Treasury monetizes gold that it has purchased from foreign monetary authorities or issues new gold certificates following an increase in the official value of gold and thus in the value of the outstanding U.S. gold stock.

Until the late 1960s the Reserve banks were required to hold gold certificate reserves equal to at least one-quarter of their combined note and deposit liabilities. The appreciably reduced role of gold in the domestic money system is underlined by the elimination of these formal "gold cover" requirements for the Reserve banks. This account also includes a special drawing rights (SDRs) certificate account established by Treasury deposit of SDRs with the Federal Reserve.

Table 8.1   CONSOLIDATED BALANCE SHEET FOR THE TWELVE
FEDERAL RESERVE BANKS, APRIL 1978
(millions of dollars)

Assets		Liabilities and Capital Accounts	
1. Gold certificate account (includes SDR certificate account)	12,968	1. Federal Reserve notes	92,331
2. Cash	324	2. Deposits	
3. Loans	1,751	Member bank reserves	28,203
4. Acceptances	290	U.S. Treasury	7,177
5. U.S. government securities (includes federal agency obligations)	111,564	Foreign and other	1,165
		3. Deferred availability cash items	6,189
		4. Other liabilities	1,420
6. Cash items in process of collection	9,087	5. Capital accounts	2,660
7. Other assets	3,161		
Total assets	139,145	Total liabilities and capital accounts	139,145

Source: Federal Reserve Bulletin, May 1978, p. A12.

Special Drawing Rights in the International Monetary Fund (IMF) are
created by the IMF on agreed occasions and are allocated to members of the
IMF by an agreed formula in order to supplement their international monetary reserves. Occasionally the U.S. Treasury may monetize some SDRs by
issuing SDR certificates to the Reserve banks.

Cash

This item represents vault cash consisting of coin and paper currency (other
than Federal Reserve notes) held by the Federal Reserve banks. Cash is
obtained through Reserve banks serving as distributive channels for Treasury
coin and paper currency.

Loans

This asset account reflects the lending activities of the Reserve banks. Member banks and others borrow reserves for which they incur a repayment obligation. About half of these borrowings from Federal Reserve banks are short-term advances secured by U.S. government and federal agency securities. These securities, which are important in commercial bank asset holdings, provide convenient collateral for these borrowings. In the role of lender of last resort, the Federal Reserve banks may loan to member banks on the basis of any satisfactory collateral, although such lending carries an interest charge a half percentage point higher than the established Federal Reserve discount rate. Under certain conditions the Reserve banks may lend to other than member banks, including private parties and foreign monetary authorities.

Acceptances

These short-term, highly liquid financial assets arise from commercial bank financing of international trade. Bankers' acceptances are primarily bills to finance the export, import, transfer or storage of goods. They are called "accepted" when a commercial bank guarantees their payment at maturity. Although there has been noticeable relative growth in these financial instruments in recent years, Federal Reserve holdings of acceptances are small.

United States Government Securities

This largest single item in the Federal Reserve's balance sheet results from the central bank's conduct of open market operations involving the purchase and sale of government securities in the open securities market. Most of these securities are owned outright and provide the largest part of the earnings of Federal Reserve banks. Open market policy constitutes the most important avenue through which the Federal Reserve controls the monetary system.

Cash Items in Process of Collection

This deferred asset account represents the total amount of checks and other cash items in the collection pipelines of the Federal Reserve banks. These uncollected cash items remain on the Federal Reserve's books until their amounts are actually deducted from the Federal Reserve deposit accounts of the member banks on which they are drawn.

Other Assets

This miscellaneous item includes accrued interest and other receivables, premiums on securities owned, balances due from foreign central banks (including convertible foreign currencies obtained via "swap" agreements), and bank buildings and fixtures. This entry concludes the major asset accounts of the Federal Reserve banks, as given in Table 8.1.

Federal Reserve Notes

Outstanding notes comprise the largest single Federal Reserve liability, and reflect the central bank's service function of providing currency in accordance with the general public's changing demand for currency. Secured by collateral primarily in the form of gold certificates and government securities, Federal Reserve notes account for the biggest part of currency in circulation.

Deposits

This second largest liability item consists largely of member bank reserve accounts, which together with their vault cash represent member bank total legal reserve holdings. Treasury deposit accounts in the Federal Reserve are disbursing accounts, that is, accounts from which Treasury payments are made. Treasury deposits are replenished by transfers from deposit accounts the Treasury maintains in most commercial banks. These tax and loan accounts (T and L's) receive tax payments and the proceeds of securities sold to the general public. Foreign central banks and governments maintain Federal Reserve deposits for transacting international payments and for monetary reserve purposes. To facilitate its service function of clearing checks at par, the Federal Reserve extends this service to nonmember banks who maintain deposits large enough for this purpose. Most of the other deposits at Federal Reserve banks are nonmember bank clearing accounts.

Deferred Availability Cash Items

This deferred liability account is linked with the asset account "cash items in process of collection." The deferred availability items represent the total dollar amount of uncollected checks that have not yet been credited to the deposit accounts of those commercial banks presenting the checks for collection by the Federal Reserve. The maximum period for credit to be deferred on uncollected checks is two business days. Since the actual time required to collect checks often exceeds the Federal Reserve's posted schedule for deferring the crediting of these items, the checks are frequently credited in favor of banks prior to their actual collection from banks against which the checks were drawn. Thus the difference between the asset account (cash items in process of collection) and the related liability account (deferred availability cash items) represents still-uncollected checks that have already been added to the reserve accounts of the commercial banks presenting them for collection. This difference between the two accounts is called *Federal Reserve float,* and its specific amount can be fairly sizable at times.

Other Liabilities

Included here are miscellaneous liabilities consisting largely of unearned discount on notes and securities and accrued dividends on capital stock of the Federal Reserve banks.

Capital Accounts

Capital accounts include paid-in capital of member banks and retained earnings of Federal Reserve banks. Membership in the Federal Reserve System requires the newly entering commercial bank to purchase capital stock in its Federal Reserve bank equivalent to 3 percent of its own capital stock and surplus. Ownership of these shares, which may not be transferred, entitles member banks to receive a cumulative annual dividend of 6 percent on their stock holdings.

KEY TERMS

Central bank   "Free" banking acts
Bankers' bank   Monetary authority
Consortia banks   Federal Reserve float
Fiscal agent

REVIEW QUESTIONS

1. What basic functions does a modern central bank perform?
2. What is meant by a bankers' bank?
3. Trace the major developments leading to the establishment of the Federal Reserve System.
4. Who is the ultimate monetary authority in the United States? Explain briefly.
5. What is meant by the relative independence of the Federal Reserve System?
6. Discuss briefly two major financial functions performed by the national government.
7. What role does the "quadriad" play in economic policy making?
8. Explain the composition, functions, and responsibilities of each of the following groups within the Federal Reserve System:
   a. Board of Governors
   b. Federal Open Market Committee
   c. Federal Advisory Council
   d. Federal Reserve banks
9. For commercial banks, what benefits and obligations arise from membership in the Federal Reserve System?
10. What was the Commission on Money and Credit?
11. What did the Commission on Money and Credit propose regarding the operations and organization of various constituent bodies within the Federal Reserve System?
12. What were some of the general recommendations of the Hunt Commission and the FINE study?

13. Discuss briefly the major asset and liability accounts in the consolidated balance sheet of the Federal Reserve banks.

SUGGESTED READINGS

Boulding, Kenneth E. "The Legitimacy of Central Banks." In *Fundamental Reappraisal of the Discount Mechanism.* Washington, D.C.: Board of Governors of the Federal Reserve System, 1969.

Burns, Arthur F. "The Independence of the Federal Reserve System." *Federal Reserve Bulletin* 62 (June 1976): 493–496.

Debs, Richard A. "Petro-Dollars, LDCs, and International Banks." Federal Reserve Bank of New York, *Monthly Review* (January 1976): 10–17.

"The Fed in Perspective: 1776–1976." Federal Reserve Bank of Chicago, *1976 Annual Report,* pp. 1–4.

"Federal Reserve Operations in Payments Mechanisms: A Summary." *Federal Reserve Bulletin* 62 (June 1976): 481–489.

The Federal Reserve System: Purposes and Functions, 6th ed. Washington, D.C.: Board of Governors, September 1974.

Helfrich, Ralph T. "Trading in Bankers' Acceptances: A View from the Acceptance Desk of the Federal Reserve Bank of New York." Federal Reserve Bank of New York, *Monthly Review* (February 1976): 51–57.

Horsefield, J. Keith. "Why a Central Bank?" *Finance and Development* 2 (September 1965): 159–166.

Humphrey, Thomas M. "The Classical Concept of the Lender of Last Resort." Federal Reserve Bank of Richmond, *Economic Review* (January–February 1975): 2–9.

Knight, Robert E. "The Hunt Commission: An Appraisal." *Wall Street Journal,* July 3, 1972, p. 6.

Maisel, Sherman J. *Managing the Dollar.* New York: W.W. Norton, 1973.

Miller, Preston J. "The Right Way to Price Federal Reserve Services." Federal Reserve Bank of Minneapolis, *Quarterly Review* (Summer 1977): 15–22.

Money and Credit: Their Influence on Jobs, Prices, and Growth. Report of the Commission on Money and Credit. Englewood Cliffs, N.J.: Prentice-Hall, 1961.

Chapter Nine

BANK RESERVES AND FEDERAL
RESERVE OPERATIONS

The operating structure of the Federal Reserve serves several functions. The most important is the conduct of monetary policy to promote economic stabilization for society. In its monetary policy actions the Federal Reserve influences the supply, cost, and availability of member bank reserves. This initial impact on reserves induces banks to modify their lending and investing activities, which in turn influence the supply of money, credit availability, and interest rates in various credit markets. These monetary and credit effects are linked to changes in consumption and investment expenditures, which determine aggregate levels of production, employment, and prices.

Since member bank reserves constitute an initial link in the process of exerting monetary control, we must examine the various factors that underlie these reserves. In this way, explicit analysis is made of the connections among bank reserves, Federal Reserve actions, and other forces affecting reserves.

THE MEMBER BANK RESERVE EQUATION

A convenient device for understanding how changes in various factors affect the reserve position of member banks, the *member bank reserve equation* summarizes Federal Reserve System accounts and Treasury monetary accounts that bear on member bank reserves. It indicates the factors supplying and absorbing (or using) reserve funds. The total for sources of reserve funds equals the total for uses of reserve funds. Since member bank reserves constitute one use of reserves, the total uses of reserve funds consist of member bank reserves and competing uses of reserves. In equation form, this can be written as follows:

Total sources of reserve funds = total uses of reserve funds

or

Total sources of reserve funds = member bank reserves + competing uses of reserve funds

or, alternatively,

Member bank reserves = total sources of reserve funds − competing uses of reserve funds

The individual components of the reserve equation are given in Table 9.1 for a recent date. The basic data for these components, on either a monthly or a weekly basis, are found in the monthly *Federal Reserve Bulletin.* Current weekly data are contained in a Federal Reserve release that is available for press publication in Thursday's or Friday's newspaper editions, and that shows results for the week ending the previous Wednesday. Over the longer run, the principal factors affecting member bank reserves are Federal Reserve bank credit, gold stock, and currency in circulation. Factors of less importance in the long run include Treasury currency outstanding, Treasury cash holdings, Treasury deposits at Federal Reserve banks, and other deposit accounts (including foreign and nonmember bank accounts) at Federal Reserve banks. Since changes in any of the components of the reserve equation can increase or decrease member bank reserves, it is enlightening to examine briefly the factors affecting each of these components.

Gold Stock

Variations in the gold stock directly affect bank reserves in that Treasury purchases of gold increase the flow of bank reserves and, alternatively, Treasury sales of gold decrease the flow of bank reserves. These reserve effects arise whether the Treasury deals with domestic parties or foreign parties (foreign treasuries or central banks) in conducting gold transactions. With the initiation of special drawing rights (SDRs) by the International Monetary Fund in 1970, Treasury dealings in SDRs (sometimes called paper gold because the value of the SDR is defined as a certain weight of fine gold) affect member bank reserves in the same way as do its gold stock transactions. Currently, the SDR certificate account of the Federal Reserve is relatively

Table 9.1 FACTORS IN THE MEMBER BANK RESERVE EQUATION:
CHANGES IN WEEKLY AVERAGES DURING THE WEEK
AND YEAR ENDED JULY 12, 1978
(millions of dollars)

FACTORS SUPPLYING RESERVE FUNDS	July 12, 1978	Change from Week Ending	
		July 5, 1978	July 13, 1977
1. Reserve Bank credit			
U.S. government securities Bought outright	106,710	−83	+9,275
Held under repurchase agreement	223	−2,373	+223
Federal agency issues Bought outright	8,168	. . .	+745
Held under repurchase agreement	80	−554	+80
Acceptances Bought outright	. . .	. . .	−37
Held under repurchase agreement	22	−950	+22
Member bank borrowings	774	−280	+665
Float	7,056	+2,445	+2,124
Other Federal Reserve assets	2,618	+12	−554
Total Reserve Bank Credit	125,782	−1,793	+12,622
2. Gold (includes SDR certificate account)	12,954	−2	+138
3. Treasury currency outstanding	11,607	+11	+467
Total	150,343	−1,784	+13,227
FACTORS ABSORBING RESERVE FUNDS			
1. Currency in circulation	107,627	+1,029	+9,706
2. Treasury cash holdings	368	+15	−71
3. Treasury deposits with Federal Reserve banks	10,511	+173	+1,489
4. Foreign deposits with Federal Reserve banks	299	−5	+28
5. Other deposits with Federal Reserve banks	727	−71	+97
6. Other Federal Reserve liabilities and capital	3,779	−387	+517
Total	123,311	+755	+11,767
Member banks reserves with Federal Reserve banks	27,027	+2,539	+1,460

Source: Wall Street Journal, July 14, 1978, p. 19.

small. As participating foreign nations increase the transfer of SDRs to the Treasury in exchange for dollars, this certificate account may become a more important factor affecting member bank reserves. Treasury actions relating to the gold stock and SDRs are examined in greater detail in Chapter 11. For purposes of analyzing the various factors in the reserve equation, it is sufficient to recognize in a general way the direct effects of Treasury gold operations, which include the gold stock and the SDR certificate account.

Treasury Currency Outstanding

This account reflects outstanding monetary liabilities of the Treasury in the form of coin and paper currency. The Treasury is empowered via congressional monetary legislation to issue currency to meet the general public's need for money to transact small monetary transactions. As shown in Chapter 2, Treasury currency comprises a small percentage of the general public's holding of currency. The issuance of Treasury currency to the general public is achieved indirectly through the facilities of the Federal Reserve banks. As shipments of Treasury currency are made to the Federal Reserve, the Treasury's deposit account in the Federal Reserve is increased, thus permitting the Treasury to make increased disbursements to cover or pay for government purchases of goods and services. When the Federal Reserve makes shipments of Treasury coin and currency to member banks, the Federal Reserve deposit accounts of member banks are reduced accordingly.

Federal Reserve Bank Credit

The largest factor supplying member bank reserves is *Federal Reserve bank credit* outstanding. Primarily reflecting discretionary policy actions on the part of the central bank, Federal Reserve bank credit consists of several components, as shown in Table 9.1. Federal Reserve holdings of United States government securities, largely bought outright, with a relatively small amount of securities held under repurchase agreement, constitute the largest element of Federal Reserve bank credit. These securities holdings are objective evidence of central bank open market operations, which are conducted primarily in United States government securities.

Open market policy is the primary device by which the Federal Reserve exerts monetary control. Conducted at the initiative of the monetary authorities, open market operations provide a countervailing force whereby seasonal and irregular movements in other factors in the reserve equation can be offset. Open market operations thus impart virtually complete discretionary control over Federal Reserve credit. Movements in Federal Reserve credit in turn dominate movements in other factors in the reserve equation, thus making possible close and sensitive control over the flow of member bank reserves. Whether conducted with commercial banks or with nonbank parties, open market purchases increase the flow of bank reserves, while open market sales decrease this flow. We will examine the specifics of open market policy in Chapter 10, which deals with the process of monetary control.

Member bank borrowings arise when Federal Reserve banks extend loans of additional reserves to member banks. Undertaken at the initiative of the member banks, these borrowings exemplify reserve creation via the discount window of the Federal Reserve. The discounting policy of the central bank determines the terms and conditions under which member banks may borrow reserves, thus according another important avenue of control to the Federal Reserve. Discounting policy and related administration of the discount window will be described in Chapter 10.

A third major element of Federal Reserve credit is float, which arises from the check clearing and collecting procedures of the central bank. This item, a not insignificant form of interest-free credit of the central bank, is roughly predictable in its dollar volume. Various factors affect Federal Reserve float: the number and dollar volume of checks written, seasonal factors arising from observance of holidays and from weather conditions, transportation and other communications technology bearing on the movement of checks in the collection pipelines, episodic events such as transportation strikes, and so on. The existence of float highlights the continuing Federal Reserve policy to promote and facilitate the use of checks to make money transfers via demand deposits.

The residual portion of Federal Reserve credit consists of miscellaneous items: bankers' acceptances, special Treasury short-term certificates of indebtedness, loans secured by gold made to foreign monetary authorities, and other Federal Reserve assets.

Currency in Circulation

The principal factor absorbing or using reserves at Federal Reserve banks is currency in circulation outside of member banks. Since November 1960 member bank total holdings of vault cash are allowed as legal reserves. This change in the law requires awareness of the meaning of currency in circulation as a specific account contained in the *Federal Reserve Bulletin* and in the Federal Reserve weekly release. As given in these sources, *currency in circulation* "comprises all coin and paper currency held outside the Treasury and Federal Reserve." Thus member bank holdings of vault cash are included in this item, indicating, of course, that a portion of currency in circulation is not a competing use of member bank reserves. Currency in circulation *outside member banks* can be calculated by subtracting currency and coin held as reserves by member banks from currency in circulation. Currency withdrawals by commercial bank depositors directly reduce member bank reserves, since these withdrawals increase currency in circulation outside member banks.

Throughout the 1960s and into the 1970s the ratio of currency to the total money supply has been increasing in the United States. Various factors contribute to the rise in demand for currency relative to demand deposits: changes in the composition of consumer spending, growing use of vending machines, increased interest in coin collecting, growth in the armed forces, and possible attempts at tax evasion. The first factor is influenced by general economic conditions. Growth in per capita personal income tends to lessen the severity of the risk of loss or theft of currency and also tends to increase the proportion of income spent on services that require currency transactions (for example, pari-mutuel betting, outlays for local transportation, and outlays for barbershop and beauty salon services).

Certain institutional developments also affect currency use by the general public. Vending machines have voracious appetites for coins: an estimated 80,000 coins per minute are fed into these machines. Coin collectors (or, more technically, numismatists) and speculators have removed an estimated $2 billion of the old 90 percent silver coins from active circulation. The increase in the armed forces' portion of the total labor force may affect the currency-deposit ratio, because many armed forces personnel are transient and thus do not establish commercial banking connections. Increased marginal and average tax rates of a progressive income tax system provide incentive for tax evasion, which can be facilitated by transactions conducted in currency rather than by checks drawn on demand deposits.

Treasury Cash and Treasury Deposits with Federal Reserve Banks

Treasury cash holdings represent essentially till or vault cash holdings accumulated by the Treasury through its monetary and fiscal operations. As these holdings increase, member bank reserves decrease. A relatively inactive account, Treasury cash consists of Federal Reserve notes, Treasury coin and currency, and free gold and free silver. The last two items are gold and silver against which certificate liabilities have not been created by the Treasury.

The Treasury deposits with the Federal Reserve show the central bank serving as fiscal agent for the national government. As the proceeds from Treasury tax collections and from the sale of Treasury securities are entered into the Treasury's deposit account at the central bank, the member bank reserves decrease. As disbursements are made by the Treasury from its deposit account at the Federal Reserve, member bank reserves increase, since the recipients of these payments deposit Treasury checks into their accounts in commercial banks. The Treasury also maintains deposit accounts in commercial banks and, since mid-1978, in nonbank financial institutions. These deposits, called tax and loan accounts (T and L's), are maintained in those institutions designated as special depositories by the secretary of the Treasury. The proceeds from tax collections and from the sale of new Treasury securities are deposited initially into T and L's. Generally, national government disbursements are made by checks drawn on the Treasury's account with the Federal Reserve. The supplementary depository system of T and L's enables the Treasury to maintain a working balance with the Federal Reserve adequate to cover daily operating needs, and simultaneously to minimize the impact of Treasury financial operations on the banking system and money market.

Foreign and Other Deposits with Federal Reserve Banks

Foreign deposit accounts with the Federal Reserve consist of deposits of foreign central banks and governments, which maintain these deposits for international settlement and foreign monetary reserve purposes. Other deposit accounts at the Federal Reserve are largely those of nonmember commercial banks and of government agencies and international organizations. Any transaction that induces a shift from member bank accounts to these other deposit accounts at the Federal Reserve tends to reduce member bank reserves, for example, a sale of World Bank bonds in the United States capital markets.

Other Federal Reserve Liabilities and Capital

Increases in other Federal Reserve liabilities, for example in miscellaneous accounts payable, tend to reduce member bank reserves unless offset by equivalent increases in Federal Reserve bank assets. Additionally, purchases of capital stock in Federal Reserve banks by a commercial bank newly admitted to Federal Reserve membership reduce reserves of member banks.

RESERVE AGGREGATES

When the various factors in the member bank reserve equation are presented in a single analytical table (see Table 9.1), it is a simple accounting exercise to derive various *reserve aggregates,* or overall measures of the reserve position of member banks. These measures, closely related to one another in an accounting sense, serve as analytical devices for relating reserve variables to the money supply and bank credit. In effect, reserve aggregates are marginal reserve benchmarks used as measures of monetary influence on the economy.

Total Member Bank Reserves and Other Aggregates

Some commonly used reserve aggregates, found in the *Federal Reserve Bulletin,* are shown in Table 9.2. These measures are related to the data in Table 9.1 in that *total member bank reserves* are the sum of member bank deposits with Federal Reserve banks and currency and coin held by member banks. Note that the total member bank reserves figure is adjusted to include waivers of penalties for reserve deficiencies in accordance with Federal Reserve Board policy effective November 19, 1975. This policy allows transitional relief on a graduated basis over a two-year period when an existing member bank absorbs a nonmember bank, or when a nonmember bank joins the Federal Reserve System. The second reserve aggregate is *required reserves,* which reserves member banks are compelled to hold to meet minimum legal require-

Table 9.2   MEMBER BANK RESERVE AGGREGATES: CHANGES IN
WEEKLY AVERAGES DURING THE WEEK AND YEAR
ENDED JULY 12, 1978
(millions of dollars)

Reserve Aggregate	July 12, 1978	Change from Week Ending	
		July 5, 1978	July 13, 1977
1. Total member bank re-serves*	36,859	−2,288	+2,224
With Federal Reserve banks	27,032	−2,538	+1,460
Cash allowed as reserves	9,760	+251	+796
2. Required reserves	37,050	−1,297	+2,679
3. Excess reserves	−191	−991	−455
4. Member bank borrowings at Federal Reserve banks	774	−280	+665
5. Free reserves	−965	−711	−1,120
6. Nonborrowed member bank reserves	36,085	−2,008	+1,559

*Adjusted to include waivers of penalties for reserve deficiencies in accordance with the Federal Reserve Board policy effective November 19, 1975, of permitting transitional relief on a graduated basis over a twenty-four–month period when a nonmember bank merges into an existing member bank, or when a nonmember bank joins the Federal Reserve System.

Source: Wall Street Journal, July 14, 1978, p. 19.

ments against their demand and time deposit liabilities. The next aggregate, *excess reserves,* measures member bank reserves held over and above the required reserves, and is computed by subtracting required reserves from total member bank reserves.

Borrowings at Federal Reserve banks (aggregate 4 in Table 9.2) reflect the dollar amount of reserves member banks have borrowed at the Federal Reserve. Finally, *free reserves* represent excess reserves net of member bank borrowings at Federal Reserve banks. The level of free reserves, which can be positive or negative (the latter sometimes referred to as net borrowed reserves), has been used by some observers as an immediate indicator of Federal Reserve policy. These observers view changes in free reserves as a gauge for judging the objectives and direction of monetary policy.

Use of free reserves as an exact benchmark for appraising monetary actions has stirred much critical comment.[1] These critics note that the two components of free reserves (excess reserves and borrowings) are distributed differently among member banks, with excess reserves concentrated in country banks and borrowings generally made by reserve city banks. This suggests that changes in borrowings largely explain the behavior of free reserves. Since member bank borrowings depend largely on the relation between the discount rate and other interest rates (particularly the Treasury bill rate, as one example), it is reasonable to presume that free reserves member banks desire to hold will vary inversely with the difference between the bill rate and the discount rate. Thus a rising bill rate relative to the discount rate tends to increase member bank borrowings and therefore to reduce desired free reserves. On the other hand, a declining bill rate relative to the discount rate tends to stimulate repayment of member bank borrowings and to increase desired free reserves. With the discount rate frequently lagging behind changes in other interest rates, it is misleading to interpret a constant level of free reserves as indicating a constant degree of monetary ease or tightness.

Some analysts, recognizing the shortcomings of the free reserves concept and preferring to use a variable that still excludes member bank borrowings, utilize a measure of *nonborrowed member bank reserves,* which is derived by subtracting member bank borrowings from total member bank reserves and is shown as the last item in Table 9.2. Empirical research conducted by the Federal Reserve indicates a predictable relation between nonborrowed member bank reserves and the money supply over a control horizon of several months.

Monetary Base

Another reserve aggregate that has achieved prominence as a measure of monetary influence on the economy is the monetary base, sometimes called "highpowered money." In general terms, the *monetary base* includes liquid assets that are generally used to discharge obligations and that are explicit monetary liabilities of the Treasury and the Federal Reserve. Two concepts

1. For a concise and articulate critique of the concept of free reserves, see Warren L. Smith, "The Instruments of General Monetary Control," *National Banking Review* 1 (September 1963): 55–59.

enter into the computation of the monetary base: the source base and reserve adjustments. The sum of these two is called the monetary base.

The source base, as illustrated in Table 9.3, is derived from the same accounts used to determine the various factors in the member bank reserve equation. It is the sum of Federal Reserve credit, monetary gold stock (including special drawing rights), and Treasury currency outstanding *less* Treasury deposits at Federal Reserve banks, Treasury cash holdings, and other deposits and accounts at Reserve banks. An alternative and simpler computation of the source base is obtained by summing the monetary liabilities of the Federal Reserve and the Treasury: member bank deposits at Reserve banks and currency held by commercial banks and the general public (equivalent to currency in circulation outside the Treasury and Federal Reserve). These monetary liabilities are referred to as "uses of the source base." Thus the source base can be viewed either as a magnitude supplied by monetary authorities or as the demand for the base by other sectors of the economy (see Table 9.3).

Reserve adjustments arise from making allowance for changes in reserve requirements and for shifts in reserves between city and country banks that are subject to different requirements. These adjustments, expressed in dollar amounts, are positive when average reserve requirements fall and negative when average reserve requirements rise. The addition of these reserve adjustments to the source base then gives the monetary base, as shown in Table 9.3.

Over long periods of time, such as six months to one year, a fairly close association exists between growth of the monetary base and growth of the money supply. In effect, the monetary base provides the reserve foundation for creation of the money supply. The relation between the monetary base and the money supply can be expressed as a *money multiplier,* that is, as the ratio of the money stock to the monetary base. This ratio shows the average number of dollars of the money stock supported by one dollar of the monetary base. The money multiplier for the United States is pretty stable; as shown in Figure 9.1, for M_1 the ratio has ranged between 2.5 and 2.7 in recent years. The concept of the money multiplier is useful for analyzing growth of the money stock. Specifically, growth of the money stock reflects (1) the influence of Federal Reserve actions, summarized in movements in the monetary base, and (2) all other factors, summarized in movements in the money multiplier.

Table 9.3 FACTORS INFLUENCING THE MONETARY BASE, MAY 1977 AND MAY 1978

(sign indicates effect on the monetary base; these are monthly averages of daily figures in millions of dollars, not seasonally adjusted)

Sources	May 1977	May 1978	Change	Percent Change in Monetary Base Attributable To
I. Federal Reserve credit	$112,694	$119,668	$ 6,974	60.2%
U. S. government securities*	106,771	111,518	4,747	40.9
Loans	200	1,227	1,027	8.9
Float plus other Federal Reserve assets	5,723	6,923	1,200	10.4
II. Other factors	$ 8,244	$ 12,673	$ 4,429	38.2
Treasury deposits with Federal Reserve	−10,997	−6,514	4,483	38.7
Gold stock plus other items†	19,241	19,187	−54	−0.5
Source base (I + II)	120,938	132,341	11,403	98.4
Reserve adjustment‡	2,039	2,229	190	1.6
Monetary base	122,977	134,570	11,593	100.0

Uses				Percent Change in Monetary Base Absorbed By
Adjusted bank reserves§	$ 39,477	$ 42,670	$ 3,193	27.5%
Currency held by the public	83,500	91,900	8,400	72.5

*Includes acceptances of $489 million in May 1977 and $204 million in May 1978.

†Includes SDRs held by Federal Reserve banks, Treasury currency outstanding, Treasury cash holdings, deposits with the Federal Reserve other than Treasury deposits and member bank reserves, and other Federal Reserve liabilities and capital accounts.

‡Adjustment for reserve requirement ratio changes and shifts in the same type of deposits between banks where different reserve requirement ratios apply. Reserve adjustment computed by this bank.

§Includes member bank deposits at Federal Reserve, and vault cash of all commercial banks, plus reserve adjustment (see previous footnote).

Source: Federal Reserve Bank of St. Louis, *Monetary Trends,* released June 27, 1978, p. 12.

Figure 9.1 MONEY MULTIPLIER: RATIO OF MONEY STOCK M_1 TO
MONETARY BASE

Averages of daily figures; seasonally adjusted.

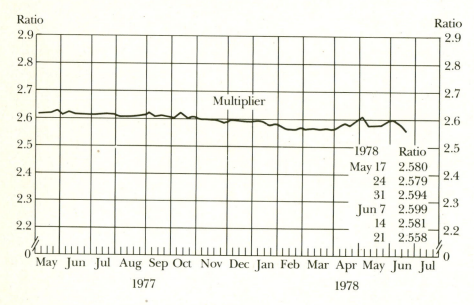

Source: Federal Reserve Bank of St. Louis, *U.S. Financial Data*, week ending June 28, 1978, p. 3.

MONETARY AGGREGATES

In addition to the reserve aggregates, analysts use other measures of monetary actions called monetary aggregates. *Monetary aggregates* are measures of magnitudes that affect income and are closely related to money. Indeed, one such aggregate is money itself; other monetary aggregates include money plus short-term liquid assets and credit, measured in various ways. Some of the more commonly used monetary aggregates are described here.

One monetary aggregate, money stock, can be defined in several ways. The simplest and most restrictive definition, presented in Chapter 2, views money as consisting of currency owned by the general public (that is, currency outside banks) and adjusted demand deposits. This narrow definition of money is sometimes designated M_1 to contrast it with other, broader, measures of money. These other measures include several different types of financial assets that perform *all* or *some* of the functions or services generally ascribed to money. Recall the three functions of money discussed in Chapter 1: as a medium of payment, as a unit of account, and as a store of economic value (or purchasing power). These three functions suggest that "money" might include whatever can be used for both current and potential transactions involving the exchange of goods and services, as well as the payment of debt.

What about the empirical definition and measurement of money? Here lies a much discussed and argued question. Not surprisingly, observers differ as to which of the various financial assets held by households and firms (including state and local government) should be included in the definition, especially as it relates to economic policy making. As the key monetary policy agency, the Federal Reserve Board currently publishes data for five measures of the money stock (see Table 9.4). These measures, each designated by an M with subscript, represent sums, or aggregates, of various liquid financial assets owned outside the federal government and the banking system.

The most commonly used measure of the money stock is M_1—the *basic money supply*. Sometimes called the "narrow" money supply, this measure most clearly satisfies the functional definition of money presented in Chapter 1. The other four published measures each add to M_1 certain interest-bearing accounts that, like M_1, serve as stores of economic value (or purchasing power). M_2 results from adding to M_1 commercial bank savings and time deposits except large CDs, which are negotiable certificates of deposit of $100,000 or more. M_3 consists of M_2 plus savings accounts in nonbank thrift institutions: mutual savings banks, savings and loan associations, and credit unions. The monetary aggregates M_4 and M_5 derive from adding large negotiable CDs to M_2 and M_3, respectively (see Figure 9.2). This list could be extended to include even higher-numbered aggregates, thus allowing for financial market innovations that widen the spectrum of assets that serve as money. The Federal Reserve, for instance, compiles but does not publish data for several other measures of the money stock beyond the five discussed here.

Note that the different components of the monetary aggregates are in turn aggregations of financial assets that can be used for current and potential transactions to varying degrees. For example, commercial bank passbook savings accounts are more readily available funds than are time deposit funds, which incur an interest penalty for early withdrawal. Nevertheless, the M_2 measure includes both passbook savings and time deposits other than large

Table 9.4 MONEY STOCK MEASURES AND COMPONENTS

(billions of dollars; averages of daily figures)

Item	1974 Dec.	1975 Dec.	1976 Dec.	1977 Dec.	1977 Oct.	1977 Nov.	1977 Dec.	1978 Jan.	1978 Feb.	1978 Mar.
					SEASONALLY ADJUSTED					
Measures*										
1. M-1	282.8	294.5	312.6	336.7	334.6	334.7	336.7	339.4	339.1	340.1
2. M-2	612.1	664.1	739.6	807.6	800.2	803.8	807.6	813.6	816.6	820.2
3. M-3	981.2	1,091.8	1,235.6	1,374.1	1,356.7	1,365.5	1,374.1	1,384.1	1,390.5	1,397.6
4. M-4	701.1	745.4	802.3	881.6	866.5	874.6	881.6	889.9	896.0	902.2
5. M-5	1,070.2	1,173.2	1,298.3	1,448.1	1,423.0	1,436.4	1,448.1	1,460.4	1,469.8	1,479.6
Components										
6. Currency	67.8	73.7	80.7	88.5	87.1	87.7	88.5	89.3	90.0	90.6
Commercial bank deposits:										
7. Demand	215.1	220.8	231.9	248.2	247.5	247.0	248.2	250.1	249.1	249.5
8. Time and savings	418.3	450.9	489.7	544.9	531.9	540.0	544.9	550.5	556.8	562.1
9. Negotiable CDs†	89.0	81.3	62.7	74.0	66.4	70.9	74.0	76.3	79.4	82.0
10. Other	329.3	369.6	427.0	470.9	465.5	469.1	470.9	474.2	477.5	480.1
11. Nonbank thrift institutions‡	369.1	427.8	496.0	566.5	556.5	561.7	566.5	570.5	573.8	577.4
					NOT SEASONALLY ADJUSTED					
Measures*										
12. M-1	291.2	303.2	321.7	346.4	334.0	336.8	346.4	345.2	333.3	335.4
13. M-2	617.5	669.3	744.8	813.0	797.5	801.2	813.0	818.3	811.4	818.7
14. M-3	983.8	1,094.3	1,237.5	1,375.5	1,351.7	1,358.5	1,375.5	1,386.5	1,383.4	1,397.5
15. M-4	707.9	752.8	809.1	888.9	865.8	872.8	888.9	894.6	888.3	899.0
16. M-5	1,074.2	1,177.7	1,301.8	1,451.4	1,420.0	1,430.1	1,451.4	1,462.9	1,460.3	1,477.7

Components										
17. Currency	69.0	75.1	82.1	90.0	86.9	88.4	90.0	88.6	88.9	89.9
Commercial bank deposits:										
18. Demand	222.2	228.1	239.5	256.4	247.0	248.4	256.4	256.6	244.4	245.5
19. Member	159.7	162.1	168.5	176.3	170.0	170.3	176.3	175.9	167.4	168.5
20. Domestic nonmember	58.5	62.6	67.5	75.8	72.7	73.8	75.8	76.3	72.8	73.0
21. Time and savings	416.7	449.6	487.4	542.5	531.8	536.0	542.5	549.4	555.0	563.6
22. Negotiable CD's†	90.5	83.5	64.3	75.9	68.3	71.6	75.9	76.4	76.9	80.2
23. Other	326.3	366.2	423.1	466.6	463.5	464.4	466.6	473.0	478.1	483.4
24. Nonbank thrift institutions‡	366.3	424.9	492.7	562.5	554.2	557.3	562.5	568.2	571.9	578.8
25. U.S. Govt. deposits (all commercial banks)	4.9	4.1	4.4	5.1	3.7	3.5	5.1	4.2	4.2	4.6

*Composition of the money stock measures is as follows:

M-1: Averages of daily figures for (1) demand deposits at commercial banks other than domestic interbank and U.S. government, less cash items in process of collection and Federal Reserve float; (2) foreign demand balances at Federal Reserve banks; and (3) currency outside the Treasury, Federal Reserve Banks, and vaults of commercial banks.

M-2: M-1 plus savings deposits, time deposits open account, and time certificates of deposit (CDs) other than negotiable CDs of $100,000 or more at large weekly reporting banks.

M-3: M-2 plus the average of the beginning- and end-of-month deposits of mutual savings banks, savings and loan shares, and credit union shares (nonbank thrift).

M-4: M-2 plus large negotiable CDs.

M-5: M-3 plus large negotiable CDs.

For a description of the latest revisions in the money stock measures see "Money Stock Measures: Revision" in the April 1978 *Bulletin*, pp. 338 and 339. Latest monthly and weekly figures are available from the Board's H.6 release. Back data are available from the Banking Section, Division of Research and Statistics.

†Negotiable time CDs issued in denominations of $100,000 or more by large weekly reporting commercial banks.

‡Average of the beginning- and end-of-month figures for deposits of mutual savings banks, for savings capital at savings and loan associations, and for credit union shares.

Source: Federal Reserve Bulletin, May 1978, p. A14.

Figure 9.2   DERIVATION OF VARIOUS MONETARY AGGREGATES M_1
THROUGH M_5, UNITED STATES, 1975

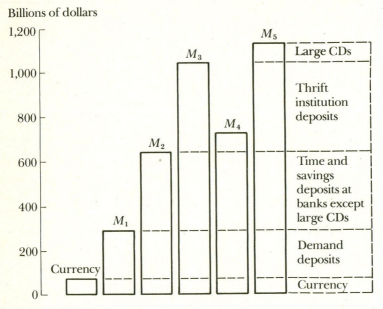

Source: Anne M. Laporte, "Monetary Aggregates Compared," Federal Reserve Bank of Chicago, *Business Conditions*, June 1976, p. 12.

CDs. Likewise, accounts in nonbank thrift institutions are composed of readily available savings deposits and less liquid time deposits. Not all components of M_1 are equally available for spending since an undetermined amount of currency is lost or is outside the country, and demand deposits include balances held to compensate commercial banks for services. Other factors blur the distinction between M_1 and the other monetary aggregates. Some noticeable regulatory and innovational developments in this area include business (in contrast to nonbusiness or household) savings accounts, negotiable orders of withdrawal (NOWs), money-market mutual funds, credit union share drafts, and the use of automatic transfer systems between customer savings accounts and checking accounts in commercial banks.

Interestingly, these developments prompted the Federal Reserve in late 1978 to devise a new monetary aggregate of sorts called "M_1 plus" (M_1+). This hybrid measure adds to M_1 the savings deposits at commercial banks, NOW accounts at nonbank thrift institutions, credit union share draft accounts, and demand deposits at mutual savings banks.

Furthermore, an article in the January 1979 issue of the *Federal Reserve Bulletin* presented proposals by the staff of the Federal Reserve Board for redefining the monetary aggregates. Inviting public comments, the Federal Reserve staff noted that "regulatory and financial innovations in recent years have fundamentally altered the character of the public's monetary assets."

Under the staff proposals, the basic money supply M_1 would be redefined to include the new transaction-related savings deposits, such as NOW accounts, share drafts, and automatic transfer accounts. As compared with the old M_1 concept, the proposed M_1 is a broader measure of *domestically* related transaction balances because it specifically excludes demand deposits of foreign commercial banks and official institutions.

Regarding other monetary aggregates included in the staff's study, the proposed M_1+ consists of the proposed M_1 plus savings balances at commercial banks. The proposed M_2 would add savings deposits at *all* depositary institutions (commercial banks and nonbank thrifts) to the proposed M_1. Finally, the proposed M_3 would consist of the proposed M_2 and all time deposits at all depositary institutions, regardless of denomination, maturity period, or negotiability. Note that the proposed measures would replace the old measures M_1 through M_5. Acceptance of these proposals by the Federal Reserve Board should provide the basis for revamped monetary aggregates that are relevant for the 1980s.

ANALYTICAL USE OF RESERVE
AND MONETARY AGGREGATES

The choice of a monetary aggregate for measuring monetary influence on the economy depends largely on the particular orientation of the analyst. For example, some analysts, viewing monetary policy as a form of debt management, concentrate their attention on the total amount of noninterest-bearing government debt that results from the actions of the monetary authority.[2]

2. For a sophisticated expression of this viewpoint, see James Tobin, "An Essay on Principles of Debt Management," in *Fiscal and Debt Management Policies,* ed. B. Fox and E. Shapiro (Englewood Cliffs, N.J.: Prentice-Hall, 1963).

They may emphasize the source base adjusted to exclude member bank borrowings, thus giving a measure of demand debt of the government. Other observers, more concerned with the commercial banking sector or the demand deposit component of the money supply, may focus on total member bank reserves or nonborrowed member bank reserves.

In recent years many economists (for example, those associated with the Federal Reserve Bank of St. Louis and with the University of Chicago) have stressed the analytical usefulness of the monetary base. According to their view, the monetary base constitutes an asset that the monetary authority supplies to the economy. Since the supply of this asset is controlled largely by the Federal Reserve (see Figure 9.3, which depicts simultaneous movements in the monetary base and Federal Reserve credit), banks and the nonbank public must adjust their holdings of real and other financial assets so as to equate the quantity demanded of the monetary base to the quantity supplied. This market adjustment of asset holdings brings changes in economic activity, prices of real assets, and interest rates. An even stronger view regarding the role of the monetary base holds that the monetary base is the principal determinant of the money stock, which affords a good indicator of the thrust of monetary forces. Proponents of the latter view regard the monetary base as the proper measure of Federal Reserve monetary actions. Analysts using the monetary base generally regard changes in the monetary base as ultimately leading to changes in the growth of aggregate demand for goods and services.[3]

However, many observers are skeptical of the usefulness of the monetary base because they regard the measure as less reliably linked to macroeconomic policy variables such as output, employment, and price level than most monetary aggregates. The measure has a technical advantage over other aggregates, however, because it is less affected by the various innovations modifying the payments mechanism.

On the other hand, an aggregate may be chosen to direct attention to the effects of certain Federal Reserve "defensive" operations, which are taken to offset changes in particular items in the member bank reserve equation. If, for example, the Federal Reserve uses open market operations to offset

3. For a detailed discussion of these views and some of their policy implications, see L. C. Andersen and Jerry L. Jordan, "The Monetary Base—Explanation and Analytical Use," Federal Reserve Bank of St. Louis, *Review* (August 1968): 11.

Figure 9.3   MONETARY BASE AND ADJUSTED FEDERAL RESERVE CREDIT

Monthly averages of daily figures seasonally adjusted. Percentages are annual rates of change for periods indicated. Latest data plotted May 1978.

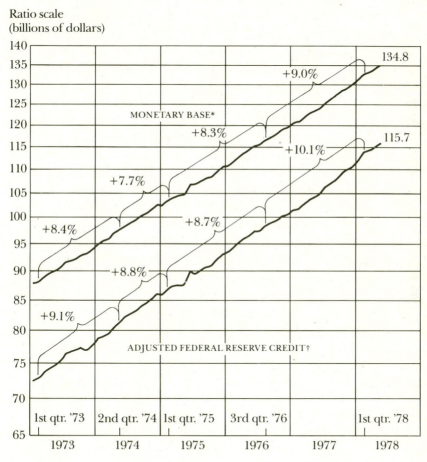

*Uses of the monetary base are member bank reserves and currency held by the public and nonmember banks. Adjustments are made for reserve requirement changes and shifts in deposits among classes of banks. Data are computed by this bank.

†Federal Reserve credit consists of Federal Reserve holdings of securities, loans, float and other assets. Adjusted Federal Reserve credit is computed by subtracting Treasury deposits at Federal Reserve banks from this series, and adjusting the series for reserve requirement ratio changes and shifts in the same type of deposits between banks where different reserve requirement ratios apply. Data are computed by this bank.

Source: Federal Reserve Bank of St. Louis, *Monetary Trends*, Released June 27, 1978, p. 7.

changes in currency outside commercial banks, an analyst could choose total member bank reserves as an aggregate indicator rather than the monetary base. In this instance, an increase in currency held outside commercial banks might induce a reduction in total member bank reserves. Reacting to this initial currency drain, the Federal Reserve could use open market operations to restore member bank reserves to their original level. Overall, then, total reserves would not be allowed to fall because of the currency movements, but the Federal Reserve's defensive response would result in an increase in the monetary base. The analyst might assume that the Federal Reserve is more concerned with maintaining a given level of total reserves than with increasing the monetary base and therefore choose the total reserves aggregate for purposes of analysis.

Finally, for many years, policy makers within the Federal Reserve had used information relating to reserve and monetary aggregates in formulating their analysis. Then, beginning in 1970, the Federal Open Market Committee (FOMC) established longer-term objectives for growth of selected monetary and reserve aggregates as a specific part of its general directive for the conduct of open market operations. Although this move did not imply any lack of concern with interest rates and financial flows, the more explicit emphasis on aggregates brought some modification in the way the committee devised its policy strategy.[4]

In early 1974, the FOMC started to include numerical specifications for short-run monetary aggregate growth in its own policy record. Following passage of the congressional resolution on March 24, 1975, the committee began announcing on a quarterly basis the desired growth rate ranges for certain monetary aggregates over the year following the most recent calendar quarter. In effect, the resolution proclaimed that the longer-run growth in the monetary aggregates be consistent with the longer-run growth potential of the economy's productive capacity. The first regularly scheduled congressional hearings held in accordance with the congressional resolution opened on May 1, 1975, at which were publicized target growth rates for certain aggregates for the period from March 1975 to March 1976.

Finally, in mid-1976, the Federal Reserve published the report of an advi-

---

4. For a detailed account of the evolution of the committee's general directive and the role of the aggregates in 1970, see "Monetary Aggregates and Money Market Conditions in Open Market Policy," *Federal Reserve Bulletin* 57 (February 1971): 79–104.

sory committee relating to the measurement, definition, and analytical use of the various monetary aggregates. The Bach committee, named for its chairman, Professor George L. Bach, considered the difficult question of relating various concepts of money to the fast-changing payments mechanism. After careful review and evaluation, the committee could recommend no one monetary aggregate as being the best gauge of the economy's need for money and credit. In assessing the several aggregates the committee observed that "each has its theoretical and practical strengths and weaknesses as a guide to, or intermediate target for, monetary-policy operations." At the very least, the Bach committee's findings suggest that effective analytical use of monetary and reserve aggregates requires awareness of the limitations of these measures and of the need for careful interpretation of their results.

KEY TERMS

Member bank reserve equation
Federal Reserve bank credit
Currency in circulation
Reserve aggregates
Total member bank reserves
Required reserves
Excess reserves

Free reserves
Nonborrowed member bank reserves
Monetary base
Money multiplier
Monetary aggregates
Basic money supply

REVIEW QUESTIONS

1. What is meant by the member bank reserve equation?
2. Indicate the various sources and uses of reserve funds.
3. Explain briefly how changes in gold stock and in Treasury currency outstanding affect member bank reserves.
4. What are the principal components of Federal Reserve bank credit?
5. How does Federal Reserve float originate?
6. Explain briefly how changes in currency in circulation affect bank reserves.
7. What factors have contributed to the rising ratio of currency to demand deposits in the United States?

8. Explain briefly how each of the following affects bank reserves:
   a. Treasury cash holdings;
   b. Treasury deposits at Federal Reserve banks;
   c. Foreign and other deposits at Federal Reserve banks.
9. What is the purpose of Treasury tax and loan accounts in commercial banks?
10. Give a general definition of reserve aggregates and indicate several commonly used reserve aggregates.
11. What concepts enter into computation of the monetary base?
12. Indicate five ways of measuring the money stock.
13. How would the Federal Reserve Board's staff redefine the monetary aggregates in order to allow for recent regulatory and financial innovations?
14. What is the significance of monetary and reserve aggregates in the formulation of Federal Open Market Committee directives?

SUGGESTED READINGS

Andersen, Leonall C., and Denis S. Karnosky. "Some Consideration in the Use of Monetary Aggregates for the Implementation of Monetary Policy." Federal Reserve Bank of St. Louis, *Review* (September 1977): 2–7.

Anderson, Paul S. "Currency in Use and in Hoards." Federal Reserve Bank of Boston, *New England Economic Review* (March–April 1977): 21–30.

Balbach, Anatol B., and Albert E. Burger. "Derivation of the Monetary Base." Federal Reserve Bank of St. Louis, *Review* (November 1976): 2–8.

Debs, Richard A. "On Fed Watching." Federal Reserve Bank of New York, *Monthly Review* (October 1974): 243–247.

Gambs, Carl M. "Money—A Changing Concept in a Changing World." Federal Reserve Bank of Kansas City, *Monthly Review* (January 1977): 3–12.

Hoel, Arline. "A Primer on Federal Reserve Float." Federal Reserve Bank of New York, *Monthly Review* (October 1975): 245–253.

Hoffman, Stuart G. "Monetary Growth Objectives." Federal Reserve Bank of Atlanta, *Monthly Review* (December 1976): 175–181.

"Improving the Monetary Aggregates: Report of the Advisory Committee on Monetary Statistics." *Federal Reserve Bulletin* 62 (May 1976): 422–426.

Laporte, Anne Marie. "Monetary Aggregates Compared." Federal Reserve Bank of Chicago, *Business Conditions* (June 1976): 11–15.

McDonough, William R. "Monetary Policy—Effectiveness of Alternative Approaches to Monetary Control." Federal Reserve Bank of Dallas, *Business Review* (August 1976): 1–7.

Monetary Aggregates and Monetary Policy. Federal Reserve Bank of New York, 1974.

"A Proposal for Redefining the Monetary Aggregates." *Federal Reserve Bulletin* 65 (January 1979): 13–42.

Rutner, Jack L. "The Federal Reserve's Impact on Several Reserve Aggregates." Federal Reserve Bank of Kansas City, *Monthly Review* (May 1977): 14–22.

Chapter Ten

THE PROCESS OF MONETARY CONTROL

Now that we have some understanding of the various ways in which the Federal Reserve attempts to exert monetary control, we must examine the different tools the central bank uses to conduct monetary policy. These policy tools are of two types: general (quantitative or indirect) and selective (qualitative or direct). *General monetary controls* include those devices that influence the overall supply, cost, and availability of money and credit. They are sometimes called indirect monetary controls because they impinge initially on bank reserves and then in turn indirectly affect the money supply. The three principal general controls are open market policy, reserve lending policy, and changes in reserve requirements.

Selective monetary controls, on the other hand, directly affect the terms and conditions relating to particular kinds or qualities of credit. In contrast to the more impersonal general controls, selective controls are directed toward specific segments of the credit and financial markets. Here the regulatory authorities interpose explicit limitations on dealings between borrowers and creditors.

This chapter describes and appraises the central bank's use of these two types of controls and concludes with a brief look at monetary controls utilized by major foreign central banks.

OPEN MARKET POLICY

Open market operations are the most important continuously used general monetary control tool available to the Federal Reserve. This tool is a delicate monetary scalpel that provides great flexibility as to both timing and the amount of funds released or absorbed. The original Federal Reserve Act gave the system legislative authority to conduct purchases and sales of securities in the open market, and in its early years the system engaged in open market operations on numerous occasions. Until the early 1920s, however, individual Federal Reserve banks conducted security transactions primarily to accrue earnings, to facilitate Treasury financing, or to acquire collateral backing for Federal Reserve bank notes, which are no longer in open circulation.

It was only in the early 1920s that the Federal Reserve perceived that the purchase and sale of government securities tended to affect credit conditions. System purchases appeared to ease credit, while sales tended to make credit less available. The explanation for this phenomenon is simple. In purchasing securities, the Federal Reserve paid with newly created funds, which, when deposited in the commercial banking system, made more reserves available for additional lending and "investing" by banks. Federal Reserve sales of securities entailed the receipt of checks drawn on deposit accounts in commercial banks, thus reducing the aggregate reserve holdings of commercial banks.

Recognizing the implications for monetary control, the Federal Reserve devised working arrangements to coordinate the buying and selling of government securities. Finally, with the passage of the Banking Act of 1935, the Federal Open Market Committee (FOMC) was established to provide more formal coordination and direction to open market policy.

The Conduct of Open Market Operations

The actual conduct of open market operations is done through the Securities Trading Desk of the New York Federal Reserve Bank. The Federal Open Market Committee issues general directives to the manager of the System Open Market Account at the Trading Desk. He or she is a senior officer of the Federal Reserve Bank of New York appointed annually by the FOMC to conduct open market purchases and sales of United States government and federal agency securities and banker acceptances. These directives, which serve as general guidelines in conducting open market operations, are necessarily given in fairly broad terms. Since 1970 they have focused on a desired rate of growth in the monetary and reserve aggregates with reasonable regard for the general state of the money market. To illustrate, the policy directive adopted at the August 1978 meeting of the Committee included these instructions:

. . . it is the policy of the Federal Open Market Committee to foster monetary and financial conditions that will resist inflationary pressures while encouraging continued moderate economic expansion and contributing to a sustainable pattern of international transactions. At its meeting on July 18, 1978, the committee agreed that these objectives would be furthered by growths of M_1, M_2, and M_3 from the second quarter of 1978 to the second quarter of 1979 at rates within ranges of 4 to 6½ percent, 6½ to 9 percent, and 7½ to 10 percent, respectively. The associated range for bank credit is 8½ to 11½ percent. These ranges are subject to reconsideration at any time as conditions warrant.

In the short run, the committee seeks to achieve bank reserve and money market conditions that are broadly consistent with the longer-run ranges for monetary aggregates cited above, while giving due regard to developing conditions in domestic and international financial markets more generally. Early in the period until the next regular meeting, system open market operations shall be directed at attaining a weekly-average federal funds rate slightly above the current level. Subsequently, operations shall be directed at maintaining the weekly-average federal funds rate within the range of 7¾ to 8¼ percent.[1]

Each FOMC directive contains a short review of economic developments, the general economic goals of the committee, and operating instructions to the account manager. These instructions are stated in terms of money market conditions and of short-term growth rates for monetary aggregates that are deemed to be consistent with desired longer-run growth rates. Special factors are also considered, for example, conditions in foreign exchange markets. Essentially, in formulating its directives, the FOMC regards the money stock as the policy instrument relating to such basic long-run economic policy goals as price-level stability and employment. On the other hand, the federal funds rate is the policy instrument linked to the short-run target: the money stock's growth rate.

1. FOMC meeting held August 15, 1978, contained in "Record of Policy Actions of the Federal Open Market Committee," *Current Economic Policy Directive*, published monthly by the FOMC. The record is released about thirty days after each meeting, and subsequently published in the monthly *Federal Reserve Bulletin*. Furthermore, records for the entire year appear in the *Annual Report of the Board of Governors of the Federal Reserve System*.

The daily task of the Trading Desk is to translate the committee's policy decision into concrete decisions to buy or sell a certain amount of securities in the open market. Following through on the committee's policy directive, the Trading Desk performs a comprehensive review of various economic intelligence data: detailed statistical reports of bank reserve positions and monetary and credit aggregates; projections of the aggregates and of factors affecting bank reserves; and up-to-the-minute assessments of developments in the money and securities markets. On the morning of each trading day the account manager holds a conference phone call with staff members of the Board of Governors and one voting Federal Reserve bank president on the FOMC to provide a briefing on present security market conditions and on the market operations proposed for that day. A wire summary of the daily program also informs the other members of the Federal Open Market Committee.[2]

Once the precise magnitude of the daily open market operation is determined, the transaction is made through some two dozen government securities dealers. The effects of the given transaction, which has immediate impact on money market banks and government securities dealers, are spread through the normal flow of funds among banks and regions and through the complex of rates in the money and government securities markets. The interest rate on federal funds is especially sensitive to Federal Reserve open market operations. Via open market transactions, the Trading Desk supplies or absorbs reserves depending on whether the federal funds rate is higher or lower than desired. These operations do not afford exact control of the federal funds rate, but they enable the Trading Desk to hold the rate within a range that is narrower than the tolerance range specified by the FOMC. In turn, the federal funds rate influences commercial bank decisions on loans to businesses, consumers, and other borrowers. Additionally, interest rates paid on other short-term financial assets, such as commercial paper and U.S. Treasury bills, roughly parallel movements in the federal funds rate. Thus the federal funds rate also influences the cost of credit obtained from nonbank lenders.

2. A detailed and fascinating account of Trading Desk operations by the manager of the System Open Market Account is given in Alan R. Holmes, "A Day at the Trading Desk," Federal Reserve Bank of New York, *Monthly Review* (October 1970): 234–238.

T Account Effects of Open Market Operations

The mechanics of open market operations can be illustrated by the use of T accounts, which were first presented in Chapter 7 to portray the process of deposit creation. In examining the effects of open market operations, we will overlook the intermediate role played by the government securities dealers and concentrate on the ultimate results for bank reserves and for the money supply. This procedure is acceptable for analytical purposes, since the securities dealers are simply intermediaries who bring together buyers and sellers of government securities.

As indicated in an earlier chapter, Federal Reserve purchases of securities tend to increase the flow of reserves to member banks, while sales of securities by the Federal Reserve tend to decrease this flow. These basic results are achieved whether the operations are conducted with member banks or with parties other than member banks. Let us first consider the case of open market purchases. The T account changes arising from purchases of securities from member banks are as follows:

FEDERAL RESERVE		MEMBER BANKS	
Securities +	Deposits of member banks +	Deposits at Federal Reserve + Securities −	

Here it can be seen that member bank total and excess reserves have increased to the full·extent of the securities purchases, with no change in the general public's money supply.

If the purchases of securities are made from other than member banks, for example, from pension funds or from wealthy private individuals, the T accounts are affected as follows:

FEDERAL RESERVE		MEMBER BANKS	
Securities +	Deposits of member banks +	Deposits at Federal Reserve +	Demand deposits +

In this situation, the securities sellers deposit the checks received from the Federal Reserve in their accounts in commercial banks; when these checks are cleared, member bank reserve accounts are increased.[3] Here member bank total reserves and the general public's money supply increase to the full extent of the securities purchases. Excess reserves of member banks increase to a lesser extent than the original securities purchase because the increase in member bank demand deposit liabilities entails an increase in required reserves of member banks.

Once again simplifying the T account analysis by ignoring the role played by securities dealers, we find the results of open market sales by the Federal Reserve are the exact opposite to those just given. If member banks purchase securities from the Federal Reserve, these changes occur:

FEDERAL RESERVE		MEMBER BANKS	
Securities −	Deposits of member banks −	Deposits at Federal Reserve − Securities +	

Here member bank total and excess reserves are reduced to the full extent of the securities sales, with the general public's money supply unaffected.

Similar destruction of member bank reserves occurs when the Federal Reserve sells securities to other than member banks:

FEDERAL RESERVE		MEMBER BANKS	
Securities −	Deposits of member banks −	Deposits at Federal Reserve −	Demand deposits −

The open market sales fully reduce total reserves and the money supply, while excess reserves are cut to a lesser extent because of the decrease in member bank deposit liabilities.

---

3. These results ultimately occur even if the securities sellers have accounts in nonmember banks, because nonmember banks maintain correspondent banking balances with member banks.

Secondary Effects of Open Market Operations

As indicated, open market operations have an immediate impact on bank reserves and the money supply. In addition, they have secondary effects on the pattern of interest rates in money and financial markets. This secondary impact occurs because open market operations, being conducted in government securities, affect their market prices. Since the securities are obligations that carry stipulated, fixed interest payments, variations in their market prices imply inverse changes in effective yields (or interest rates). This inverse (or opposite) relation between market price and effective yield emerges simply from the arithmetic involved in computing the current yield of a debt security such as a bond. A bond earns a fixed number of dollars in interest each year. The current yield is computed by dividing the fixed annual dollar amount of interest by the bond's market price. Changes in this market price (or in the price of any other type of fixed interest security), therefore, are reflected automatically in changes in the opposite direction in the effective yield.

For example, an open market purchase by the Federal Reserve tends to increase the demand for marketable securities and, with supply assumed to remain unchanged, raises their market prices. An increase in market prices is equivalent to a decrease in the effective yields (or interest rates) of these securities. Open market sales, on the other hand, tend to lower market prices of securities, and hence to increase their effective yields. The degree to which interest rates (or yields) are affected is determined largely by the magnitude of the open market operation, the maturity class of the security, and the particular conditions existing in the market for government securities.

Official Policy Governing Open Market Operations

Official views about the conduct of open market operations have changed since World War II. For several years following the end of hostilities, the Federal Reserve continued its policy, initiated in World War II, of using open market purchases to support the market for government securities. These support operations implied the abandonment of open market policy as an effective monetary control for economic stabilization purposes. Rising criticism of this bond support policy, together with the mounting price inflation following the outbreak of the Korean War in 1950, led to the Treasury–Federal Reserve Accord of March 1951, by which open market operations would be used for monetary control purposes rather than to support the prices of government securities. At the same time, it was agreed that the Federal Reserve would temporarily support the market for government securities whenever disorderly markets would otherwise occur. Subsequently, after carefully analyzing how best to achieve a smoothly functioning market for government securities, the FOMC announced a *bills-only* (or bills-preferably) *policy* in March 1953. This policy, followed for some eight years, stipulated that, under normal conditions, open market operations would be conducted in short-term securities, preferably Treasury bills. The exception to this official approach arose only when the Federal Reserve conducted appropriate open market operations to correct disorderly market conditions.

The rationale for the bills-only policy was that confining open market operations to short-term securities lessened the Federal Reserve's disruptive effects on free market forces in the government securities market. In effect, the policy would allow securities prices and yields to seek their own levels in the market, while the authorities would use open market operations to affect the flow of bank reserves for purposes of monetary control.

Controversy arose about the bills-only policy, both within and outside of the Federal Reserve System. Officials of the New York Federal Reserve Bank, for example, assailed it as abandoning explicit, direct concern for the impact of open market operations on the pattern of interest rates. They reasoned that at certain times it is advantageous for open market operations to be conducted in longer-term securities in order to affect intermediate- and long-term interest rates. Official defense of the bills-only doctrine emphasized that the short end of the government securities market was characterized by a "breadth, depth, and resiliency" that would minimize the disruptive impact of open market operations on free market forces. In addition, the official view was that open market operations conducted in the short end of the market would initially affect short-term interest rates, and that these changes, by competitive market adjustments, would be transmitted quickly to intermediate- and long-term rates.

However, the bills-only policy was abandoned in February 1961 when the FOMC authorized the purchase of intermediate- and longer-term securities with maturities up to ten years. This action, which was followed later by removal of the maturity limitation, reflected official concern for painfully high levels of unemployment and for mounting deficits in the international balance of payments. Confronted by these two problems, the authorities revamped the orientation of open market operations to meet the new situation. Referred to as Operation Twist, the new policy called for appropriate open market operations to raise short-term interest rates and thus dampen short-term capital outflows, while at the same time easing long-term credit in order to spur domestic investment and growth. Since 1961 Federal Reserve open market operations have been conducted in various maturity groupings, thus imparting a more flexible stance to open market policy. Nevertheless, the majority of these operations (measured on a dollar-volume basis) have been carried out in the short end of the market, largely because short-term securities comprise the biggest segment of outstanding marketable government securities.

FEDERAL RESERVE LENDING
OPERATIONS

The most traditional general monetary control involves Federal Reserve lending operations, which include both discount policy and changes in discount rates. *Discount policy*, sometimes called the discount mechanism, refers to the various conditions governing member bank borrowing from the central bank. Discount policy sets the framework within which member banks may have access to Reserve bank credit at the discount window. The discount rate provides a means of influencing the cost to member banks of this access.

Both discount policy and the discount rate played major roles in the early operations of the Federal Reserve System. The original Federal Reserve Act, relying heavily on the real-bills doctrine, or commercial loan theory of credit,[4] limited lending to member banks solely on the basis of discounts of short-term paper that these banks had "issued or drawn for agricultural, industrial, or commercial purposes." In other words, in providing credit by the discount mechanism, the Federal Reserve banks were restricted to discounting short-term working-capital loans that member banks had made. This restrictive view of loans was based on the belief that Reserve bank credit would adjust automatically to the varying needs of commerce and business. The havoc worked by the Great Depression revealed the deficiencies of this approach: it

---

4. The real-bills doctrine and its relation to commercial bank liquidity were examined in Chapter 5.

unduly restricted central bank lending and did not automatically provide a volume of bank reserves appropriate for sustaining high levels of production and employment with reasonably stable prices.

Finally, the Banking Act of 1935 amended the Federal Reserve Act by permitting loans to member banks on the basis of any assets acceptable to Federal Reserve banks. Under section 10(b) of the act, the rate of interest charged for these loans, which are secured by assets other than eligible paper or United States government securities, is a half percentage point higher than the established discount rate. This broadened authority for Federal Reserve lending effectively marked the demise of the commercial loan theory of credit.

In the latter half of the 1930s, as a huge influx of gold and weak demand for credit brought a large build-up of excess reserves and low interest rates, the significance of the discount apparatus waned. During World War II and the immediate postwar period, Federal Reserve support of the market for government securities gave member banks ready access to Reserve bank credit. With the Treasury–Federal Reserve Accord of March 1951, discount policy and the discount rate regained significance. Increasing numbers of member banks resorted to the discount window to cover reserve deficiencies. The discount mechanism regained some of its early standing as an instrument of monetary policy, but was overshadowed by the importance of open market operations.

Administration of the Discount Window

In addition to broadening member bank access to Federal Reserve credit, the Federal Reserve Act (as amended) recognizes the importance of effective administration of the discount window to the maintenance of sound credit conditions. Viewing borrowing from a Reserve bank as a privilege and not as an automatic right accorded to member banks, the act directs each Reserve bank to examine carefully the general character and volume of bank lending to determine whether undue use is being made of bank credit for speculative purposes or for other purposes inconsistent with the promotion of sound credit conditions. Furthermore, the discount window is to be administered impartially, and the Board of Governors is authorized to establish regulations explicitly defining conditions under which credit can be extended to member banks. These specific regulatory aspects are contained in Regulation A of the Board of Governors.

Implicit within this regulation is the view that proper administration of the discount window requires something more than mechanical rules. Essentially, the regulation provides general guidelines relating to member bank borrowing. A safety-valve function is recognized whereby loans to member banks ease the temporary stresses arising from the many business and financial factors that constantly shift funds among banks. Reserves are channeled directly to the banks that need them. When the need passes, member banks repay their borrowings and reserves are extinguished. In addition, unlimited access to the discount window is viewed as being inconsistent with sound credit conditions and a forceful monetary policy.

In 1968 the Federal Reserve completed a three-year study of the discount mechanism.[5] This study prompted strong support for a plan that would grant each member bank an assured line of credit at the Federal Reserve. Called a basic borrowing privilege, the plan was aimed at lessening member banks' present embarrassment at having to resort to formal discount window borrowing to meet temporary and emergency needs for reserves. This privilege would also serve as an inducement to smaller banks to provide more ample credit.

In light of this view, the Federal Reserve in April 1973 instituted changes in discount procedures designed to assist small member banks to meet seasonal credit needs in their localities. This new approach, called the *seasonal borrowing privilege,* provides seasonal lines of credit to member banks that have no reliable access to private borrowing sources. These banks operate in areas with heavy seasonal businesses, such as agriculture and tourism. According to Federal Reserve estimates, the seasonal borrowing privileges would apply to some 2,000 member banks, most of which have deposits of less than $50 million.

Other developments have generated even greater access to the Federal Reserve's discount window in recent years. The circumstances surrounding the collapse of the Franklin National Bank in October 1974 brought a major change in Federal Reserve lending operations. The Federal Reserve provided

---

5. See *Reappraisal of the Federal Reserve Discount Mechanism: Report of a System Committee,* 1968. In connection with this study, a series of papers was prepared by Federal Reserve researchers and by academic economists. These papers constitute a veritable library of professional analysis of various facets of the discount mechanism.

some $1.75 billion in loans in an attempt to keep the distressed bank afloat over a period of several months. The outgrowth of this experience is that the Federal Reserve stands ready to provide substantial loans over prolonged periods (greater than two months) to individual member banks whose continued liquidity is deemed essential for maintaining stability of the financial system. Such credit accommodation carries an interest rate that is greater than the basic discount rate.

Finally, in the midst of the mounting municipal fiscal crisis of New York City in late 1975, the Federal Reserve stood ready to lend to nonmember commercial banks to offset any severe financial repercussions. Authority for such lending is given in the last paragraph of section 13 of the Federal Reserve Act, whereby loans secured by U.S. government securities may be made "to individuals, partnerships, or corporations other than member banks." These loans also carry an interest rate higher than the Federal Reserve discount rate. Fortunately, the expected financial storm from New York City's troubles did not occur and this assistance was not required. The significant point, however, is the ready willingness of the central bank to use this extraordinary authority should circumstances force it to do so.

Effects of Discount Rate Changes

The general principles guiding administration of the discount window do not change over the business cycle. On the contrary, the discount rate is used as a tool for combatting inflationary and recessionary tendencies in the economy.

An obvious effect of a change in the Federal Reserve discount rate is on the cost of member bank borrowing from the Federal Reserve banks. Other factors remaining equal, a rise in the discount rate makes borrowing more expensive and thus tends to discourage member bank borrowing, whereas a reduction tends to have opposite effects. The cost effect of a change in the discount rate constitutes only one of several factors influencing the volume of member bank borrowing. For example, a major factor is whether conditions generate a need by banks for additional funds. If so, cost does become a factor influencing member bank willingness to borrow from the Federal Reserve.

Although member banks may be reluctant to borrow from the Federal Reserve, a discount rate that is lower than other rates on money market claims makes borrowing at the discount window more attractive. For example, a high Treasury bill rate in relation to the discount rate induces member banks to

Figure 10.1   MEMBER BANK BORROWINGS AND SHORT-TERM
INTEREST RATE DIFFERENTIAL

Monthly averages of daily figures. Latest data plotted June 1977.

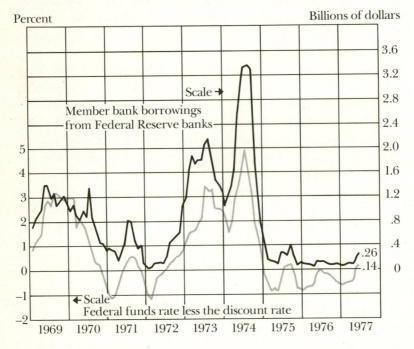

Source: Federal Reserve Bank of St. Louis, *U.S. Financial Data*, week ending July 20, 1977, p. 1.

borrow from the Federal Reserve rather than sell off Treasury bills in order to acquire more funds. Similarly, a high federal funds rate relative to the discount rate provides incentive for the banks to use the discount window, particularly if the economy is booming and bank credit demand is strong. Figure 10.1 traces the response of member bank borrowings to short-term interest rate differentials in the 1970s. Note especially the borrowings surge during the years 1973 and 1974, when the Federal Reserve discount rate was much lower than the federal funds rate. The Federal Reserve controls the volume and profitability of discount window borrowings by aligning the discount rate more closely with other short-term interest rates, such as the Treasury bill rate and the federal funds rate.

Changes in the discount rate can affect total spending through psychological effects, known as *announcement effects*. Since changes in the discount rate are formally announced, the public may regard these changes as signaling a turn in Federal Reserve credit policy and thus tend to alter their expectations of future business and economic conditions. These changed expectations in turn modify the behavior of economic decision-making units, which may or may not have countercyclical effects. For example, a reduction in the discount rate may generate rising expectations of easier money and credit conditions and create anticipation of favorable future business prospects, thus tending to strengthen spending. On the other hand, the same reduction could be interpreted as a sign of official anticipation of slackening business activity, thus contributing to a bearish mood with initially adverse effects on aggregate spending.

It is difficult to predict public reaction to a change in the discount rate. The great uncertainty surrounding these psychological effects makes the announcement impact of a change in the discount rate of dubious value for monetary control purposes. Furthermore, rather than representing a turn in official monetary stance, a change in the discount rate may be only a technical adjustment to realign the discount rate with market rates so as to maintain the existing degree of restraint or ease.

**CHANGES IN RESERVE
REQUIREMENTS**

A powerful but little used monetary control available to the Board of Governors is the power to vary member bank reserve requirements within specified limits. The original Federal Reserve Act established fixed required reserve ratios for member banks and specified what assets could be counted as legal reserves. In 1933 Congress gave the Board of Governors temporary authority to vary required reserve ratios between set limits, and the Banking Act of 1935 established this authority on a permanent basis. Subsequently, in 1959, the Federal Reserve Act was amended to allow the Board of Governors discretion in including vault cash, in addition to member bank deposits at Federal Reserve banks, as part of legal reserves. In July 1966 the Board of Governors applied structured reserve requirements to various specified dollar amounts of net demand deposits and time deposits of member banks.

Then, effective November 9, 1972, the Federal Reserve restructured reserve requirements on a more equitable basis and adopted new check-collection procedures. The revamped reserve requirements apply the same requirement ratio to all member banks of equal size regardless of their location (see Table 10.1). Furthermore, all member banks with net demand deposits exceeding $400 million are considered reserve city banks. This classification contrasts with the previous approach, in which the *reserve city* designation applied generally to larger banks in larger cities, with all others commonly called country banks.

The new regulation governing check collection requires all banks served by the Federal Reserve's collection facilities to make payment on the same day the checks are presented. Previously, most banks located outside cities with Federal Reserve facilities or outside payment areas served by the system's newly formed Regional Check-Processing Centers could delay payment by one day.

Currently, the board may set required reserve ratios for demand deposits at between 10 and 22 percent for reserve city banks and between 7 and 14 percent for other banks. For time deposits, the specified minimum and maximum reserve ratios are 3 and 10 percent for both classes of banks. As indicated in Chapter 5, in 1969 and 1970 the authorities modified the regulatory definition of bank deposits subject to reserve requirements to include Eurodollar borrowings exceeding a specified base amount and bank-related commercial paper, where the proceeds are used to purchase assets from the related bank.

Changes in reserve requirements work in two ways. First, although they have no effect on total reserves, these changes directly affect excess reserves by altering the amount of reserves required against existing deposits. A reduction in reserve requirements releases reserves and tends to produce an expansion in bank credit and the general public's money supply. Increases in requirements have the opposite effect and are used mainly to absorb excess reserves. Second, changed reserve requirements alter the amount of deposits a given volume of reserves can support. For example, a required reserve ratio of 10 percent permits a given dollar amount of reserves to support up to ten times this amount in the form of deposits, in a simplified model. A reserve ratio of 20 percent lowers the maximum multiple to five.

Changes in reserve requirements constitute the least subtle or flexible instrument of monetary control, since a fractional percentage change in

Table 10.1   RESERVE REQUIREMENTS ON DEPOSITS OF MEMBER BANKS

(requirements are in percent of deposits)

Type of Deposit, and Deposit Interval in Millions of Dollars	Requirements in Effect April 30, 1978		Previous Requirements*	
	Percent	Effective Date	Percent	Effective Date
Net demand†				
0–2	7	12/30/76	7½	2/13/75
2–10	9½	12/30/76	10	2/13/75
10–100	11¾	12/30/76	12	2/13/75
100–400	12¾	12/30/76	13	2/13/75
Over 400	16¼	12/30/76	16½	2/13/75
Time†‡				
Savings	3	3/16/67	3½	3/2/67
Other time:				
0–5, maturing in—				
30–179 days	3	3/16/67	3½	3/2/67
180 days to 4 years	2½§	1/8/76	3	3/16/67
4 years or more	1§	10/30/75	3	3/16/67
Over 5, maturing in—				
30–179 days	6	12/12/74	5	10/1/70
180 days to 4 years	2½§	1/8/76	3	12/12/74
4 years or more	1	10/30/75	3	12/12/74

	Legal limits, April 30, 1978	
	Minimum	Maximum
Net demand		
Reserve city banks	10	22
Other banks	7	14
Time	3	10

*For changes in reserve requirements beginning 1963, see Board's *Annual Statistical Digest, 1971–1975* and for prior changes, see Board's *Annual Report* for 1976, Table 13.

†(a) Requirement schedules are graduated, and each deposit interval applies to that part of the deposits of each bank. Demand deposits subject to reserve requirements are gross demand deposits minus cash items in process of collection and demand balances due from domestic banks.

(b) The Federal Reserve Act specifies different ranges of requirements for reserve city banks and for other banks. Reserve cities are designated under a criterion adopted effective Nov. 9, 1972, by which a bank having net demand deposits of more than $400 million is considered to have the character of business of a reserve city bank. The presence of the head office of such a bank constitutes designation of that place as a reserve city. Cities in which there are Federal Reserve banks or branches are also reserve cities. Any banks having net demand deposits of $400 million or less are considered to have the character of business of banks outside of reserve cities and are permitted to maintain reserves at ratios set for banks not in reserve cities. For details, see the Board's Regulation D.

(c) The Board's Regulation M requires a 4 percent reserve against net balances due from domestic banks to their foreign branches and to foreign banks abroad. Effective Dec. 1, 1977, a 1 percent reserve is required against deposits that foreign branches of U.S. banks use for lending to U.S. residents. Loans aggregating $100,000 or less to any U.S. resident are excluded from computations, as are total loans of a bank to U.S. residents if not exceeding $1 million. Regulation D imposes a similar reserve requirement on borrowings from foreign banks by domestic offices of a member bank.

‡Negotiable orders of withdrawal (NOW) accounts and time deposits such as Christmas and vacation club accounts are subject to the same requirements as savings deposits.

§The average of reserves on savings and other time deposits must be at least 3 percent, the minimum specified by law.

Source: Federal Reserve Bulletin, May 1978, p. A9.

requirements affects a large volume of excess reserves. In addition, since changes in required reserve ratios apply to each individual bank included within the particular classification of member banks subject to the new ratios, careful advance study must be made of the impact on individual member banks.

The heavy impact of reserve requirement changes is shown in the reserve requirements that became effective in early November 1972. Reserve restructuring, along with the temporary waiver of penalties for reserve deficiencies arising from this restructuring and from the changed check-collection procedures, released an estimated $3.5 billion of reserves to the banking system. This reserve injection was offset partly by a $2 billion reduction in Federal Reserve float stemming from the collection arrangements. Defensive open market operations neutralized the impact on the monetary system of the $1.5 billion net release of reserves.

Just as in the case of discount rate changes, changes in reserve requirements carry considerable psychological or announcement effects through their influence on the expectations of businesspeople and financial institutions. Here again the precise nature and extent of these effects are largely uncertain and unpredictable.

Some Proposals Relating to Reserve Requirements

Various observers have recommended modifications in policy governing reserve requirements. One view, recognizing that reserve requirement changes constitute a powerful weapon that is too cumbersome for frequent use, suggests that reserve requirements be permanently fixed at an appropriate level and that uniform reserve requirements for demand deposits be established for all commercial banks.[6] This approach stresses the absence of any logical basis for differentiating among banks in the application of reserve ratios against demand deposits and regards uniform requirements as enhancing the precision of open market policy as a device for controlling monetary aggregates.

Another proposal involves the application of structured reserve requirements against bank assets rather than deposit liabilities. The rationale for this

6. Warren L. Smith, "The Instruments of General Monetary Control," *National Banking Review* 1 (September 1963): 75.

approach is that setting required reserve ratios at different levels for different kinds of assets would tend to encourage banks to extend credit to specified types of borrowers. Since reserve requirements specify the percentage of deposits that must be held as reserves, that is, bank funds not available to the banks for lending and investing, the level of reserve requirements is inversely related to bank profitability. Hence a differential reserve requirement upon assets would tend to induce banks to hold those assets with the lowest reserve requirements. Proponents of this view would have the central bank actively assist such sectors as housing and agriculture, whose economic well-being is judged to be so essential to the nation's welfare as to require special measures ensuring their credit accommodation.

The proposal for asset reserve requirements raises several difficult administrative and philosophical issues. Some of the more obvious questions are the following:

1. What social priorities and what authority shall determine the relative asset reserve requirements?

2. How would nonmember banks and the nonbank sector of the money and capital markets be included in such a scheme?

3. How will the timing and the degree of change in relative asset reserve requirements be instituted to have the desired impact on credit allocation?

4. What is the effect of asset reserve requirements on the relation between reserves and the money supply?

Given satisfactory answers to these complex questions, we can still criticize the use of asset reserve requirements. This approach still overlooks the basic source of the problem, which is not bank portfolio behavior but the existing structure and functioning of financial markets.[7]

A SELECTIVE APPROACH TO MONETARY CONTROL

The authorities can utilize selective as well as general monetary controls. A selective approach to monetary control, which can include either compulsory

7. See Arnold Dill, "Selective Credit Controls: The Experience and Recent Interest," Federal Reserve Bank of Atlanta, *Monthly Review* (May 1971): 85f.

or voluntary features, attempts to supplement general or quantitative controls by affecting the terms and conditions surrounding particular kinds of credit. The Federal Reserve has relied mainly on the use of general monetary instruments to affect the total supply of money and credit and the general level of interest rates, thus allowing market forces to allocate credit among various uses.

Although the central banking system concerns itself primarily with aggregate, rather than specific, credit flows, the United States has had considerable experience with selective credit controls. Especially during wartime, direct credit controls on consumer installment credit and on real estate credit (the latter instituted during the Korean War) attempted to conserve financial resources for the war effort and to lessen inflationary pressures. During peacetime, selective credit controls have been employed particularly when special factors restrained the use of general monetary controls or when their use might have produced undesirable side effects. These peacetime efforts have been directed toward limiting the growth of specialized types of credit—namely, stock market credit and foreign lending—without retarding the expansion of other types of credit.

Compulsory Selective Controls

Compulsory selective controls have covered three areas: stock market credit, consumer installment credit, and real estate credit. Currently, stock market credit is the only area subject to compulsory control.

The Securities Exchange Act of 1934 authorized the Board of Governors of the Federal Reserve System to establish margin requirements for the purchase and carrying of securities listed on national exchanges. *Margin requirements* determine the percentage downpayment required when borrowing to finance purchases or holdings of these securities. These requirements apply to credit extended by various lenders: brokers and dealers (via Regulation T), banks (via Regulation U), and other lenders (via Regulation G). Table 10.2 shows margin requirements over various periods. Note that Regulation G and special margin requirements for bonds convertible into stocks were adopted by the Board of Governors effective March 11, 1968. The effectiveness of these controls has been enhanced by their wide coverage of sources of stock market

---

Table 10.2 MARGIN REQUIREMENTS
(*percent of market value*)

Type of Security on Sale	Mar. 11, 1968	June 8, 1968	May 6, 1970	Dec. 6, 1971	Nov. 24, 1972	Jan. 3, 1974
1. Margin stocks	70	80	65	55	65	50
2. Convertible bonds	50	60	50	50	50	50
3. Short sales	70	80	65	55	65	50

Note: Regulations G, T, and U of the Federal Reserve Board of Governors, prescribed in accordance with the Securities Exchange Act of 1934, limit the amount of credit to purchase and carry margin stocks that may be extended on securities as collateral by prescribing a maximum loan value, which is a specified percentage of the market value of the collateral at the time the credit is extended. Margin requirements are the difference between the market value (100 percent) and the maximum loan value. The term *margin stocks* is defined in the corresponding regulation.

Regulation G and special margin requirements for bonds convertible into stocks were adopted by the Board of Governors effective Mar. 11, 1968.

Source: Federal Reserve Bulletin, May 1978, p. A10.

---

credit and by generally favorable support among the financial community and the general public.[8]

Regulation of consumer installment credit was imposed during World War II and twice in the immediate postwar period as well as during the Korean War. Regulation W of the Board of Governors stipulated minimum downpayments and maximum repayment periods for purchase of major consumer durables.

In 1951–1952, at the height of the Korean War effort, Federal Reserve Regulation X pertaining to real estate was instituted, along with companion regulations by the Federal Housing Administration and Veterans Administration. These regulations set maximum loan values and maturities for credit extended for purchasing new one- or two-family houses. Administrative difficulties inherent in this area of control are evidenced by the fact that

---

8. Under provisions of the Foreign Bank Secrecy Act of 1970, the Board of Governors is authorized to extend margin requirements to borrowers. Regulation was extended to borrowers in the fall of 1971, whereby all United States citizens and residents must comply with margin requirements when borrowing from domestic or foreign lenders on securities transactions.

Regulation X was amended some ten times during 1951, while Regulation W was amended five times in the same period. Particular difficulties affecting real estate credit control included the large amount of building already under way, a heavy overhang of financing commitments outstanding, and the exclusion of loans on existing property.

Voluntary Approaches to Credit Control

In addition to the more rigid compulsory selective controls just described, voluntary cooperation by various lending institutions has been sought in allocating credit among different uses. Here, rather than relying on strict coercion, the authorities apply *moral suasion,* that is, friendly persuasion, to influence lenders' actions along desired lines. Some prominent examples of voluntary programs can be cited.

After the outbreak of the Korean War in June 1950 the demands of the military build-up coincided with a cyclical upswing in economic activity, marked by growing price inflation. The imposition of direct controls on consumer installment credit and real estate credit in the fall of 1950 was followed by the Federal Reserve's initiation of a Voluntary Credit Restraint Program in March 1951. Enlisting the support of representatives from the major financial industries, the program attempted to channel credit into areas of "essential production" and away from areas that served only to achieve transfers of ownership, speculative purchases of property or commodities, or the production of "nonessential" items. In judging the program a success, the Board of Governors noted several special conditions surrounding the successful undertaking of this voluntary effort: rapid price inflation, accompanied by rising speculation and appreciable growth in private credit; vigorous use of general credit restraints; and selective credit regulations in those specific areas where experience indicated they could be effective. Without these conditions, the board observed, it would have been difficult to generate community acceptance and support, which are vital underpinnings for a voluntary program.

Furthermore, in an effort to reduce large and persistent deficits in the United States balance of payments, the authorities instituted the Voluntary Foreign Credit Restraint Program in February 1965. The program requested banks and other financial institutions to keep holdings of foreign loans and securities within limits, expressed as a percentage of earlier outstanding levels. In the following month (March 1965) the Voluntary Cooperation Program invited the cooperation of nonfinancial firms in dampening capital outflows by returning more foreign earnings to the United States, repatriating short-term funds attracted abroad by higher interest earnings, adhering to target levels of direct investment spending in developed countries, and resorting to more borrowing from abroad. At the start of 1968 the Voluntary Cooperation Program became mandatory, and other programs bearing on the balance-of-payments problem were expanded.

Finally, beginning in November 1971, President Nixon's new economic program included a Committee on Interest and Dividends. Headed by Arthur F. Burns, chairman of the Federal Reserve's Board of Governors, the committee's role involved obtaining voluntary restraint of both interest rates and dividend payments. For example, the committee recommended that cash dividend payments for 1972 on common stock be held to a 4 percent increase over the highest dividend payment for any fiscal year ending in the three-year period from 1969 through 1971. These programs ended in early 1974.

In March 1973 the committee opposed several large commercial banks in their half-point hike in the prime interest rate, the minimum rate charged their most credit-worthy business borrowers. In this confrontation the committee stressed that boosts in lending rates must be justified by increases in the cost of deposits and other funds. Although the committee could not compel a rollback in rates, the president had such authority under the provisions of the Economic Stabilization Act of 1970, which provided the legislative basis for Nixon's economic game plan.

After grudgingly assenting to two quarter-point increases that nudged the prime rate to 6.5 percent in March 1973, the committee adopted a dual rate system in April of that year. Under this system, commercial banks could make more frequent rate increases on loans to prime business customers but were expected to make few changes in rates charged small businesses and consumers. With this new arrangement, the prime business loan rate reached 10 percent by mid-September 1973. This record level reflected fourteen separate quarter-point adjustments in the rate since March 1973. The committee ceased operations in April 1974.

The double-digit price inflation of 1974 prompted the Federal Advisory Council of the Federal Reserve in September 1974 to warn all member commercial banks against making loans for speculative purposes. Then, in October, President Ford announced a highly publicized voluntary effort against inflation. This "jawbone" approach exhorted all citizens to act to "whip inflation now" (WIN) and to demonstrate their support by wearing a specially designed WIN button.[9] The enthusiastic promotion of the WIN campaign was short-lived, as mounting evidence indicated that the United States economy was suffering from both its worst recession and its worst inflation since World War II. These and other instances show the temporary appeal but ultimate ineffectiveness of voluntary efforts in economic stabilization programs within the United States.

SELECTIVE CREDIT CONTROLS: SOME LESSONS LEARNED

Generally, the United States has been marginally successful in its use of selective credit controls. At the same time, operating results indicate that selective controls engender some serious administrative and enforcement difficulties. Together with a general distaste for direct economic regulation, these difficulties partly explain the limited emphasis on selective controls in the United States.

Administrative costs constitute an obvious limitation in the use of selective devices. Once the controls and designation of the administrative authority are authorized, considerable staff work is required to draft, execute, and enforce the regulations. Groups subject to the regulations need to be informed of their responsibilities, particularly with regard to maintaining files and submitting reports. Compliance must be checked and, in the case of compulsory controls, legal action taken against offenders. Constant review of operating results suggests frequent need to amend regulations to eliminate loopholes and to adjust the effects of the controls. These red-tape aspects generate considerable public and private expense, especially as controls grow in complexity and coverage.

A major shortcoming of selective credit controls is the difficulty of effective enforcement, aggravated by ease of evasion arising from the substitutability of various sources and types of credit. For example, sometimes securities speculators have indirectly financed their portfolios by financing durable goods or mortgaging real estate holdings. The easy substitutability of various

---

9. A brief, humorously written but factual account of the inception of the WIN button campaign is given in "The Talk of the Town: Button, Button," *The New Yorker,* October 21, 1974, pp. 32–33.

sources of credit implies that effective control can only be achieved if regulations cover all sources of a given type of credit.

Formidable enforcement problems emphasize the basic need for strong public support in order to achieve reasonable compliance with selective controls. Such public support was generally evident during periods of wartime emergency, when there was widespread acceptance of the necessity for government interference in economic decisions. As the height of the emergency passed, however, compliance tended to deteriorate, as evidenced by the experience with installment credit regulations after World War II and near the end of the Korean War. Overall, the record of United States experience with selective credit controls indicates that despite inherent administrative and operational difficulties, these controls will be used to supplement general monetary policies, especially as new forces and conditions impinge on economic stabilization policy.

MONETARY CONTROLS OF
FOREIGN CENTRAL BANKS

We can supplement the analysis of monetary controls used by the Federal Reserve by examining briefly the major instruments of monetary control utilized by important foreign central banks.[10] Table 10.3 compares the monetary operations conducted by eleven foreign central banks. The information contained in the table indicates a wide range of activities and endeavors that are not ordinarily pursued by the Federal Reserve.

It is evident that most of the foreign central banks are quite active in channeling credit into priority uses. Also, balance-of-payments considerations loom large in the activities of many of these banks. Although these considerations influence United States monetary policy, they are a less sensitive factor for the United States than for most other countries.

Open market policy, the most important monetary control of the Federal Reserve, plays a significant role in the operations of the central banks of West

10. This section is based largely on information presented in Nicholas A. Lash's article "Commentary on Central Bank Activities," Federal Reserve Bank of Chicago, *Business Conditions* (April 1971): 6–11. The article summarizes the main results of a survey of activities of eleven central banks, contained in *Activities by Various Central Banks to Promote Economic and Social Welfare Programs*, House Committee on Banking and Currency, 91st Congress, 2d Session, 1970.

Table 10.3   A COMPARISON OF CENTRAL BANK OPERATIONS FOR MAJOR COUNTRIES

Country	I Market Too Weak for Open Market Operations*	II Differential Discount Policy†	III Differential Reserve Requirements‡	IV Foreign Exchange Considerations§	V Significant Use of Moral Suasion
Banque de France France	•	•	•	•	
Reserve Bank of India India	•	•			•
Bank of Israel Israel	•	•	•	•	•
Banca D'Italia Italy	•	•	•	•	•
Nihon Ginko Japan	•	•			•
Banco de Mexico Mexico	•	•	•	•	
Nederlandsche Bank Netherlands	•			•	•
Sveriges Riksbank Sweden	•		•	•	•
Bank of England United Kingdom			•	•	•
Federal Reserve System United States					
Deutsche Bundesbank West Germany		•	•	•	
Natodna Banka Jugoslavize Yugoslavia	•	•			•

*Market too weak for extensive operations compared with the United States.
†Certain classes of loans given preference at discount windows.
‡Certain classes of loans allowed to satisfy reserve requirements.
§Monetary policy complicated significantly by foreign exchange considerations.

Source: Nicholas A. Lash, "Commentary on Central Bank Activities," Federal Reserve Bank of Chicago, *Business Conditions* April 1971, pp. 8, 9.

Table 10.3   (cont.)

Country	VI Direct Credit Controls	VII Exports	VIII Housing	IX Agri-culture	X Indus-tries for Economic Growth	XI State & Local Govern-ment
				Support of		
Banque de France France	•	•	•	•	•	•
Reserve Bank of India India	•	•		•	•	•
Bank of Israel Israel	•	•				
Banca D'Italia Italy	•		•	•		•
Nihon Ginko Japan	•	•	•	•	•	•
Banco de Mexico Mexico		•	•	•	•	•
Nederlandsche Bank Netherlands	•	•				
Sveriges Riksbank Sweden	•	•	•	•	•	
Bank of England United Kingdom	•	•				
Federal Reserve System United States						
Deutsche Bundesbank West Germany	•			•		•
Natodna Banka Jugoslavize Yugoslavia		•			•	

Germany and the United Kingdom. It is little used in other European countries, however, because money and capital markets are either underdeveloped or are linked sensitively to the European money market. The central banks in Israel and Japan place minor emphasis on open market operations, and other non-European countries even less. On the other hand, many of the eleven foreign central banks rely more heavily on discount and reserve requirement policies than does the Federal Reserve. For example, discount policy is a major control of the Bank of Japan, which has financed an appreciable part of Japan's rapid economic growth via credit extended to commercial banks.

Most of these foreign central banks often employ the device of moral suasion, that is, persuasive influence on commercial bank activities. Commercial banking in these countries is highly concentrated or owned largely by the national government. These features permit more effective use of moral suasion than in the United States, with its thousands of privately owned commercial banks. The Bank of England, for example, traditionally holds strong persuasive influence in the close-knit London banking community. In Italy, effective moral suasion is supported by heavy government ownership of commercial banking, prestige accorded the governor of the central bank, and threats of sanctions against banks. Moral suasion is sometimes linked with direct credit controls in order to encourage banks to provide credit for certain uses. The Bank of Sweden's annual credit agreement, an important feature in its monetary operations, suggests recommended areas for credit granting by commercial banks.

Some foreign central banks, as shown in Table 10.3, use various measures to channel credit into specific areas: exempting certain kinds of loans from credit ceilings, according preference to these loans for rediscounting purposes, and allowing certain loans to satisfy reserve requirements. Typically, sectors accorded such favorable treatment include housing, agriculture, state and local governments, exports, and industries essential for economic development.

Some U.S. officials want the Federal Reserve to copy the credit allocation activities of foreign central banks to some extent, especially those banks in Western Europe. However, several significant issues need clarification regarding this policy question. These foreign experiences have incurred certain costs, especially through the reduction of competition within financial markets and the greater extension of administrative controls. Furthermore, relatively little information exists about the effectiveness of these foreign credit allocation programs. Finally, American financial markets differ greatly from those of Western Europe, particularly in their level of development, extent of restriction, and degree of competition.

In examining these different techniques of monetary control, note that measures effectively used in other countries may not necessarily be appro-

priate for the United States. Basic differences in the economic structure and composition of financial and commercial markets, as well as fundamental philosophical differences, suggest that no uniform guidelines exist for planning monetary strategies in various nations.

KEY TERMS

General monetary controls
Selective monetary controls
Open market operations
Bills-only policy
Discount policy

Seasonal borrowing privilege
Announcement effects
Margin requirements
Moral suasion

REVIEW QUESTIONS

1. Distinguish between general and selective monetary controls used by the Federal Reserve.

2. Summarize briefly the evolution of Federal Reserve open market operations prior to 1935.

3. Explain briefly how Federal Reserve open market operations are actually conducted.

4. Using T accounts, illustrate the monetary effects of Federal Reserve open market purchases and sales of securities.

5. What secondary effects are associated with Federal Reserve open market operations?

6. Indicate briefly the meaning and significance of each of the following developments affecting Federal Reserve open market operations:
    a. bond-support policy
    b. Treasury–Federal Reserve accord
    c. bills-only policy
    d. Operation Twist

7. In the early years of the Federal Reserve, how was discount policy affected by the real-bills doctrine?

8. Outline current Federal Reserve views relating to administration of the discount window.

9. Examine briefly the effects that changes in the discount rate have on member bank borrowing.

10. Trace briefly the evolution of Federal Reserve policy relating to reserve requirements.

11. Explain how changes in reserve requirements affect bank reserves and the money supply.

12. What are some proposals to modify policy governing reserve requirements?

13. What is the rationale in the use of selective credit controls?

14. Contrast the use of compulsory and voluntary approaches to selective credit controls in the United States.

15. What limitations affect the use of selective credit controls?

16. In general, how do techniques of monetary control used by major foreign central banks compare with those of the Federal Reserve?

SUGGESTED READINGS

Boehne, Edward G. "Falling Fed Membership and Eroding Monetary Control: What Can be Done?" Federal Reserve Bank of Philadelphia, *Business Review* (June 1974): 3–15.

Cacy, J.A. "Reserve Requirements and Monetary Control." Federal Reserve Bank of Kansas City, *Monthly Review* (May 1976): 3–13.

"Complying with Consumer Credit Regulations: A Challenge." *Federal Reserve Bulletin* 63 (September 1977): 769–774.

Kaminow, Ira, and James M. O'Brien. "Selective Credit Policies: Should Their Role Be Expanded?" Federal Reserve Bank of Philadelphia, *Business Review* (November 1976): 3–22.

Lang, Richard W. "The Federal Open Market Committee in 1977." Federal Reserve Bank of St. Louis, *Review* (March 1978): 2–21.

Knight, Robert E. "Reserve Requirements Part I: Comparative Reserve Requirements at Member and Nonmember Banks." Federal Reserve Bank of Kansas City, *Monthly Review* (April 1974): 3–20.

Knight, Robert E. "Reserve Requirements Part II: An Analysis of the Case for Uniform Reserve Requirements." Federal Reserve Bank of Kansas City, *Monthly Review* (May 1974): 3–15.

O'Brien, James M. "Central Banking Across the Atlantic: Another Dimension." Federal Reserve Bank of Philadelphia, *Business Review* (May 1975): 3–12.

O'Brien, James M. "Federal Regulation of Stock Market Credit: A Need for Reconsideration." Federal Reserve Bank of Philadelphia, *Business Review* (July-August 1974): 23–33.

Poole, William. "The Making of Monetary Policy: Description and Analysis." Federal Reserve Bank of Boston, *New England Economic Review* (March-April 1975): 21–30.

Chapter Eleven

THE TREASURY AND MONETARY CONTROL

The Treasury comprises the third major sector of any modern monetary system, although its primary power is fiscal. As in the cases of the commercial banking system and the central banking system, certain activities of the national Treasury can affect the supply, cost, and availability of money and credit. These monetary influences can arise from various Treasury operations. For example, the Treasury has certain monetary authority accorded it by law. Prior to the establishment of the two-tier gold market in March 1968, Treasury policy governing the buying and selling of gold represented an important use of its statutory monetary powers. Less obvious but more significant monetary effects arise from Treasury fiscal activities involving deficit-financing operations and from the handling of tax surpluses. Finally, varied monetary influences are inherent in the Treasury's management of the existing public or national debt. This chapter examines these different aspects of Treasury influence on monetary conditions as well as some implications for monetary policy.

MONETARY POWERS OF THE TREASURY

Although the Federal Reserve exercises primary control over the monetary system, the Treasury possesses some statutory authority that affects the working of the monetary system. Federal Reserve policy actions allow for the monetary impact of these and other Treasury operations. The Treasury's specific monetary powers arise largely from monetary legislation enacted by Congress. Treasury monetary actions relate essentially to the issuance of

Treasury currency and to its gold operations. Historically, Treasury policy governing silver had an impact on the monetary sector, but today silver plays no role in the monetary system.

Issuance of Treasury Currency

As shown in an earlier chapter, the Treasury issues a small fraction of the coin and paper currency used by the general public. This issuance of Treasury currency is reflected in Treasury currency outstanding, a factor supplying reserves in the member bank reserve equation. Treasury currency is issued in response to the needs of the general public for pocket money or "hand-to-hand money." The monetary effects connected with Treasury issuance of currency can be illustrated by the following T accounts:

FEDERAL RESERVE

Cash items +	Deposits: Treasury +(−) Member banks (+)

MEMBER BANKS

Deposits at Federal Reserve (+)	Demand deposits (+)

In the first instance, the shipment of Treasury currency to the Federal Reserve creates an equivalent increase in the cash items asset account and in the Treasury's deposit account in the Federal Reserve. Subsequently, as the Treasury draws checks on its Federal Reserve account and as the recipients of these checks make primary deposits in member banks, the reserve account of member banks increases, with an appropriate decline in the Treasury's account. The changes for the second-phase transactions are shown in parentheses. The initial increase in Treasury currency outstanding has caused an increase in member bank reserve holdings. In this transaction the Treasury utilizes the Federal Reserve as a channel through which Treasury currency is eventually routed to the general public. As the general public requires Treasury currency, the currency shipments will be made from the Federal Reserve to the commercial banks, which will then meet their customers' requests for deposit withdrawals.

Treasury Gold Operations

Prior to 1968 the Treasury's monetary power relating to gold was an important factor in the monetary system. Erection of the two-tier gold market in March 1968 and the closing of the United States gold window to official foreign holders of dollars in August 1971 ended Treasury gold operations on any sustained basis. Nevertheless, when conducted, Treasury gold operations have a direct effect on member bank reserves and the money supply. Gold purchases, for example, increase member bank reserves and the money supply, whereas gold sales have the opposite effect. Since August 1971, Treasury gold operations have been fairly infrequent, except for two developments. One of these developments relates to the two increases in the official price of gold in the early 1970s; the other involves the piecemeal and infrequent sale of Treasury gold following legalization of gold ownership for U.S. citizens at the very end of 1974.

The United States, along with other major nations, announced an increase in gold's official price to $38 per ounce at the Smithsonian Agreement of December 1971; a subsequent price increase to $42.22 was declared in February 1973. In turn, the United States Congress twice enacted legislation—in May 1972 and in October 1973—directing the Treasury, as the official custodian or holder of the gold stock, to value gold at the new price. In effect, on these two separate occasions the Treasury accrued an "inventory valuation profit" on a gold stock of more than 275 million ounces. Specifically, the Treasury obtained some $2 billion in profit from these two increases in gold's official price: $800 million from the rise to $38 per ounce in May 1972 and $1.2 billion from the increase to $42.22 per ounce in October 1973. On the basis of the increased valuation for its gold stock, the Treasury issued additional paper gold certificates to the Federal Reserve banks, thus increasing the Treasury's deposits at the Federal Reserve by $2 billion. When the Treasury spends these funds by drawing checks on its Federal Reserve deposit account, it monetizes the increased dollar value of the gold stock, which ultimately results in an increase in member bank reserves and the money supply. This expansionary effect on the monetary sector is a one-time effect and can be offset partially or wholly by discretionary Federal Reserve actions affecting its open market operations. Data for the Federal Reserve's average holdings of government securities indicate that the Federal Reserve allowed the expansionary effects to occur following the May 1972 gold monetization, but offset them following the October 1973 gold monetization by means of open market sales.

After the United States legalized gold ownership for its citizens on December 31, 1974, the Treasury sold gold twice during 1975. In January 1975 some three-quarters of a million ounces of gold were sold, followed in June by the sale of about one-half million ounces, at an average bid price in each instance of approximately $165 per ounce. The immediate monetary effects of these two gold sales were contractionary: member bank reserves and money supply M_1 decreased as the gold buyers' checks were deposited in the Treasury's deposit account at the Federal Reserve. These changes ultimately occur whether the gold is sold to domestic or to foreign buyers. In order to buy gold from the Treasury, a foreign buyer must have dollars. Hence when payment is made for the gold, foreigners' demand deposits at U.S. commercial banks decrease. Since the U.S. money stock includes foreign-owned deposits, the analysis would be the same as when demand deposits of U.S. residents decline. Finally, note that the Treasury accrued some profit because it sold gold valued on its books at $42.22 an ounce to buyers at an average price of over $165 an ounce. This capital appreciation produced an increase in the Treasury's net worth of some $155 million.

For the foreseeable future the Treasury most likely will not buy gold either from other central banks or from the market, but may ocasionally sell some of its gold stock. For example, in the spring of 1978 the Treasury announced plans to sell gold at a series of monthly public auctions. Some 300,000 ounces of gold were to be sold at each of the first six auctions. The Treasury would then review the results of these auctions to determine whether the gold amounts offered at future auctions should be changed. In May 1978 the Treasury's first gold auction in almost three years brought an average price of over $180 an ounce. By November 1978 these monthly gold offerings had more than doubled to 750,000 ounces. In December 1978 Treasury gold offerings had increased greatly to a monthly volume of 1.5 million ounces.

MONETARY ASPECTS OF
FISCAL POLICY

The Treasury can and does exert a considerable impact upon the economy in the area of *fiscal policy,* which involves actions affecting the federal government's receipts and expenditures for the purpose of promoting economic stabilization. Fiscal policy, in contrast to monetary policy, directly affects aggregate demand by changing the income available to spending units via tax and expenditure policies. Technically, Congress ultimately determines fiscal policy by taxing and spending legislation. As is often said, "The administration proposes and the Congress disposes." In turn, the Treasury is primarily responsible for executing fiscal policy. This responsibility relates especially to Treasury tasks that apply when an imbalance exists between tax receipts and expenditures. A deficit or a surplus in the budget necessitates the raising or disposition of Treasury funds. These financial actions carry important effects on bank reserves and the money supply. Thus fiscal policy not only has direct effects on income but also generates indirect effects on the monetary system. To fully appreciate the Treasury's role in the monetary sphere we must examine these monetary aspects of fiscal policy. Essentially, these aspects include the impact on bank reserves and on the money supply of various approaches to financing a tax deficit or to disposing of a tax surplus.

DEFICIT-FINANCING
ALTERNATIVES

Several options are open for financing a net tax deficit. A simple, though limited, short-run expedient is for the Treasury to cover the extra spending by running down its cash balances. In this case, the spending of funds from the Treasury's disbursing accounts in the Federal Reserve banks would tend to increase the general public's money supply and bank reserves. However, if the Treasury replenished its Federal Reserve accounts by making a subsequent call on its tax and loan accounts in commercial banks, then bank reserves would be reduced to their original level. Since the Treasury requires adequate cash balances for day-to-day operating purposes, there is some urgency in rebuilding these depleted cash balances. Use of cash balances to finance a deficit simply provides breathing space for the Treasury until other, long-run sources of funds can be tapped, for example, through borrowing.

Treasury borrowing through the issuance of new government securities is the major method for financing a budget deficit. Several alternatives are open for Treasury borrowing, each of which has different effects on the money supply and bank reserves. Thus depending on who buys the new securities from the Treasury, the effects on the monetary system will differ greatly. Buyers of new Treasury securities can be classified into three general groups: (1) the nonbank (or general) public, including individuals, business corporations, and nonbank financial institutions; (2) commercial banks; and (3) Federal Reserve banks. The monetary effects of Treasury borrowing from each of these three groups can be illustrated by use of the now-familiar T accounts.

Borrowing from the Nonbank Public

Borrowing from the nonbank public has relatively neutral effects on the monetary system in that the money supply and bank reserves are unchanged. The T accounts shown in Table 11.1 illustrate the effects of each of the constituent phases or transactions connected with borrowing from the general public to cover a current tax deficit. Transaction 1 indicates the sale of the new Treasury securities to the bond-buying groups in the general public, with the decline in the demand deposits of the general public offset by an equivalent increase in tax and loan accounts of the Treasury. Transaction 2 shows the inevitable effects on commercial banks of the Treasury's call on tax and loan accounts: bank reserves decrease to the extent of the call. Transaction 3, reflecting the Treasury's drawing on its disbursing accounts in the Federal Reserve, shows the restoration of the general public's demand deposits and bank reserves as primary deposits are made by individuals receiving checks from the Treasury and as these checks clear against the Treasury's accounts in the Federal Reserve.

Stated simply, the Treasury has borrowed funds from the bond buyers in the general public and then has returned these funds to the general public to cover expenditures in excess of current tax receipts. What one hand has taken away by borrowing, the other hand has returned by the payment of amounts owing to the general public. Although the money supply and bank reserves are unchanged by this approach to financing a tax deficit, the average velocity

Table 11.1   T ACCOUNTS SHOWING THE MONETARY EFFECTS OF
DEFICIT FINANCING
(Treasury borrows from general public)

Trans-action Number	Transaction	Federal Reserve		Member Banks	
1.	Sale of new Treasury securities to general public				Deposits of securities buyers −
					Tax and loan accounts +
2.	Treasury call on tax and loan accounts		Deposits: Member banks − Treasury +	Deposits at FR −	Tax and loan accounts −
3.	Treasury draws checks to pay accounts payable and checks clear		Deposits: Member banks + Treasury −	Deposits at FR +	Deposits of payees +
	Net results of all transactions	No net changes		No net changes	

or rate of turnover of money may be increased. This velocity effect arises from the increase in net claims of the public against the government as a result of the public's acquisition of new Treasury securities. The growth in net claims tends to push up interest rates, with varied effects: (1) private spending on goods and services may decline; (2) individuals economize on their cash holdings; and (3) banks adjust their reserve positions by increased borrowings and reductions in excess reserve holdings. The net impact of these reactions, linked with the initial government spending, is to raise velocity.

Borrowing from Commercial Banks

If the Treasury borrows by selling new securities to commercial banks with excess lending capacity, the commercial banking system monetizes the federal government's debt, thus eventually enlarging the money supply of the general

Table 11.2   T ACCOUNTS SHOWING THE MONETARY EFFECTS OF
DEFICIT FINANCING
(Treasury borrows from commercial banks)

Transaction Number	Transaction	Federal Reserve		Member Banks	
1.	Sale of new Treasury securities to commercial banks			Securities +	Tax and loan accounts +
2.	Treasury call on tax and loan accounts		Deposits: Member banks − Treasury +	Deposits at FR −	Tax and loan accounts −
3.	Treasury draws checks to pay accounts payable and checks clear		Deposits: Member banks + Treasury −	Deposits at FR +	Deposits of payees +
	Net results of all transactions	No net changes		Securities +	Deposits of payees +

public. As shown in the T accounts in Table 11.2, the net effect of Treasury borrowing from commercial banks is to increase demand deposits owned by the general public. The increase in deposit liabilities of the commercial banking system, with no change in total reserve holdings, implies a reduction in excess reserves for commercial banks.

However, if commercial banks were fully loaned up, their purchase of new Treasury securities would require liquidation of an equivalent amount of loans or investments. This liquidation would decrease the general public's money holdings, offsetting the increase resulting from the excess of government expenditures over tax receipts. In adjusting their portfolios, commercial banks substitute new Treasury securities for other loans or investments, with an increase in net claims against the government. Thus the net results for the monetary system would be the same as if the Treasury had borrowed from the nonbank public, as described in the previous section. Furthermore, as indicated earlier, a deficit means that the Treasury is a net *demander* of funds and thus tends to put upward pressure on interest rates.

Table 11.3 T ACCOUNTS SHOWING THE MONETARY EFFECTS OF
DEFICIT FINANCING
(Treasury borrows from the Federal Reserve)

Trans-action Number	Transaction	Federal Reserve		Member Banks	
1.	Sale of new Treasury securities to Federal Reserve	Securities +	Deposits: Treasury +		
2.	Treasury draws checks to pay accounts payable and checks clear		Deposits: Member banks + Treasury −	Deposits at FR +	Deposits of payees +
	Net results of all transactions	Securities +	Deposits: Member banks +	Deposits at FR +	Deposits of payees +

Borrowing from the Central Bank

Finally, Treasury borrowing from the Federal Reserve is the most monetarily inflationary way of financing a tax deficit, since both money supply and bank reserves increase. The T accounts given in Table 11.3 indicate that these effects arise when recipients of the Treasury's checks deposit the checks in commercial banks for clearance and collection against Treasury accounts in the Federal Reserve. Since both the money supply and bank reserves increase by the full amount of the Treasury's expenditures of borrowed funds, commercial banks gain excess reserves that can provide the basis for additional deposit creation via lending and "investing." The Federal Reserve is limited to an outstanding amount of $5 billion of securities purchased directly from the Treasury. Generally, the Treasury regards this as a temporary source of borrowing, and in practice it is seldom used. The Federal Reserve, however, is not limited effectively in its purchases in the *old* (secondary) issues market for government securities. Federal Reserve open market purchases in the secondary market can supply additional bank reserves, which in turn may be used by commercial banks to monetize *new* Treasury debt issues sold to commercial banks.

In our examination of the varied monetary effects of the different deficit-financing alternatives, we stressed the impact on money supply and bank reserves. In addition to these more obvious results, borrowing by the sale of new Treasury securities will affect prices and yields in the market for government securities. The precise extent of this impact depends on the dollar volume and type of securities sold as well as on the various factors underlying the demand for Treasury securities. Furthermore, Treasury borrowing to cover a tax deficit may have "crowding-out effects" on private borrowing in financial markets. Chapter 20 analyzes some of the macroeconomic implications of the crowding-out hypothesis.

ALTERNATIVES FOR HANDLING
A TAX SURPLUS

In the presumably happy and infrequent situation of disposing of a tax surplus, the Treasury must consider the different monetary effects of alternative uses of the tax surplus. A tax surplus occurs when tax revenues exceed government expenditures during a given fiscal period. Several options exist for disposing of the surplus. An obvious and relatively simple approach would be for the Treasury to use the tax surplus to build up its cash balances. On the other hand, the Treasury could employ the tax surplus to retire outstanding national debt. Here the net monetary effects of disposing of the surplus would depend on who is selling the securities to the Treasury: the general (nonbank) public, commercial banks, or the Federal Reserve banks.

Surplus Held Idle

If the Treasury chose simply to hold the tax surplus idle in its cash balances, then the initial reduction in the general public's money supply arising from the generation of the tax surplus is allowed to persist; that is, there is a reduction in the money stock M_1. A subsequent transfer of the tax surplus to the Treasury's accounts in the Federal Reserve would also reduce bank reserves. In effect, if the Treasury "sits on" the tax surplus, the monetarily deflationary effects from the initial build-up of the tax surplus continue. These results are shown in the following T accounts:

FEDERAL RESERVE		MEMBER BANKS	
	Deposits: Treasury (+) Member banks (−)	Deposits at Federal Reserve (−)	Deposits: General taxpaying public − Tax and loan accounts + (−)

The build-up of the tax surplus is shown in a reduction of demand deposits of the general taxpaying public and an equivalent increase in Treasury tax and loan accounts in commercial banks. Should the Treasury shift the surplus to its Federal Reserve accounts by making a call on tax and loan accounts, bank reserves would decline, as shown by changes in parentheses.

Retirement of Securities Held by the General (Nonbank) Public

Generally, the Treasury is more likely to use a tax surplus to retire outstanding securities. If securities held by the general (nonbank) public are retired, then the Treasury buys back the securities with the proceeds of the tax surplus. What was extracted from the taxpaying public in the form of the tax surplus is now returned to the bond-holding groups within the general (nonbank) public. Thus, overlooking any possible effects on the velocity of money, retirement of securities held by the general (nonbank) public has neutral effects on the money supply and bank reserves. These results, broken down by phases in the overall operation, are shown in the T accounts in Table 11.4.

Retirement of Securities Held by Commercial Banks

Retirement of securities held by commercial banks permits the original reduction in the general (nonbank) public's money supply to persist, since the tax surplus is not returned to the general public. In this case the demand deposits of the general public have been extinguished through retirement of securities held by commercial banks, as shown in the T accounts presented in Table 11.5. The reduction in commercial bank deposit liabilities, with no change in total reserve holdings, implies an increase in excess reserves for

Table 11.4 T ACCOUNTS SHOWING THE MONETARY EFFECTS OF DISPOSING OF TAX SURPLUS

(Treasury retires securities held by general public)

Trans-action Number	Transaction	Federal Reserve		Member Banks	
1.	Collection of tax surplus and transfer to Treasury account at Federal Reserve		Deposits: Member banks − Treasury +	Deposits at FR −	Deposits of taxpayers −
2.	Treasury draws checks to pay securities holders and checks clear		Deposits: Member banks + Treasury −	Deposits at FR +	Deposits of securities holders +
	Net results of all transactions	No net changes		No net changes	

Table 11.5 T ACCOUNTS SHOWING THE MONETARY EFFECTS OF DISPOSING OF TAX SURPLUS

(Treasury retires securities held by commercial banks)

Trans-action Number	Transaction	Federal Reserve		Member Banks	
1.	Collection of tax surplus and transfer to Treasury account at Federal Reserve		Deposits: Member banks − Treasury +	Deposits at FR −	Deposits of taxpayers −
2.	Treasury draws checks to pay securities holders and checks clear		Deposits: Member banks + Treasury −	Deposits at FR + Securities −	
	Net results of all transactions	No net changes		Securities −	Deposits of taxpayers −

Table 11.6   T ACCOUNTS SHOWING THE MONETARY EFFECTS OF
DISPOSING OF TAX SURPLUS

(Treasury retires securities held by Federal Reserve)

Trans-action Number	Transaction	Federal Reserve		Member Banks	
1.	Collection of tax surplus and transfer to Treasury account at Federal Reserve		Deposits: Member banks − Treasury +	Deposits at FR −	Deposits of taxpayers −
2.	Treasury draws checks to pay securities holders and checks clear	Securities −	Deposits: Treasury −		
	Net results of all transactions	Securities −	Deposits: Member banks −	Deposits at FR −	Deposits of taxpayers −

commercial banks. Monetization of private debt by commercial banks could thus restore the general public's money supply in a subsequent period. The results shown in the T accounts illustrate only the use of the tax surplus to retire securities held by the commercial banks and do not portray any lending by banks on the basis of excess reserves generated by the decline in the taxpayers' demand deposits.

Retirement of Securities Held by the Federal Reserve

Finally, securities held by the Federal Reserve could be retired with a tax surplus. As indicated in the T accounts given in Table 11.6, this alternative for retiring outstanding Treasury securities has maximum deflationary effects on the monetary system, since it reduces both money supply and bank reserves by the amount of the surplus. Assuming the banking system holds excess reserves at the start of the retirement operation, then excess reserves are decreased also. These net monetary effects emerge because the surplus funds do not reappear in the hands of the general public or in the reserve accounts of the member banks. Interestingly, identical results occur when the Treasury holds the surplus idle in its Federal Reserve accounts. In most cases, it is politically more expedient for the Treasury to use a tax surplus to retire outstanding debt than to allow a build-up of its cash balances. Strong public pressure exists for retiring Treasury securities with a tax surplus because of sensitivity to the size of the federal debt and to the not inconsiderable interest-carrying charge on the debt. Thus if debt retirement is to be compatible with economic stabilization efforts, the Treasury must exercise discretion in determining which securities will be retired with a tax surplus.

DEBT-MANAGEMENT POLICY

The varied monetary effects of alternative approaches for financing a tax deficit or for disposing of a tax surplus emphasize the unavoidable impact on monetary conditions of the Treasury's management of the national (or federal) debt. This debt, which reflects the accumulation of tax deficits of prior fiscal years, requires continuous Treasury management operations that can have important implications for the monetary sector.

In an ultimate sense, congressional fiscal policy actions (via taxation and spending legislation) largely determine the size or amount of the national debt. Furthermore, a large part of the national debt is held within the federal government itself, that is, by federal governmental agencies and trust funds and by the Federal Reserve banks, which are quasi-governmental bodies (see Table 11.7). Treasury *debt-management operations* can be defined as actions that affect the composition or structure of the national debt, especially that portion of the national debt held outside the federal government. Specifically, these actions affect various structural aspects of the national debt, such as ownership composition, average term to maturity, interest rates or yields, and other technical offering terms. Strictly speaking, debt management's scope includes all facets of the national debt, except changes in its dollar amount.

The Scope of Debt-Management Operations

That the Treasury's debt-management task is herculean is shown by the fact that each year tens of billions of dollars of new securities are issued to meet cash needs and to refund maturing obligations. Annual Treasury borrowing exceeds that of corporations and state and local governments. Even a budgetary surplus does not necessarily preclude the need for Treasury borrowing.

Table 11.7 ESTIMATED OWNERSHIP OF PUBLIC DEBT SECURITIES, 1972–1978

| | | Held by Gov't Accounts | Held by Federal Reserve | Held by Private Investors | | | | | | |
	Total			Total	Commercial Banks	Mutual Savings Banks and Insurance Companies	Corporations	State & Local Gov'ts	Individuals	Misc. Investors
1972	426.4	111.5	71.4	243.6	60.9	10.2	9.3	26.9	73.2	63.2
1973	457.3	123.4	75.0	258.9	58.8	9.6	9.8	28.8	75.9	76.0
1974	474.2	138.2	80.5	255.6	53.2	8.5	10.8	28.3	80.7	74.2
1975	533.2	145.3	84.7	303.2	69.0	10.6	13.2	31.7	87.1	91.5
1976	620.4	149.6	94.4	376.4	92.5	16.0	24.3	39.3	96.4	107.9
1977	698.8	155.5	104.7	438.6	99.8	20.5	23.3	53.0	103.9	138.1
1978:										
Jan	721.6	151.5	97.0	473.1	100.9	20.9	23.4	56.7	106.1	165.1
Feb	729.8	154.2	98.5	477.1	102.2	20.8	22.3	58.6	106.6	166.6
Mar	738.0	152.7	101.6	483.7	101.1	20.6	20.8	61.2	106.9	173.1
Apr	736.6	153.6	103.5	479.5	100.7	20.4	19.9	61.2	107.1	170.2
May	741.6	159.1	102.8	479.7	98.4	20.5	19.7	60.2	107.7	173.2
Jun	749.0	161.1	110.1	477.8	98.5	20.2	19.0	62.7	108.1	169.3
Jul	750.5	159.3	108.9	482.3	97.7	20.6	20.0	61.7	108.5	173.9
Aug	764.4	163.7	111.7	489.0	95.8	20.6	22.4	69.2	108.9	172.1
Sep	771.5	168.0	115.3	488.3	95.3	20.5	21.5	67.8	109.3	173.9
Oct	776.4	166.3	115.3	494.7	94.3	20.7	21.0	67.1	109.8	181.8
Nov	783.0	167.4	113.3	502.3	93.5	20.4	20.9	69.1	110.2	188.2
Dec	789.2	170.0	110.6	508.6	—	—	—	—	—	—

Source: *Economic Report of the President*, January 1979, p. 272.

For example, in fiscal year 1969, a year marked by a $3.2 billion budgetary surplus, the Treasury had to borrow some $11 billion to meet temporary cash needs in the first half of the fiscal year, which at that time ran from July 1 to June 30.

A major chore facing Treasury debt managers is the refunding, or refinancing, of securities already issued as part of the gross federal debt outstanding. *Refunding* involves the Treasury retiring existing debt by selling new securities in financial markets. The dollar volume and frequency of refunding operations are appreciable. During fiscal 1970, for example, the Treasury exchanged or redeemed for cash about $37 billion in maturing marketable notes and bonds. These operations were in addition to the weekly refinancing of some $3 billion of maturing 91-day and 182-day Treasury bills and a monthly roll-over of at least $1.5 billion of maturing nine-month and one-year bills. By mid-1976 the Treasury was conducting weekly auctions of about $6 billion in three-month and six-month Treasury bills, as well as regular monthly sales of some $5.5 billion in one-year bills and two-year Treasury notes.

Another significant aspect of debt-management operations involves the maturity composition of the public debt. Since the Treasury can ordinarily shift large amounts of debt among various maturities, its actions affecting the average maturity of outstanding debt can have major implications for the cost and availability of funds in various credit markets.

In addition, federal government securities are an important part of the financial fabric of society. Not only do Treasury obligations have a large place in various financial institution portfolios, but short-term government securities (primarily Treasury bills) provide a convenient device for commercial banks and other institutions to use in adjusting their cash positions. Treasury debt-management decisions affecting the liquidity of these debt holdings can have a powerful impact on the cost and availability of credit and thus on private decisions to spend.

Furthermore, annual interest payments on the national debt are now almost $40 billion. These interest outlays not only redistribute national income, but they create additional pressure on the Treasury's cash financing needs. The rise in interest costs reflects both the increase in the absolute size of the national debt and the higher yields on Treasury securities. However, interest outlays ranged only between 8 and 9 percent of total U.S. budget outlays over the past two decades.

Goals of Debt Management

Since debt management can have repercussions on the monetary sector and the overall economy, the Treasury attempts to coordinate its efforts with monetary and fiscal policy in order to achieve economic stabilization objectives. These objectives consist primarily of high-level employment at stable prices in an economy marked by the achievement of orderly growth and reasonable balance in international payments.

In addition to its macroeconomic objectives, the Treasury has certain technical considerations relating to debt-management operations. These suggest some other, more immediate, objectives for debt-management policy, such as the need to fashion a balanced debt structure, to minimize interest-carrying charges, to accommodate liquidity requirements of the economy, to increase the average maturity of outstanding debt, and to reduce short-term borrowing (especially via the commercial banking system). These various objectives are not always compatible, nor are they always consistent with economic stabilization goals. Furthermore, the relatively recent (since 1965) sharp growth in debt issued by federal and federally sponsored agencies has compelled the Treasury to coordinate its debt-management efforts with financing by these agencies. These agencies, which are discussed in Chapter 3, greatly expanded their lending (particularly in the housing and agricultural sectors) as credit conditions tightened in the late 1960s. Offering low-risk obligations with attractive yields, they compete actively for short-term investment funds. The increasing frequency and growth of agency debt offerings make them an important element in Treasury planning of financing operations.

PROBLEMS RELATING TO THE MATURITY STRUCTURE

Of the many technical considerations that occupy the attention of Treasury debt managers, none are more vexing than those related to the maturity structure of the national debt. Of particular note is the fairly short average term to maturity of the debt (see Table 11.8), which reflects the Treasury's difficulties in selling bonds (coupon securities with long-term maturities of five years or more). The Treasury's hands are tied by a 4.25 percent *interest rate ceiling* on marketable bonds that was originally imposed during World

Table 11.8 AVERAGE LENGTH AND MATURITY DISTRIBUTION OF MARKETABLE INTEREST-BEARING PUBLIC DEBT HELD BY PRIVATE INVESTORS, 1972–1978

End of Fiscal Year or Month	Amount Out-standing	Maturity Class					Average Length	
		Within 1 Year	1–5 Years	5–10 Years	10–20 Years	20 Years and Over	Years	Months
		Millions of Dollars						
1972	165,978	79,509	57,157	16,033	6,358	6,922	3	3
1973	167,869	84,041	54,139	16,385	8,741	4,564	3	1
1974	164,862	87,150	50,103	14,197	9,930	3,481	2	11
1975	210,382	115,677	65,852	15,385	8,857	4,611	2	8
1976	279,782	151,723	89,151	24,169	8,087	6,652	2	7
1977	326,674	161,329	113,319	33,067	8,428	10,531	2	11
1978								
Jan	355,374	177,642	123,692	32,712	9,733	11,595	2	11
Feb	358,320	175,195	130,715	29,853	9,719	12,838	3	0
Mar	362,693	178,474	132,501	29,414	9,635	12,669	2	11
Apr	355,144	170,272	130,884	31,816	9,571	12,601	3	0
May	356,892	166,094	135,524	31,758	9,847	13,668	3	1
June	353,660	162,533	137,543	30,458	9,766	13,360	3	1
July	358,255	163,619	139,017	30,573	11,512	13,533	3	1
Aug	359,919	163,512	136,462	33,603	11,407	14,936	3	3
Sept	356,501	163,819	132,993	33,500	11,383	14,805	3	3
Oct	362,443	165,337	136,064	33,476	12,746	14,820	3	2
Nov	367,256	170,492	133,876	33,695	13,879	15,314	3	4
Dec	365,239	174,231	128,293	33,604	13,833	15,278	3	4

Source: Economic Report of the President, January 1979, p. 273.

War I. With market rates on high-grade bonds being well above this legal limit since mid-1965, the Treasury has had to conduct its financing operations (both for refunding maturing debt and for borrowing new money) by short- and intermediate-term obligations, which are not subject to the statutory limitation.

A possible way around the 4.25 percent interest rate ceiling would be for the Treasury to sell bonds at a discount from their par value. The Treasury has not used this loophole, largely because the action might be viewed as violating the spirit, if not the letter, of the law. In recent years, Congress has eased the limitation in two ways. As of 1978 the Treasury had authority to issue up to $32 billion in bonds without regard to the statutory interest rate ceiling. Furthermore, by successively changing the definition of bond maturity from five to seven to ten years, Congress effectively has exempted a wider range of maturities from the ceiling.

Impact on Liquidity

The declining maturity structure of the debt is regarded by some observers as a source of inflationary pressures within the economy. Two lines of argument are stressed. In the first case, increased public holdings of short-term securities relative to holdings of longer-term securities enhance the public's liquidity and thus tend to induce additional spending. In effect, short-term government securities are substituted for money holdings, lowering money demand and driving down market rates of interest.

In addition, this view recognizes that commercial banks hold short-term government securities as secondary reserves that can be liquidated when the demand for bank loans is rising. Thus, it is argued, large holdings of short-term obligations by commercial banks facilitate a more sensitive response by banks to rising private demand for credit and therefore a less sensitive response to monetary restraint.

Effects on Interest Rates

The second line of argument against a shortened maturity structure stresses the impact of changes in debt maturity on the pattern of interest rates. According to this view, Treasury replacement of long-term bonds with shorter-term securities would tend initially to lower long-term interest rates and, at the same time, to buoy up short-term interest rates as the supply of short-term debt increases. If investment spending is sensitive to changes in long-term rates, then it would tend to increase, thus strengthening aggregate demand for goods and services. If these results occur at a time of high-level employment, then the general price level would rise.

Not all observers agree with this analysis. Some insist that the impact of shortened maturities on the pattern of interest rates is removed quickly as market participants adjust their holdings of short- and long-term securities. These critics, who emphasize the role of expectations in determining the term structure of interest rates, regard shifts in debt maturity as having little, if any, effect on the structure of market rates. Even granting that shortening the maturity of the public debt carries an impact on the pattern of interest rates, the ultimate effects on investment spending cannot be determined, since some investment expenditures are discouraged while others are encouraged.

Although they generally agree that a close association exists between private spending and the overall level of liquidity in the economy, some economists question whether marginal shifts in debt maturity bring appreciable changes in the economy's liquidity and, in turn, in the level of private spending. This view, which holds that there is no significant difference in liquidity between long- and short-term government debt, regards Treasury debt management as a weak tool for economic stabilization. Furthermore, any disturbing economic effects arising from changes in maturity structure are considered to be easily offset with appropriate fiscal and monetary policies.

Professional opinion is divided regarding the precise inflationary results of a shorter maturity structure for the national debt. Nevertheless, the considerably short average maturity of the debt poses some fairly serious technical problems for Treasury debt managers. Hampered by its inability to sell long-term bonds since 1965, the Treasury encounters large refunding operations that require frequent and sizable debt offerings. An increase in the size and number of these refinancings can complicate Treasury borrowing operations, make security sales by private long-term borrowers more difficult, and even interfere with the effective conduct of monetary policy.

An Even-Keel Policy

Generally, the Federal Reserve avoids major changes in monetary policy when the Treasury is in the market for issuing or refunding debt. This central bank practice, sometimes called an *even-keel policy* for maintaining stable conditions in financial markets, applies not to all Treasury financings but usually to coupon-issue financings. Occasionally, even-keel policy delays the central bank from taking positive action for promoting economic stabilization. In a market unable to absorb newly issued Treasury securities at current market prices, an even-keel policy may require the supplying of additional bank reserves by Federal Reserve open market purchases. Unless they are absorbed later, these extra reserves provide the basis for monetary expansion through lending and "investing" activities of the commercial banking system.

Frequent short-term Treasury borrowing adds to the congestion of financing operations in securities markets and tends to increase deposit volatility at commercial banks and nonbank financial institutions. Increased volume of short-term Treasury offerings raises interest rates on these securities and tends to buoy up other short-term market yields. Liquid obligations issued by savings and loan associations and other thrift institutions become less attractive to financial investors, since earning rates are usually raised only after a considerable lag. Thus, disintermediation can result, with reduced flow of funds into the mortgage market and other areas usually attractive to thrift institutions.

A COMPROMISE APPROACH
TO DEBT MANAGEMENT

Many observers, recognizing the inherent difficulty and complexity of using Treasury debt-management policy as a major tool for economic stabilization purposes, propose a compromise approach. In their view, a workable policy of debt management emphasizes those economic stabilization results that involve the least cost for the Treasury. In effect, the Treasury would give first priority to minimizing the interest cost of the national debt, and less emphasis to any economic stabilizing actions that are compatible with this least-cost objective.

We can illustrate this pragmatic approach by looking at the question of the proper timing of Treasury sales of long-term bonds. Following the Treasury–Federal Reserve accord of 1951, long-term Treasury issues have been floated when market conditions have been deemed to ensure successful financing with minimum repercussions on the rest of the market. This policy precludes selling bonds when private demand for long-term credit is strong.

Over the past several years (especially since 1965), sustained and strong private demand in United States capital markets provides the basis for a suggested change in the Treasury procedure for issuing long-term bonds. The new procedure would entail regularly scheduled offerings of fairly constant amounts of Treasury long-term securities. For example, the Treasury might conduct on an annual basis one or two new bond offerings of $2 billion to $4 billion each. Adoption of this method would require complete repeal of the existing 4.25 percent interest rate ceiling and major revamping of the mechanics of bond sales. Some possible advantages of this approach include a reduction in the market uncertainty that usually marks Treasury bond sales, a simplification of bond-issuing procedures, and an increase in the average maturity of the debt, thus according better control to debt managers.

A willingness on the part of the Treasury to try new debt-management techniques might facilitate achievement of economic stabilization. At the very least, a better rationalization of these techniques might lessen some of the economic destabilizing effects of debt management, thus strengthening the effectiveness of monetary-fiscal policy in promoting economic stability.

KEY TERMS

Fiscal policy   Interest rate ceiling
Debt-management operations   Even-keel policy
Refunding

REVIEW QUESTIONS

1. What are the main avenues of Treasury influence on the monetary sector?
2. Explain how issuance of Treasury currency affects the monetary sector.
3. Explain briefly the effects of Treasury gold operations on the U.S. monetary system after the closing of the gold window in August 1971.
4. Summarize by means of T accounts the monetary effects of the various alternatives for Treasury borrowing to cover a current tax deficit.
5. What options are open to the Treasury in disposing of a tax surplus?

6. Show with the aid of T accounts the monetary effects of Treasury use of a tax surplus to retire outstanding securities.

7. Define and explain the scope of Treasury debt-management operations.

8. How can Treasury debt-management operations promote economic stabilization?

9. What are some implications for the monetary sector of a declining maturity structure for the national debt?

10. What is implied in a pragmatic approach to Treasury debt-management policy?

SUGGESTED READINGS

Bedford, Margaret E. "Recent Developments in Treasury Financing Techniques." Federal Reserve Bank of Kansas City, *Monthly Review* (July-August 1977): 12–24.

Behravesh, Nariman, and Donald L. Raiff. "Tax Cuts and Economic Activity: The Role of 'Financing'." Federal Reserve Bank of Philadelphia, *Business Review* (January-February 1976): 13–23.

Brewer, Elijah. "Treasury to Invest Surplus Tax and Loan Balances." Federal Reserve Bank of Chicago, *Economic Perspectives* (November-December 1977): 14–20.

Burger, Albert E. "Monetary Effects of the Treasury Sale of Gold." Federal Reserve Bank of St. Louis, *Review* (January 1975): 18–22.

———. "The Monetary Economics of Gold." Federal Reserve Bank of St. Louis, *Review* (January 1974): 2–7.

Cacy, J.A. "Budget Deficits and the Money Supply." Federal Reserve Bank of Kansas City, *Monthly Review* (June 1975): 3–9.

Carlson, Keith M. "Large Federal Budget Deficits: Perspectives and Prospects." Federal Reserve Bank of St. Louis, *Review* (October 1976): 2–7.

Hamblin, Mary. "Treasury Deposits and the Money Supply." Federal Reserve Bank of Kansas City, *Monthly Review* (February 1977): 14–20.

Kasriel, Paul L. "The Federal Debt and Commercial Banks." Federal Reserve Bank of Chicago, *Business Conditions* (October 1975): 3–9.

Lang, Richard W., and Robert H. Rasche. "Debt Management and the Own Price Elasticity of Demand for U.S. Government Notes and Bonds." Federal Reserve Bank of St. Louis, *Review* (September 1977): 8–22.

Roley, V. Vance. "Federal Debt Management Policy: A Re-Examination of the Issues." Federal Reserve Bank of Kansas City, *Economic Review* (February 1978): 14–23.

Part Four

THE INTERNATIONAL MONETARY
PROCESS

Chapter Twelve

THE INTERNATIONAL ECONOMY
AND THE MONETARY PROCESS

Economic activity takes place on both a domestic and an international scale. In both contexts money and the monetary process play an important role in the allocation of scarce resources and in aggregate economic performance. Just as the domestic monetary system facilitates the conduct of trade and exchange within national boundaries, the international monetary payments mechanism makes possible trade and exchange across national boundaries.

This chapter examines some important aspects of the international sector that bear on the working of the monetary process. Specifically, the fundamentals of international trade and financial activity are summarized and their effects on the domestic monetary system are explored. Next, the rudiments of balance-of-payments accounting are explained. And finally, the highlights of the United States payments experience and the nation's international role in the post–World War II era are reviewed.

THE FUNDAMENTALS OF
INTERNATIONAL TRADE

Put simply, international trade arises from differences between prices of domestically produced goods and prices of goods produced abroad. An item will be imported when an entrepreneur determines that the foreign price converted to domestic currency units, allowing for transportation costs and other added charges, is lower than the domestic price he or she hopes to get for it (providing its profitability is equal to or greater than that of the alternatives). The problem has been to explain why the differences in prices exist internationally.

Comparative Advantage

Economists have sought a comprehensive explanation for international trade for over two hundred years. In the simplest case we would expect international trade to exist whenever demand conditions justify importing a product that is either totally unavailable domestically (with no close domestic substitutes) or is in insufficient supply, for example, diamonds from South Africa. However, a large percentage of international trade involves products not meeting these restrictive conditions.

For those products that do not meet the first condition—of domestic unavailability—the initial explanation was in terms of absolute advantage. *Absolute advantage* exists whenever one country can produce a product for a lower cost than another country. Then, in the nineteenth century, David Ricardo showed by the principle of *comparative advantage* that even if country A had an absolute advantage in the production of several goods compared to country B, it generally was to country A's benefit not to produce all those goods. Country A would gain if country B produced some of the goods in which country A had an absolute advantage and country A traded for them. A country's comparative advantage exists where it has either the greatest absolute advantage or the least absolute disadvantage.

Traditionally, the explanation of comparative advantage has stressed certain differences between countries. Originally, a country's comparative advantage was regarded as being based on international differences in labor productivity. However, this explanation has lost favor since it ignores other factors of production, such as land and capital.

Comparative advantage is now regarded as based on the concept of opportunity costs. *Opportunity costs* define the implied real cost of each good in terms of what a country has to sacrifice by producing that good instead of another good. A country would tend to produce and trade those goods that are relatively cheap at home as compared to overseas. Whether a product is relatively cheap or expensive is explained by the *Heckscher-Ohlin theory,* which states that (1) different products require different factors of production, and (2) countries are endowed with different factor proportions.[1] Hence, in sim-

---

1. The Heckscher-Ohlin theory was first presented in English in Bertil Ohlin, *Interregional and International Trade* (Cambridge, Mass.: Harvard University Press, 1933). Much of the theory as explicated by Bertil Ohlin (1899–1979), Nobel laureate in economics in 1977, was based in large part on research done by his professor, Eli F. Heckscher (1879–1952).

ple terms, the most abundant resources in each country would tend to be cheaper than in other countries. Each country would enjoy a comparative advantage in those goods whose production requires more of the abundant factor, because the costs of production would be relatively lower. With resource endowments changing over time, countries enjoy no permanent comparative advantage in the same items. The pattern of comparative advantage in trade shifts as differences in the resource endowments of different nations emerge from varying growth rates in their populations, incomes, capital formations, and available natural resources.[2]

The emphasis on differences in resource endowments as underlying international trade suggests that the largest trade volume should be between countries with the widest differences in relative endowments of factor proportions. And yet, interestingly, most of the trade in manufactures occurs between highly developed countries with fairly similar demand structures and relative endowments of labor and capital. This situation may reflect greater opportunities for profitable trade arising from increased specialization linked with industrialization.[3]

A country's comparative advantage, especially in manufactured goods, may be explained by influences arising from innovations, economies of scale, and marketing strategies. The country in which a particular product innovation occurs gains a temporary edge in world markets that may be sustained through economies of scale and marketing strategies. Per-unit costs decrease as output increases, as unskilled labor is substituted for skilled labor (when more sophisticated capital equipment is used), as the product becomes standardized, and as per-unit marketing costs become less after initial market penetration is achieved.

However, a country with a comparative advantage in product innovation may lose the advantage gained from any particular product innovation. As the

---

2. For a more complete treatment of comparative advantage, see Charles P. Kindleberger and Peter H. Lindert, *International Economics*, 6th ed. (Homewood, Ill.: Richard D. Irwin, 1978), esp. Chapter 2.

3. One extremely interesting study done by Wassily Leontief, Nobel laureate in economics in 1973, indicated that U.S. imports had a higher capital content than exports while U.S. exports had a greater labor content than imports, which is contrary to what one might expect. See Wassily Leontief, "Domestic Production and Foreign Trade: The American Position Re-examined," *Economia Internazionale*, VII (February 1954): 3–32; reprinted in an abridged form in *Readings in International Economics*, ed. Richard E. Caves and Harry G. Johnson (Homewood, Ill.: Richard D. Irwin, 1968), pp. 503–528.

technique used for producing a product becomes widely known and as the product gains general acceptability, other firms may begin to produce close substitutes. Hence a country with a comparative advantage based partially on product innovation due to heavy spending on research and development must be prepared to strive continuously or it will lose its edge over its trading partners.

Benefits from Trade

Importing a good that is difficult or impossible to produce domestically is clearly beneficial should demand conditions warrant it. The gain from trade in lower-priced foreign goods that are relatively close substitutes for domestically produced goods is not so obvious. Imports of this type compete with home production and thus stir more controversy.

International trade occurs when the domestic economy imports goods and services that are relatively cheap abroad and specializes in the production of export goods and services that are relatively cheap at home. Thus commodity prices influence entrepreneurs' production decisions. In a freely competitive economy, commodity prices tend to mirror opportunity costs in that they reflect the production costs in terms of the opportunity forgone by not producing something else. Through the market mechanism, exchange rates translate differing international opportunity costs into differing monetary costs.

We can illustrate the benefits from international trade by stating the problem in terms of prices. Suppose that an importer can obtain for $3 a foreign-produced shirt that is identical to a domestically produced shirt that costs $5. An opportunity for private profit exists in importing such shirts. More importantly, however, benefits accrue to the overall economy from such a transaction. Assuming that imports and exports of goods pay for each other, it becomes clear that resources released by importing goods can be devoted to the production of other desired goods, and that the national economy enjoys a net gain from the transaction. The domestically produced shirt absorbs domestic resources that otherwise could be allocated to the production of $5 worth of other goods. By forgoing domestic production of a shirt, sufficient resources are released to pay for an imported shirt with $3 worth of exports *and* to produce $2 worth of additional goods. In this situation, international trade enhances real income by permitting the more efficient use of scarce resources.

International capital movements can be explained in much the same terms. Purchases of foreign capital goods or foreign securities occur only if the expected rate of return exceeds that for domestic capital goods and securities. The country selling the securities benefits by obtaining a scarce resource to improve the efficiency of its productive process.

The foregoing explanation of the bases of international trade is somewhat simplified. In the real world the smooth working of the price mechanism encounters frictions that detract from the use of prices as accurate reflections of opportunity cost and comparative advantages. In a national economy, price distortions result from such factors as imperfectly competitive markets, tax laws and regulations, factor immobilities, externalities, and so on. In the international economy, prices are distorted by factors that impede trade by raising, directly or indirectly, the prices of foreign goods and services; for example, transportation and insurance costs, marketing costs, and tariff and nontariff trade barriers. Any developments lessening these impediments would tend to let market prices reflect more accurately underlying opportunity costs and comparative advantages among nations.

INTERNATIONAL PAYMENTS AND
THE MONETARY SYSTEM

International trade and finance require a system for making international payments. For domestic trade transactions, the payment of debts involves only an exchange of domestic currency, or more typically, a check drawn on the debtor's bank and paid to the creditor. International trade transactions, however, involve more complicated payments, since the debtor and creditor reside in different countries with different units of exchange. Ordinarily, dollars do not circulate freely abroad, nor do foreign currencies generally circulate in the United States. Consequently, some means must be found to permit traders to convert their domestic currencies into foreign currencies. Here is where the international monetary payments mechanism plays an important role in facilitating the conversion of domestic money into foreign money.

For purposes of illustration, suppose that an American purchases a

Japanese motorcycle. This transaction requires payment in yen to the Japanese exporter. To obtain the needed foreign exchange in the form of Japanese yen, the United States importer pays dollars by writing a check to his or her own bank. The bank would then pay to the Tokyo bank of the Japanese exporter the designated amount in either United States dollars or Japanese yen. Finally, the yen are paid to the Japanese exporter by the Tokyo bank. In essence, the entire process was conducted by the banks in both countries serving as intermediaries without any dollars or yen actually crossing the ocean, yet its result was to increase the amount of yen held by Japan and to reduce the amount of dollars held by the United States.

Role of the Commercial Bank

The major banks of the different countries participate in an international correspondent banking network by holding accounts in banks in the various financial centers of the world. Use of these accounts permits them to transact international financial payments. Banks may increase their foreign balances by purchasing such credit instruments as commercial bills of exchange from exporters; they reduce the·e foreign balances when they sell various credit instruments to importers. Thus import transactions generate a demand for foreign exchange, while export transactions provide a supply of foreign exchange.

Since foreign-owned deposits in United States banks are linked with United States international payments experience, it is not surprising that these foreign deposits have grown, largely as a result of the mounting deficits since 1950 in the United States balance of payments. When foreigners accrue more dollars than they spend here, their deposits in United States banks tend to increase. Because the build-up of these deposits influences both the distribution and volume of member bank reserves, it carries implications for domestic monetary and credit conditions. Let us examine some of these repercussions on the United States monetary system.

International Payments and Bank Reserves

Aggregate bank reserves are usually not affected by a net transfer of deposits from Americans to foreigners. Under normal conditions foreigners will hold, temporarily at least, their new deposits with United States commercial banks, thus leaving total bank reserves unchanged.

Newly acquired foreign deposits in United States commercial banks are generally not held as demand deposit balances. They may be invested partly in time deposits, in a variety of United States government securities or in privately issued securities, depending on the relative liquidity preferences of the holders. The rate of return on alternative financial investments in relation to their respective liquidity is a major factor influencing foreigners' choices among various alternatives for holding dollar credits. Relatively high short-term rates, for example, induce foreigners to hold less in the form of demand deposits than they would otherwise while relatively high rates paid on time deposits generate larger holdings by foreigners in this form.

Shifts among alternative forms of investments bring varied results for member bank reserves. A shift to time deposits from demand deposits reduces required reserves and, *ceteris paribus*—that is, all other variables being held constant—provides excess reserves for further debt monetization by commercial banks. Similarly, deposit shifts between banks subject to different minimum reserve ratios alter required reserves and excess reserves of member banks. These effects pose no real difficulty for monetary authorities, however, since they can easily be offset by open market operations.

In addition to adjusting their financial investment holdings in the United States, foreign recipients of dollar credits can also sell dollar deposits to their own central banks. Foreigners can convert these dollars into their own or any other national currency. These sales transactions shift deposits at United States banks from foreign private holders to foreign central banks. Typically, foreign central banks maintain part of their dollar deposits at the Federal Reserve rather than at commercial banks. Thus these sales transactions may induce a shift of deposits and reserves from the commercial banking system to the Federal Reserve, thereby producing a net reduction in total banking reserves. Conversely, purchases of United States dollars by private foreigners from their own central banks usually precipitate a transfer of deposits from the Federal Reserve to commercial banks and a resulting increase in bank reserve holdings. Such shifts are one repercussion that foreign deposits have on bank reserves.

Role of Foreign Central Banks

Foreign central banks and other official institutions frequently use some of their deposits in United States banks to purchase United States government

Table 12.1   ILLUSTRATION OF MONETARY EFFECTS ARISING FROM
SALE OF DOLLARS BY PRIVATE FOREIGNER TO HIS OR
HER CENTRAL BANK

Federal Reserve		Member Bank	
	(b) Member bank deposits −	(c) Deposits at Federal Reserve −	(d) Foreign demand deposits −
	(a) Foreign deposits +		

securities. Bank reserve losses arising from a previous shift of deposits from foreign private holders to foreign official accounts in the Federal Reserve are offset, since such security purchases by foreign official groups tend to shift deposits and reserves back to commercial banks. At several times during 1972, for example, foreign central banks made large-scale purchases of United States government securities in order to reduce their dollar holdings, which had swelled greatly prior to and following the Smithsonian Agreement of December 1971. Changes in these foreign central bank balances at the Federal Reserve usually imply inverse changes in member bank reserves. Thus foreign deposits at the Federal Reserve are one of several factors in the member bank reserve equation.

T Account Changes and International Transactions

The impact of foreign deposit shifts on bank reserves can be illustrated through T accounts. Suppose, as shown in Table 12.1, that a private foreigner sells dollar deposits held at a member bank to his or her own central bank, which subsequently deposits the funds with the Federal Reserve. This transaction is initiated when the private foreign party draws a check payable to his or her own central bank. The foreign central bank deposits the check in a Federal Reserve bank, thus increasing foreign deposits at the Federal Reserve [change (a)]. When the check clears, member bank reserves at the Federal Reserve decline by an equivalent amount [change (b)], and member bank reserves [change (c)] and foreign deposits [change (d)] decline on the books of

Table 12.2   T ACCOUNTS SHOWING MONETARY EFFECTS OF
FOREIGN CENTRAL BANK PURCHASES OF
TREASURY SECURITIES

Federal Reserve		Member Bank	
	(c) Member bank deposits + (d) Foreign deposits −	(b) Deposits at Federal Reserve +	(a) Domestic demand deposits +

the member bank. Thus, a shift of foreign deposits from commercial banks to the Federal Reserve, ceteris paribus, decreases bank reserves.

Foreign official transactions in the open market for United States government securities also have an impact on the domestic monetary system. For example, Table 12.2 illustrates the monetary effects of a foreign central bank's purchase of United States Treasury securities from a government securities dealer by drawing down its deposit at the Federal Reserve. Initially, the dealer deposits the check in a checking account at a member bank [change (a)]. When the check clears through the Federal Reserve, member bank reserves increase [changes (b) and (c)], while foreign deposits at the Federal Reserve decrease [change (d)].

In conclusion, we should emphasize that foreign deposits comprise only one of several factors affecting bank reserves in the domestic monetary system, as detailed in Chapter 9. Considering all the factors affecting reserves, foreign deposits generally play a minor role. In recent years, however, the growth of foreign deposits arising from mounting United States balance-of-payments deficits has made this a more pressing element in the Federal Reserve's conduct of day-to-day open market operations.

**BALANCE OF PAYMENTS:
SOME BASICS**

A country's *balance of payments* measures that country's economic and financial transactions with the rest of the world by providing a summary record of all international transactions by its private residents, businesses, and government over a specified period. As an accounting device, the balance-of-payments statement adheres to the principles of double entry bookkeeping. By the double entry approach, the amount involved in each transaction is entered on each of the two sides of the balance-of-payments accounts. The balance-of-payments account is like any other ledger in that it records every transaction as a credit and a debit. Therefore, the sums of the two sides of the balance-of-payments account must always be the same. In this sense, the balance of payments always balances, since credits (or receipts) equal debits (or payments).

However, there is no bookkeeping requirement that the sums of the two sides of *selected* balance-of-payments accounts should be the same. The imbalances shown by selected accounts are referred to as surpluses or deficits in the balance of payments, and it is these imbalances that carry analytical significance for policy makers. Essentially, then, the analytical content of the balance-of-payments account emerges when the individual transactions are grouped in a particular way to describe the behavior of United States and foreign governments, businesses, and private residents.

Table 12.3 gives the United States balance of payments or international transactions for 1978. Note that signs (pluses or minuses) in front of the data imply the direction of the flow of funds resulting from various transactions. Transactions that bring dollars or foreign currencies into the United States are preceded by a plus; those that cause an outflow of dollars or other currencies to foreign countries are designated by a minus.

Note also that three balances are given in the body of the table (lines 11, 13, and 15). These balances are usually listed as *memoranda,* as is the *balance on merchandise trade* (line 25). However, we feel that these balances are more helpful when presented in this form.[4] The *balance on the current account* (line 15) measures the difference between the total of United States exports of goods and services and the total of United States imports of goods and

---

4. If readers compare balance-of-payments data before and after June 1976, they will note many changes in the presentation. One of the major changes is a reduction in the number of *balances* given and listing those retained as *memoranda.* The decision to reduce the number of balances calculated and not to list those retained in the body of data was not unanimous by the group whose duty was to study the question of a desirable presentation of balance-of-payments data and make recommendations. For a series of essays dealing with the various items of debate, see Robert M. Stern, *et al., The Presentation of the U.S. Balance of Payments: A Symposium, Essays in International Finance,* No. 123 (Princeton, New Jersey: Princeton University Press, 1977).

Table 12.3 UNITED STATES INTERNATIONAL TRANSACTIONS, 1978
(billions of dollars)

(1)	Export of goods and services		+218,024
(2)	Merchandise	+141,844	
(3)	Services	+23,451	
(4)	Receipt of income on U.S. assets abroad	+29,244	
(5)	Transfers under U.S. military agency sales contracts	+5,213	
(6)	Imports of goods and services		−228,909
(7)	Merchandise	−175,988	
(8)	Services	−24,143	
(9)	Payment of income on foreign assets in U.S.	−21,599	
(10)	Direct defense expenditures	−7,179	
(11)	*Balance on goods and services*		−10,885
(12)	Net remittances		−2,048
(13)	*Balance on goods, services and remittances*		−12,933
(14)	U.S. government grants*		−3,028
(15)	*Balance on current account*		−15,961
(16)	U.S. assets abroad (net)		−58,748
(17)	Private (net)	−54,963	
(18)	U.S. official reserve (net)	+872	
(19)	U.S. government (other than line 18)	−4,657	
(20)	Foreign held assets in U.S. (net)		+63,260
(21)	Foreign official (net)	+33,967	
(22)	Other foreign assets	+29,293	
(23)	Allocation of special drawing rights		0
(24)	Statistical discrepancy		+11,449
	Memorandum:		
(25)	*Balance on merchandise trade*		−34,144

Note: These data are subject to revision. Details may not add to totals due to rounding.

*Excluding military

Source: Survey of Current Business, March 1979.

services. We turn first to an examination of the items that comprise the current account.

In Table 12.3, *merchandise exports* and *imports* (lines 2 and 7) are simply the current dollar value of all goods exported from and imported into the United States. No services are included. Combining these data gives us the balance on merchandise trade (line 25).

Services under exports and imports (lines 3 and 8) have several components. For example, when Americans traveling to or in a foreign country are using insurance or transportation supplied by a foreign country, they are adding to foreign service imports, whereas foreigners using those services provided by domestic United States companies are adding to service exports. Royalties and fees earned by Americans in other countries or those earned by foreigners in the United States are also part of service exports or imports, respectively.

When earnings from United States investment overseas are repatriated, they are an export item since the United States gains dollars or foreign currencies; this is known as *receipt of income on U.S. assets abroad*. The opposite situation is entered under *payment of income on foreign assets in U.S.* (line 9). *Transfers under U.S. military agency sales contracts* represent military equipment sold to foreigners. *Direct defense expenditures* under imports include such items as payments on overseas military bases. If the data from *export of goods and services* (the sum of lines 2 through 5) and *imports of goods and services* (the sum of lines 7 through 10) are combined, the *balance on goods and services* results.

Net remittances include private transfers like gifts or similar payments from Americans to foreigners or from foreigners to Americans. The negative sign indicates that Americans are making more of these payments than they are receiving. When added to the balance on goods and services, it gives the *balance on goods, services, and remittances* (line 13).

The last item under the *current account, U.S. government grants,* includes grants and loans made by the government to other nations. This entry is also preceded by a negative sign showing that the flow of funds is out of the United States. When this amount is added to the previous balance, we have the *balance on current account* (line 15).

The remainder of the balance of payments is composed of United States claims on foreign-issued assets, foreign-held assets issued in the United States, the allocation of special drawing rights, and an entry for statistical discrepancies.

The entry *allocation of special drawing rights* SDRs (line 23) is generally a blank. The International Monetary Fund (IMF), the organization that creates SDRs,[5] does so on an irregular basis. Since the balance of payments measures *changes* in various entries on either an annual or quarterly basis, and not totals held from previous periods, this item will usually be zero.

Statistical discrepancy (line 24) is calculated on an *ex post* basis. Since all transactions are theoretically recorded twice, those that are not "seen" by the government will be recorded only once in a different form elsewhere. When various tallies do not agree, then an unrecorded transaction occurred and a balancing entry must be made. Generally the amount is not overly large, but it may be. In 1971 the statistical discrepancy (or *errors and omissions,* as it was called previously) amounted to $10.8 billion. Given the international monetary crisis taking place that year, a sizeable statistical discrepancy might have been expected as individuals and institutions moved large sums to different countries to protect themselves from potential currency depreciation. Many times these individuals and institutions were not overly careful that the government was aware of these movements.

U.S. assets abroad (the sum of lines 17 through 19) are broken into two parts—those held by the government (public) and those held by the private sector. Examples of items under the private sector entry would be the purchase of a foreign company by an American company or the purchase of a foreign-issued security by an institution or individual in the United States.

United States governmental holdings are in turn broken into two groups—*U.S. official reserves* (line 18) and *other* (line 19). Official purchases of foreign currency to stabilize exchange-rate fluctuations,[6] for example, would be included under line 18. A foreign country repaying a loan made by the United States government would be entered in the *other* account (line 19) and would be preceded by a positive sign. The loan itself when made by the United States government for nonmilitary purposes to a foreign government would have been included in the *other* account also. Since the flow of funds in this latter instance was from the United States, the sign would have been negative. The minus sign for line 19 indicates a net outflow of funds from the United States in 1978.

Foreign-held assets in U.S. is broken into *foreign official* and *other;* hence it is the sum of lines 21 and 22. Of the $29.3 billion entered under *other foreign*

5. For a discussion of SDRs and their creation, see Chapter 13.
6. For a discussion of exchange rates, see Chapter 13.

assets, $5.6 represented direct investment in the United States by foreigners. That is not very high considering that of the $55.0 billion from the private sector flowing overseas from the United States (line 17), $15.4 billion was direct investment by United States individuals and institutions.

For 1978, the balance on the current account was −$16.0 billion, which implies a net outflow from the United States of dollars or other currencies. Hence for the entries below line 15, there must be a similar net increase in foreign-held United States securities or dollars if the balance of payments is ultimately, in fact, to balance. The securities may be either privately or publicly issued. An example of a privately issued security would be shares in an American company whereas one issued publicly would be a Treasury bill.

To the degree that foreigners become increasingly unwilling to hold United States dollars or securities, an adjustment in the value of the dollar *vis-à-vis* other currencies is required. No country can run either a net outflow or a net inflow of funds continually. Some type of adjustment has to occur. Presently, with flexible exchange rates, a dollar outflow (inflow) should cause a decrease (increase) in the value of the dollar, thus making it cheaper (dearer) for foreigners to buy dollars and more (less) expensive for Americans to obtain other currencies. This in turn would cause American exports to become more (less) attractive and imports less (more) so. Hence, due to exchange-rate adjustments, balance-of-payments difficulties would become less trying.

THE UNITED STATES PAYMENTS EXPERIENCE: AN OVERVIEW

The fundamentals of balance-of-payments accounting, summarized in the previous section, provide an analytical base for a review of the highlights of the United States payments experience in recent years and of the nation's role in the international economy in the post–World War II period.

The Emergence of United States Deficits

The United States was the only major nation to emerge from World War II relatively unscathed in terms of damage to its economy. This was in marked contrast to the economic upheavals of continental Europe, England, and the major Far Eastern nations, especially Japan. An immediately pressing task was the restoration of the economic viability of these war-devastated countries. In the immediate postwar period, massive United States economic and financial aid flowed abroad, and by the mid-1950s noticeable results had been achieved. Not only had the productive capacity of these nations been largely restored but the normalization of their former trade patterns had proceeded apace, with a consequent improvement in their balance-of-payments position relative to the United States. The restoration of currency convertibility in Western Europe by the end of 1958 was evidence of the strengthening of the world economy.

In retrospect, the United States generally experienced payments deficits. Until the last three years of the Eisenhower administration, these deficits were relatively small and stirred no strong official concern. By 1959, however, they had mounted to such an extent that foreign central banks began to accumulate dollars. In turn, heightened conversion of dollars into gold by central banks abroad elicited official reaction to the large United States gold outflows. This reaction surfaced in the form of a restrictive United States monetary policy. Following the recession of 1960–1961, the economy operated below capacity for several years, thus dampening inflation. Between 1960 and 1964, for example, wholesale prices in the United States were largely unchanged, in marked contrast to 1.9 percent average increase for other major industrial countries. Improved price performance in the United States tended to lessen payments deficits largely because export growth outstripped the rise in imports.

The benefits of monetary restraint for the United States payments position during the late 1950s and early 1960s were deflected partly by mounting outflows of long-term capital. Long-term U.S. net foreign investment grew steadily from $1.6 billion in 1959 to more than $4 billion in both 1964 and 1965.

Although a variety of actions taken in the latter half of the 1960s tended to dampen these capital outflows from the United States, the United States current account surplus receded after 1964. This situation reflected divergent price trends between home and abroad. Sparked by stimulative domestic monetary policy, strong inflation appeared beginning in 1965, and between 1964 and 1968 United States wholesale prices rose at a 2 percent annual rate compared with a 1.4 percent rate for other major countries. Another factor affecting the balance on current account was the appreciable increase in direct United States overseas military outlays.

Capital Flows

During 1969 and 1970 capital flows were the main cause of changes in the United States balance-of-payments position. Heightened net outflows of long-term capital generated an increase in the deficit balance. In 1970 the decline in interest rates in the United States triggered a drop in Eurodollar interest rates, which in turn precipitated a massive conversion of dollars into local currencies by private foreigners.

These rising and persistent payments deficits generated an increased supply of dollars for foreign residents far beyond their needs for liquidity purposes and for purchase of American goods and financial instruments. After the mid-1960s private foreigners showed less willingness to hold these additional dollar deposits (or dollar claims). At this time, outstanding dollar claims were greater than the available United States gold stock, and private foreigners sold dollars to their central banks with increasing intensity. These chronic dollar deficits, linked with the declining willingness of foreigners to hold dollar balances, finally impeded the effective working of the international monetary system in 1971. In May of that year, official foreign agencies balked at accumulating additional dollar holdings. Subsequently, on August 15, the United States renounced its long-standing policy of absorbing balance-of-payments deficits by announcing the suspension of dollar convertibility into gold and its intention to press for a realignment of parity rates and for ultimate reform of the international monetary system.

AUGUST 1971: A MILESTONE

The dramatic events of mid-August 1971 marked a major milestone in the evolution of United States international payments policy. This significant date divided reactions to the United States payments deficit in 1971 into two time periods. The major developments in each of these two periods should be reviewed, since they set the international monetary system on an entirely new course.

Pre-August 15 Period

Increased reserve accumulation among foreign industrial countries started in 1970, but little reaction was evident at that time. Many nations that had

Table 12.4 OFFICIAL RESERVES OF SELECTED INDUSTRIAL
COUNTRIES, 1968–1971

(billions of dollars; end of period)

Country	1968	1969	1970	1971 March	1971 June	1971 September	1971 December*
United States	15.7	17.0	14.5	14.3	13.5	12.1	13.2
United Kingdom	2.4	2.5	2.8	3.3	3.6	5.0	6.6
Belgium	2.2	2.4	2.8	3.1	3.2	3.4	3.5
France	4.2	3.8	5.0	5.5	5.7	7.3	8.2
Italy	5.3	5.0	5.4	6.0	6.1	6.7	6.8
Netherlands	2.5	2.5	3.2	3.5	3.5	3.6	3.8
West Germany	9.9	7.1	13.6	15.8	16.7	17.0	18.4
Canada	3.0	3.1	4.7	4.8	4.9	5.0	5.7
Japan	2.9	3.7	4.8	5.9	7.8	13.4	15.4
Sweden	0.8	0.7	0.8	0.9	1.0	1.0	1.1
Switzerland	4.3	4.4	5.1	4.6	5.1	6.5	7.0

Note: These figures include $3.4 billion SDRs allocated on January 1, 1970, and $2.9 billion allocated on January 1, 1971. The United States share in these allocations was $867 million and $717 million, respectively.
    *Reserve figures are restated to reflect the anticipated rise in the dollar price of gold from $35 to $38 an ounce and the realignment of currencies in late December.

Source: International Monetary Fund, as quoted in C. L. Bach, "U.S. Balance-of-Payments Problems and Policies in 1971," Federal Reserve Bank of St. Louis, *Review*, April 1972, p. 9.

experienced some reduction in the foreign exchange component of their international reserves from earlier years enjoyed reserve inflows in 1970, which restored their reserve holdings to previous levels. However, as the United States deficit surged in 1971, the reserve build-up stirred some concern (see Table 12.4).

In early April 1971 the dollar felt mounting pressures in foreign exchange markets, reflecting appreciable interest rate differentials between the United States and abroad as well as rising foreign expectations of an impending formal devaluation of the dollar. Several industrial nations abroad felt the heat of domestic inflation, a situation that complicated their responsibilities in maintaining exchange rate stability under the rules of the International Monetary Fund. Under these IMF stipulations, nations had to limit exchange rate fluctuation to a range of ± 1 percent of parity.

In contrast to relatively calm conditions in the first quarter of 1971, the Eurodollar market felt increasing speculative pressures in the second quarter. These forces mounted as exchange rate uncertainties increased. By late July and August the Eurodollar borrowing rate surged to almost 9 percent, with the overnight rate rocketing to 200 percent at the end of August.

In the first half of 1971 West Germany was the country most buffeted by the United States deficit and churning international financial conditions. Pressed by a torrent of dollar inflows, strong domestic inflation, and domestic interest rates appreciably above the Eurodollar and most European money market rates, the Bundesbank suspended its foreign exchange operations following a $1 billion inflow over May 3 and 4 and a further $1 billion inflow in the initial forty minutes of trading on the morning of May 5. Subsequently, the Frankfurt market reopened on May 10 with the Bundesbank's announcement of temporary suspension of trading limits for the mark. These moves allowed West German stabilization policies to remain restrictive and even to be reinforced by higher reserve ratios applied to commercial banks.

These German actions fairly quickly diverted speculative pressures to other strong national currencies. Following in this speculative wake, the Netherlands allowed the guilder to float and Belgium reinforced its two-tier exchange rate system (one official and one financial) and permitted the financial exchange rate to fluctuate. In addition, Switzerland and Austria appreciated their currencies by some 7 and 5 percent, respectively.

The second quarter of 1971 showed a marked deterioration in the United States balance-of-payments position. Total United States international reserve assets, which stood at $14.6 billion at the start of 1971, had eroded to some $12.1 billion by mid-August, with almost half of the $2.5 billion decline occurring in early August. Mounting pressures abroad to convert dollars into other currencies and ultimately into United States reserve assets became irresistible. This well-nigh intolerable situation forced the United States to suspend dollar convertibility into gold.

Post-August 15 Period

After having been closed for one week following President Nixon's announcement, the reopened European exchange markets saw France as the only major industrial nation that sought to keep the value of its currency against the dollar within the 1 percent upper ceiling. In these French efforts the foreign exchange market was split into two tiers. One tier consisted of a market for dollars arising from international trade transactions, and in this market official intervention maintained the franc's parity value. The second tier covered all other exchange transactions conducted in "financial francs," whose exchange rate was allowed to float.

At the same time, the Japanese initially tried to officially purchase all dollars offered at the ceiling rate, but a dollar deluge of $4.4 billion in August forced them to retreat to a policy of limited intervention whereby the yen appreciated some 5 percent relative to the dollar in the following month. Other nations applied restrictions to foreign exchange dealings while simultaneously allowing the value of their currencies to float relative to the dollar. Occasionally in ensuing months, intervention in foreign exchange markets was used to control the extent of this float.

In early December 1971 an array of regulated exchange rates between foreign currencies and dollars showed marked changes from the beginning of the year. The *Smithsonian Agreement* of December 18, 1971, largely took these new exchange rates as temporary "central values." This realignment of exchange rates of other nations relative to the dollar and to each other was accompanied by the announced United States intention to devalue the dollar with respect to gold by raising the dollar price of gold by 8.57 percent. At the same time, most nations agreed to an allowable band of exchange rate fluctuations of ± 2.25 percent of the central value. Based on the new central rates for fourteen leading industrial nations, effective devaluation of the dollar amounted to over 10 percent, weighted by the shares of these countries in world trade. With all the results in for the year 1971, the United States balance of payments registered a deficit of almost $30 billion.

AFTER AUGUST 1971

The United States balance-of-payments experience in 1972 raised increasing doubt that the modifications in exchange rates established by the Smithsonian monetary agreement could achieve effective results within a reasonable period. There was continued concern about the size of the United States balance-of-payments deficit, even though it had decreased from $29.8 billion in 1971 to $10.3 billion in 1972. The merchandise-trade balance, despite the benefits expected from the dollar's December 1971 devaluation, grew from a $2.9 billion deficit in 1971 to a $7.0 billion deficit in 1972. This large trade deficit emerged as the strongly expanding domestic economy attracted imports while the relatively weak pace of the economies of major trading partners hampered the growth of United States exports. By late 1972 United States liquid liabilities to foreign official holders totaled some $61 billion, for an increase of $36 billion in two years' time. Although developments had not reached an explosive point, the dollar's value in relation to other nations' currencies was under downward pressure several times during 1972.

The year 1973 brought increased awareness of the growing need for further realignment of exchange rates. This charged setting sparked massive speculative flows of liquid funds among various financial centers and culminated in a flood of dollars into West Germany. Within a week's time, the German central bank bought some $6 billion in exchange for marks, to keep the mark-dollar rate from piercing its ceiling established by the Smithsonian Agreement.

In the face of these irresistible pressures, the United States announced on February 12, 1973, a 10 percent dollar devaluation to reinforce the 8.57 percent devaluation of December 1971. The Japanese government, allowing the market to establish a price for the yen, watched it appreciate some 18 percent relative to the dollar within approximately five weeks. Other countries (Belgium, Denmark, France, Germany, the Netherlands, Norway, and Sweden) decided to let their currencies float relative to the dollar while maintaining constant rates among their currencies.

The value of the dollar continued to fall through mid-year. However, an upward pressure on the value of the dollar appeared in August, and became considerably stronger in the last quarter of 1973. This development was due to the continuing improvements in trade surpluses caused by the previous devaluations, the expectation that the United States would cope with oil-embargo difficulties better than most other countries, a generally lower inflation rate, and improved conditions for agricultural exports.[7]

The dollar again lost value in the second quarter of 1974, partly as a result of the greater-than-anticipated trade deficit after the end of the petroleum

7. Hans H. Helbling, "Recent and Prospective Developments in International Trade and Finance," Federal Reserve Bank of St. Louis, *Review* (May 1974): 17–18.

embargo. In fact, large petroleum imports caused a deficit in the merchandise trade balance. Other factors influencing the value of the dollar were a more severe decline in United States output than expected, and an increase in the inflation rate. This downward movement in the value of the dollar was reversed in mid-May due to improved economic conditions, including a decrease in the growth rate of the money supply and a resulting rise in interest rates.[8]

Whereas resumed petroleum shipments played a significant role in 1974 on the international scene, the sharp, deep contraction in economic activity that began late in 1973 and continued through the early part of 1975 overshadowed most other influences on economic affairs. While OPEC imports from the United States grew substantially and agricultural exports continued strong, the recession produced a pronounced decrease in United States imports.

The decreased value of the dollar in 1975 was due mostly to short-term capital outflows resulting from a decline in domestic interest rates. Then, beginning in the second quarter and continuing through the year, the dollar increased in value as economic conditions seemed to improve, and interest rates began to rise, leaving the dollar overall by the end of the year in a stronger position than at the beginning.[9]

Also in 1975, events transpired by which the United States dollar began to lose some of its role as *the* international currency. In March, four major petroleum-producing countries (Iran, Saudi Arabia, Kuwait, and Qatar) decided to tie their currencies to Special Drawing Rights (SDRs) or "paper gold" of the IMF. In the same month, the European Economic Community (EEC) tied its unit of account to a market basket of goods in place of the dollar to eliminate problems in its own internal financial settlements created by changes in the international value of the dollar.

While the dollar remained relatively strong during 1976, four currencies—the Italian lira, the British pound sterling, the Mexican peso, and the Australian dollar—all took serious declines. These currencies also changed from having their prices "pegged" to being determined more by the

8. Hans H. Helbling, "International Trade and Finance Under the Influence of Oil—1974 and Early 1975," Federal Reserve Bank of St. Louis, *Review* (May 1975): 12–13.

9. Hans H. Helbling, "Foreign Trade and Exchange Rate Movements in 1975," St. Louis Federal Reserve Bank, *Review* (January 1976): 11–12.

market. This action tended to perpetuate the trend toward floating exchange rates that had begun earlier for other currencies. In fact the IMF proposed changes in its Articles of Agreement that would permit members to allow exchange rates to fluctuate. This was a radical change from previous provisions, which generally required intervention to stabilize exchange rates.[10]

During 1977 and continuing well into 1978, the United States balance of payments has run at record or near record deficit levels. However, a long-run adjustment seems to be occurring. While the value of the United States dollar measured against all its major trading partners on a trade-weighted basis has decreased somewhat, its value has changed significantly against specific currencies. For example, the United States continues to run a large deficit with the Japanese. Even though the Japanese have been adamant in not permitting greater levels of imports, their exports now face an increasing competitive disadvantage due to an appreciation of the yen. In 1977 the yen appreciated or increased in value against the United States dollar by 22.3 percent; in 1978 (through October'30) the yen increased in value by an additional 43.4 percent (again using its value on January 1, 1977 as the base). As a consequence, Japanese goods are increasing in price rapidly in the United States and their sales should, ceteris paribus, decrease.

Other currencies appreciating against the dollar over the same periods are the British pound sterling (12.8 and 10.9 percent in the two periods, respectively), the German mark (12.5 and 24.8 percent), the French franc (5.5 and 19.2 percent), the Swiss franc (23.0 and 43.7 percent), and the Dutch guilder (8.7 and 23.7 percent). Over the same periods, the Canadian dollar depreciated by 7.8 and 5.6 percent. These changes in the value of the United States dollar versus specific currencies promise to be a partial cure for the United States balance-of-payments deficits given sufficient time.

On November 1, 1978, the United States government announced several measures to alleviate part of the pressure that was causing the dollar to depreciate so severely against some of its trading partners. The Federal Reserve bank raised the discount rate by a full percent to 9.5 percent (an historical high at the time), and the administration announced an anti-inflation program involving wage and price guidelines. As a result the dollar has recovered some of its value against these currencies.

---

10. Donald S. Kemp, "U.S. International Trade and Financial Developments in 1976," St. Louis Reserve Bank, *Review* (December 1976): 9–14.

Internationally, events seem to have returned to a more mundane progression. The feeling of desperation that existed in 1971 through 1973, when it was feared that the entire international payments system might collapse, has faded. This worry exists in the background still—especially should petroleum prices again be raised beyond many countries' ability to pay. Clearly the future promises to remain interesting as far as international monetary considerations are concerned—even frightening should a Middle East peace settlement turn out to be impossible.

KEY TERMS

Absolute advantage

Comparative advantage

Opportunity costs

Heckscher-Ohlin theory

Ceteris paribus

Balance of payments

Balance on merchandise trade

Balance on current account

Smithsonian Agreement

REVIEW QUESTIONS

1. Explain how the basis of the comparative advantage concept has changed over the years.

2. Can international payments arising from international trade affect bank reserves? Discuss.

3. Since World War II, what general trends in the United States balance of payments are apparent? Can you suggest explanations for these trends?

4. What changes have occurred in the United States balance of payments since the most recent data given in the text?

5. Trace movements (or the lack thereof) in the value of the United States dollar against the following currencies from November 30, 1978, on and account for them if possible:

    a. Swiss franc

    b. Japanese yen

    c. British pound sterling

    d. German Deutschemark

    e. Canadian dollar

    f. Italian lira

SUGGESTED READINGS

Hetzel, Robert L., and Thomas A. Lawler. "The Cause of the Dollar Depreciation." Federal Reserve Bank of Richmond, *Economic Review* (May-June 1978): 15–26.

Kvasnicka, Joseph G. "Measuring the International Value of the U.S. Dollar." Federal Reserve Bank of Chicago, *Economic Perspectives* (May-June 1977): 17–22.

Westerfield, Janice M. "A Lower Profile for the U.S. Balance of Payments." Federal Reserve Bank of Philadelphia, *Business Review* (November-December 1976): 11–17.

Chapter Thirteen

INTERNATIONAL MONETARY
ADJUSTMENT AND POLICY

The system of adjustment utilized in international economics for approximately the last thirty years is virtually no more. Established under the guidance of Lord Keynes in 1944 at Bretton Woods, New Hampshire, the *Bretton Woods system,* as it is called, is rapidly evolving away from one of continuous supervision to one governed more by market forces. Yet the goals of international monetary policy have remained essentially the same.

Just as domestic monetary policy attempts to promote economic stability within a country's borders, the international monetary system facilitates the exchange of goods, services, and productive capital among nations with differing internal monetary systems. Like the monetary systems of individual countries, the international monetary system has evolved in response to the changing nature of economic activity in the world economy. Although divergent national interests have impeded desirable changes in the international monetary arena, recent years have seen a rising spirit of cooperation toward the resolution of common problems. These collective efforts unfold in the context of pressing economic issues.

In this chapter we will first derive the demand and supply curves for a currency to determine the equilibrium price or exchange rate. Next we will explain and evaluate the fixed, or pegged, exchange rate system, and then the floating, or freely fluctuating, exchange rate system. We will follow with a consideration of two other proposals offered for reforming the international adjustment system. Finally, we shall look at the present situation of the International Monetary Fund (IMF) and the question of international reserves.

**DERIVATION OF DEMAND AND
SUPPLY FUNCTIONS FOR A
CURRENCY**

The Demand Function

In this section we will derive first the demand function, and then the supply function, for the United Kingdom's pound sterling. The demand function for the pound is generally negatively sloped, indicating that as the dollar value of the pound decreases, a greater quantity of pounds will be demanded. Foreigners will demand a greater quantity of pounds at $1.65 than at $1.75 to buy goods and services produced in the United Kingdom, since these goods are cheaper when the pound costs $1.65 than when the pound costs $1.75. For example, a £100 suit when the price of the pound is $1.75 would cost an American $175. At $1.65 per pound, the suit would cost $165 even though its domestic or British price remained the same.

The increase in the quantity of pounds demanded when there is a decrease in the price of the pound sterling depends on the price elasticity of demand for British exports. As we know, *price elasticity of demand* is the percentage change in quantity demanded, given some percentage change in price; that is,

$$PE_D = \frac{\%\Delta Q_D}{\%\Delta P}\,(-1) = \frac{\Delta Q/Q}{\Delta P/P}\,(-1) \tag{13.1}$$

The price elasticity of demand for a country's exports will be a function of the type of goods being exported and of whether or not the importing country has industries that produce import-competing goods. If a country exports goods that are basic either to the development of less-developed economies or to the operation of other economies, the price elasticity of demand for these goods tends to be very inelastic. If the price elasticity of demand were zero, like demand function D_1 in Figure 13.1a, then changes in the price of an exporting country's currency will not bring about a change in the quantity of that country's currency demanded. Other countries will require the same quantity of the good(s) irrespective of the price. Since the domestic price is assumed constant, the total quantity of pounds demanded remains the same. This would result in a demand function like $D_{£1}$ in Figure 13.1b.

As the goods exported become less essential and more choice is involved in

Figure 13.1 DEMAND CURVES FOR EXPORTS OF THE UNITED
KINGDOM AND RELATED DEMAND CURVES FOR
POUND STERLING

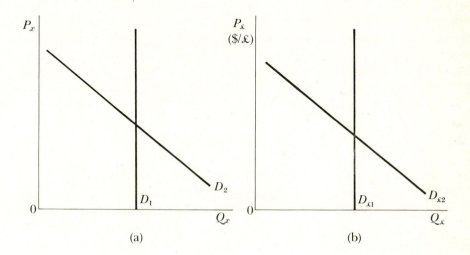

(a)

(b)

their use, the price elasticity of demand for both the goods and the exporting
country's currency becomes more elastic. As a consequence, changing the
price of the exporting country's currency and hence the international price of
its exports will alter the quantity of exports demanded and the quantity of the
exporting country's currency demanded. An increase (decrease) in the price
of the exporting country's currency will result in a decrease (increase) in the
quantity of exports demanded as well as a decrease (increase) in the quantity
of currency demanded, ceteris paribus.

Similarly, the existence in the importing countries of industries that can
produce close or perfect substitutes for their imports will influence the price
elasticity of demand for both the imports (the exporting country's exports)
and the currency of the exporting country. As we have seen, increases or
decreases in the price of the exporting country's currency will increase or
decrease the quantity of exports demanded. As the exporting country's currency increases in price, its exports become more expensive. Hence importing
countries will substitute domestic products for the more expensive imports.
Since the domestic price of the exporting country's products is assumed

constant, a decrease in the quantity of the exporting country's currency demanded occurs.

Furthermore, as one exporting country's export prices rise, importing countries if possible will switch to other foreign sources of the same product, again making the demand for the exporting country's product and currency more elastic, ceteris paribus. Consequently, a price elasticity of demand for a country's exports that is greater than zero will result in a price elasticity of demand for the country's currency that is greater than zero.[1] Hence a demand for a country's exports like D_2 in Figure 13.1a will result in a demand function for pounds like $D_{£_2}$ in Figure 13.1b.

The Supply Function

The supply function for pounds $S_£$ indicates that as the dollar value of the pound increases, a greater quantity of pounds will generally be supplied. An increase in the price of the pound from \$1.65 to \$1.75, for example, means that individuals and institutions will be more willing to sell pounds. The supply function for pounds reflects the British demand for imports. In order to buy foreign goods, individuals in the United Kingdom must use pounds to buy the foreign currency of the country where they wish to purchase these imports. The slope of the supply function for pounds will be a function of the price elasticity of demand for British imports.

Table 13.1 contains data referring to a hypothetical British demand for some American product, the infamous product "*x*" in this case. The price elasticity of demand indicated by the data is greater than unity (>1), using the British or pound price of the good. Column 1 of Table 13.1 contains the quantities of the good that will be demanded when the price is stated in terms of the pound. The prices of the good in *pounds*, found in column 5, are calculated by dividing the dollar price of the good (column 2) by the dollar price of the pound (column 4). We assume that the price of the good in dollars is constant (column 2) at \$1.00 per unit. Column 3 measures the total revenue received in dollars by the American suppliers. Column 6 shows the total quantity of pounds supplied, which is computed by multiplying the quantity

---

1. Price elasticities of demand are always negative given a negatively sloped demand curve. Therefore, economists generally multiply them by a -1, thus reversing the sign. It is in this sense that we write "greater than zero."

Table 13.1 DATA RELATED TO AN ELASTIC DEMAND FOR
BRITISH IMPORTS

Q_x^D (1)	$P_{x(\$)}$ (2)	$TR_{(\$)}$ (3) $(1)\times(2)$	$P_{£(\$)}$ (4)	$P_{x(£)}$ (5) $(2)\div(4)$	$TR_{(£)}$ (6) $(1)\times(5)$
100	$1.00	$100	$1.75	0.571	57.1
90	$1.00	$ 90	$1.65	0.606	54.5
80	$1.00	$ 80	$1.55	0.645	51.6

of the good demanded (column 1) by the pound price of the good (column 5).
As we can see in the final column, the total pounds generated decrease as the
dollar price of the pound decreases. Hence the supply function of pounds is
positively sloped when the price elasticity of demand for imports is elastic
(>1).[2]

2. A negatively sloped supply function for pound sterling would result if the price elasticity of
demand for British imports were inelastic (<1), as in the following table (plot column 6 against
column 4).

Q_x^D (1)	$P_{x(\$)}$ (2)	$TR_{(\$)}$ (3) $(1)\times(2)$	$P_£$ (4)	$P_{x(£)}$ (5) $(2)\div(4)$	$TR_{(£)}$ (6) $(1)\times(5)$
100	$1.00	$ 100	$1.75	0.571	57.1
100	$1.00	$ 100	$1.65	0.606	60.6
100	$1.00	$ 100	$1.55	0.645	64.5

A perfectly vertical supply function for pound sterling would result if the British demand for
imports had a unitary price elasticity of demand (= 1), as approximated in the following table
(plot column 6 against column 4).

Q_x^D (1)	$P_{x(\$)}$ (2)	$TR_{(\$)}$ (3) $(1)\times(2)$	$P_{(\$)}$ (4)	$P_{x(£)}$ (5) $(2)\div(4)$	$TR_{(£)}$ (6) $(1)\times(5)$
100	$1.00	$100	$1.75	0.571	57.1
95	$1.00	$ 95	$1.65	0.606	57.6
89	$1.00	$ 89	$1.55	0.645	57.4

Figure 13.2   DETERMINATION OF POUND STERLING EXCHANGE
RATE WITH SUPPLY AND DEMAND FUNCTIONS

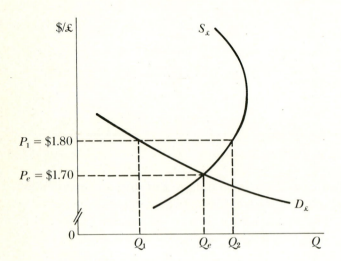

The price elasticity of demand for British imports is determined by the
same sorts of considerations as is the price elasticity of demand for British
exports. These considerations are the type of goods being imported and the
existence of domestic substitutes. The less (more) essential the imports are,
the greater (smaller) the price elasticity of demand for imports. The more
numerous (fewer) the industries that produce import competing goods, the
higher (lower) the price elasticity of demand for British imports.

Figure 13.2 shows a supply and demand function for pound sterling. We
assume that the demand curve for pound sterling is other than perfectly
inelastic. We also assume that the demand curve for British imports (that is,
American exports) is linear and negatively sloped. We know that for a linear,
negatively sloped demand function the price elasticity of demand is unitary at
the midpoint of the demand function, elastic above the midpoint (>1), and
inelastic below the midpoint (<1). This will result in a supply function for
pounds that looks like that in Figure 13.2. The negatively sloped part of the
supply function for pounds is derived from the inelastic portion of the
demand function for imports. When the price elasticity of demand for imports is unitary, the supply function of pounds is vertical, that is, perfectly

inelastic. And when the price elasticity of demand for imports is elastic, the supply function for pounds will be positively sloped. All things considered, we shall assume that the demand for imports is elastic, that is, that the supply function for a currency is positively sloped over its *relevant* range.

As usual in supply and demand analysis, the equilibrium price and quantity will be where the supply and demand functions intersect. The equilibrium price for the pound P_e is here assumed to be $1.70; the equilibrium quantity Q_e. If a price higher than $1.70 existed for the pound—for example, P_1, which we will assume is $1.80—the quantity of pounds supplied Q_2 would exceed the quantity of pounds demanded Q_1 and a downward pressure on the price of the pound would exist, that is, pressure for a *depreciation* of the pound. (A depreciation is the lowering of the price of one currency in terms of another currency.) The price of the pound would fall until it reached the equilibrium price unless some sort of intervention took place to support the price of $1.80. (You are left to analyze the situation where a price lower than P_e exists and an appreciation or rise in the price of the pound will be called for.)

A decrease in the dollar price of the pound implies an increase in the pound price of the dollar. At $1.80 per pound, the quantity of dollars demanded will generally be greater than the quantity of dollars supplied. Hence the pressure will be for an increase in the value of the dollar to bring about equilibrium in the dollar market, that is, to decrease the quantity of dollars demanded and increase the quantity supplied.

ADJUSTMENT MECHANISM:
FIXED EXCHANGE RATES

As we have noted, from 1946 until the early 1970s exchange rates were not set on a day-to-day basis by market forces. Under the IMF Articles of Agreement, nations had to maintain established exchange or parity rates. In order to develop consistent parity rate definitions, each member nation effectively defined its currency in terms of gold or the dollar, which was officially convertible into gold. Therefore, all currencies were linked to gold and indirectly to each other.

For a group of nations with fully convertible currencies in which one particular nation's currency served double duty as domestic and international money, the number of exchange rates that could be independently defined was one less than the total number of nations.[3] If all countries tried to define their parity rates independently, conflict would emerge if one country sought to raise a parity that another country was trying to lower. Therefore, at least one country had to follow a passive course in defining its own parity rate. Under the operational Bretton Woods system, the passive country was the United States.

Once parity rate definitions were established, participating nations had to decide how to fulfill their responsibilities for maintaining stable exchange rates. Typically, member country officials controlled exchange rate fluctuations by using dollars to conduct transactions in the foreign exchange market.

In effect, foreign official agencies assured stable exchange rates through exchange market interventions involving dollar purchases when the price of the dollar was declining in terms of foreign currencies and vice versa. On the other hand, the United States *fixed* (*pegged*) the dollar's *exchange rate* by assuring convertibility of foreign officially held dollars into gold at $35 an ounce. These features of the original Bretton Woods system actually formed an operational dollar exchange standard, since the dollar's price was fixed in terms of gold and all other currency prices were fixed in terms of the dollar.

As we have indicated, maintaining or defending a given parity price for a currency meant that excess supply or demand situations had to be accommodated. In Figure 13.3 we find supply and demand functions for the pound. Assume that originally price P_2 was an equilibrium price determined by the intersection of supply and demand. Due to a change in some variable, the supply function for the pound has shifted so a new equilibrium price P_1 is called for. However, under IMF control, supply and demand were not allowed to establish a new price unless a *fundamental disequilibrium* situation exists.

At price P_2, the old equilibrium price, the quantity of pounds supplied Q_2 is greater than that demanded Q_1. Hence an excess supply situation exists, and under flexible exchange rates a depreciation of the pound would occur as market forces brought the price down to P_1. Since a country has to defend the established or pegged price for the currency, the excess supply of pounds

---

3. The principle is the same as that used in describing the efficiency of using one good (money) as a unit of account to reduce the number of prices required in an economy. The equation $n(n - 1)/2$ found in Chapter 1 applies here also, but n now refers to the number of countries or national currencies instead of to goods.

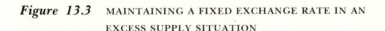

Figure 13.3   MAINTAINING A FIXED EXCHANGE RATE IN AN
EXCESS SUPPLY SITUATION

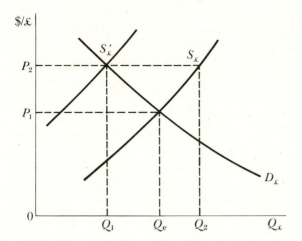

$Q_2 - Q_1$ must be taken off the market. The excess supply country has to buy up the excess currency using either gold or other foreign exchange reserves, such as British holdings of United States dollars in this instance. This would shift the supply function to the left (to $S_£'$), temporarily eliminating the excess supply of pounds.

In the short run a solution like this is feasible. Temporary payment deficits can be met by drawing down a country's international reserves, including its IMF reserve position.[4] As the period lengthens over which excess pounds have to be purchased, however, Britain would begin to exhaust its holdings of gold (if it cannot mine gold) or its foreign exchange reserves that were accumulated previously. When a country can no longer defend the old price or no longer wishes to, it has one of two choices: it may announce a new official price for its currency that is more defensible given current market conditions, or it may attempt to modify the situation by domestic economic policies.

Domestic economic policies can decrease or eliminate the excess supply of a

4. For a discussion of IMF reserve position including SDRs, see later in this chapter.

domestic currency, but usually not very rapidly. The cure would most likely involve a slowdown of the domestic economy. A lower level of economic activity would decrease imports while not affecting the export level very significantly. The decreased imports would imply a shift to the left in the supply function for pounds (that is, the demand function for dollars). However, most nations are loath to engineer an economic slowdown that may turn into a recession. Sacrificing domestic employment rates for solutions to international economic problems is difficult politically to sell to the public. Thus countries given the choice between a depreciation of their currency and diminished economic growth rates usually opt for the depreciation. Unfortunately, most countries under the fixed exchange rate system refused to face their international problems until forced to. Usually economic conditions brought about a depreciation without the country making a choice, thus leading to a less than orderly process that was not envisioned when the IMF was established.

A depreciation of the domestic currency does *not* imply that no real changes occur, however. With a depreciation, all imports become more expensive. This will cause many costs to rise, creating inflationary pressures (especially if the country has to import significant amounts of petroleum). As the price of the domestic currency falls, exports should increase, resulting in a greater share of the country's output being exported. All this may well mean that a country will be worse off as far as the real standard of living is concerned. If the country is already close to or at full employment, then inflationary pressures will increase; if there is substantial unemployment, increased exports and decreased imports will mean a greater aggregate demand and a higher level of output. Domestically, in either situation exporting industries will be favored over those producing mostly or solely for the local population.

Under the fixed exchange rate system, an excess demand situation will exist if the exchange rate to be defended is less than that called for by market forces. In Figure 13.4 price P_1 is the pegged exchange rate and P_2 would be the equilibrium rate. At price P_1, the quantity demanded is Q_2 and the quantity supplied Q_1. In one sense this is an easier situation to deal with than the opposite case. The market calls for a greater supply of pounds, and in this example Britain can print pounds as fast as she wishes, thus shifting the supply function out to S' to maintain price P_1. While it is easier for a country to obtain greater supplies of its own currency, however, supplying greater quantities generally increases the inflationary pressures. Thus a country like

---

Figure 13.4   MAINTAINING A FIXED EXCHANGE RATE IN AN
EXCESS DEMAND SITUATION

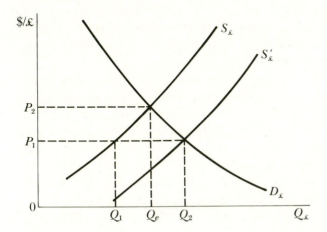

the Federal Republic of Germany, which over several years experienced an excess demand situation and continuous pressures for an appreciation of the Deutschemark, complained of being forced to import inflation because supplying increased amounts of the domestic currency tends to increase the money supply. An alternative would have been to expand the German economy, which would have increased imports and eliminated part of the excess demand for the mark. However, over much of this period the German economy was already operating at full employment, and an expansionary policy would simply have increased inflation rates. Nevertheless, the Germans did not wish to appreciate their currency and incur the costs as the domestic economy adjusted to its exports such as Volkswagens becoming more expensive.

Implications for Domestic Stabilization Policy

As indicated, a fixed exchange rate system can create a serious impediment to effective pursuit of domestic stabilization policies. Consider the hypothetical case of a nation facing domestic inflation but no payments imbalance for the time being. To dampen inflationary pressures, the nation's central bank pursues open market sales of government securities. This restrictive policy causes interest rates and security yields to rise. Emerging yield differentials between domestic and foreign securities stimulate arbitrage activity, whereby domestic investors sell their foreign assets and purchase domestic securities. In addition, funds are borrowed abroad, where interest costs are lower. The resulting capital inflow generates a payments surplus for the country, which at the same time experiences a slowing of economic activity that dampens imports and further expands the surplus.

Committed to maintaining a fixed exchange rate for its currency, the country's central bank intervenes in exchange markets by purchasing the excess supply of foreign currency. As shown earlier, the monetary result of these operations is similar to that of open market purchases of government securities by the central bank. The expansion of the domestic money supply tends to negate, or at least blunt, the impact of the original restrictive monetary policy. In this setting, a resurgence of economic activity stimulates an increase in imports. In turn, in the wake of declining interest rates and security yields, capital inflows are reduced, thus restoring the nation's balance of payments to its earlier state. Hence a domestic monetary policy aimed at dampening inflation is impeded by concern for holding the exchange rate stable. Figure 13.5 depicts clearly the incompatibility of these two goals.

Recognizing these limitations, foreign agencies have attempted to improve the working of monetary policy by applying various direct controls to the foreign activities of their countries' banking institutions. These controls, devised to limit capital inflows during periods of restrictive monetary policy, include (1) credit ceilings to limit the expansion of bank credit, thus making borrowing incentives less attractive; (2) stiffer reserve requirements against bank liabilities to foreigners than against liabilities to residents, thus making borrowing abroad relatively more costly; (3) absolute limits on net foreign liabilities; (4) regulations stipulating that a bank's current (spot) foreign assets and liabilities should be equal; and (5) interest bans on foreign-owned deposits.

These direct approaches provide only temporary breathing room for a domestic restrictive monetary policy, because a waning level of economic activity cuts spending on foreign goods and services. Beyond impeding the efficient allocation of financial resources, these direct controls simply postpone the balance-of-payments effects on the domestic monetary system until repercussions in the real sector are felt.

While adherence to a fixed exchange rate scheme limits the effectiveness of

Figure 13.5 ILLUSTRATION OF CONFLICT BETWEEN INTERNAL
AND EXTERNAL STABILIZATION GOALS FOR
MONETARY POLICY

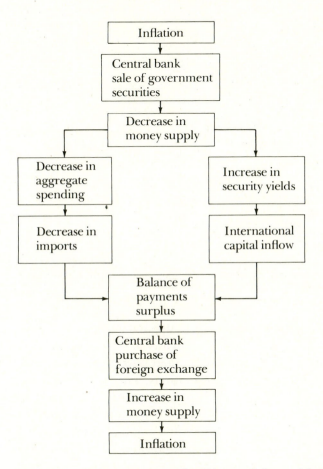

Source: George W. McKenzie, "International Monetary Reform and the 'Crawling Peg,'" Federal Reserve Bank of St. Louis, *Review*, February 1969, p. 18.

Figure 13.6   ILLUSTRATION OF COMPATIBILITY BETWEEN
INTERNAL AND EXTERNAL STABILIZATION GOALS
FOR FISCAL POLICY

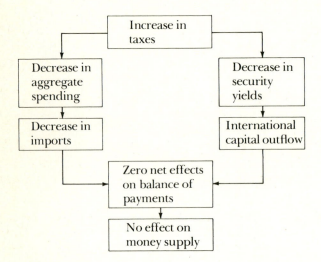

Source: George W. McKenzie, "International Monetary Reform and the 'Crawling Peg,'" Federal Reserve Bank of St. Louis, *Review*, February 1969, p. 19.

domestic monetary policy, fiscal policy remains unimpeded at home. In terms of the hypothetical case just discussed, an anti-inflationary fiscal policy may entail an increase in the nation's tax rates. Augmented government tax revenues tend to decrease government financing operations. The weaker pace for government financing tends to reduce the supply of securities offered in markets, thus bringing a rise in domestic security prices and a decline in yields. Interest rate differentials between home and abroad induce capital outflows, and hence the nation's payments position deteriorates. However, the fiscally induced cut in the nation's disposable income slows domestic economic activity, thus reducing imports and offsetting the deterioration in the country's capital account. In sum, this adjustment process tends to restore balance-of-payments equilibrium, to have no net effect on the domestic money supply, and most important, to maintain an anti-inflationary pace for economic activity. Figure 13.6 shows the chain of effects generated by the initial fiscal action of raising taxes.

Note that the schematic diagram in Figure 13.6 ignores serious drawbacks affecting the timely implementation of fiscal policy, especially in relation to political considerations.[5] Furthermore, changes in interest rates and total spending take time to work their full effects on the real and financial sectors of the economy. In addition, both tariff and nontariff barriers affecting international economic relations impede the working of the adjustment process.

Finally, economic goals may conflict in the short run. In those settings marked by either lagging employment and a payments surplus or domestic inflation and a balance-of-payments deficit, stabilization actions affecting aggregate spending can achieve a solution for both simultaneously. However, when there exists either an unacceptable rate of domestic unemployment and a payments deficit or domestic inflation and a balance-of-payments surplus, policy makers are hard pressed to achieve both domestic and international goals. Actions that cut total spending and reduce a payments deficit will tend also to increase domestic unemployment. Alternatively, efforts to eliminate a payments surplus by expanding aggregate spending and employment within the home economy may kindle strong inflationary pressures. These dilemmas facing policy makers reflect the difficulties of weighing domestic social-political goals against the costs associated with payments imbalances.

ADJUSTMENT MECHANISM:
FLEXIBLE EXCHANGE RATES

On August 15, 1971, President Nixon's momentous announcement of the suspension of dollar convertibility into gold heralded the end of the international monetary system's adherence to the gold-exchange standard. It was felt that the best way to get the international adjustment system functioning again after its breakdown was simply to allow market forces (with some minimal intervention by governments) to establish new rates for currencies. Owing to either a willingness on the part of various governments or a lack of choice because economic conditions would permit nothing else, more and more currencies have been turned loose to find their price in terms of other

5. See Chapter 21 for a discussion and comparison of monetary and fiscal policy lags. See also Chapter 22, the section entitled "Coordination of Stabilization Policies."

currencies in the foreign exchange market. The adjustment mechanism in use is not a perfect free-market system but one referred to as a *dirty float*, characterized by some day-to-day governmental intervention to smooth out changes, but no obligation to maintain any given exchange rate.

What began as a temporary situation prior to the reinstitution of the old system has worked so well that the movement now *seems* irrevocably in the direction of permanent market control, that is, *freely fluctuating (flexible, floating) exchange rates.* However we would be remiss if we did not say that there are strong arguments for and proponents of continuing with the old system (given a hiatus of several years). Hence it would come as a mild surprise but no shock if the plans for a permanent flexible exchange rate system were scrapped and the international system were returned to one of a modified pegged, or fixed, exchange rate.

Under a flexible exchange rate system, as we have noted, the price of a currency in terms of another currency is set by the market, that is, the forces of supply and demand.[6] The supply and demand functions for a currency are not fixed. A change in any variable other than the exchange rate will cause shifts in one or both of these curves if the variable affects the supply of, or demand for, a currency. Variables important in determining the position of the supply and demand functions for a currency include the inflation rate in the domestic country compared to foreign economies, changes in expectations concerning the stability of the domestic government and the economy, changes in the quality of products produced, or changes in people's preferences for certain country's goods.

For example, assume that a 5 percent inflation rate per year exists in the United Kingdom, the same rate as in the United States. Now assume inflation increases to 10 percent annually in the United States while it remains at 5 percent in Britain. Goods from the United States are now becoming more expensive *vis-à-vis* goods in Britain. Hence the demand for British goods and services will increase. In Figure 13.7 we show this increased demand for

6. The classic modern statement on flexible exchange rates is Milton Friedman's essay, "The Case for Flexible Exchange Rates," written in 1950 and published subsequently in his *Essays in Positive Economics* (Chicago: University of Chicago Press, 1953), pp. 157–203; abridged version in R.E. Caves and H.G. Johnson (eds.), *Readings in International Economics* (Homewood, Ill.: Richard D. Irwin, 1968), pp. 413–437. For an article that gives the argument both for and against flexible and fixed exchange rates, see Harry G. Johnson, "The Case for Flexible Exchange Rates, 1969," in *Further Essays in Monetary Economics* (Cambridge, Mass.: Harvard University Press, 1973), pp. 198–222.

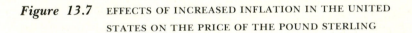

Figure 13.7 EFFECTS OF INCREASED INFLATION IN THE UNITED STATES ON THE PRICE OF THE POUND STERLING

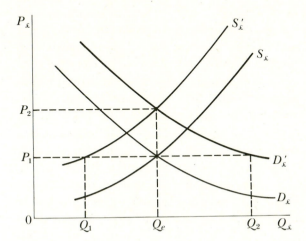

British goods and services as an increased demand for pounds, a shift from $D_£$ to $D_£'$. Since American goods are becoming more expensive relative to those from the United Kingdom, the demand for American goods decreases. This decrease is represented as a decrease in the supply of pounds, a shift from $S_£$ to $S_£'$. This decreased supply of and increased demand for pounds means that at the initial equilibrium price P_1, the quantity supplied Q_1 is now less than that demanded Q_2. Thus the price of the pound will be bid up, an appreciation, until a new equilibrium price is established at P_2 where the quantity demanded and that supplied are again equal.[7] The decreased demand for United States goods and increased demand for British goods because of the higher inflation rate in the United States results in an increased price for the pound and a decreased price for the dollar.

If expectations about the stability of the British government or its ability to overcome economic problems are lowered relative to those concerning the United States government, the opposite set of events would occur. The price of the pound would fall and that of the dollar would increase, ceteris paribus.

A flexible exchange rate system permits foreign exchange rates to respond

7. In this model, the old and the new equilibrium quantities are the same, Q_e; this need not be so.

freely to changing supply-demand relations, without government imposed restrictions on rate movements. In effect, exchange rates would serve the same function as does market price in any free unregulated competitive market. Since an exchange rate is simply a price, a flexible exchange rate regime allows price to perform its equilibrating function of maintaining balance between market demand and supply. Exchange rates would react automatically to an incipient payments imbalance, so that in the case of a United States payments deficit, the prices of foreign currencies would rise at home while the dollar would depreciate in exchange markets abroad. Emergent disequilibrium in a country's balance of payments would prompt rate changes that would tend to restore a payments balance. Foreign exchange markets would be cleared without resort to rationing, subsidies, or stockpiling. Private speculators in exchange markets would perform a stabilizing role by purchasing foreign exchange when its price fell (that is, the domestic currency appreciated in terms of other currencies) and selling foreign exchange when its price rose (that is, the domestic currency depreciated in terms of foreign currencies).

It should be stressed that a system of flexible exchange rates does not necessarily imply wildly gyrating or unstable exchange rates, as some critics contend. Freedom of rates to respond to market forces would precipitate extremely erratic rate movements only if underlying forces affecting supply and demand were inherently unstable. In this extreme situation, any international adjustment mechanism would face severe strains. Since a freely floating system permits quick adjustment of exchange rates, large disparities among rates would generally not develop. Yet there is no inherent feature in this system to preclude official intervention in foreign exchange markets to lessen or avoid disruptive and disorderly rate fluctuations.

The flexible adjustment of rates would speed up the adjustment process and tend to decrease the pressure on nations' holdings of international reserves. Since changes in exchange rates would also provide the basic equilibrating force affecting the flow of international transactions, nations' price-cost structures would be largely separate from one another. In effect, countries could follow completely independent domestic economic policies without shunting painful adjustments onto others. For example, a government pursuing an expansive inflationary policy at home would generate a rise in demand for imports and a decline in demand for its exports. Instead of running a chronic payments deficit and thereby exporting its inflation abroad, the depreciation in the international value of this nation's currency will force an elimination of its import surplus. Therefore, the real burden stemming from domestic policy excesses would be borne largely at home.

A CRITICAL APPRAISAL OF
FLEXIBLE EXCHANGE RATES

Proponents of freely fluctuating exchange rates base their argument on the view that their system affords the only reasonable approach between two highly unattractive alternatives: nationally imposed controls on international trading activities, or wide swings in the domestic economy. Rather than compelling the domestic economy to adjust to a pre-established fixed exchange rate, a flexible approach would allow the exchange rate itself to do the adjusting.

Exchange rate fluctuations do not imply that the internal economy is left unchanged. Since exchange depreciation increases import prices relative to domestic prices, consumption patterns shift toward domestic goods and away from competing import goods. Furthermore, additional productive resources would be directed into export industries. Opposite changes in the patterns of consumption would occur in a surplus country, whose currency appreciates in the foreign exchange market.

Theoretically, both systems—involving either fixed rates or flexible rates— require similar adjustments in the economy. Therefore, why all the fury of discussion surrounding them? The answer lies in the operational results felt in the real economy. Price-wage rigidities in the actual economy imply that the deflationary process required to erase a deficit under a fixed rate regime would carry adverse effects for employment. Although exchange depreciation via floating rates would involve some painful reduction in real income, it presumably would be free from employment effects linked with internal price-wage rigidities. Hence fluctuating exchange rates could make rigid domestic prices and wages flexible in terms of foreign currencies.

Possible Trade Disruptive Effects

A major criticism of the flexible rate system is that exchange rate fluctuations might seriously disrupt international trade. This implicitly assumes that international trade and financial activity require stable rates. It is presumed that in the face of fluctuating exchange rates international traders would be disheartened by uncertainty surrounding future exchange rates (even if the rates did not gyrate wildly); consequently, trade volume would dwindle.

Several points counter this criticism. First, over the long run, pegged exchange rates are not absolutely certain, because official par values can be changed abruptly. Second, in the short run, effectively operating forward exchange markets can minimize business uncertainty arising from temporary fluctuations in exchange rates. For example, assume that a United States importer contracts to purchase goods from West Germany, the German exporter to be paid in German marks upon delivery of the goods in three months. Since the dollar-mark exchange rate could change over this period, the United States importer would be uncertain what the dollar cost of the goods would be if he waited three months to buy marks. Purchase of marks for future delivery in the forward exchange market would permit the United States importer to avoid this uncertainty. Specifically, the importer's bank could agree to deliver, three months hence, the marks required by the importer at that time and could also indicate *today* the rate of exchange (or dollar price) that would have to be paid for the marks at that time. This contractual arrangement is sometimes referred to as a *purchase of forward cover*.

Granting this role of the forward exchange market, critics retort that the market would buckle under pressures generated by a system of floating exchange rates. They argue that with flexible rates the demand for forward cover would increase sharply, the forward exchange market would be overburdened, and hence international commerce would be crippled.

Recent experience affords some insight into the ability of the forward exchange market to withstand strains emanating from freely fluctuating rates. The Canadian dollar has been allowed to float since June 1, 1970, and most of the other major currencies were permitted to float for a time in 1971. Results of a sample survey of United States firms doing business with Canadians during the flotation of the Canadian dollar suggest an unimpaired ability of the forward exchange market to provide forward cover for transactions between United States and Canadian parties.[8] Further evidence on whether

8. Federal Reserve Bank of Boston, *Canadian-United States Financial Relationships*, Conference Series No. 6 (September 1971). During the period 1950–1962 Canada experimented with flexible exchange rates. This earlier experience saw a rising level of Canadian international trade and investment activity. Furthermore, empirical evidence suggests the absence of any destabilizing

exchange rate flexibility weakens the viability of forward exchange markets emerges from a Federal Reserve survey of 167 United States nonbanking firms transacting business with West German residents during the period May 10, 1971, through December 17, 1971. The study found no major, and almost no minor, complaints by these firms regarding the operation of the mark-dollar forward market during this period. This finding is reinforced by two factors: the appreciable change in the mark-dollar exchange rate during this flotation period, and the prolonged uncertainty surrounding the setting of a new rate.[9]

This same study observed that some forward exchange markets performed poorly during this period, especially the forward market for the Japanese yen. This creaky performance was attributed to government controls and restrictions on institutions serving these markets rather than to inherent weaknesses in these institutions.

This finding gives at least partial support to critics of a fixed rate system who contend that official efforts to protect a fixed rate may create more adverse repercussions on traders and investors than would the adjustment such actions attempt to avoid. Involved here is a basic choice: the risk of exchange fluctuation must be compared with the alternative risks stemming from direct controls and other restrictive devices utilized to maintain fixed rates.

Balance-of-Payments Discipline

Finally, another criticism raised against flexible rates is that such an approach removes a major disciplinary restraint against domestic inflationary policies. This argument holds that under a fixed rate system, inflationary policies worsen the balance of payments, thus inducing a loss of gold or foreign exchange reserves. In turn, this reserve loss eventually compels policy makers to take more restrictive actions against domestic inflation. However, such disciplinary pressure is not restricted to fixed rates. Under freely floating

exchange rate fluctuations arising from speculation in exchange markets. See George W. McKenzie, "International Monetary Reform and the 'Crawling Peg,'" Federal Reserve Bank of St. Louis, *Review* (February 1969): 21ff.

9. Norman S. Fieleke, "Exchange-Rate Flexibility and the Forward-Exchange Markets: Some Evidence from the Recent Experience with the German Mark," Federal Reserve Bank of Boston, *New England Economic Review* (May-June 1972): 9.

rates, nations' inflationary policies would lead to depreciation of their currencies relative to other currencies, and this exchange depreciation may be something to be avoided. Exchange depreciation tends to raise import prices and generally worsens a country's terms of trade.

The question of whether reserve losses or exchange depreciation exert greater disciplinary effects for inflationary policies may be misleading. The fundamental point may well be that inflation is undesirable per se and should be avoided. Essentially, no international payments system can compel, or substitute for, responsible domestic economic policies.

OTHER PROPOSED REFORMS OF THE ADJUSTMENT MECHANISM

The preceding discussion focused on a distinction between completely free exchange rates and fixed exchange rates. In the real world, however, the choices for selecting an international adjustment mechanism are not so clear-cut. Political, social, and other factors make authorities reluctant to devise an adjustment mechanism incorporating completely free exchange rates. Instead, officials and other observers have considered various alternatives for achieving more limited forms of rate flexibility that do not depart completely from the fixed exchange rate system.

These compromise suggestions attempt to capture some of the assumed advantages of exchange flexibility within the basic context of the fixed rate system. These proposals for limited flexibility typically involve some version of "wider bands," "crawling pegs," or a combination of the two.

The Band Proposal

One frequently suggested proposal, called the *band proposal,* is to widen the range within which exchange rates are allowed to fluctuate. For example, the Smithsonian Agreement of December 18, 1971, enlarged the band of permissible exchange rate variation to ±2.25 percent of the newly agreed central values. This change from the previous range of ±1 percent was presumably to enable exchange rates to play a bigger part in inducing adjustments necessary to correct payments imbalances. Then, following the great upheaval in foreign exchange markets in early 1973, major industrial nations agreed to allow some unspecified float in exchange rates between the United States dollar and other leading currencies. At the same time, eight European nations (including six European Economic Community members) agreed to hold their currency fluctuations within a narrow 2.25 percent band of each other while the currencies floated as a bloc against the dollar.

Operationally, a major advantage of a wider band is that it affords more leeway for the conduct of domestic stabilization policies. Greater swings in exchange rates tend to lessen the pressure of payments imbalances on international reserves, and policy makers have more flexibility in taking actions to stabilize the domestic economy. However, a greater range for rate swings would still be ineffective in the face of a fundamental disequilibrium in the balance of payments or a massive speculative attack on a currency.

The Crawling Peg Proposal

A moving or *crawling peg system* involves a gradual, but continuing, adjustment in a currency's par value up to a predetermined maximum rate. The speed of adjustment might be set, for example, at a maximum of one-sixth of 1 percent per month. In a year this could generate a 2 percent change in par value. The result would be a relative short-run stability of rates that would accord a degree of certainty to international transactions. In the longer view, the gradual change in parity values allows for variations in price-cost structures among nations and facilitates payments corrections before massive dislocations occur.

An important question in devising a crawling peg system involves the use of automatic versus discretionary changes in parity. A discretionary arrangement would require government decisions on the timing and extent of alterations in the parity rate, much like the traditional system of stable parities linked with very narrow bands. Administratively enacted, frequent and small changes in parity could smooth disruptive capital flows, but at times officials might have to face decisions that could stir unpopular domestic reactions. Thus officials might procrastinate in making necessary decisions.

An automatic arrangement would permit market forces to determine fluctuations in parity, with the margins about the parity rate free to change up to a predetermined maximum annual rate in either direction. Note that official action is required in establishing the marginal limits. A fully automatic approach to parity changes would strengthen the adjustment mechanism, but it would require a partial surrender of national sovereignty over exchange rates.

Which of these exchange rate adjustment mechanisms will be used depends on the countries involved. It would appear that most of the developed and Western countries are planning to stick with a flexible exchange rate system, resorting to minor governmental intervention only. However, other countries may decide to peg their currency to that of one of the larger, more developed nations. Thus some Latin American countries may tie their currency to the United States dollar, for example. Since the United States represents their largest international market, they may well opt for a pegged exchange rate. At the same time, a country choosing to tie its currency to the dollar might also decide to use wider bands.

With the adoption of flexible exchange rates, the United States dollar has been freed from unnecessary restraints, thus permitting the United States and other countries to make required adjustments more easily, given the international sector. The nations constituting the greatest portion of international trade are also seeking a way to free the United States from its role of providing the majority of international reserves required for international trade. One possible solution is the increased use of special drawing rights (SDRs) by the IMF.

INTERNATIONAL MONETARY POLICY

The International Monetary Fund is the official organization through which many of the nations of the world help formulate international trade and monetary policy. It provides a forum in which member nations can raise and debate the issues of interest to them. The IMF is particularly interested and actively engaged in assisting member nations to solve their balance-of-payments problems.

The IMF was established after World War II as an attempt to avoid a repetition of the disastrous situation that occurred before the war, when international trade came almost to a complete stop. The volume of international trade grew smaller year by year as nations constructed barriers to trade to protect themselves and engaged in competitive devaluations, causing great uncertainty worldwide. The IMF was instituted in the belief that increased international trade would help nations develop and prosper. One of the requirements for increased international trade appeared to be a system providing a high degree of international financial stability. This stability was to be guaranteed by a fixed exchange rate system that was tied to gold.

Amendments to the IMF Articles of Agreement indicate that fundamental changes are required in the international monetary system. The first amendment to the Articles, officially accepted in 1969, allowed the IMF to create *special drawing rights (SDRs),* or "paper gold," as they have been called due to their connection to gold. (This connection disappeared when the second amendment to the Articles entered into force in April 1979.) The principle of SDRs and their operation had originally been approved (though not officially) at the 1967 meeting of the IMF at Rio de Janeiro. SDRs were introduced to increase the supply of international reserves for international trade. Under a system of fixed exchange rates, the dollar amount of trade increased yearly, necessitating greater amounts of international reserve assets to facilitate trade between countries. Faced with an essentially static gold supply (except for limited increases from South Africa and indirectly from the USSR[10]) and a weakened United States dollar (caused by successive balance-of-payments deficits), the IMF created SDRs. These served as a substitute for gold and the dollar (or any other single national currency used as international reserve assets). Note that the creation and use of SDRs in lieu of the United States dollar decreases United States seigniorage. *Seigniorage* is the difference between the value of a unit of currency (for example, a $1 bill) and the cost of producing that unit of currency.

The idea that led to the creation of an international currency or asset in the late 1960s was not new. At Bretton Woods in 1944, John Maynard Keynes had suggested a new reserve asset to replace gold, which he named the "Bancor." Robert Triffin in the 1950s also recognized the difficulties gold presented and the need for increasing international reserves over time, and offered the "Triffin Plan." Various other solutions have also been offered from time to time.[11]

10. While the USSR mines gold, it reaches the rest of the world only when the Russians choose to use it to buy goods from the West. The Russians and the Eastern bloc nations are not members of the IMF.

11. For a more complete description of various plans suggested, see Raymond F. Mikesell,

Obtaining acceptability for the idea of an international reserve asset has been difficult, however. Nations historically mistrust each other's motives and intentions. As a consequence, without an appreciable say in the decision-making process about the way in which the system was to operate, they refused to participate. What finally led to the acceptance of the SDR plan in the late 1960s was the realization that a gold solution would neither be acceptable to a majority of the nations nor be able to accomplish the tasks necessary to solve the liquidity problems facing much of the world. Furthermore, participating nations no longer wished to allow the United States to create the other reserve asset, the dollar, over which they had virtually no control. Hence some asset like SDRs seemed to offer the least objectionable solution.

SDRs are created in much the same way that the Federal Reserve System creates assets in the United States, in effect by fiat. In order for SDRs to be issued, 60 percent of the IMF members and 80 percent of the voting power had to approve the amendment. Voting strength in the IMF is apportioned on the basis of the quotas assigned to each country. The quotas are a function of a country's volume of international trade, national income, and international reserve holdings in relation to other countries. The purpose of the stringent voting requirements for acceptance of the SDR plan was to guarantee substantial agreement for what at the time was a relatively radical move.

The distribution of the assets created by the Federal Reserve System is not a major problem whereas the distribution of assets created by the IMF is. The Federal Reserve does not have to worry about which countries are going to receive its assets; the IMF does. Third World nations argued, for example, that SDR issues should be distributed to them initially as they could use the purchasing power to command resources for development. This was not a widely accepted viewpoint among the members with the voting power, and consequently the SDRs have been distributed according to the size of a country's quota.

Several features make SDRs unique. First of all, they differ markedly from IMF borrowings in several ways. For one thing, SDRs are allocated among all participating nations, while borrowings initially augment the reserves of borrowing countries only. Since SDRs are not extended through lending, they

Financing World Trade: An Appraisal of the International System and of Proposals for Reform (New York: Thomas Crowell, 1969), pp. 75–111.

theoretically do not have to be repaid. A nation's average holdings of SDRs must comprise a minimum of 30 percent of its average cumulative allocations over a specified base period. If this minimum percentage is not met, a country must then reconstitute its SDR holdings prior to the end of the specified base period to once again attain the average ratio requirement. This provision seeks to preclude a member nation from depending solely on SDRs for financing balance-of-payments deficits and also to promote SDR holdings as part of a nation's monetary reserves.

Another distinguishing feature of SDRs is that participating countries must accept them in exchange for convertible currencies and are committed to hold unneeded SDRs up to an overall amount triple the size of total allocations. Furthermore, a country may not use them merely to alter the composition of its reserve holdings by exchanging them for gold or a reserve currency. Finally, SDR holdings in excess of a given nation's total allocations earn a low interest yield, thus enhancing their acceptability as a reserve asset.

These distinguishing provisions were instituted to give SDRs the acceptability necessary for success. They tended to make SDRs and gold almost equally acceptable. By agreeing to accept SDRs in official IMF settlements, member nations limited the possibility that they would become less desirable than other assets, which is true of the position of many national currencies.

Initially the SDR was given a value of a certain amount of gold. Since gold's value was given in dollar terms, the SDR had a stated dollar value: SDR 1 equaled U.S. $1. Then two events caused participating countries to decide that the SDR would no longer be valued so that it was equal to U.S. $1: in 1971 the United States ceased dollar convertibility into gold, and in that year and in 1973 the dollar was devalued. Hence most countries felt that it was undesirable to have the SDR's value denominated in dollars since the value of their assets (SDRs) decreased when the United States dollar did. Therefore, since 1974 a "basket" of sixteen currencies has been used to value SDRs. When one currency depreciates, other currencies necessarily appreciate by comparable amounts. The value of the SDR thus remains fairly constant.

In the period from 1970 to 1972, the IMF issued SDR 9.3 billion (at the time equivalent to U.S. $9.3 billion). While SDR 9.3 billion is a sizable amount, it is small compared to official gold holdings and foreign exchange of SDR 180 billion. An additional SDR 12 billion has been provided for, one-third to be created on the first day of 1979, and the other thirds on the first days of 1980 and 1981, respectively.

This second amendment effects changes in the operation of the IMF that reflect the current economic environment. The changes of most concern to us are in three areas: the international adjustment or exchange mechanism, the role of gold, and the future of SDRs.

As we mentioned at the beginning of this chapter, the international monetary adjustment system seems to be evolving away from one of fixed exchange rates to one of floating exchange rates. Each year more countries seem to be letting the market determine the international value of their currency. This is technically illegal under the present IMF Articles of Agreement, which require pegged exchange rates.

The approved second amendment to the Articles allows countries to choose their own system of adjustment—fixed, flexible, or some combination of the two. For example, a member could choose to go from one fixed exchange rate to a new one, using a flexible exchange rate system in between, as long as the process was orderly and the member fulfilled its obligations to the IMF required under the Articles of Agreement.

The second area of reform under the second amendment is in the role of gold. Gold would become considerably less important in international transactions. Officially, gold would no longer be used in setting the value of the SDR. Secondly there would no longer be an official price for gold; the market would be left to determine its price. Individual members would be permitted to trade in gold at the market-determined price. However, the IMF would not have a gold tranche[12] and would not accept gold except under unusual circumstances. In line with these changes, the IMF will dispose of all of its gold holdings, generally by selling them on the market. Finally, and this is not part of the accepted second amendment, many of the major members of the IMF have agreed to cease using gold officially. Hence the international role of gold appears to be severely circumscribed. It will henceforth become in many ways simply another product like potatoes—shiny, perhaps, but still potatoes.

The last area of change involves the use of SDRs. SDRs would replace gold as the official reserve asset of the IMF. The method of determining the value of the SDR would be decided by a high majority of the voting power (85 percent). However, the "basket" of sixteen national currencies would probably

12. Each member of the IMF has a quota or subscription of monetary assets it must contribute. Of that quota, 25 percent was composed of gold, the so-called gold tranche.

continue to be used to define the value of the SDR as long as it seemed satisfactory, since it has the backing of major nations already. (In 1978, the nations whose currencies define the "basket" were rearranged; some were dropped, others added. The currencies defining the basket are not fixed.) Furthermore, the allowable uses of SDRs by the members would be broadened. SDRs would still be restricted to official institutions of the member nations, however; so they would not be used by private individuals and institutions.[13]

One of the major questions facing the international monetary system at the moment is what will be required in the way of reserves in the future. One of the supposed benefits of a system of flexible exchange rates is that reserves do not have to be increased as international trade increases, as was true under a system of fixed exchange rates. Whether or not they will have to be increased as rapidly as under the fixed exchange rate system has yet to be seen. Thus we do not know the amount of SDRs that will be created in the future. Clearly one of the factors determining the answer to this question will be the number of countries that select a flexible exchange rate system given the freedom permitted under the recent second amendment to the IMF's Articles of Agreement. For an answer to this question, we will simply have to wait.[14]

KEY TERMS

Bretton Woods system	Freely fluctuating (flexible,
Price elasticity of demand	floating) exchange rates
Depreciation	Purchase of forward cover
Appreciation	Band proposal
Fixed (pegged) exchange rate	Crawling peg system
Fundamental disequilibrium	Special drawing rights (SDRs)
Dirty float	Seigniorage

13. A beginning in the direction of a supranational currency is seen in current negotiations in the European Economic Community (Common Market).

14. For a more complete discussion of all the changes under the second amendment to the IMF Articles of Agreement, see *IMF Survey,* April 3, 1978, pp. 97–105.

REVIEW QUESTIONS

1. Explain how the price elasticity of demand for a country's exports determines the slope of the foreign demand function for that country's currency.

2. What considerations explain the price elasticity of demand for a country's exports?

3. a. From the following data, derive a supply curve for the pound sterling based on the British demand for an American good:

Q_x^D	$P_{x(\$)}$	$P_{£(\$)}$
900	$6.00	$2.20
800	$6.00	$2.00
700	$6.00	$1.80

   b. What can you say about the British price elasticity of demand for this American good?

4. Assuming the current price for a country's currency with respect to another currency is greater than the equilibrium rate justified by supply and demand conditions, explain how a depreciation of that currency effects a return to equilibrium.

5. What circumstances led to the abandonment of the fixed exchange rate system established at Bretton Woods in 1944?

6. Discuss the pros and cons of fixed versus flexible exchange rates.

7. What are SDRs and what purpose do they serve?

8. Under what conditions would a fixed exchange rate system impede the effective operation of domestic stabilization policy? Explain.

SUGGESTED READINGS

Balbach, Anatol B. "The Mechanics of Intervention in Exchange Markets." Federal Reserve Bank of St. Louis, *Review* (February 1978): 2–7.

Cornell, W. Bradford, and J. Kimball Dietrich. "The Efficiency of the Market for Foreign Exchange Under Floating Exchange Rates." *The Review of Economics and Statistics* LX (February 1978): 111–120.

Mudd, Douglas R. "International Reserves and the Role of Special Drawing Rights." Federal Reserve Bank of St. Louis, *Review* (June 1978): 9–14.

Part Five

MONEY IN THE ECONOMIC PROCESS

Chapter Fourteen

SOME INTRODUCTORY BASICS

Economic *theory* provides a framework for tracing the role that money plays in the economic system. Without a theory the difficulties of analyzing the influence of money in the economy would greatly increase. If one were simply to imagine, on the basis of the discussion of money up to this point, trying to describe the effects of an increase in the money supply on the level of employment or on the balance-of-payments situation, one would understand that theory is amazingly useful. To suggest changes in either of these variables is to use theory, either explicitly or implicitly, however complete or incomplete.

In this section we discuss the economic theory that has been developed to explain the relation between money and other economic variables. In addition, we present some of the major variations in theory concerning the role of money, emphasizing that the role money plays in the economy is interpreted differently by various observers.

THE SIGNIFICANCE OF THEORY

The significance of theory in general is that it provides a framework within which the effects of certain variables on other variables may be discussed. Theory is a common tool that all individuals may utilize for analyzing the phenomena in a given area of study.[1]

There is necessarily an opportunity cost incurred with the use of theory.

---

1. For an interesting treatment of the importance of theory to any discipline, especially a general theory that is widely held by those in a field of study, see Thomas S. Kuhn, *The Structure of Scientific Revolutions,* 2d ed. (Chicago: University of Chicago Press, 1970).

Part of that cost is that not all data can be included; a good many must be ignored if the theory is to have general applicability. Then, as the theory is applied to a particular problem and is made more specific, it loses its general applicability. Yet the opportunity cost of not using theory must be understood to be much greater than the cost resulting from its use. The skill of the theoretician is indicated by the ability to take a general theory and modify it to fit the specific case under study.

A general theory does not offer answers to specific problems. What it does is to indicate a means for analyzing some unknown or incompletely understood relation. For example, the so-called law of supply and demand is part of the general theory of economics. Yet the supply-demand model does not indicate how a tax would affect price and output. To find the effects of the tax on price and output, it is necessary to specify, in addition to the type of tax, the conditions under which the tax is being applied. One can then modify the supply-demand model to reflect these conditions.

Furthermore, it is only by applying theory to particular problems that one can see when the general theoretical bases of a discipline are deficient. When the theories that explain specific problems no longer fit into the general theoretical framework, a revision of the latter is required. The time necessary for conceiving a new general theory is a function of the brilliance of those working in the field. A Newton or an Einstein or a Keynes is a rare occurrence.

VARIETIES OF MONETARY THEORY

You may find it surprising, and perhaps somewhat disconcerting, to discover that there is no single monetary theory that is accepted by all economists, not even all economists who profess an expertise in the field of monetary economics. It might be said that there are two general views of monetary theory: the so-called Keynesian (or nonmonetarist) view, and the monetarist view.[2] Moreover, different interpretations or formulations of both the Keynesian and monetarist views exist.

2. A third view of monetary theory exists, according to some observers, that represents an amalgamation of the stronger points of the general Keynesian and monetarist views.

The classical quantity theory of money was the basic monetary theory for at least two hundred years, until it was displaced by the Keynesian theory during the 1940s and 1950s. Even though *The General Theory of Employment, Interest and Money,* by John Maynard Keynes, was published in 1936, several years passed before it began to have any general acceptance and significant influence in academic circles, let alone in the government policy area.[3]

The classical quantity theory (to Keynes, "classical" meant any macroeconomics before Keynes, that is, B.K.) held that some relationship existed between the quantity of money and the level of economic activity. In contrast, the Keynesian view holds that money is only one of several assets. Hence control of the money supply, in the Keynesian liquidity preference theory, is of less than overwhelming importance; at times it is held that control of the money supply is virtually useless. For Keynesians, regulation of the economy might well be better effected through tax and fiscal measures, since they question any suggestion that money has a direct influence on the equilibrium income level.

The pre-Keynesian or classical quantity theory of money, being no longer the predominant monetary theory, has been rewritten, in part because of the objections raised by Keynesians, who in turn were attempting to eliminate weaknesses in Keynes's theory. The present-day monetarists have restored money to a place of importance, now based on a more solid theoretical foundation and backed by improved empirical evidence. In fact, they claim that the relation between the money supply and the level of income is impossible to ignore. The relation is so strong, they assert, that controlling the growth of the money supply is the most powerful tool that exists for controlling the economy.

---

3. It is probably fair to say that much of the lag in the acceptance of *The General Theory* was due to a lack of precision in the book. *The General Theory* certainly does not have the focus and rigor of, say, Einstein's works on relativity, where the major impediments were simply (or not so simply) to get people to understand theory that was a quantum leap from that of Newton and to test it empirically. Some feeling for the deficiencies in *The General Theory* can be gained by a perusal of a retrospective review of the book by Harry G. Johnson (and the following discussions). While the review is at times technical, much of its flavor and content are understandable after a first year's course in macroeconomic and monetary theory. See Harry G. Johnson, "The *General Theory* after Twenty-five Years," *American Economic Review* 51 (May 1961): 1–25.

Interestingly, 1971 Nobel laureate Paul Samuelson writes that "Keynes himself did not truly understand his own analysis" until he had seen the mathematical models developed by others to explain *The General Theory.* See Paul A. Samuelson, "Lord Keynes and the *General Theory,*" *Econometrica* 14 (July 1946): 188.

And yet, as we shall see, monetarists generally argue against the active use of monetary policy. Many monetarists agree with the Keynesians that the primary means of controlling the economy is fiscal policy—changes in taxes and governmental expenditures. Although they may view control of the money supply as the most important tool available, they would prefer to use fiscal policy as the discretionary, countercyclical tool because they believe that an active, vigorous use of monetary policy cannot be carried out correctly. At the same time, many other monetarists would choose not to use fiscal policy in this fashion either.

It is clear that the monetary policy used today represents an acceptance of some monetarist positions. However, whether the general Keynesian view, the monetarist approach, or an intermediate position will carry the day is yet to be seen. Since no unanimity exists as to which is the more useful theory, both the Keynesian and monetarist views of monetary theory will be developed in this book. After presenting the classical quantity theory in Chapter 16, we will explain the Keynesian liquidity preference theory in Chapter 17 and the monetarist position in Chapter 19. Before proceeding to the discussion of these theories, however, we must consider the subjects of national income accounting and changes in the price level.

NATIONAL INCOME ACCOUNTING

To lay some foundation for the chapters following, we must briefly discuss the process of national income accounting and the national income accounts themselves. In the national income accounts, data from all sectors of the economy are aggregated to give the value of different macroeconomic concepts such as gross national product, gross investment, or gross consumption. The importance of understanding the process of national income accounting and what the various concepts imply cannot be underestimated. Only when students of macroeconomics master the essentials of national income accounting will they realize, for example, what gross national product is and what it is not.

The national income accounts are developed through two basic approaches—a products approach and an incomes approach. Either approach should, theoretically, result in the same value for any specified con-

Table 14.1 GROSS NATIONAL PRODUCT BY THE PRODUCT
APPROACH, 1978
(billions of dollars)

Personal consumption expenditures				1,340.1
Durable goods			197.5	
Nondurable goods			526.5	
Services			616.2	
Gross private domestic investment				345.6
Fixed investment			329.6	
Nonresidential		222.6		
Structures	77.8			
Producers' durable equipment	144.8			
Residential structures		107.0		
Nonfarm	103.8			
Farm	1.4			
Producers' durable equipment	1.7			
Change in business inventories			16.0	
Net export of goods and services				−12.0
Exports			204.8	
Imports			216.8	
Government purchases of goods and services				433.9
Federal			153.8	
National defense		99.5		
Other		54.3		
State and local			280.2	
Gross national product				2,107.6

Note: Data may not add due to rounding.
Source: Survey of Current Business, March 1979.

cept, such as gross national product or net national product. They in fact do
not. By the products approach, gross national product, for example, is found
by summing the values of the products and services that compose gross
national product (see Table 14.1). By the incomes approach, the incomes
generated in the production of the applicable goods and services are aggregated. However, this total measures *national income,* which is less than *gross
national income* (see Table 14.2).

Table 14.2   NATIONAL INCOME BY THE INCOMES APPROACH, NET
NATIONAL PRODUCT, AND GROSS NATIONAL
PRODUCT, 1978
(billions of current dollars)

Compensation of employees			1,301.4
Wages and salaries		1101.0	
Government and government enterprises	216.1		
Other	884.8		
Supplements to wages and salaries		200.5	
Employer contributions for social insurance	94.5		
Other labor income	105.9		
Proprietor income			113.2
Farm		25.3	
Nonfarm		87.8	
Rental income of persons			23.4
Corporate profits and inventory valuation adjustment			177.7
Profits before tax		202.1	
Profit tax liabilities	83.9		
Profits after tax	118.2		
Dividends	49.3		
Undistributed profits	68.9		
Inventory valuation adjustment		−24.4	
Net interest			106.3
National income			1,703.8
+Indirect business tax and nontax liability			178.3
+Business transfer payments			10.7
+Statistical discrepancies			1.7
−Subsidies less current surplus of government enterprises			3.9
Net national product			1,890.7
+Capital consumption allowance			216.9
Gross national product			2,107.6

Source: Survey of Current Business, March 1979. Data may not add due to rounding.

Eliminating Double Counting

The most important feature of national income accounting is the elimination of *double counting*—that is, when a good or service produced in the economy gets counted twice. Double counting is avoided by three different techniques—two of which apply to the products approach and one that applies to the incomes approach.

The two techniques for eliminating double counting that apply to the products approach to national income accounting involve either (1) summing only *final* goods and services produced, or (2) aggregating the *value added* at each stage of production for each product. The technique applying to the incomes approach to national income accounting is the addition of the incomes generated within an economy in a specified period of time.

The elimination of double counting by aggregating only final goods and services means that intermediate products are not counted. Intermediate products are those used in the production of other goods and services. For example, the lumber used in the production of a door is an intermediate good. The door would be the final good if sold to a consumer. The door would be an intermediate good, however, if sold to a contractor building a house; the house would then be the final good. The goods that are counted as being final are those for private consumption, investment, public consumption (those purchased by the government), and net exports.

A second technique for eliminating double counting involves summing the value added for each product at each stage of production. For example, lumber, locks, door handles, varnish, and other products purchased from other producers are used in the production of prefabricated doors. These products are combined to produce a door that will, hopefully for the producer, have a value greater than the goods that went into the door's construction. The difference between the cost of the materials purchased from other manufacturers and the value of the door is the *value added* at this stage of production for this good. If the value added were computed at previous stages of production in the manufacture of the lumber, locks, and so on used in the production of the door and then summed, the aggregate value added should equal the value of the door—the door itself being the final good in this instance.

Finally, the incomes approach for avoiding double counting involves aggregating the incomes generated in production of goods and services. In the example of prefabricated doors, labor was required to modify the products purchased from other manufacturers to produce doors. This labor received some remuneration, an income. Similarly, labor was required to produce the lumber used in making the doors; that labor also received some return. The total found by adding the incomes generated in the production process should be equal to the value of the products created (if it were not for the existence of the government).[4] The value added technique from the product side and the incomes generated technique amount, in fact, to the same thing.

Various Macroeconomic Concepts

Gross national product (GNP) is probably the most commonly encountered macroeconomic concept. It may be defined through either the products approach or the incomes approach. By the products approach, gross national product is defined as the summation of expenditures on consumer goods C, the amount of gross investment I_g,[5] those goods and services purchased by the government G, and net exports $Xp - Mp$ (that is, gross exports minus gross imports):[6]

$$\text{GNP} = C + I_g + G + (Xp - Mp) \tag{14.1}$$

By the incomes approach, the equation for gross national product may be written as

$$\text{GNP} = C + S + T \tag{14.2}$$

which states that incomes may be disposed of in three ways: spent on con-

---

4. The value of a product must be equal to the sum of the returns—incomes paid the various factors of production: land or natural resources, labor, capital, and entrepreneurial ability—involved in its production. Changes in the profit level keep the value of the goods equal to the total factor payments. Profits increase or decrease as the difference between the price the product sells for and the costs of production changes.

5. Gross investment is the value of all capital goods produced in a given time period, including changes in inventories.

6. Note that only final goods and services are being included so that no double counting occurs.

sumption goods C, saved S, or paid in taxes T. Combining these two equations, we derive what will be referred to as the income equation:

$$\text{GNP} = C + S + T = C + I_g + G + (Xp - Mp) \tag{14.3}$$

While it may appear otherwise, gross national product is a deficient measure of the economic value of all goods and services produced in a year. For example, the value of leisure is not included, nor is the value of the work done by members of a family around their own home or around someone else's home if they are not paid. (This work would be counted if it were done by someone else who was paid.) Gross national product does include an approximation of the rental value of owner-occupied housing. If a rental value is placed on owner-occupied housing, national income data will not be increased or decreased by long-run changes in the percentage of households owning their own homes. It is well to remember that gross national product consistently understates the value of total economic production.

Other common economic aggregates are net national product, national income, personal income, and disposable income. *Net national product*, NNP, is gross national product reduced by the amount of depreciation D (capital consumption allowance), where $I_n = I_g - D$:

$$\text{NNP} = \text{GNP} - D = C + I_n + G + (Xp - Mp) \tag{14.4}$$

Depreciation is the value of capital goods that have worn out over a given period. Thus replacement capital is not included in net national product. As has been pointed out elsewhere, including replacement capital is analogous to counting the population by taking the original population and adding those born without deducting those who have died. Consequently, many feel that net national product is a more usable and correct aggregate than gross national product because it includes only net changes in the capital stock.

National income is net national product with indirect business taxes and other items excluded. One type of indirect business tax is the property tax on businesses; another is an excise tax. *Personal income* is national income excluding incomes people earn but never receive, such as social security contributions and retained corporate profits, and including transfer payments. Examples of transfer payments are social security payments to the retired and disability payments. If personal taxes are deducted from personal income, *disposable income* results.

PRICE LEVEL CHANGES

Before considering monetary theory, we must discuss one additional subject: price level changes. Looking at either gross national product or net national product data for various years, we note changes and would like to know what these changes actually indicate. For example, if GNP has increased each year for the past three years, has the output of goods and services increased or not? Since GNP represents the aggregation of each good and service q_i, multiplied by the price of the good or service p_i, it could be written as follows:[7]

$$\text{GNP} = \sum_{i=1}^{n} q_i \cdot p_i \qquad (14.5)$$

Legitimately, any of several different conclusions may be drawn if the data show that GNP has increased for three successive years. For example, the output of goods and services alone might have increased, or the production of goods and services might have decreased but prices increased by a greater percentage than output had decreased, etc.

The difficulty is that gross national product includes two variables: prices and output. Since money serves as the unit of account, it would be convenient if the value of money did not change. When the overall price level changes, reflecting a general movement in most prices, the value or purchasing power of the dollar changes. If the price level rises, the value of money decreases; if the price level falls, the value of money increases.

Two common measures of price level changes frequently used are the consumer price index (CPI) and the producer price index (PPI). A third measure of price level changes, not often observed by the layperson, is the implicit price index.

The *consumer price index* (CPI), which is computed by the United States Bureau of Labor Statistics, is the most widely known of the three indices and is associated generally with the overall cost of living. Coverage includes prices of such items as food, clothing, shelter, recreational goods, professional fees, repair costs, transportation and public utility costs, and sales, excise, and real estate taxes.

---

7. The equation would be read, gross national product is the summation of the value of the ith good, $q_i \cdot p_i$, where $i = 1, \ldots, n$.

As of January 1978, two consumer price indices are calculated instead of one. The old index that applied to urban wage earners and clerical workers has been retained. But now a new index that includes not only the above groups but also salaried workers, the self-employed, and those retired as well as the unemployed is computed. The second consumer price index should come closer to representing the true cost-of-living changes for the average citizen. In addition, new weights have been assigned to expenditure groups. A new sample of items priced in the survey has also been drawn up, as well as an enlarged sample of locations for price-data gathering. Finally, new statistical methods are used. However, given these changes, 1967 is still the base year (1967 = 100). (The consumer price index found in Table 14.4 is that for urban wage earners and clerical workers.)

The *producer price index* (PPI) is the result of revising the old wholesale price index, WPI. The wholesale price index was designed to measure average price changes in commodities sold in primary markets of the United States. It covered commodities sold at the factory or farm level. While the revision for the consumer price index has been completed, that on the wholesale price index has not. However, as of late 1977 the Bureau of Labor Statistics has been emphasizing its producer price index on finished goods (PPI). The PPI will reflect price changes for producers' goods that are in the form to be sold to final users, thus eliminating producers' goods that have more processing to be done. The two types of finished goods to be included are those to be used by producers (capital goods) and those to be used by consumers (food, durables, and nondurables). This index differs from the consumer price index in that producer finished goods are included while services purchased by consumers are not. The revision under way is substantial, and will take at least until 1983 to complete.

Changes in the general price level of all final goods and services produced in the economy during a given period are measured by the GNP *implicit price index* sometimes called the GNP deflator. The GNP implicit price index is not obtained by direct price measurement as the consumer and wholesale price indices are. In developing the GNP implicit price deflator, the United States Department of Commerce adjusts for price change in each component of GNP in as fine detail as possible. For example, the consumer expenditures component of GNP is deflated by dividing each category of consumer spending by the appropriate index of consumer prices. The applicable index of wholesale prices is used to deflate business expenditures for capital equip-

Table 14.3   GROSS NATIONAL PRODUCT IN CURRENT AND
CONSTANT DOLLARS (BILLIONS) AND THE GROSS
NATIONAL PRODUCT DEFLATOR, 1967–1978

Year	GNP (Current Dollars)	GNP (1972 Dollars)	GNP Deflator (1972=100)
1967	796.3	1,007.7	79.02
1968	868.5	1,051.8	82.57
1969	935.5	1,078.8	86.72
1970	982.4	1,075.3	91.36
1971	1,063.4	1,107.5	96.02
1972	1,171.1	1,171.1	100.00
1973	1,306.6	1,235.0	105.80
1974	1,412.9	1,217.8	116.02
1975	1,528.8	1,202.3	127.15
1976	1,700.1	1,274.7	133.76
1977	1,887.2	1,332.7	141.61
1978	2,106.9	1,385.3	152.09

Sources: Economic Report of the President, 1979; Survey of Current Business, April 1979.

ment, raw materials, or semifinished goods. Hence, the CPI and WPI play a part in determining the implicit price deflator. In addition, indices of construction costs, prices paid by farmers, import prices, and so on permit deflation of other components of GNP. After the specific GNP components are adjusted for price changes, they are then aggregated to obtain GNP in constant dollars. The aggregate GNP deflator is computed by dividing current dollar GNP by constant dollar GNP and multiplying by 100.[8] In this roundabout way, the GNP deflator provides an implicit price index.

8. For example, if gross national product in some year were found to be $895.3 billion when measured in current dollars and $845.6 billion when measured in constant dollars (that is, prices were not allowed to change), the GNP deflator would be 105.9.

$$\frac{\text{GNP (current dollars)}}{\text{GNP (constant dollars)}} \cdot 100 = \text{GNP deflator}$$

$$\frac{\$895.3}{\$845.6} \cdot 100 = 105.9$$

Table 14.4 COMPARISON OF MOVEMENTS IN THE CONSUMER
PRICE INDEX, PRODUCER PRICE INDEX, AND GNP
DEFLATOR, 1967–1978
(with annual percentage changes in each)

Year	Consumer Price Index (1967 = 100)		Producer Price Index* (1967 = 100)		GNP Deflator (1972 = 100)	
1967	100.0	(3.0)	100.0	(0.2)	79.02	(2.9)
1968	104.2	(4.7)	102.5	(2.5)	82.57	(4.5)
1969	109.8	(6.1)	106.5	(3.9)	86.72	(5.0)
1970	116.3	(5.5)	110.4	(3.7)	91.36	(5.4)
1971	121.3	(3.4)	114.0	(3.3)	96.02	(5.1)
1972	125.3	(3.4)	119.1	(4.5)	100.00	(4.1)
1973	133.1	(8.8)	134.7	(13.1)	105.80	(5.8)
1974	147.7	(12.2)	160.1	(18.9)	116.02	(9.7)
1975	161.2	(7.0)	174.9	(9.2)	127.15	(9.6)
1976	170.5	(5.8)	183.0	(4.6)	133.76	(5.2)
1977	181.5	(6.5)	194.2	(6.1)	141.61	(5.9)
1978	195.5	(7.7)	209.3	(7.8)	152.09	(7.4)

*Prior to 1978 data are for the Wholesale Price Index.

Sources: *Economic Report of the President, 1979; Survey of Current Business,* April 1979.

Table 14.3 shows gross national product both in current dollars and in constant dollars as well as the GNP deflator for the period from 1967 to 1978. The base year is 1972, that is, the 1972 dollar has a value of 1.00. The steady rise in prices over this time as reflected in the index implies a decline in the purchasing power of the dollar.

The data in Table 14.3 show the effect that price increases have on GNP. Between 1973 and 1974 GNP in current dollars increased. When GNP using 1972 dollars is considered, it becomes apparent that the entire increase in GNP when measured in current dollars was a function of a rise in the general price level. In fact, one notes that real GNP declined in 1974 from the 1973 level. This decline reflects the economic recession of the time. The rise in prices was more than sufficient to disguise the absolute decrease in the output of goods and services.

Subtracting the GNP deflator for one year from that for a different year and dividing by the deflator for the earlier year will determine the rate of inflation (or deflation, if it occurred). Thus between 1973 and 1974 the general price level rose by 9.7 percent.

Table 14.4 gives data for the consumer price index, the producer price index and the GNP deflator for the years 1967 through 1978. Note that the base year for the consumer and producer price indices is 1967, while the base year for the GNP deflator is 1972.

KEY TERMS

Theory	Disposable income
Double counting	Consumer price index
Gross national product	Producer price index
Net national product	Implicit price index (GNP deflator)
National income	

REVIEW QUESTIONS

1. Define double counting and discuss methods used to eliminate it.

2. What is the explanation for the revision of the consumer price index and the producer (wholesale) price index?

3. What revisions have been made in the consumer price index?

4. From either the *Survey of Current Business* or the *Federal Reserve Bulletin* obtain data and compute on a quarterly basis percentage changes in GNP (in both current and constant dollars) and the GNP deflator from the first quarter of 1979 to the present. Note the success or lack of success in slowing the rate of inflation.

5. In August 1971 voluntary wage and price controls were introduced by President Nixon to fight inflation; in October 1978 voluntary wage and price controls were instituted by President Carter for the same purpose. Compare the succeeding events in the two periods, explaining differences and similarities where possible and discussing the effectiveness of the controls in containing inflation.

SUGGESTED READINGS

Economic Report of the President. Washington: Government Printing Office, various years.

Kuhn, Thomas S. *The Structure of Scientific Revolutions*. 2d ed. Chicago: University of Chicago Press, 1970.

Shapiro, Edward J. *Macroeconomic Analysis*. 4th ed. New York: Harcourt Brace Jovanovich, 1978. Especially Chapter 2 and Appendix.

Chapter Fifteen

AGGREGATE INCOME
DETERMINATION

Before the role of money in the economy is discussed, the determinants of the equilibrium level of income must be understood. This requires that the concepts of equilibrium in general and the equilibrium level of income be defined.

In the aggregate expenditures model of income determination, the components are derived from the four sectors constituting the economy: the households, whose expenditures are termed consumption C; business, which gives rise to investment I; the government, which is the source of public consumption G; and the foreign sector, whose component is net exports, the difference between gross exports and gross imports $(Xp - Mp)$. Each of these will be examined in turn.

The model developed here explains equilibrium in the real goods sector as opposed to the monetary sector. Hence, no important role for money is assumed initially other than that of *numeraire*, that is, other prices can be stated in relation to the common price of money. Secondly, prices will be assumed constant.

In Chapter 18 the *IS-LM* model is presented. The *IS-LM* model is an integration of the real goods sector and the monetary sector. The *IS*, or real goods, part of the model will be based on the various parts of the model developed here.

EQUILIBRIUM AND THE
EQUILIBRIUM LEVEL OF INCOME

Economists have traditionally developed theories based on the concept of *equilibrium*. As has often been pointed out, the equilibrium concept is borrowed from the sciences, where it means a balancing of opposing forces.[1] In economics this takes on a particular meaning. Economic systems are composed of human beings, who possess a volitional nature *vis-à-vis* their activities. Yet while human beings have some choice as to their activities, they are not totally unconstrained; there are limits or parameters to their alternatives. Consequently, the term *equilibrium* is used differently in the economic sphere than in the sciences. Equilibrium exists when, as H. T. Koplin states, "no one who *can* make a change *wants* to, and no one who *wants* to make a change is *able* to do so."[2]

An equilibrium level of income will exist when the individuals (or individual firms) constituting an economy find themselves in this position. To state it somewhat differently, an equilibrium income level implies that the forces tending to increase the level of income are just offset by those tending to decrease it.

CONSUMPTION AND SAVING

From the national income accounts, we know that the following identity exists:

$$Y \equiv C + S + T \equiv C + I + G + (Xp - Mp) \qquad (15.1)$$

Assuming a two-sector economy only (removing government and the foreign sector), the economy will consist of a household sector and a business sector. Then the income identity becomes

$$Y \equiv C + S \equiv C + I \qquad (15.1a)$$

The only goods and services produced will be for consumption or investment, and the ways to allocate income will be limited to spending or saving. It will be

1. John S. Chipman, "The Nature and Meaning of Equilibrium in Economic Theory," in *Functionalism in the Social Sciences: The Strength and Limits of Functionalism in Anthropology, Economics, Political Science, and Sociology,* ed. Don Martindale (Philadelphia: American Academy of Political and Social Science, 1965), p. 36.
2. H. T. Koplin, *Microeconomic Analysis: Welfare and Efficiency in the Private and Public Sectors* (New York: Harper & Row, 1971), p. 37.

Figure 15.1 CONSUMPTION FUNCTION RELATING THE LEVEL OF
CONSUMPTION TO THE LEVEL OF INCOME

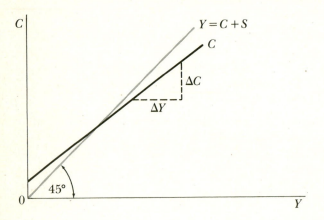

assumed that only households save—that the business sector does not.[3] A
consumption function or saving function explains on what basis the decision to
consume or save is made. Of the many variables of which consumption is a
function, the most important seems to be *disposable income* Y_d, which is income
from which taxes have been deducted. Other variables that appear to have
some influence in determining consumption are the rate of interest i; the real
wealth of an individual w; expectations concerning such things as changes in
the general price level and future employment x; and the distribution of
income d. The consumption function may be written

$$C = f(Y_d, i, w, x, d) \tag{15.2}$$

Since there is no government in this simplified model, disposable income is
identical with income, that is, $Y_d = Y$. If consumption is plotted against
different income levels, the consumption function is assumed to look like C in
Figure 15.1.

We assume the consumption function is linear, that is, a linear relationship

---

3. To simplify the model, we are assuming that businesses do not save, when in fact they do.

exists between consumption and income.[4] The equation for a straight line is $a + bY$, where a is the intercept and b is the slope of the line. However, we write the consumption function in this book as

$$C = \overline{C} + cY_d \tag{15.3}$$

substituting $\overline{C}$ for a and c for b. $\overline{C}$ refers to the autonomous or fixed part of the consumption function and c refers to the induced part of the function. $\overline{C}$ is simply where the consumption function intersects the vertical axis. The other part of the equation, cY_d, states that consumption will change as disposable income changes, where c is the *marginal propensity to consume,* defined as the change in consumption induced by a change in income. In Figure 15.1 the change in consumption brought about by a change in income, $\Delta C/\Delta Y$, is the slope of the line.[5] The illustrated consumption function is based on the assumption that the marginal propensity to consume is greater than zero and less than one, that is, out of an additional dollar of income, consumption will increase by less than one dollar.

The 45-degree line labeled $Y = C + S$ is equidistant from the C and Y axes. At present it shows where income and consumption would be equal. Alternatively, it shows where consumption plus saving are equal to income.

The consumption function shown is a short-run analytical consumption function. It may be derived empirically from cross-sectional data showing the consumption of families at different income levels in the same time period. John Maynard Keynes used this consumption function in his *General Theory* in 1936. The consumption hypothesis on which it is based is known as the *absolute income hypothesis.*[6]

4. The consumption function need not be linear. This assumption simplifies the model but does not destroy its value.

5. The slope of a line is measured by the rise divided by the run, the vertical distance divided by the horizontal distance.

6. Two consumption theories have been developed after Keynes' absolute income hypothesis. They are the relative income hypothesis of James Duesenberry and the permanent income hypothesis of Milton Friedman. The above consumption function may be applicable to either of these consumption theories in the short run as well as to Keynes'. Both the relative and permanent income hypotheses do imply distinct differences, though. The interested reader should consult the following for additional information on consumption theories: Robert Ferber, "General Theories of Spending or Saving Behavior," *American Economic Review* 52 (March 1962): 20–32, also included in *Macroeconomics: Selected Readings,* ed. Edward Shapiro (New York: Harcourt, Brace and World, 1970), pp. 3–17.

Figure 15.2 CONSUMPTION AND SAVING FUNCTIONS

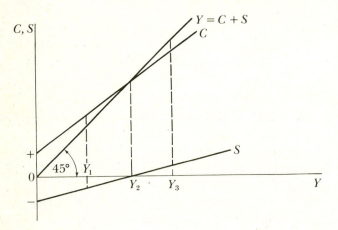

From the consumption function, a saving function can also be derived. Since saving S is what is not consumed in this simple two-sector economy, and $Y = Y_d$,

$$S = Y - C = Y - (\overline{C} + cY) \tag{15.4}$$

$$S = Y - C - cY = -\overline{C} + Y - cY$$

$$S = -\overline{C} + (1 - c)Y \tag{15.5}$$

where $(1 - c)$ is the *marginal propensity to save,* which is the change in saving per dollar change in income. The marginal propensity to consume plus the marginal propensity to save is equal to one. The marginal propensity to save will be less than one, since the marginal propensity to consume is assumed to be greater than zero.

In Figure 15.2 both the consumption function and the saving function are drawn. Note that where the consumption function intersects the 45-degree line, income level Y_2, saving is zero. Consumption is equal to income; therefore nothing remains to be saved. To the left of that income level, Y_1, for example, consumption is greater than income, so saving must be negative; to the right, Y_3, consumption is less than income, so saving must be positive.

To solve algebraically for consumption and saving, all that is needed is a consumption or saving function. Assume that the consumption function is C

= 40 + 0.8Y_d, and $Y_d = Y$. At income $Y = 0$, consumption is 40 + 0.8(0) = 40. The saving function is $S = -40 + 0.2Y_d$. Therefore, when $Y = 0$, saving must equal $-40 + 0.2(0) = -40$. At $Y = \$100$, $C = \$120$ and $S = -\$20$. At $Y = \$200$, $C = \$200$ and $S = \$0$.

INVESTMENT

The goods produced for purchase by the business sector are known as *capital goods*. The acquisition of capital goods is *investment*. Capital is a *stock concept* in that it is the amount of capital that exists at a certain point in time. Investment is the related *flow concept*, since investment is the change in the capital stock between two time periods.

Entrepreneurs and Investment

An entrepreneur (that is, a businessman or businesswoman), in considering whether or not to make an investment, must have some way of judging the profitability of the investment. One technique is to compare the internal rate of return on that investment with the external rate of return, or interest rate, that defines the opportunity cost of using funds available.

The *internal rate of return* on an investment is calculated by equating the cost or price of the capital good with the revenues that will be generated by that capital good. However, although the cost of the capital good is generally borne immediately, the revenues are generated over the life of the capital good, which means that the two cannot be equated as is. First, the *present value* PV of the revenues must be calculated by discounting the stream of future revenues. The following equation is used to determine present value:

$$PV = \frac{R_1}{1 + r} + \frac{R_2}{(1 + r)^2} + \cdots + \frac{R_n}{(1 + r)^n} \tag{15.6}$$

R represents the net revenues from the use of a capital good in future time periods, 1 through n, and r is the discount rate. The correct discount rate or internal rate of return for an investment is one that will equate the present value of future revenues with the price of the capital good.

The reason future income has to be discounted is that $100 today is worth

Figure 15.3   RANKING OF POSSIBLE INVESTMENTS FOR A FIRM

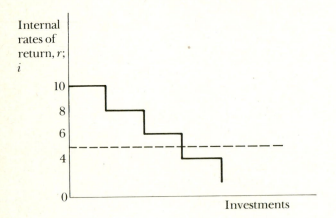

more than $100 in the future. At 5 percent interest, $100 would be worth $162.88 in ten years. Consequently, future income must be discounted to find its present value; that is, $162.88 ten years from now is worth only $100 today if the anticipated interest rate over the period is 5 percent.

The Marginal Efficiency of Investment and the Interest Rate

Figure 15.3 shows the ranking of possible investment projects facing a firm. The internal rates of return, or discount rates, for the projects are measured on the vertical axis; the level of investment measured in dollar amounts is indicated on the horizontal axis. The interest rate, or external rate of return, can also be shown on the vertical axis since it too is measured in percentage terms.

The investments the entrepreneur would be willing to make are those where the internal rate of return is equal to, or greater than, the external rate of return. The *external rate of return* is assumed to be represented by the interest rate i, which, because it defines the opportunity cost of available funds, determines which investments will be made.

It does not pay to buy a capital good that will return only 5 or 6 percent if money has to be borrowed for 7 percent. Even if one need not borrow, it would be more efficient to lend money to some other entrepreneur at 7

Figure 15.4   DETERMINATION OF LEVEL OF INVESTMENT

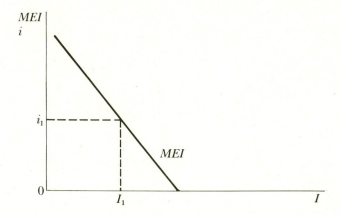

percent than to purchase a capital good whose return would be less.[7] Conversely, it would be foolish not to invest where the internal rate of return is greater than the interest rate. Thus if the interest rate is 5 percent, those investments earning a greater return would be made. Those earning less than 5 percent would not be made.

If the demand for investment for all firms is aggregated, an investment function like that in Figure 15.4 can be derived. Again, different levels or dollar amounts of investment are indicated on the horizontal axis, and the interest rate is found on the vertical axis. However, the discount rate or internal rate of return that equates the price of capital with the discounted stream of future revenues earned from capital is now defined as the *marginal efficiency of investment* (*MEI*). Just as for the individual firm, the interest rate determines the level of investment that will occur for the economy as a whole. Investment projects earning higher rates of return than the interest rate are undertaken, ceteris paribus, while those that earn lower rates of return are not. At interest rate i_1, I_1 investment occurs.

The *MEI* function is negatively sloped, showing that decreases in the interest rate will increase the level of investment that is economically feasible; increases in the interest rate bring about a decrease. Lower interest rates encourage more capital-intensive or *roundabout techniques of production,* that is,

7. For simplicity we are assuming that the borrowing and lending rates are the same.

Figure 15.5   AUTONOMOUS AND INDUCED INVESTMENT
FUNCTIONS

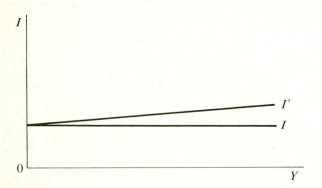

techniques that require higher percentages of capital relative to other inputs.
More roundabout techniques generally provide output at lower per unit costs
of production *when interest payments are excluded from costs.* More capital-
intensive techniques of production clearly require greater dollar amounts of
investment. Hence the more roundabout or capital intensive the technique,
ceteris paribus, the more important interest payments become. Thus higher
interest rates discourage more capital intensive production techniques while
lower interest rates tend to make them economically feasible.

After determining the level of investment that will occur in any given time
period, one can graph it against the level of income, as in Figure 15.5.
Initially, it is assumed that investment is *autonomous* of the level of income, that
is, that investment is not a function of the level of income and hence does not
increase as the income level increases. This investment function would appear
as I. If the investment were a function of the level of income, an *induced*
investment function like I' would result, where investment increases as income increases. (Actually, I' is partially autonomous and partially induced.
The equation describing I' would be $I' = \bar{I} + \hat{i}Y$, where $\bar{I}$ is the autonomous part and $\hat{i}$ is the induced part, the marginal propensity to invest. (The
symbol $\hat{i}$ is used instead of i since the latter i is used throughout the book to
refer to the interest rate.)

Figure 15.6 DETERMINATION OF EQUILIBRIUM INCOME LEVEL

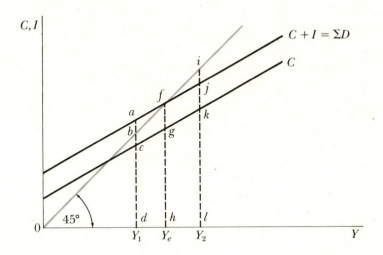

The Two-Sector Economy

A simple *two-sector economy* composed of households and business may now be constructed. Income is made up of goods and services for consumption and investment goods. Consumption and investment in a two-sector economy constitute aggregate demand—the total demand for goods and services in an economy. Graphically, the economy may be described as in Figure 15.6. It is assumed that only households save.[8] Further, since there is no government sector, disposable income equals income, $Y_d = Y$. The *equilibrium income level* is determined by the intersection of the aggregate demand curve and the 45-degree line.

The 45-degree line now becomes the reference line. It shows that if income for a given period were $500, there would be $500 worth of goods and services produced in that time period. The value of the goods and services produced, which is measured on the vertical axis, is equal to the income, which is measured on the horizontal axis.

8. Businesses do save, but for simplicity we assume that business saving is equal to zero.

Aggregate demand, ΣD, is the vertical summation of an autonomous investment function and the consumption function. Investment, therefore, is equal to the vertical distance between the C and the $C + I$ lines.

At this point, we must recognize that *planned* saving and investment may not necessarily equal *actual* saving and investment. In Figure 15.6 the vertical distance between the C and $C + I$ lines is planned investment. The consumption function C represents the planned consumption at each income level. Thus the difference between the 45-degree line and the consumption function represents planned saving. It is assumed that the amount households plan to save is the amount they actually save. However, those saving and those investing are not necessarily the same individuals.

Investment decisions are made by persons working to a large degree independently of each other. Simultaneously, households are making the decisions relating to saving. Hence no reason exists for planned saving to equal planned investment. If planned saving and planned investment should differ, equilibrium could not exist, because what is planned for investment will be different from what actually occurs. Those individuals making investment decisions will change their investment plans when they observe that what they planned is not what has taken place. And that implies a nonequilibrium situation.

Where aggregate demand and the 45-degree line intersect in Figure 15.6, an equilibrium income level Y_e is determined. Aggregate demand ΣD is equal to fh, which is equal to income produced and the value of goods and services supplied. Planned consumption is gh; hence planned savings is equal to fg. The vertical distance between the C and $C + I$ (ΣD) curves is planned investment, which equals fg. We assume that households actually save what they plan to save (that is, fg). Those goods not consumed in a two-sector economy become investment goods because investment includes net changes in inventories. Thus actual investment must be fg, which is the same as planned and actual saving. Businesses find that they are actually investing what they planned or wished to invest, which is equal to that amount households planned to save. Therefore income level Y_e is an equilibrium income level.

Note that the condition for an equilibrium income level is that planned or *ex ante* saving S_p equals planned or *ex ante* investment I_p:

$$S_p = I_p \tag{15.7}$$

The fact that actual or *ex post* saving S_A equals actual or *ex post* investment I_A is true by definition; it is an identity because unplanned changes in inventories will always make them equal in a two-sector economy:[9]

$$S_A \equiv I_A \tag{15.8}$$

For income levels to the right of Y_e, such as Y_2, aggregate demand is less than the total value of the final goods and services produced. The total value being produced is *il*; aggregate demand *jl* is composed of planned consumption *kl* and planned investment *jk*. Planned saving is *ik*. Since planned saving and actual saving are equal by assumption and actual saving and actual investment equal by definition, actual investment will equal *ik*. Since there are more goods and services being produced than purchased, an unplanned increase in inventories *ij* will be experienced. This net change in inventories is unplanned investment, and production will be curtailed in the time period following. Again, the expectations of those in business are not being fulfilled because actual investment *ik* is greater than planned investment *jk*. Therefore, an equilibrium income level does not exist at Y_2.

At income levels less than Y_e, aggregate demand is greater than the value of the goods and services supplied. For example, at Y_1, income generated is equal to *bd*. Aggregate demand is *ad*, planned consumption is *cd*, and planned investment is *ac*. Thus aggregate demand is greater than goods supplied by the amount *ab*. With planned consumption equal to *cd*, planned saving (and by assumption, actual saving) is equal to *bc*. Since actual saving equals actual investment by definition, actual investment must also equal *bc*, which is less than the planned investment of *ac*.

An economy can consume and invest an amount greater than that being produced only by drawing down previously accumulated inventories. Since inventories are part of investment, an *unplanned* decrease in inventories *ab* implies that actual investment *bc* will be less than planned investment *ac*. Those in business will find that their investment plans are not being met by the amount of the decrease in inventories. Consequently, they will employ

9. *Ex ante* and *ex post* are the Swedish economist Knut Wicksell's terms for "planned" and "actual." Wicksell was the first to analyze this problem. As Leijonhufvud points out, Keynes completely misunderstood Wicksell's use of the terms. Alex Leijonhufvud, *On Keynesian Economics and the Economics of Keynes* (New York: Oxford University Press, 1968): 62–63n.

Figure 15.7 DETERMINATION OF EQUILIBRIUM INCOME LEVEL

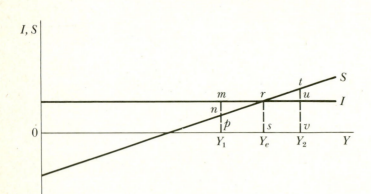

additional factors of production and increase the level of output, and therefore income, in the next time period in order to fulfill investment plans. Thus income will be increased, and income level Y_1 cannot be an equilibrium level because those able to change are doing so.

By means of a similar technique, we can use the saving and investment functions to determine the equilibrium income level. The investment and saving functions are shown in Figure 15.7. Investment is assumed to be autonomous, as in the previous example. The saving function is derived from the consumption function.

The saving-investment technique of income determination gives an equilibrium income level where *planned* investment equals *planned* saving. The saving function is planned saving and the investment function is planned investment. At Y_e, what is planned for saving is just equal to what is planned for investment, *rs* in both instances.

At income level Y_1, planned investment is *mp*, but planned saving is *np*; thus households are consuming too much and saving too little relative to investment plans. An unplanned *disinvestment* (a negative investment) of *mn* in the form of a decrease in inventories will thus occur. Actual investment will be *np*, which is less than planned investment *mp*. Since this is other than what the entrepreneurs had planned, production plans will be increased in the next period, and income level Y_1 cannot be an equilibrium level.

At income Y_2, planned investment is *uv* and planned saving is *tv*. Since

Figure 15.8   DETERMINATION OF EQUILIBRIUM INCOME IN A
TWO-SECTOR ECONOMY USING BOTH THE
AGGREGATE DEMAND AND SAVING-INVESTMENT
TECHNIQUES

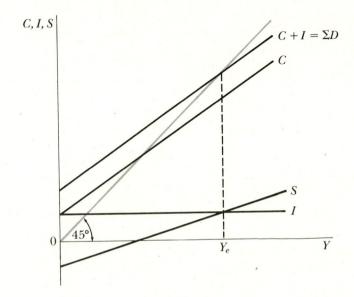

planned saving is too much relative to the amount planned for investment,
inventories will be accumulated by the amount *tu*. Actual investment *tv* will be
greater than planned investment *uv*, and the income level will decrease in the
following time period as production plans are cut back by entrepreneurs
determined to see that an unplanned increase in inventories does not occur
again.

Note that although the investment level assumed here is autonomous, it is
subject to change. If the entrepreneurs decide that the current investment
level is undesirable, it may be altered. Since the equilibrium level of income is
determined where planned saving equals planned investment, the equilibrium income will change as planned investment is changed, ceteris paribus.

If Figures 15.6 and 15.7 are combined as in Figure 15.8, the equilibrium
income level determined by the aggregate demand technique is the same as
that determined by the saving-investment technique. The saving function is

derivable from the consumption function and 45-degree line. The level of investment is the same as the vertical distance between the consumption function and the aggregate demand function. Note that the reasoning is the same as to why income levels to either the right or left of Y_e are not equilibrium levels of income, regardless of which technique is used.[10]

The equilibrium level of income may be determined algebraically. Again, two techniques exist for determining the equilibrium level—the aggregate-demand technique and the saving-investment technique. Setting the unknown equilibrium income level equal to aggregate demand,

$$Y = C + I \tag{15.9}$$

where

$$C = 40 + 0.8Y_d$$

and

$$I = 30$$

we can solve for the unknown income level.

The assumption that income and disposable income are the same still holds.

$$
\begin{aligned}
Y &= 40 + 0.8Y + 30 \\
Y - 0.8Y &= 40 + 30 \\
0.2Y &= 70 \\
Y &= 350
\end{aligned}
$$

The saving-investment technique can also be used to solve for the equilibrium income level. Saving is equal to income minus consumption in the present model.

$$Y - C = C + I - C \tag{15.10}$$

thus

$$Y - C = S = I$$

10. We suggest that readers graphically analyze for their own benefit the situation where investment is induced rather than autonomous.

and

$$S = I \qquad\qquad (15.11)$$

If

$$C = 40 + 0.8Y_d$$

then

$$S = -40 + 0.2Y_d$$

and if

$$I = 30$$

then

$$-40 + 0.2Y = 30$$
$$0.2Y = 30 + 40 = 70$$
$$Y = 350$$

Thus whichever approach is used, the same equilibrium income level is found.[11]

MULTIPLIER IN A TWO-SECTOR ECONOMY

If we were to introduce a change in investment ΔI, either an increase or a decrease, we would expect a change in income ΔY, ceteris paribus. In Figure 15.9 we have an aggregate demand curve, ΣD_1 ($= C + I$). Where ΣD_1 intersects the 45-degree line, an equilibrium income level Y_1 is determined. With a change in the level of investment—an increase, in this instance—a new aggregate demand curve is derived, ΣD_2 ($= C + I + \Delta I$), which is raised vertically above ΣD_1 by the amount of ΔI. A new equilibrium income level is determined at Y_2. The change in the equilibrium income level ΔY is greater than the

11. If investment were assumed to be induced rather than autonomous, it would be written, for example, as $I = 30 + 0.1Y$. Substituting the new investment function for the old, a new equilibrium level of income will be found. Again, we suggest that readers solve for the equilibrium income level algebraically, using both techniques.

Figure 15.9   THE EFFECTS OF A CHANGE IN INVESTMENT ON THE
EQUILIBRIUM INCOME LEVEL

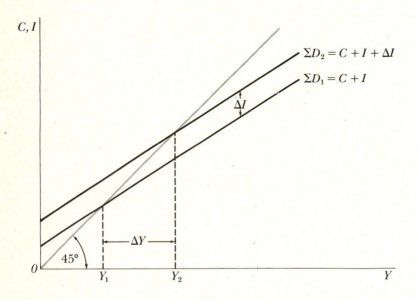

change in investment ΔI. The *multiplier k* expresses the predictable change in
the equilibrium income level brought about by a change in investment.

We can gain an understanding of this multiple effect if we consider the
following. An initial increase of $10 in investment ΔI occurs. Of that, 0.8, or
the marginal propensity to consume c, is spent in the next time period by
those who received that $10 ($c\Delta I$). In the period after that, 0.8 of 0.8 × $10
(0.64 × $10 or $c^2\Delta I$) is spent, and so on. Hence if the $10 increase in
investment is permanent, the change in the income level ΔY is a multiple of
the original change in investment n periods later. This process is shown in
Figure 15.10.

Algebraically, we can derive the multiplier in the following fashion. Aggregate demand ΣD in a two-sector economy is equal to consumption plus
investment,

$$\Sigma D = C + I \tag{15.12}$$

Figure 15.10   MULTIPLIER EFFECTS ON INCOME OF A CHANGE IN
THE LEVEL OF INVESTMENT

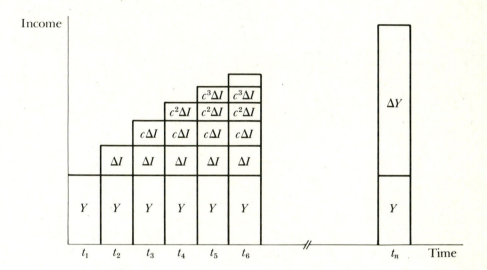

where

$$C = \bar{C} + cY_d \qquad\qquad\qquad [15.3]$$

Because taxes are nil in this model, disposable income Y_d is equal to income
Y. Furthermore, investment is assumed to be autonomous, $\bar{I}$. Then setting the
equilibrium income level equal to aggregate demand,

$$Y = \bar{C} + cY + \bar{I} \qquad\qquad\qquad (15.13)$$

and rearranging terms we have,

$$Y - cY = \bar{C} + \bar{I}$$
$$Y(1 - c) = \bar{C} + \bar{I}$$

and finally

$$Y = \left(\frac{1}{1 - c}\right)(\bar{C} + \bar{I}) \qquad\qquad\qquad (15.14)$$

Now if we assume an increase in investment that would bring about a new income level, we could write it as follows:

$$Y + \Delta Y = \left(\frac{1}{1-c}\right)(\bar{C} + \bar{I}) + \left(\frac{1}{1-c}\right)\Delta \bar{I} \tag{15.15}$$

Then subtracting equation 15.14 from equation 15.15, we would have,

$$\Delta Y = \left(\frac{1}{1-c}\right)\Delta \bar{I} \tag{15.16}$$

or

$$\frac{\Delta Y}{\Delta I} = \frac{1}{1-c} = k \tag{15.17}$$

where k is the multiplier.

If the level of autonomous investment were $30 and the consumption function C were equal to $40 + 0.8Y_d$, the equilibrium income level would be $350. If investment were increased $10, from $30 to $40, the equilibrium income level would increase to $400. By using the multiplier just derived, we could have predicted that result. The change in the income level ΔY is equal to the multiplier, $1/(1 - c)$, times the change in investment, $10. With c equal to 0.8, the value of the multiplier k is

$$k = \frac{1}{1-c} = \frac{1}{1-0.8} = \frac{1}{.2} = 5$$

With ΔI equal to 10, then ΔY equals $50 (= 5 \times 10). Adding $50 to the previous equilibrium income level of $350 gives a new income level of $400.

The multiplier just derived is not restricted in use to changes in investment. It would apply equally well to changes (whether increases or decreases) in the autonomous part of the consumption function.

GOVERNMENT

The government or public sector in this model is composed of two parts: government expenditures G and taxes T. The government sector as used here includes all levels of government—federal, state, and local. Government expenditures are for such things as national defense, public transportation, the operation of the various government units, the parks and recreational services, schools, and all types of social services, including social security, health, and welfare. It is through taxes and borrowing that the public sector finances its spending.

In this model we will assume that government expenditures are determined in the political sphere and hence are independent of income. Thus government spending will be autonomous and will not vary with changes in the income level. Clearly, this is not totally realistic, as some government expenditures such as unemployment insurance will definitely vary with changes in the income level.

With the inclusion of the government sector, one significant modification must be made. Without any public sector, income and disposable income were identical. But with the government added, disposable income is now less than income by the amount of taxes. Therefore, the consumption function may no longer be described as a function of income directly. The consumption function is written, as before,

$$C = \bar{C} + cY_d \qquad [15.3]$$

but now

$$Y_d = Y - T \qquad (15.18)$$

so

$$C = \bar{C} + c(Y - T) \qquad (15.3a)$$

Graphically, the economy may now be depicted as in Figure 15.11. It is now a *three-sector economy*, composed of households, business, and government. Aggregate demand will be the summation of the demand for goods and services by these sectors. As in the previous case, where the economy was composed of households and business only, the equilibrium income level is determined by the intersection of the aggregate demand curve and the 45-degree line.[12]

---

12. In previous graphs we could simply draw consumption as a function of income, since Y equaled Y_d. When taxes are introduced and disposable income no longer equals income, we have

Figure 15.11 AGGREGATE DEMAND IN A THREE-SECTOR
ECONOMY

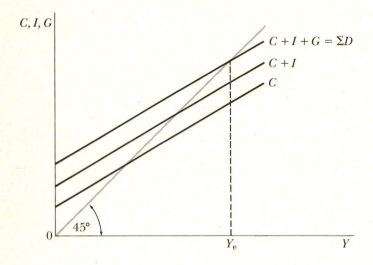

to modify the consumption function. In the graph shown, consumption function C is drawn as a function of income where Y equals Y_d. Now if taxes are introduced, Y is unequal to Y_d, and the

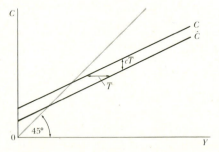

consumption function would have to be shifted down by the amount $c\bar{T}$, assuming taxes are all autonomous. ($\hat{C} = \bar{C} + cY_d = \bar{C} + c(Y - \bar{T}) = \bar{C} + cY - c\bar{T}$.) Consumption is reduced by less than the full amount of taxes, $c\bar{T}$, since part of taxes will come from savings, $(1 - c)\bar{T}$. Shifting the consumption function down by $c\bar{T}$ is the same as shifting it to the right by the amount $\bar{T}$. Since an autonomous tax function is being utilized here, C and $\hat{C}$ are parallel. Hence it is the $\hat{C}$ function to which investment and government expenditures are added in Figure 15.11.

Using the values for the various functions found later in this section, readers should solve for C and $\hat{C}$ holding income constant (for example, equal to $395), which shows how far the consumption function must be reduced. Alternatively, they should hold consumption constant (for example, equal to $100) to show how far the $\hat{C}$ function would have to be shifted to the right.

Figure 15.12 DETERMINATION OF EQUILIBRIUM INCOME LEVEL
USING THE MODIFIED SAVING-INVESTMENT
APPROACH

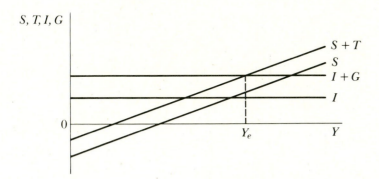

For a two-sector economy, we found that at equilibrium, planned investment was equal to planned saving. In a three-sector economy, modifications
must be made. If the income equation is written to include three sectors,

$$Y = C + S + T = C + I + G \tag{15.1b}$$

and consumption is eliminated, the following equality will hold:

$$S + T = I + G \tag{15.11a}$$

Household saving is a function of disposable income, just like consumption in
the previous example. Taxes are a constant amount, which may be added
vertically to the saving function. Investment and government expenditures
may also be added vertically; and where the $I + G$ and $S + T$ functions
intersect, as in Figure 15.12, the equilibrium income level is determined.[13]
Providing that consistent values for the variables are used in both approaches,
the same equilibrium income will result.[14]

13. The saving function in Figure 15.12 is the saving function in Figure 15.7 shifted down by the
amount $(1 - c)\overline{T}$, that is, $s\overline{T}$, or to the right by the amount of taxes, just as the consumption
function was shifted in footnote 12 (see above).
14. Readers should graphically employ both approaches for determining the equilibrium income
on the same graph to verify this.

The equilibrium income level may be solved for algebraically, again by two approaches. As before, in the aggregate-demand approach, the unknown equilibrium income Y is set equal to aggregate demand:

$$Y = C + I + G \qquad (15.9a)$$

where

$$C = \bar{C} + c(Y - T) \qquad [15.3a]$$

Hence

$$Y = \bar{C} + c(Y - T) + I + G \qquad (15.13a)$$

Assuming

$$C = 40 + 0.8Y_d$$
$$I = 30$$
$$G = 25$$
$$T = 20$$

and substituting,

$$Y = 40 + 0.8(Y - 20) + 30 + 25$$
$$= 40 + 0.8Y - 16 + 30 + 25$$
$$Y - 0.8Y = 40 - 16 + 30 + 25$$
$$0.2Y = 79$$
$$Y = 395$$

Or using the saving-investment approach, where taxes and government expenditures are included:

$$S + T = I + G \qquad [15.11a]$$

Then

$$S = Y_d - C \qquad (15.4a)$$
$$= Y_d - (40 + 0.8Y_d)$$
$$Y_d = Y - T \qquad [15.18]$$
$$S = -40 + 0.2(Y - T) \qquad (15.5a)$$

With I, G, and T having the same values as before,

$$-40 + 0.2(Y - 20) + 20 = \mathbf{30 + 25}$$
$$-40 + 0.2Y - 4 + 20 = 55$$
$$0.2Y = 55 + 40 + 4 - 20$$
$$= 79$$
$$Y = 395$$

Again, either approach determines the same equilibrium income. One point to note immediately is that an equilibrium income level in no way implies that government expenditures and taxes are equal. In fact, in the present example, they have purposely been made unequal.

MULTIPLIERS IN A THREE-SECTOR ECONOMY

In a three-sector economy where governmental expenditures are assumed to be autonomous $(G = \bar{G})$ and taxes are nil $(T = 0)$, we can solve for an equilibrium income level by setting aggregate demand equal to income. Using our regular consumption function we have:

$$Y = C + I + G = \bar{C} + cY + \bar{I} + \bar{G} \qquad (15.13\text{b})$$

Then

$$Y - cY = \bar{C} + \bar{I} + \bar{G}$$

and

$$Y(1 - c) = \bar{C} + \bar{I} + \bar{G}$$

thus

$$Y = \frac{1}{1 - c}(\bar{C} + \bar{I} + \bar{G}) \qquad (15.14\text{a})$$

Then introducing a change in the level of governmental expenditures $\Delta \bar{G}$ will bring about a change in the equilibrium income level ΔY. As we can see, the multiplier that is applicable to changes in investment or the autonomous part of consumption also applies to changes in government spending.

$$Y + \Delta Y = \frac{1}{1-c}(\bar{C} + \bar{I} + \bar{G}) + \frac{1}{1-c}\Delta\bar{G} \qquad (15.15a)$$

where

$$\Delta Y = \frac{1}{1-c}\Delta\bar{G} \qquad (15.16a)$$

and thus

$$\frac{\Delta Y}{\Delta\bar{G}} = \frac{1}{1-c} = k_G \qquad (15.17a)$$

Hence a $10 increase in governmental expenditures will result in a $50 increase in the income level if $k = 5$ just as would a $10 increase in $\bar{C}$ or I.

When taxes are introduced, a *tax multiplier* k_T can be derived. Since taxes are not zero, disposable income is no longer equal to income; hence $Y_d = Y - T$. Then, assuming the tax function is of an autonomous nature and setting the unknown equilibrium income level equal to aggregate demand (where the consumption, investment, and governmental expenditure functions are as previously), we have the following:

$$Y = \bar{C} + cY_d + \bar{I} + \bar{G} = \bar{C} + c(Y - \bar{T}) + \bar{I} + \bar{G} \qquad [15.13a]$$

Then

$$Y = \bar{C} + cY - c\bar{T} + \bar{I} + \bar{G}$$

and

$$Y - cY = \bar{C} - c\bar{T} + \bar{I} + \bar{G}$$

or

$$Y(1-c) = \bar{C} - c\bar{T} + \bar{I} + \bar{G}$$

$$Y = \frac{1}{1-c}(C - c\bar{T} + \bar{I} + \bar{G}) \qquad (15.14b)$$

With a change in taxes we would expect a change in the equilibrium income level:

$$Y + \Delta Y = \frac{1}{1 - c}(\bar{C} - c\bar{T} + \bar{I} + \bar{G}) + \frac{1}{1 - c}(-c\Delta\bar{T}) \qquad (15.15b)$$

Then subtracting equation 15.14b from 15.15b, we have

$$\Delta Y = \frac{1}{1 - c}(-c\Delta\bar{T}) = \frac{-c}{1 - c}\Delta\bar{T} \qquad (15.16b)$$

or

$$\frac{\Delta Y}{\Delta T} = \frac{-c}{1 - c} = k_T \qquad (15.17b)$$

If we assume a marginal propensity to consume equal to 0.8, then the tax multiplier is -4; that is, $-0.8/(1 - 0.8) = -0.8/0.2 = -4$.

The first thing to notice about the tax multiplier is that it is negative. The negative sign is understandable if we consider that a tax increase, ceteris paribus, should cause a decrease in the equilibrium income level because aggregate demand would decrease. Second, the absolute value of the tax multiplier is less than the governmental expenditures multiplier given the same data. Intuitively we can understand this by considering the case of a tax decrease. If taxes were decreased, part of the additional funds now available to households would be spent, but part would be saved. The part that is saved, which is specified by the marginal propensity to save, should cause income to increase by less than it would if those funds had been spent since they do not increase aggregate demand. In the instance of increased governmental expenditures, the entire amount is spent in the initial round; none is saved. Hence the increase in aggregate demand would be larger.

Using the tax multiplier of -4, a \$10 increase in taxes would be predicted to bring about a \$40 decrease in income. A \$10 decrease in governmental expenditures would cause a \$50 drop in income, using k_G.

A final multiplier that can be derived at this point is the so-called *balanced-budget multiplier*. Assume an increase in governmental expenditures that is equal to an increase in taxes, that is, $\Delta G = \Delta T$. Using the multipliers just derived, the change in the income level would be equal to the change in governmental expenditures times its multiplier plus the change in taxes times its multiplier. Thus

$$\Delta Y = \frac{1}{1 - c} \Delta G + \frac{-c}{1 - c} \Delta T \tag{15.19}$$

and

$$\frac{\Delta Y}{\Delta G = \Delta T} = \frac{1}{1 - c} + \frac{-c}{1 - c} = \frac{1 - c}{1 - c} = 1 = k_{\Delta G = \Delta T} = k_{BB} \tag{15.17c}$$

In other words, the multiplier, where the changes in taxes and governmental expenditures are equal, is unitary. Thus if G is increased by \$10 as are taxes, the equilibrium income level will increase by \$10; if both are decreased by \$20, the income level will decrease by \$20.

Even though this multiplier is often called the balanced-budget multiplier, it by no means implies that governmental expenditures and taxes are equal, that is, that the budget is balanced. Rather it applies to situations where governmental expenditures and taxes are changed by *like* amounts. Hence if the governmental budget was not balanced to begin with, equal changes in both will mean that the budget is still not balanced.

THE FOREIGN SECTOR

Since any single economy does not include the entire world, and to the extent that the individuals in any economy have some economic contact with the remainder of the world, a foreign sector exists. The foreign sector takes account of all the dealings of the individuals in an economy with individuals in other countries. The foreign sector in this model is composed of exports Xp and imports Mp.

We now have a *four-sector economy*, consisting of households, business, the government, and the foreign sector. The income equation for a four-sector economy is generally written in the following form:

$$Y = C + S + T = C + I + G + (Xp - Mp) \tag{[15.1]}$$

where $Xp - Mp$ is *net exports*, which may be positive, negative, or zero. Imports are subtracted since we are trying to measure the economy's productivity for

Figure 15.13   DETERMINATION OF NET EXPORT FUNCTION

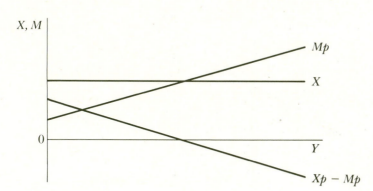

a given time period and imports represent production outside the domestic economy.

In the present model we will assume that exports are determined completely outside the domestic economy. Consequently, the export function will be assumed to be autonomous with respect to the income level. In fact, the export function is not completely independent of the income level in the domestic economy. However, since there is no certain relation between the domestic income level and the level of exports, nor can it generally be very large, no real damage is done to the validity of the model.

Yet whereas the export function is assumed to be autonomous of the income level, the import function will be assumed to be induced and, like other functions, linear. As the income level increases, the individuals in an economy will experience a desire to import more goods and services. Therefore, the import function Mp, export function Xp, and net export function $Xp - Mp$ will appear as in Figure 15.13. Just as the algebraic notation implies, the net export function is obtained by subtracting the import function from the export function. Where the export function intersects the import function, net exports will be zero. At any income level greater than that, net exports will be negative.

The equilibrium income level may now be determined graphically by the aggregate demand approach, as in Figure 15.14. Note that aggregate demand, $\Sigma D = C + I + G + (Xp - Mp)$, over part of its range lies below the combined demand from households, business, and government alone. This

Figure 15.14 DETERMINATION OF EQUILIBRIUM INCOME LEVEL
IN A FOUR-SECTOR ECONOMY

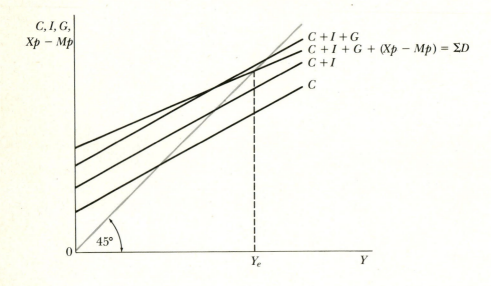

represents the fact that over part of its range the net export function is negative. As usual, the equilibrium income is determined where aggregate demand intersects the forty-five-degree line at income level Y_e. In this model investment is assumed to be autonomous.

If the saving-investment approach is to be utilized to find the equilibrium income level, one further modification must be made in the form of the approach where $S + T = I + G$ when a three-sector economy was assumed. For a four-sector economy, the income equation is written

$$Y = C + S + T = C + I + G + (Xp - Mp) \qquad [15.1]$$

Rewriting,

$$Y = C + S + T + Mp = C + I + G + Xp$$

Subtracting consumption leaves

$$S + T + Mp = I + G + Xp \qquad (15.11b)$$

Figure 15.15 DETERMINATION OF EQUILIBRIUM INCOME LEVEL
IN A FOUR-SECTOR ECONOMY USING THE MODIFIED
SAVING-INVESTMENT APPROACH

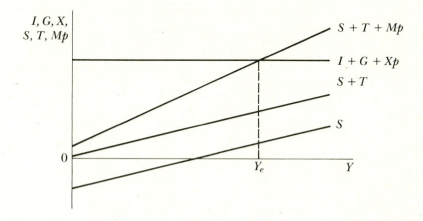

Thus, graphically presented as in Figure 15.15, the equilibrium income level is determined where the $S + T + Mp$ function intersects the $I + G + Xp$ function. In the present example, investment, government spending, and exports are all assumed to be autonomous of the income level. The $S + T$ function is that found in Figure 15.12. The $S + T + Mp$ function is obtained simply by adding the import function to the $S + T$ function. The increasing vertical distance between the $S + T$ function and the $S + T + Mp$ function represents the induced nature of the import function assumed.

Finally, the equilibrium income may be found algebraically using the aggregate demand approach. Assume the following values for various functions:

$$C = 40 + 0.8Y_d$$
$$I = 30$$
$$G = 25$$
$$T = 20$$
$$Xp = 10$$
$$Mp = 5 + 0.1Y$$

Setting income equal to aggregate demand,

$$Y = C + I + G + (Xp - Mp) \tag{15.9b}$$

and substituting,

$$
\begin{aligned}
Y &= 40 + 0.8\,(Y - 20) + 30 + 25 + 10 - (5 + 0.1Y) \\
&= 40 + 0.8Y - 16 + 30 + 25 + 10 - 5 - 0.1Y \\
Y - 0.8Y + 0.1Y &= 40 - 16 + 30 + 25 + 10 - 5 \\
0.3Y &= 84 \\
Y &= 280
\end{aligned}
$$

The equilibrium income can also be found by using the modified saving-investment approach, where $S + T + Mp = I + G + Xp$.[15]

MULTIPLIERS IN A
FOUR-SECTOR ECONOMY

With the addition of the foreign sector, we must make some alterations in the multipliers we have derived. Assume as previously an autonomous level of investment, taxes, and governmental expenditures; assume also a consumption function of the form $C = \bar{C} + cY_d$. Now if the export function is autonomous of the income level and the import function is induced ($\overline{Mp} + mY$), we again can set the income level equal to aggregate demand:

$$Y = \bar{C} + c(Y - \bar{T}) + \bar{I} + \bar{G} + \bar{X}p - (\overline{Mp} + mY) \tag{15.13c}$$

Solving for the multiplier that applies to governmental expenditures (in addition to investment, the autonomous part of consumption, and now exports and the autonomous part of imports) in the same manner as previously, we have:

$$\frac{\Delta Y}{\Delta G} = \frac{1}{1 - c + m} = k_G \tag{15.17d}$$

---

15. It is now suggested that the reader in fact solve for the equilibrium income using the functions just given and applying the investment-saving approach.

If the marginal propensity to consume is 0.8 and the marginal propensity to import is 0.1, then $k_G = 3.33$, $1/(1 - 0.8 + 0.1) = 1/0.3 = 3.33$. Thus a \$20 increase in G would lead to a \$66.7 increase in the equilibrium level of income, ceteris paribus, $\Delta Y = 20(3.33)$; a \$40 decrease in G would result in a \$133.3 decrease in income.

Deriving the tax multiplier as before, we see that

$$\frac{\Delta Y}{\Delta T} = \frac{-c}{1 - c + m} = k_T \qquad (15.17e)$$

Given the same values for the marginal propensity to consume and the marginal propensity to import, 0.8 and 0.1 respectively, the value of the tax multiplier is $-0.8/(1 - 0.8 + 0.1) = -0.8/0.3 = -2.67$. This allows us to calculate changes in the income level given changes in taxes.

With the addition of the foreign sector, the so-called balanced-budget multiplier is no longer equal to one. Adding the multipliers that apply to changes in governmental expenditures and taxes when governmental expenditures and taxes are assumed to change by the same amounts, $\Delta G = \Delta T$, we have

$$\frac{\Delta Y}{\Delta G = \Delta T} = \frac{1 - c}{1 - c + m} = k_{\Delta G = \Delta T} = k_{BB} \qquad (15.17f)$$

Assuming values for the marginal propensities to consume and import the same as in the two preceding examples, the balanced budget multiplier equals $(1 - 0.8)/(1 - 0.8 + 0.1) = 0.2/0.3 = 0.67$. While the multiplier is no longer equal to one, note that an equal *increase* in governmental expenditures and taxes still has an *expansionary* effect on the income level, ceteris paribus. Similarly, an equal decrease in both would bring about a decrease in the income level.

THE EQUILIBRIUM INCOME AND
THE FULL-EMPLOYMENT INCOME

So far it has been assumed that the *full-employment income level* is identical to the equilibrium income level. At this point, it must be recognized that this is not

Figure 15.16 RELATION BETWEEN THE EQUILIBRIUM AND THE
FULL-EMPLOYMENT LEVELS OF INCOME

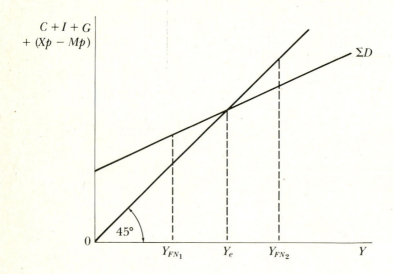

necessarily true; in fact, this would not be true the great majority of the time if measures were not taken to manipulate the aggregate demand so as to alter the equilibrium income level.[16]

In Figure 15.16 the 45-degree line and an aggregate demand function are drawn. The equilibrium income will be at Y_e. However, the full-employment income level may be at Y_{FN_1}, for example, or at Y_e, or at Y_{FN_2}. If full employment is at Y_{FN_1}, the equilibrium income is greater than full employment. Inflation will result, since the economy is being operated at an income level greater than full employment. If full employment is at Y_{FN_2}, the equilibrium income is less than the full-employment income and unemployment exists.

Since neither unemployment nor inflation is desirable, efforts are made to see that the equilibrium income level is modified so that its coincident occurrence with that of full employment is more likely, ceteris paribus. Methods for

16. This in no way denies that many manipulations of aggregate demand, whether intentional or not, move the equilibrium level of income further away from the full-employment level.

modifying the equilibrium income level fall under two broad headings: fiscal policy and monetary policy.

Fiscal policy is essentially the alteration of government expenditures, taxes, or both to change aggregate demand. Altering government expenditures changes the G part of aggregate demand directly—increases in G will increase aggregate demand, and decreases will decrease aggregate demand. Altering taxes influences aggregate demand by changing consumption, investment, or net exports, or some combination of the three.

Monetary policy involves changing the size of the money supply and using selective controls to effect changes in aggregate demand. Different ways of viewing the working of monetary policy will be explained in the following chapters.

KEY TERMS

Equilibrium

Disposable income

Marginal propensity to consume

Marginal propensity to save

Investment

Internal rate of return

Present value

External rate of return

Marginal efficiency of investment

Roundabout techniques of production

Autonomous investment

Induced investment

Two-sector economy

Equilibrium income

Ex ante

Ex post

Multiplier

Three-sector economy

Tax multiplier

Balanced-budget multiplier

Four-sector economy

Net exports

Full-employment income level

REVIEW QUESTIONS

1. Given

$C = 30 + 0.75Y_d$

$I = 60$

$G = 45$

T $= 10$
Xp $= 15$
$Mp = 6 + 0.1Y$

determine the following:

$Y_e =$
$C =$
$S =$
$Xp - Mp =$
$G - T =$
$k =$
$k_t =$
$k_{\Delta G = \Delta T} =$

2. Explain why planned or *ex ante* investment must equal planned or *ex ante* saving if an equilibrium is to exist.

3. Explain how a business investor would decide whether or not to make an investment.

4. Fiscal policy is altering taxes and/or governmental expenditures to bring about changes in aggregate demand. Show how altering taxes and/or governmental expenditures affects the income level.

5. Assuming a three-sector economy, derive the tax multiplier.

6. If the budget is running at a deficit (or surplus), an equilibrium income level cannot exist. Discuss.

7. A balanced-budget multiplier is of little use since the government budget is seldom balanced. Discuss.

SUGGESTED READINGS

Duesenberry, James. *Income, Saving and the Theory of Consumer Behavior.* Cambridge, Mass.: Harvard University Press, 1949.

Keynes, John M. *The General Theory of Employment, Interest and Money.* New York: Harcourt, Brace, 1936.

Samuelson, Paul A. "Interactions Between the Multiplier Analysis and the Principle of Acceleration." *Review of Economic Statistics* 21 (May 1939): 75–78.

Chapter Sixteen

QUANTITY THEORY OF MONEY

In the previous chapter money played no role except as a numeraire; that is, the prices of goods and services could be stated in terms of a common unit of account. Now we must recognize that money does play a role in the determination of the income level. In this chapter we develop the role of money as seen by classical economists. This model is generally known as the *quantity theory of money*.

We will initially discuss the general characteristics of the quantity theory. Then we will concentrate on the development of the two major interpretations of the role of money: the Fisher, or transaction-velocity, approach and then the Cambridge, or cash-balances, approach. D. H. Robertson, the famous Cambridge economist, characterized the difference between these two views as "money on the wing" and "money sitting."[1] In Chapter 17 we will present the Keynesian model for money, and in Chapter 19 the monetarist model as developed by Milton Friedman and others. The monetarist model is derived to a large extent from the quantity theory found in this chapter.

GENERAL CHARACTERISTICS

In general, those individuals who are now classified as quantity theorists argued that a relationship exists between the quantity of money and the value of economic output over a given period of time. More specifically, they believed that a direct relationship exists between changes in the quantity of

1. Sir Dennis H. Robertson, *Money* (Chicago: University Chicago Press, 1959), p. 28.

money and changes in the price level. For example, as the quantity of money increases and the price level rises, the purchasing power of money declines.

The classical quantity theory of money was the predominant paradigm in monetary economics for decades prior to its displacement by Keynesian monetary economics in the latter 1940s and 1950s, after the publication of the *General Theory* in 1936. Jean Bodin in the sixteenth century is accepted as the first quantity theorist. According to Bodin, the inflation in Europe at that time was a result of Spain's importation of precious metals from her colonies. However, although we use the term quantity theory to describe the monetary theory spanning over four hundred years, the theory was not as homogenous as the name implies, as we shall see. We now turn to a discussion of the basic characteristics generally found in the monetary economics classified under the quantity theory label.

One of the basic tenets of the quantity theory is that the price level is a function of the quantity of money. Generally, quantity theorists held that the price level varies in direct proportion to the quantity of money; that is, if the money supply doubles, the general price level (but not necessarily specific prices) should also double. This means necessarily that the demand for money is a stable function and that at any given real income level, a given quantity of real money balances is demanded. If the demand for money were not stable, there would be no reason to believe that doubling the money supply would necessarily result in a doubling of the general price level.

Quantity theorists also argued that changes in the money supply explain or cause changes in the price level and not vice versa. More specifically, they claimed that changes in the money stock in circulation are the best explanation for changes in the price level. The price of a specific good may change for other reasons—for example, improvements in technology—but these nonmonetary factors were not considered adequate explanations for changes in the general price level.

Furthermore, quantity theorists held that money is neutral when changes in real output at different equilibrium states are compared, but not necessarily during the periods of transition between equilibrium states. Factors such as technology, the productivity of capital, growth in the labor force, and so on explain real output changes when the system is in equilibrium. Thus changes in the quantity of money would not affect the level of aggregate economic output in the long run, but could do so in the short run. Much of Irving Fisher's important work, for instance, is concerned with the effect of changes in the money supply on business cycles or fluctuations, that is, the changes occurring during periods of transition. He argued that varying growth rates in the money supply are the best explanation for business cycles.

Finally, proponents of the quantity theory of money generally believed that the nominal stock of money is *exogenously* determined, meaning that the money supply is a function of variables outside the economic model. More specifically, this means that the money supply is *not* a function of the interest rate. If it is argued that the money supply is a function of the interest rate, it is said to be partially or completely *endogenously* determined; that is, as the interest rate changes, the nominal money supply changes, either increasing or decreasing.

Quantity theorists were careful to distinguish between the *nominal money supply* and the *real money supply*. The real money supply is the nominal money supply M deflated (or inflated, depending on the direction of price-level changes) by a price-level index, that is, M/P. If the price level rises while the nominal money stock remains constant, the real money supply decreases. Hence the real money stock is partially endogenously determined because it is altered by changes in the price level, which is a variable generated in the model. The nominal money stock, on the other hand, is held to be exogenously determined, that is, not a function of the interest rate. If the nominal money supply is exogenously determined, then it is susceptible to a greater degree of control by the central bank than if it were held to be partially endogenously determined.

We now turn to a consideration of the Fisher and Cambridge versions of the quantity theory. We pay particular attention to their views on demands for money, which will help us understand the Keynesian view on demand for money as an evolutionary development.

IRVING FISHER—THE TRANSACTIONS-VELOCITY APPROACH

Irving Fisher (1867–1947) taught at Yale University from 1895 to 1935. Joseph Schumpeter, in his exhaustive *History of Economic Analysis,* asserts that Fisher was "one of two stars of the first magnitude that glorify Yale's scientific record."[2] According to Fisher's view, often called the *transactions-velocity approach*, prices are a function of the money supply M, the goods and services being traded in all transactions T, and the velocity of money V:[3]

$$P = f(M, V, T) \tag{16.1}$$

The money supply is composed of coin and currency M, and demand deposits M'.[4] The goods and services being bought and sold in all transactions T are the physical goods or services. The variable T includes not only final goods and services but also intermediate goods and services, transactions in financial markets, and the transfer of assets. The *velocity of money* V refers to the rate at which money turns over, that is, how many times a given stock of money is used in a given time period. Of these four variables, Fisher viewed the price level P as the most passive; in other words, the price level is influenced more by M, V, and T than M, V, or T is influenced by the others. Hence the functional relation is written as in equation 16.1.

Using these variables, we may write the *equation of exchange* in the following fashion:

$$MV + M'V' = PT \tag{16.2}$$

2. Joseph A. Schumpeter, *History of Economic Analysis* (New York: Oxford University Press, 1954), p. 871. The other "star," according to Schumpeter, was the physicist Willard Gibbs.

3. As Schumpeter points out, the variables T, V, and M exert a direct influence on the price level P as they have been defined here. Yet Fisher recognized that there were variables with an indirect effect on the price level that could not be ignored. These variables, which Fisher discussed in *The Purchasing Power of Money*, Rev. ed. (New York: Macmillan, 1920), Chapters 5 and 6, must be seen as working through T, V, and M. Thus T, V, and M represent more than their relatively simple definition indicates. Schumpeter, *History of Economic Analysis*, p. 1102.

4. Fisher and the Americans included demand deposits in the money supply; the contemporary European treatment left demand deposits out of the money supply. The Europeans treated demand deposits as affecting the velocity of money; that is, demand deposits made the use of money more efficient and increased the turnover rate of the money supply. If this treatment of demand deposits sounds somewhat strange, a perfect counterpart exists in monetary theory at present. Many assets, such as time deposits and accounts at savings and loan and similar institutions, display many of the characteristics of money. These assets or accounts are called near-monies. Some economists prefer to count some of these near-monies as part of the money supply. For example, Milton Friedman prefers to define the money supply so that time deposits are included. Other economists would include more of these near-monies as part of the money supply; many would include none of them. Those not including near-monies in the money supply recognize the existence of these assets as affecting the velocity of money. Thus one may adopt a strict definition of money (coin, currency, and demand deposits) or a broader definition (adding some of the near-monies), but the near-monies not included are seen to affect the velocity of money V.

Each type of money—coin and currency M and demand deposits M'—has its own respective velocity. The product PT can be viewed as either the average price of all goods and services times output, or as the aggregation of each product and service multiplied by its price. This product must be equal to the money supply, composed of both demand deposits and coin and currency multiplied by the number of times that the money supply was used. Simplifying by aggregating the two types of money, we may rewrite equation 16.2 as

$$MV = PT \tag{16.3}$$

This equation takes account of all transactions within an economy. Eliminating both double counting and certain transactions permits us to discuss changes in the money supply with respect to some national income concept like GNP. Rewriting equation 16.3 so that Q is substituted for T and only final goods and services are represented, we have

$$MV = PQ = Y \tag{16.4}$$

PQ is of a smaller magnitude than PT and equal, for example, to GNP or national income, which we may designate as Y. If we assume that the money supply is the same, a new value for the velocity of money is required in equation 16.4.[5]

This equation can be viewed in two ways. It can be understood in a strict identity sense, in which the money supply multiplied by the velocity must equal the value of the goods and services traded in a given period of time. Or it can be viewed as Fisher intended it, as indicating something about the influence of these variables on each other—more specifically, the influence of the money supply on the price level. A given money supply would *tend* to bring about a compatible price level.[6] Fisher could reach this conclusion

---

5. The reader will note that different V's exist, depending upon which concept is used on the right side of the equation. The value of V per se is not important, for different values of V may be consistent with each other, given different quantities (PT or PQ, for example) on the right side of the equation. What is important is whether or not V changes over time when looking at a specific V—for example, the V derived when PQ implies GNP.

As Schumpeter notes, the different "velocities" were not recognized for what they were until A. C. Pigou pointed them out in *Industrial Fluctuations*. (A. C. Pigou, *Industrial Fluctuations*, London: Macmillan and Co., 1927, Part I, Chapter XV.) J. A. Schumpeter, *History of Economic Analysis*, p. 1098.

6. Schumpeter, *History of Economic Analysis*, p. 1096.

because of his assumptions about the nature of Q and V. That is why equation 16.4 is not written as

$$MV \equiv PQ \equiv Y \qquad (16.4a)$$

Fisher does not intend that it be understood as an identity.

The output of goods and services Q, as seen by the classical school and Fisher, was determined in the real goods sector. Assuming perfect wage and price flexibility, they saw a full-employment economy as existing always.[7] The demand for, and the supply of, labor were both assumed to be functions of the real wage rate W/P—the money wage rate W modified by changes in the price level P. The demand for, and the supply of, labor are depicted in Figure 16.1a. The quantity of labor N is measured on the horizontal axis and the real wage rate W/P on the vertical axis.

Given the usual assumptions, the demand curve shows that as the amount of labor demanded increases, the marginal product of labor decreases.[8] Consequently, the real wage rate employers are willing to pay decreases. Where supply and demand intersect, the equilibrium real wage rate W/P' and the equilibrium quantity of labor N' are determined.

The production function is drawn in Figure 16.1b. It shows what output of goods and services Q can be produced by any given amount of labor N.[9] With equal increases in labor, the increase in output becomes less and less, reflect-

---

7. This is not strictly true. The classical school of thought and Fisher did not overlook the existence of business fluctuations. However, fluctuations in the output of real goods and services were considered aberrations, given their assumptions.

8. Assuming that diminishing marginal productivity of labor holds and that perfect competition in the buying and selling of inputs and the selling of the output exists, an employer would hire units of labor up to the point where the marginal physical product of labor MPP_L, multiplied by the price of goods produced, P_x was equal to the wage rate W:

$$W = MPP_L \cdot P_x$$

Rewriting the equation and generalizing, we find that the real wage rate will be equal to the marginal physical product of labor:

$$W/P = MPP_L$$

9. It is assumed here that the capital stock remains constant. If the capital stock were to increase, then the production function would rotate up, ceteris paribus. Similarly, technology is assumed to remain constant. An improvement in technology would be seen as a rotation upward in the production function, showing an increase in output with the same amount of labor.

Figure 16.1   EMPLOYMENT AND OUTPUT ACCORDING TO THE
                CLASSICAL SCHOOL

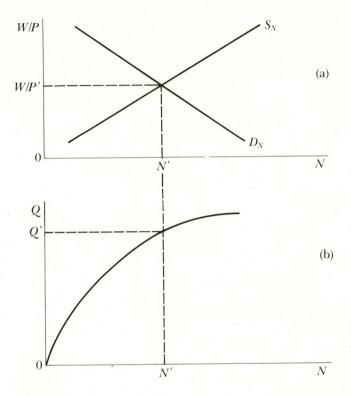

ing the assumption of diminishing marginal productivity of labor. Hence the demand for labor in Figure 16.1a is obtained from the production function in Figure 16.1b.[10]

When the amount of labor employed N', which is determined from the supply of, and demand for, labor, is plugged into the production function, it determines the level of output Q'.[11] In the short run, the full-employment

10. It is useful to recall that marginal physical product will be the derivative of the total physical product curve, that is, the production function. Since the derivative is the slope of the total curve, the marginal physical product of labor, which defines the demand curve for labor in the classical model, is seen in the decreasing slope of the production function.

11. Q will be determined if we are primarily concerned with a national income concept where

level N' should be fairly stable; hence, output in the short run would remain constant.[12]

For quantity theorists, the velocity of money was understood to be a function of people's spending habits, how often they were paid, and other variables. Many of these variables would be unlikely to change in the short run, and velocity might tend to be more stable in the short run. However, the quantity theorists asserted that the velocity would not necessarily be constant in the short run. As people saw prices rising (falling), they would be inclined to purchase goods sooner (later), thus increasing (decreasing) the velocity of money. Therefore, during transition periods the velocity of money might change.

Initially, we may assume that equation 16.4 has two constants, the velocity of money V, and the output of goods and services Q:

$$M\bar{V} = P\bar{Q} \qquad (16.5)$$

Fisher and other early quantity theorists held that people desired money for one purpose only, to buy goods and services. When the money supply is increased, people find themselves with greater amounts of money, which they then spend. Since the velocity of money is assumed constant and the output of goods and services cannot be increased because the economy is fully employed, prices must rise to take account of the greater money supply being spent. Thus changes in the money supply are seen to have a direct effect on the price level. Since Fisher viewed the price level as being the most passive of all the variables, he held that it would change as required, given changes in the other variables. Therefore, if the money supply were doubled, the price level would double; if the money supply were decreased by 10 percent, the price level would decrease by 10 percent.

Now we must recognize that Fisher perceived that the velocity of money V and output Q could not be constants in the short run, which he termed "pe-

---

intermediate goods are ignored, like GNP or NNP. T will be determined if *all* goods and services are counted, that is, if double counting is not avoided, which would be the case if we were interested in all transactions.

12. Simultaneously, we are assuming that the stock of capital and technology remain constant. While employment and hence output may be seen as being relatively constant in the short run, as the labor force would be able to increase only in the long run, Fisher saw output as increasing and then decreasing somewhat in the short run because of fluctuations during "periods of transition." These fluctuations were caused primarily by changes in the money supply.

riods of transition." Both V and Q could be expected to change. If V and Q change with changes in the money supply M, there is no guaranteed change in P that can be predicted. However, Fisher held that changes in Q would be slight and changes in V would not be sufficient to destroy the main relation between changes in M and changes in P. Thus if the money supply were doubled in the short run, the price level would *tend* toward doubling; if the money supply were decreased by 10 percent, the price level would *tend* to decrease by 10 percent.

In Fisher's transactions-velocity approach to monetary theory, money is assumed to be useful primarily for making purchases, that is, meeting one's transactions needs. The rapidity with which money turns over is the important interpretation of velocity.

THE CAMBRIDGE VIEW—THE
CASH BALANCES APPROACH

Whereas the Fisher view of money is referred to as the transactions-velocity approach, the Cambridge view is often referred to as the *cash balances approach*. The economists at the University of Cambridge in England saw the quantity theory differently than Irving Fisher. If equation 16.4 is rewritten so that V appears on the right side of the equation, we have:

$$M = \left(\frac{1}{V}\right) PQ \tag{16.6}$$

Letting $k = 1/V$, we may write equation 16.6 in the following form:

$$M = kPQ. \tag{16.7}$$

This is the so-called *Cambridge equation* containing the famous Cambridge k. Like the equation of exchange of Fisher, the Cambridge equation may be interpreted in two ways. It may be seen as an identity where the money supply *must* equal some national income concept like GNP, PQ, multiplied by the reciprocal of the velocity of money. This interpretation of the Cambridge equation is of no theoretical interest any more than $S \equiv I$ in an *actual* or *ex post* sense is important theoretically. It is true by definition.

The theoretical interest in the Cambridge equation is evident when one recognizes that the Cambridge k is being used to call attention to the holding of money. Instead of defining V as how fast money turns over, as Fisher did, the Cambridge economists asked why money remains idle as long as it does, why people do not spend it faster.

The Cambridge economists agreed with Fisher that people hold money to meet transactions in the future. But a second reason offered was that people might choose to hold money because of uncertainty.[13] People do not know what is going to happen in the future; consequently, they may decide to hold money to protect themselves. Hence, according to the Cambridge view, money has some utility itself. It is good for something other than just buying goods and services; it can serve as protection.

The Cambridge k can now be better understood not as the reciprocal of the velocity of money but as the proportion of income that one wishes to hold as money, that is, as the money balances people wish to maintain. We can illustrate by rewriting equation 16.7 and isolating k:

$$k = \frac{M}{PQ} = \frac{M}{Y} \tag{16.8}$$

Viewing k as the ratio of money to income forces us to recognize that money is being held for some reason.

This marks the major shift in emphasis between the Fisher view and the Cambridge view. According to Fisher, people want money for transactions purposes only; consequently, the demand for money is relatively unimportant and the analysis is primarily oriented to the supply of money. The Cambridge view, in asking why money remains idle as long as it does, raises the demand for money to a position equal to the money supply function. While M in equations 16.6 and 16.7 refers to the money supply, it is assumed that the demand for money is equal to the supply of money, thus preserving the significant difference between the Fisher and Cambridge views. Thus, equation 16.7 would be written:

$$M_s = M_d = kPQ \tag{16.9}$$

13. Milton Friedman, "A Theoretical Framework for Monetary Analysis," *Journal of Political Economy* 78 (March–April 1970): 201.

Economists at Cambridge University who helped develop the Cambridge cash balance approach, such as Alfred Marshall and A. C. Pigou, passed the Cambridge heritage in economic thought along to John Maynard Keynes. Keynes then virtually rewrote monetary theory over a period of years, rejecting the idea of a stable demand for money. As a consequence, he almost completely buried the quantity theory for approximately three decades.

KEY TERMS

Quantity theory of money
Exogenous
Endogenous
Nominal money supply
Real money supply
Transactions-velocity approach

Velocity of money
Equation of exchange
Cash balances approach
Cambridge equation
k

REVIEW QUESTIONS

1. Explain the general characteristics of the quantity theory of money.
2. Why does Fisher argue that a doubling of the money supply need not result in a doubling of the price level? Is his time reference the long or short run? Explain.
3. Discuss the differences between the following equations as they relate to the classical theory of money:

$$MV = PQ$$

and

$$M = kPQ = kY$$

4. Discuss whether the transactions-velocity approach or the cash balances approach seems to be better. What criterion or criteria are you using to decide?
5. Explain why no single correct series of values for *V* exists.

SUGGESTED READINGS

Anderson, Paul S. "Behavior of Monetary Velocity." Federal Reserve Bank of Boston, *New England Economic Review* (March-April 1977): 8–20.

Fisher, Irving. *The Purchasing Power of Money,* rev. ed. New York: Macmillan, 1920. Especially chapters 2, 4, 5 and 6.

Humphrey, Thomas M. "The Quantity Theory of Money: Its Historical Evolution and Role in Policy Debates." Federal Reserve Bank of Richmond, *Economic Review* (May-June 1974): 2–19.

Patinkin, Don. "The Chicago Tradition, the Quantity Theory, and Friedman." *Journal of Money, Credit, and Banking* I (February 1969): 46–70.

———. *Money, Interest and Prices.* 2d ed. New York: Harper & Row, 1965.

Chapter Seventeen

KEYNES ON MONEY

After the publication of John Maynard Keynes' *General Theory* in 1936, the quantity theory of money passed into relative obscurity over a period of several years.[1] Keynes' *liquidity preference theory*, which will be developed in this chapter, recognized explicitly that money would be held by people according to how liquid they desired their assets to be. The Cambridge or cash balances view of the quantity theory was, as we shall see, a definite movement in the direction of the Keynesian liquidity preference theory of money. However, as Schumpeter cautions, this view was *not* a liquidity preference theory.[2]

In this chapter, we develop the role of money in the Keynesian system. This role is explained by the demand for, and the supply of, money. The demand for and supply of money also determine the interest rate. After describing the role of money as seen by Keynes, we combine the real goods or production sector from Chapter 15 and the monetary sector developed in this chapter into a single model. This model, frequently referred to as the *IS-LM* model, is presented in Chapter 18.

1. It is not surprising that the Keynesian liquidity preference theory evolved from the Cambridge view of money. John Maynard (Lord) Keynes (1883–1946) was a member of the economics faculty at Cambridge. (However, he was neither Dr. Keynes nor Professor Keynes. When A.C. Pigou retired from the professorship at Cambridge in 1943, the chair was offered to Keynes, who turned it down in favor of D.H. Robertson.) His father, J. N. Keynes (1857–1949), was also an economist at Cambridge. Many individuals feel that one reason the Keynesian revolution was so complete was because of Keynes' Cambridge heritage. He was part of the Cambridge group, and his ideas, as revolutionary as they were, were not completely alien to those they displaced.

2. Joseph A. Schumpeter, *History of Economic Analysis* (New York: Oxford University Press, 1954), p. 1109.

THE DEMAND FOR MONEY

In the monetary sector, as elsewhere, when equilibrium exists, a price is determined as well as an equilibrium quantity. According to the Keynesians, the relevant price in the monetary sector is the interest rate; in other words, the interest rate is the price of money. (The monetarist, on the other hand, believes that the interest rate is the price of credit.) As usual, the equilibrium price is the result of the forces of supply and demand—in this instance, the supply of, and demand for, money. Consequently, if we are to understand the determination of the interest rate, we must examine these two sides of the monetary sector.

In the Keynesian monetary system the distinguishing feature is the demand for money. As formulated by Keynes, the demand for money is composed of three parts: (1) a transactions demand D_t; (2) a precautionary demand D_p, which when added to the transactions demand gives $D_t + D_p$; and (3) a speculative demand D_{sp}. Combining all three demands for money gives us the total demand for money M_d: $D_t + D_p + D_{sp} = M_d$. We will briefly examine each of these demands for money.

Transactions Demand

Since each spending unit—whether consumer, business, or government—does not have a cash *inflow* that is perfectly synchronized with its cash *outflow*, spending units must keep a certain amount of money on hand. For example, individuals generally are paid on a monthly or semimonthly basis, yet their expenditures take place daily. As a consequence, people need to hold an amount of money for these transactions. Should all expenditures be made, for example, on Friday of every other week, which would also be the day on which the individual is paid, he or she would have no need to carry money around for day-to-day purchases.

The *transactions demand* for money is the aggregate demand for money balances for transactions purposes in the economy. The size of the transactions demand is directly related to the level of income of the consuming units. Presented graphically, the transactions demand for money D_t might appear as in Figure 17.1, where the quantity of money balances demanded for transactions purposes M_t is measured on the vertical axis, and income Y on the horizontal axis. The transactions demand for money is assumed to be a linear

Figure 17.1   THE TRANSACTIONS DEMAND FOR MONEY AS A
FUNCTION OF THE LEVEL OF INCOME

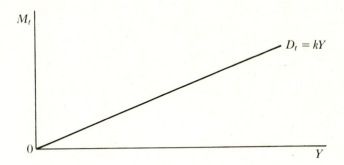

function. The function indicates that there is a given ratio between the level of income and the size of the transactions demand for money. Here it is assumed that for every four dollars of income, one dollar must be kept for transactions purposes; that is, in Figure 17.1, $k = \frac{1}{4}$ where k is the ratio of transactions balances to income. Hence we can write the transactions demand for money as a function of income.

$$D_t = f(Y) \qquad (17.1)$$

For each individual spending unit, the value of k is a function of personal preference. For example, the more frequently a person is paid, ceteris paribus, the smaller the cash balances required for transactions purposes, and hence the smaller the value of k. All that is assumed here is that there is an average value for k for the economy.

Another variable that might influence the transactions demand for money is the interest rate. For example, a higher interest rate calls for fewer dollars held for transactions purposes. Since the interest rate would define in a sense the opportunity costs of holding money idle for transactions purposes, an increase in the interest rate would be an incentive for individuals to put part of their transactions balances in some earning asset.[3]

3. For the classic article on the theoretical relationship between transactions balances and the interest rate, as well as income, see William Baumol, "The Transactions Demand for Cash: An Inventory Theoretic Approach," *Quarterly Journal of Economics* 66 (November 1952): 545–556.

Figure 17.2   TRANSACTIONS AND PRECAUTIONARY DEMANDS FOR
MONEY AS A FUNCTION OF THE INTEREST RATE WITH
INCOME HELD CONSTANT

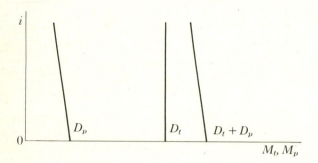

However, it is unlikely the average individual would be able to place half of the transactions balance, for example, in an earning asset for one or two weeks. Time deposits cannot be used in that fashion because individuals are penalized when withdrawals exceed a small, specified number within a three-month period. And the minimum dollar amount required to enter the Treasury bill market is considerably beyond the average individual's reach. Therefore, it is not surprising that Keynes assumed that the transactions demand for money is perfectly *interest inelastic*; that is, changes in the interest rate do not bring about changes in the balances held for transactions.[4] In Figure 17.2 the transactions demand D_t is drawn so that it is completely inelastic with respect to the interest rate. The interest rate i is measured on the vertical axis and the quantity of money demanded is measured on the horizontal axis.

Precautionary Demand

The *precautionary demand* for money as envisioned by Keynes reflects money balances held by individuals for unforeseen events, whether good or bad. Since people generally do not suffer from omniscience, they may well decide

---

4. Not all transactions balances are held by the average individual who lives on a salary or wage; those held by wealthier individuals and corporations will be responsive to changes in the interest rate. Since it will not seriously affect the model to ignore these aspects of the transactions demand for money, Keynes' assumption of an inelastic transactions demand will be retained here.

to retain a certain amount of money for unexpected occurrences—such as five dollars so designated in one's checking account or perhaps tucked away in the wallet in case of an emergency, whether a flat tire or an impromptu party.

The amount of money a person would retain for precautionary purposes would be in part a function of personality—the pessimist, for example, being perhaps more inclined to keep a larger amount for precautionary purposes because of suspicions that something is going to go wrong. Another factor influencing money balances held to meet precautionary demands would be an individual's occupation. An individual with a regular income as opposed to one whose employment is seasonal, for example, would need to retain smaller balances for precautionary purposes. A person's income level would also influence the size of precautionary balances. The wealthier individual is able to allow ten or twenty dollars for precautionary purposes, whereas the poorer student may have to be satisfied with putting a fifty-cent piece in his or her shoe or dreaming of the day when he or she will be able to afford to have some money "just in case."

Finally, the precautionary demand for money may be partially a function of the interest rate. If so, it is probably more interest elastic than the transactions demand. As the rate of interest increases, the opportunity cost of holding money for unforeseen and unpredictable events becomes greater. Consequently, an individual may take the risk of not having emergency money immediately available and put the money where it can earn 5 or 6 percent.

Income and interest rates are the basic economic determinants of the precautionary demand for money. Our general assumption is that, just as for the transactions demand, the larger percentage of the change in precautionary balances is explained by income changes. However, we assume generally that a greater percentage of the changes in precautionary balances is explained by interest rate changes than is true for balances retained to meet transactions demand; that is, the precautionary demand for money is generally more *interest elastic* than the transactions demand.

The transactions and precautionary demands for money balances are shown in Figure 17.2. Money balances held for precautionary purposes would probably utilize a significantly smaller percentage of one's income than balances held for transactions purposes, which is why the precautionary demand for money D_p is drawn to the left of the transactions demand for money in Figure 17.2. Again assuming a linear function, the precautionary demand for money is shown to be somewhat more elastic with respect to the rate of

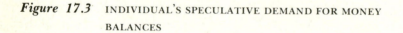

Figure 17.3   INDIVIDUAL'S SPECULATIVE DEMAND FOR MONEY
BALANCES

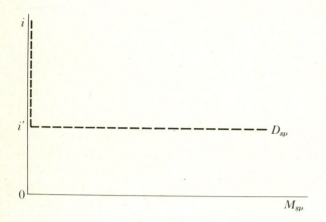

interest than the perfectly inelastic transactions demand. Adding the transactions and precautionary demands for money gives the combined demand function $D_t + D_p$.

Speculative Demand

According to Keynes, an individual has an additional demand for money that is primarily a function of the rate of interest, which he called the *speculative demand*. The amount of money a person decides to hold for speculative purposes depends on the current interest rate and expected changes in that interest rate.[5]

In the analysis used by Keynes, the individual's demand for speculative balances D_{sp} looks like that in Figure 17.3, where the interest rate is on the vertical axis and money balances held for speculative purposes M_{sp} are meas-

5. Initially in the *General Theory*, as Harry G. Johnson points out, the role of the precautionary demand for money was concerned with the problem of uncertainty of future interest rates and its avoidance; the speculative demand for money was defined in terms of the less important problem of changing prices on an organized market for securities. Later in the *General Theory*, both roles were attributed to the speculative demand while the precautionary demand was as described above. Harry G. Johnson, "The *General Theory* after Twenty-five Years," *American Economic Review* (May 1961): 8.

ured on the horizontal axis. At some interest rate i', the individual is indifferent between holding all available wealth for speculative balances in either interest or other earning assets *or* in money balances. At interest rates higher than i' the individual holds only earning assets, and at rates lower than i' only speculative money balances. Interest rate i' itself is a function of the perceived *normal interest rate,* which is the rate that the individual believes interest rates will tend toward in the long run.

A person would hold relatively large amounts of wealth in the form of money when the current interest rate is lower than i' because anticipated changes in the current rate make it profitable to do so. Changes in the rate of interest will cause changes in the prices of assets such as bonds or stocks. If current interest rates are below what individuals consider the normal rate of interest, likely changes in the interest rate would imply an increase; and an increase in the interest rate would mean a decrease in the price of assets.

The influence of changes in the interest rate on the price of an asset can be seen in the following equation:

$$\text{Present value} = \frac{R_1}{(1 + i)} + \frac{R_2}{(1 + i)^2} + \cdots + \frac{R_n}{(1 + i)^n} + \frac{S_n}{(1 + i)^n} \qquad (17.2)$$

where R is the contract (or promised) interest in a given period of time, i the current interest rate, and S the value of the asset when sold at maturity. One can see that if the current interest rate should rise—that is, if the rate at which the returns are being discounted is increased—the present value of the asset will decline. For example, the contract (or promised) interest on a government security is fixed; hence the price must change so that the guaranteed return will imply a given rate of return. Consequently, should current interest rates rise, the price of the asset would have to fall in order for the return to equal the new current interest rate. People would not buy an asset that earns an effective 5 percent if they could get 7 percent elsewhere, assuming similar risk and maturity conditions.

Therefore, if the current interest rate is below the normal interest rate, below i' in Figure 17.3, an individual should hold funds available for speculative purposes in speculative balances and not buy other assets like stocks and bonds. Since the current rate is below the normal rate, one would expect that the current rate will rise as it moves in the direction of the normal rate. Therefore, holding wealth in the form of money instead of other assets would

Figure 17.4   THE SPECULATIVE DEMAND FOR MONEY

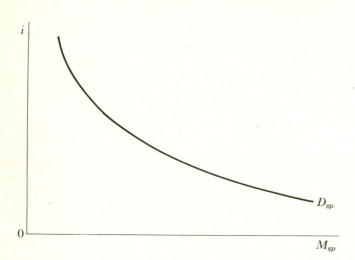

be rational where the likely change in the interest rate would imply a decrease in the value of these assets, that is, a capital loss. Thus we find the individual holding all money and no assets in the situation shown in Figure 17.3.

In the case where the current interest rate is above the normal interest rate—above i'—the individual would hold no speculative balances, only earning assets like stocks or bonds. With the current interest rate higher than the normal rate, a decline in the current rate would be expected were interest rates to change. A decline in the current interest rate would mean that the prices of assets like stocks or bonds would increase. Hence individuals would hold these assets in order to benefit from the anticipated capital gain.

If individual speculative demands for money balances were aggregated, a speculative demand for money like that in Figure 17.4 would be derived. The aggregate speculative demand for money is a smooth, convex from below, negatively sloped curve. It does not resemble the individual's specula-tive demand for money because of a key assumption made by Keynes that not everyone has the same idea as to what the normal interest rate is. Thus i' will not be the same for everyone.[6] As a consequence, when the speculative

6. While in simplest terms we could assume that the interest rate i' and the normal interest rate are equal, we would find that they are not upon more careful analysis; i' will be greater than the

Figure 17.5 THE TOTAL DEMAND FOR MONEY WITH INCOME
HELD CONSTANT

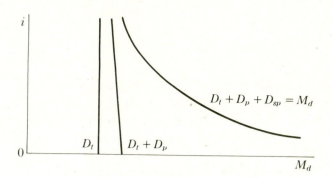

demands for money balances for all individuals are aggregated, society's speculative demand for money looks like that shown in Figure 17.4. Should all individuals have the same concept of the normal interest rate, then the aggregate speculative demand for money would look like that in Figure 17.3.[7]

As a further explanation for the shape of the speculative demand for money, we might at this time suggest the following: the lower the current interest rate becomes, the lower becomes the opportunity cost of holding wealth in the form of money. In turn, the higher current interest rates are, the greater the opportunity cost of holding wealth in the form of cash balances. If the current interest rate is 1 percent, an individual loses only that by not holding wealth in the form of an earning asset; a 6 percent current interest rate, however, would increase the implied cost of holding speculative balances substantially. Hence as the interest rate rises, there is an increasing incentive to hold wealth in some form other than money balances.

When all three components of the demand for money are graphically presented as in Figure 17.5, the transactions demand for money D_t is seen to be interest inelastic, the transactions-precautionary demand for money $D_t +$

---

normal interest rate. For a more complete analysis, see Fred R. Glahe, *Macroeconomics: Theory and Policy*, 2d ed. (New York: Harcourt Brace Jovanovich, 1976), pp. 167–168.

7. A derivation of the speculative demand for money, using indifference curve analysis, that precludes the aggregate speculative demand for money from looking like that in Figure 17.3 was presented by James Tobin. See James Tobin, "Liquidity Preference as Behavior Toward Risk," *Review of Economic Studies* 25 (February 1958): 65–86.

D_p somewhat more elastic, and the transactions-precautionary-speculative demand for money, or total demand for money, very responsive to the interest rate, reflecting the effect of the speculative demand for money.

THE SUPPLY OF MONEY

The money supply is a function of several variables, among which is the monetary base, or high-powered money, as it is also known. The *monetary base* is composed of total reserves plus the coin and currency in circulation. Other variables important in determining the money supply are the desired level of excess reserve holdings and the size of the currency drain. In the simplest model, assuming that the monetary base is a given, that the money supply is fully expanded, and that the amount of excess reserve holdings is not a function of the interest rate, a money supply function like M_{s_1} in Figure 17.6 would result.

However, we already know that these assumptions are in part unrealistic.[8] Changes in the interest rate may affect several of the variables that determine the money supply, which in turn depends on a given size of the monetary base. As interest rates increase—or, more specifically, as the difference between the lending rate and the rate that financial intermediaries must pay to borrow money increases—commercial banks will probably become more and more willing to do with fewer excess reserves because the opportunity cost of holding excess reserves increases as the interest rate rises. Decreased holdings of excess reserves will mean an increase in the money multiplier and hence an increase in the money supply.[9]

The holding of excess reserves should be viewed as including other items, such as a change in borrowing from the federal funds market. While this does not increase the monetary base, its use permits a more efficient utilization of the existing reserves.

Reserves themselves may be increased if commercial banks are induced to go to the discount window at the Federal Reserve and make increased discounts or advances. As the lending rate increases relative to the discount rate, it becomes more attractive for the commercial bank to use the discount

8. See Chapter 5 for a discussion of portfolio management by commercial banks.
9. See Chapter 7 for a consideration of the money multiplier.

Figure 17.6   TWO MONEY SUPPLY FUNCTIONS, ONE INDEPENDENT
OF THE INTEREST RATE, THE OTHER A FUNCTION OF
THE INTEREST RATE

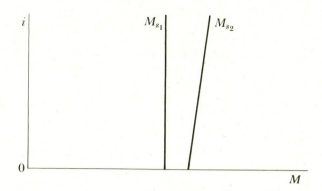

window temporarily rather than pass up profitable loan potentials. Increases
in reserves from discounts and advances enlarge the monetary base and hence
the money supply supported by it. Consequently, the money supply function
would be more accurately represented by a function like M_{s_2} than it is by M_{s_1}
as in Figure 17.6.

On the other hand, changes in the interest rate might affect the ratio of
time deposits to demand deposits. If funds are shifted from demand deposits
to time deposits as the interest rate rises, the ratio increases. Using the money
multiplier developed in Chapter 7,

$$m = \frac{1 + c}{r_D + c + x + r_T \cdot t} \tag{17.3}$$

where t is the ratio of time deposits to demand deposits, an increase in t
would imply a decrease in the money supply, ceteris paribus. Thus an inverse relationship between the money supply and the interest rate would exist, resulting in a negatively sloped money supply. We shall assume that the
money supply function is not negatively sloped. A money supply function that
is partially a function of the interest rate, like M_{s_2}, is said to be partially
endogenously determined, whereas a money supply function like M_{s_1}, which is
not a function of the interest rate, is said to be *exogenously* determined.

Figure 17.7   DETERMINATION OF THE EQUILIBRIUM INTEREST
RATE WITH INCOME HELD CONSTANT

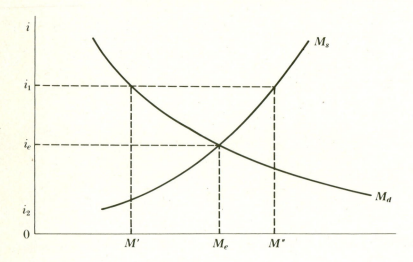

INTEREST RATE
DETERMINATION

Now that we have developed a money supply function and the Keynesian
demand for money, we can find the interest rate. In Figure 17.7, the supply of
money and the demand for money functions are both presented graphically,
with the interest rate emerging from the model as the equilibrium price for
money, i_e.

If the interest rate were higher than the equilibrium rate—for example,
i_1—a disequilibrium situation would exist. At i_1 the quantity of money demanded M' would be less than the quantity of money being supplied M''.
Individuals would find that they had more money than they wished at the
current interest rate. The excess money balances would be used to buy bonds
or other assets. The increased demand for these assets would increase their
price, ceteris paribus, and decrease their effective rate of return. Thus a lower
interest rate would come about. This process would continue until the current
interest rate would fall to the equilibrium interest rate.

If the interest rate were lower than the equilibrium rate—i_2, for example—the quantity of money demanded would be greater than that supplied. Individuals would sell assets to obtain more money, decreasing the price of the assets and driving the interest rate higher.

Using the material developed in this chapter and in Chapter 15, we may now develop a general equilibrium model. This model permits us to combine the real goods sector with the monetary sector presented in this chapter and note the interrelatedness between the two.

KEY TERMS

Liquidity preference theory   Interest elastic
Transactions demand   Speculative demand
Interest inelastic   Normal interest rate
Precautionary demand   Monetary base

REVIEW QUESTIONS

1. Explain why the Keynesian demand for money seems to be a logical extension of the Cambridge cash balances approach.
2. Why are balances held for transactions purposes considered to be more responsive to changes in income than interest rates?
3. Discuss the role of the normal rate of interest as it relates to the speculative demand for money.
4. Discuss the factors that might affect whether or not the money supply is exogenously determined and how.
5. Assuming a negatively sloped demand curve for money and a positively sloped supply curve, designate the equilibrium interest rate. Now assume an increase in the money supply. Explain the process by which a new equilibrium interest rate would be established.
6. Would an optimist be inclined to keep larger or smaller balances for precautionary purposes than a pessimist (of the same absolute degree)? Discuss.

SUGGESTED READINGS

Baumol, William. "The Transactions Demand for Cash: An Inventory Theoretic Approach." *Quarterly Journal of Economics* 66 (November 1952): 545–556.

Hansen, Alvin. *A Guide to Keynes.* New York: McGraw-Hill, 1953.

Tobin, James. "Liquidity Preference as Behavior Toward Risk." *Review of Economic Studies* 25 (February 1958): 65–86.

Chapter Eighteen

GENERAL EQUILIBRIUM:
THE *IS-LM* MODEL

In the preceding chapter we developed a model to explain the Keynesian view of the monetary sector. Placing this model in a slightly different framework, along with the material discussed in Chapter 15 on aggregate income determination, enables us to present a general equilibrium model, the *IS-LM* model. This general equilibrium model will combine the monetary and real-goods sectors. It must seem somewhat artificial to discuss the real-goods sector as if money had no role in it, or the monetary sector as if the real-goods sector had no influence. The model that will now be presented will overcome this artificiality to a certain extent.

The *IS-LM*, or general equilibrium, model developed here was first suggested by Sir John R. Hicks, the British Nobel laureate in economics.[1] The *LM* or monetary sector equilibrium is developed first, followed by the *IS* or real-goods sector equilibrium.

LM—MONETARY SECTOR
EQUILIBRIUM

To develop the *LM schedule,* which describes *monetary sector* equilibrium, we begin with the demand for money. The quantity of money balances M is measured on the horizontal axis and the interest rate i on the vertical axis. In Figure 18.1 the demand for money balances is broken into two parts, the transactions demand (a) and the speculative demand (b). (We assume that the precautionary demand for money can be added to the transactions demand

1. The original presentation of this model by J. R. Hicks was in his article "Mr. Keynes and the 'Classics': A Suggested Interpretation," *Econometrica* 5 (April 1937): 147–159.

Figure 18.1   DERIVATION OF MONEY DEMAND FUNCTIONS FOR
DIFFERENT INCOME LEVELS

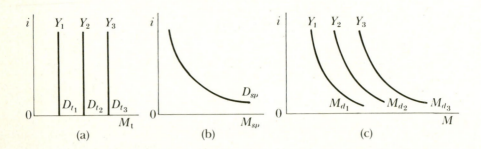

(a)   (b)   (c)

because we also assume that the greater percentage of the changes in money
balances held for these purposes are explained by changes in the income level
and not the interest rate.) Both the transactions demand and the speculative
demand for money are graphed against the interest rate. However, in part (a)
of Figure 18.1, the transactions demand for money is drawn such that it is not
a function of the interest rate; that is, it is perfectly interest inelastic. Three
transactions demands for money are shown, each for a different income level.
As the income level increases ($Y_1 < Y_2 < Y_3$), the transactions demand for
money balances increases. In part (b) the speculative demand for money
is shown. In part (c), the aggregate demand for money for each income
level is drawn, with the speculative demand added to each of the transactions demands.

Figure 18.2a is part (c) of Figure 18.1. The money supply function shown is
assumed to be completely exogenously determined, that is, not a function of
the interest rate (like M_{s_1} in Figure 17.6). With these money demand functions
and a money supply function, we can now derive an *LM* schedule. In part (b)
of Figure 18.2 the interest rate is measured on the vertical axis and the income
level on the horizontal axis. The money supply function intersects the money
demand function M_{d_1} at interest rate i_1. The money demand function M_{d_1}
exists for income level Y_1. Hence where i_1 and Y_1 intersect, we have an
equilibrium point where the demand for money balances is equal to the
supply of money balances, given the interest rate and the income level.
Performing this procedure for each of the money demand functions pertaining to a given income level, we will derive the entire locus of points where the
demand for money and the supply of money balances are in equilibrium.

Figure 18.2   DERIVATION OF *LM* SCHEDULE

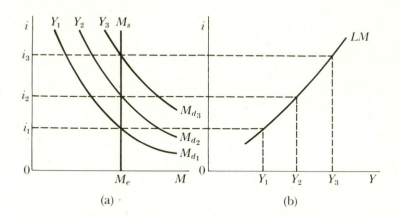

(a)   (b)

The *LM* schedule describes the various equilibria possible in the monetary sector. It shows the relation between the income level and the interest rate. As the income level increases, the interest rate increases also. This relation between the income level and the interest rate reflects the influence of a relatively fixed money supply. As the income level increases, more money is demanded for transactions-precautionary purposes. However, the money supply is not increased to compensate; consequently, money is taken from balances held for speculative purposes. For speculative balances to decrease, ceteris paribus, the interest rate must increase. To state the process differently, with increases in income, the demand for money will shift to the right. With no shift in the money supply function and assuming that it is not perfectly elastic, the interest rate will rise.

Up to this point we have assumed that the transactions (plus precautionary) demand for money is perfectly interest inelastic. We know, however, that the amount of money balances held for these purposes may be a function of the interest rate. Consequently, the transactions demand will look more like that in Figure 18.3. As the interest rate rises, money balances held for transactions purposes decrease for any given income level. This implies that the total demand for money is more elastic, ceteris paribus, than it was in part (c) of Figure 18.1. Using these more elastic aggregate money demand functions (for different income levels), we can derive a new *LM* schedule as we did in Figure 18.2. The *LM* schedule will be flatter because the aggregate demand for

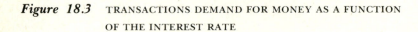

Figure 18.3   TRANSACTIONS DEMAND FOR MONEY AS A FUNCTION
OF THE INTEREST RATE

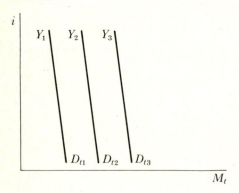

money is more elastic.[2] As the interest rate rises and individuals and institutions economize on balances held for transactions purposes, any given money supply will now be able to support a higher income level at a given interest rate than it would have when the transactions demand was perfectly inelastic.

We should also note that the money supply function may be a function of the interest rate, that is, partially endogenously determined (as money supply function M_{s_2} in Figure 17.6). Assuming that the aggregate money demand functions for each income level, Y_1 through Y_3, are given in part (a) in Figure 18.4, we are given two money supply functions, M_{s_1} and M_{s_2}. Using these two money supply functions, we can derive two *LM* curves. The *LM* curve derived using M_{s_1} is LM_1; the *LM* curve from M_{s_2} is LM_2, which is flatter than LM_1. As the interest rate increases, money balances supplied increase using M_{s_2}. With a greater money supply, more balances are available to meet increased transactions demands due to the higher income level. As a consequence, the income level supportable in the monetary sector is greater with a partially endogenously determined money supply than with a completely exogenously determined money supply function.

2. The reader should derive a new *LM* schedule using a more interest-elastic aggregate demand for money to determine what happens to its slope.

Figure 18.4 DIFFERENCE IN EFFECTS ON *LM* SCHEDULE OF
EXOGENOUS AND ENDOGENOUS MONEY SUPPLY
FUNCTIONS

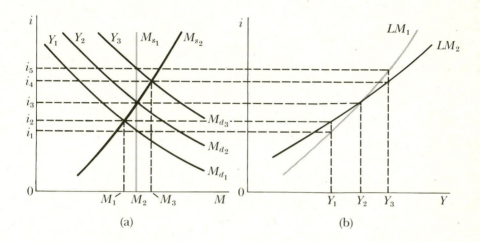

(a)

(b)

IS—REAL-GOODS SECTOR
EQUILIBRIUM

To obtain the *IS schedule,* which describes *real-goods sector* equilibrium, we
simply use the material developed in Chapter 15. The marginal efficiency of
investment *MEI* is pictured in Figure 18.5b, showing the relation between the
interest rate and the amount of investment. The saving function is drawn in
Figure 18.5c. In part (d) the condition represented is that at equilibrium
income levels, planned saving and planned investment are equal; hence this
curve is a 45-degree line.

Using these functions, we derive the *IS* schedule in part (a). Beginning at
point Z' in part (b), we find that at interest rate i', I' worth of investment will be
made. If an equilibrium income level is to exist, I' investment must be offset
by an equal amount of saving—S', determined in part (d). In part (c) the
saving function shows that income level Y' is required to provide saving S'. In
part (a) we combine income Y' and interest rate i' and obtain an initial point
on the *IS* schedule, X'. Doing this for all possible points, we obtain the entire
IS schedule.

Figure 18.5   DERIVATION OF *IS* SCHEDULE

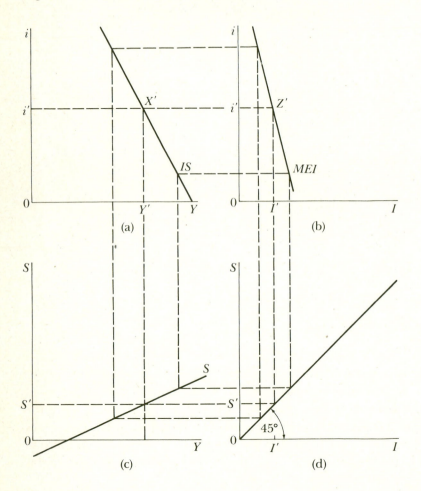

The *IS* curve shows the various points of equilibrium possible in the real-goods sector. Just like the *LM* curve, the *IS* curve is a relation between the interest rate and the income level. To increase the output of goods and services in the real-goods sector—that is, to increase the income level—it is necessary to lower the interest rate, which raises the investment level and increases consumption. Thus as the interest rate decreases, the equilibrium income level in the real-goods sector will increase.

Figure 18.6   DETERMINATION OF THE EQUILIBRIUM INTEREST
RATE AND INCOME LEVEL

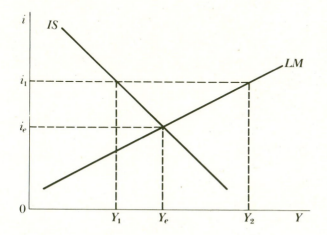

GENERAL EQUILIBRIUM

Now that the *IS* and *LM* schedules have been derived individually, they can be combined in a single model—a *general equilibrium* solution that takes account of the monetary and real-goods sectors.

The *IS* and *LM* schedules are drawn in Figure 18.6. Where they intersect determines the interest rate and income level that can exist in both sectors simultaneously. Of all the equilibria that are possible in the monetary sector and in the real-goods sector, only one interest rate i_e and one income level Y_e can exist simultaneously.

If an interest rate higher than the equilibrium interest rate were to exist, such as i_1, the level of income called for in the monetary sector would be Y_2. The interest rate i_1 is that required to keep money balances held for speculative purposes at a given level. The remainder of the balances available for speculative purposes are to be used to purchase earning assets. However, the real goods sector at i_1 will allow an income level of Y_1 only. At i_1 the interest rate chokes off sufficient investment and consumption so that the income level from the real-goods sector is not equal to that in the monetary sector. A relative deficiency in investment possibilities will exist for those individuals

Figure 18.7   EFFECTS OF SHIFTS IN THE *IS* SCHEDULE

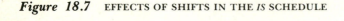
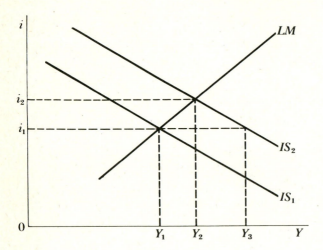

trying to buy earning assets with speculative balances. Hence bonds or similar assets will be purchased with these balances, which will drive up bond prices. The increase in bond prices must in turn decrease the interest rate. The decrease in the interest rate will encourage investment. The process will continue until an interest rate is reached that will call forth the same income level in both sectors of the economy. The reader should work through the implications of an interest rate existing below the equilibrium rate.

Shifts in the IS Schedule

When the meaning of the *IS-LM* intersection is understood, it is important to note how changes in various factors can be analyzed through this model. First we consider those factors that cause shifts in the *IS* schedule; then those that bring about shifts in the *LM* schedule.

One factor that causes the *IS* curve to shift is changes in the *MEI* function. For example, a shift to the right in the *MEI* schedule due to improved expectations or a capital-using technological improvement will cause the *IS* schedule to shift to the right, from IS_1 to IS_2 in Figure 18.7, which in turn will cause a higher level of equilibrium income, but at a higher interest rate.

The shift to the right in the *MEI* function shifts the *IS* schedule to the right. In the real-goods sector more goods and services are now being produced, reflecting the improvement in investment. At interest rate i_1, with a shift in the *IS* curve to IS_2, the income level might be expected to rise to Y_3. However, the monetary sector must be reckoned with. Money must be raised to make the added investment. The only way to entice people to make the additional funds available for investment is to offer them a higher rate of return, that is, to raise the interest rate. But the rise in the interest rate will eliminate some of the previously profitable investment possibilities (and to a degree, perhaps, some consumption). Hence the income level will rise to Y_2 instead of Y_3 from Y_1, and the interest rate will rise to i_2.

An increase in saving, ceteris paribus, would shift the *IS* curve to the left, from IS_2 to IS_1, implying a lower level of income at a lower interest rate. A change in taxes would have to be represented indirectly, since taxes do not appear explicitly. An increase in taxes can be seen to operate through the saving function, causing the saving function (saving plus taxes in this instance) to shift up.[3] The increase in taxes would cause the *IS* schedule to shift to the left.

A change in government spending ΔG would in turn be analyzed by shifting the *MEI* (or *MEI* + *G*) function; an increase would shift the *MEI* + *G* function to the right by the amount of the increase in public-sector spending. The resulting shift in the *MEI* + *G* function has at this point the same effect as the simple shift in the *MEI* function due to improved expectations discussed above.[4] This shift in the *MEI* + *G* function will cause a shift to the right in the *IS* curve (for example, IS_1 to IS_2).

Changes in the foreign sector of the economy can be handled as well. Exports Xp are added to the *MEI* (or *MEI* + *G*) function. A decrease in exports, ceteris paribus, would shift the *MEI* + *G* + *Xp* function to the left, which in turn would shift the *IS* curve to the left, decreasing the income level and lowering the equilibrium interest rate. A change in the autonomous part of imports $\Delta \overline{Mp}$ is most easily handled by adding imports to the saving (or *S* + *T*) function. An increase in the autonomous part of imports would shift the $S + T + Mp$ function up and bring about a shift to the left in the *IS* curve.

---

3. Recall that the saving function cannot simply be shifted up by the amount of taxes or the increase in taxes. See Chapter 15, the section on "Government."

4. For a possible complication, see Chapter 22, the section on "'Crowding-Out' Effect."

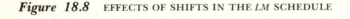

Figure 18.8 EFFECTS OF SHIFTS IN THE *LM* SCHEDULE

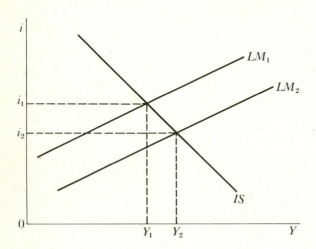

(A change in the induced part of the import function *m* would bring about a rotation—that is, a change in the slope—of the $S + T + Mp$ function. An increase in the marginal propensity to import would rotate the $S + T + Mp$ function up.)[5]

Shifts in the LM Schedule

Changes in factors on the monetary side can also occur. For example, an increased speculative demand for money would cause a shift to the left in the *LM* curve, from LM_2 to LM_1 in Figure 18.8. The most important factor for monetary policy is probably the money supply. An increase in the money supply can be brought about through changes in reserve requirements on time and demand deposits, changes in open market operations, a different discount policy by the Federal Reserve, or changes in other variables. An increase in the money supply, everything else remaining the same, would mean a shift to the right in the *LM* schedule, and hence an increase in the income level from Y_1 to Y_2 and a decrease in the interest rate from i_1 to i_2.

5. The reader should draw the related models and analyze the effects.

Note that an increase in the money supply shifting the *LM* curve from LM_1 to LM_2 means that interest rate i_1 and income level Y_1 no longer constitute an equilibrium situation. At interest rate i_1, investment possibilities are insufficient, given the money people are trying to invest. Consequently, other goods like bonds and similar assets will be purchased, raising their prices and decreasing the interest rate until interest rate i_2 and income level Y_2 are established. Altering the money supply to affect the equilibrium income level is the essence of monetary policy.

THE TERM STRUCTURE OF INTEREST RATES

Perhaps a brief comment is in order concerning interest rates. Up to this point, the discussion has referred to the interest rate as if there were a single interest rate. All of us are aware that there are many interest rates. Different rates exist for short-term government securities as opposed to long-term securities. Rates differ for various types of corporate debt as well as other types of debt. Many different rates get published, and those that do are far outnumbered by those that do not.

Interest rates vary in part because of differences in maturity and the degree of risk involved in any given debt. If all debt were made similar with respect to risk, maturity, and other characteristics, then in fact we would expect a single interest rate.

The variation in interest rates with respect to maturity is known as the *term structure of interest rates*. Since not all debt is of the same maturity, it would be desirable if some theory existed to explain the difference in interest rates one observes on loans of varying maturities when other characteristics of the loans are the same. Unfortunately, no adequate theory exists at present. Two theories predominate: the segmented market theory and the expectations theory.

The *segmented market theory* of the term structure of interest rates is based on the assumption that loans of different maturities are not perfect substitutes for each other; that is, that borrowers and lenders are not indifferent between holding debt of one maturity and holding debt of another maturity. If borrowers and lenders have preferences as to maturity of debt, then the interest rate or yield for any given maturity will depend upon the supply of, and demand for, debt of that maturity. Since short-term and long-term debt are not perfect substitutes, changes in the interest rate for one maturity will not directly affect the interest rate on debt of another maturity. Thus if the supply of funds for short-term debt of a given maturity were increased, the return or yield would be expected to decline, but the return on debt of a different maturity would not necessarily be affected.

The *expectations theory* of the term structure of interest rates assumes that borrowers and lenders are essentially indifferent as to the maturity of debt. It argues that differences in short-term rates as opposed to long-term rates reflect expected changes in short-term interest rates. The long-term rate for a given maturity is seen to be some function of the expected short-term rates that will exist over the life of the long-term debt. For debt or loans that differ only in maturity and not in other characteristics, the expectations theory holds that short-term rates will be the same as long-term rates if short-term rates are not expected to change. Thus if short-term rates are expected to remain at 5 percent for twenty years, the long-term rate for debt of twenty years will be 5 percent also. If the short-term rates are expected to rise, then the long-term rate will rise. It will rise to reflect these expectations, so that those committing their funds for the longer term will not lose because they did not lend their funds for a shorter term. As we stated earlier, neither of these theories has been shown to be more correct as yet.

KEY TERMS

LM schedule	General equilibrium
Monetary sector	Term structure of interest rates
IS schedule	Segmented market theory
Real-goods sector	Expectations theory

REVIEW QUESTIONS

1. Explain equilibrium in the monetary sector as shown by the *LM* schedule.
2. Explain the effect of the following on the *LM* schedule:
   a. The demand for money becomes more elastic with respect to the interest rate.

b. The money supply function changes from being partially endogenously determined to being totally exogenously determined.

3. Derive the *IS* schedule and explain why the real-goods sector equilibrium is a negatively sloped curve.

4. Assuming initially an equilibrium using *IS* and *LM* schedules, describe the effect of each of the following:

a. a decrease in government expenditures;

b. an increase in the money supply;

c. an improvement in expectations of entrepreneurs concerning investment;

d. an increase in the demand for money.

5. Using *IS* and *LM* schedules and assuming that initially an interest rate lower than the equilibrium rate exists, describe the process by which the interest rate returns to equilibrium.

SUGGESTED READINGS

Hicks, J.R. "Mr. Keynes and the 'Classics': A Suggested Interpretation." *Econometrica* 5 (April 1937): 147–159.

Malkiel, Burton G. *The Term Structure of Interest Rates.* Princeton, N.J.: Princeton University Press, 1966.

Scott, Robert H. "Estimates of Hicksian *IS* and *LM* Curves for the United States." *Journal of Finance* 21 (September 1966): 479–487.

Smith, Warren L. "A Graphical Exposition of the Complete Keynesian System." *Southern Economic Journal* 23 (October 1956): 115–125.

Chapter Nineteen

MONETARISM

As we said earlier, after the publication of the *General Theory,* the liquidity preference approach gradually supplanted the quantity theory as the orthodox monetary theory. Today the liquidity preference approach still predominates, but less so each year. The fact that the quantity theory was replaced by the Keynesian approach does not mean that it has seen its day and has no further relevance to contemporary economics. Instead of relegating it to the heap of used theories, today's monetarists have reformulated the quantity theory to answer some of the objections raised by Keynesians. It is now a more defensible theory than it once was.

It is important to recognize that the monetarist model is generally long run in nature—much more so than the Keynesian model. For example, a state of equilibrium where the natural rate of unemployment holds (a concept discussed later in this chapter) is attained only after the economy returns to equilibrium after being disturbed by a change in some variable like money-supply growth rates. The reader must keep this time reference in mind.

Initially we shall set out the demand for money function as formulated by Professor Milton Friedman, now retired from the University of Chicago and Nobel laureate in economics in 1976. Then we shall note alternatives or changes in the monetarist demand for money function suggested by other economists. Finally we shall develop what might be seen as the remainder of the general monetarist position, focusing specifically on the interest rate, the natural rate of unemployment, and inflation.

THE DEMAND FOR MONEY

Milton Friedman, probably the most widely known monetarist at present, states in his essay on the reformulation of the quantity theory that three characteristics define monetarism: first, the function expressing the demand for money must be stable; second, the factors affecting the supply of money must be different, to a large extent, from those affecting the demand for money; and third, the demand for money function must be of a certain form and composition.[1]

First, referring to the *demand for money,* Friedman states that it is important to the monetarist position that the demand for money be a stable function. By this he means that the demand for money should change only with changes in the variables specified in the demand for money function. Moreover, not only must the demand for money be a stable function but it must be a stable function of a *limited* number of variables. Quantity theorists or monetarists must be prepared to enumerate explicitly the variables that they feel will explain the demand for money. Friedman explains that for monetarists to argue that the demand for money is a stable function of an unlimited number of variables is to argue that the demand for money is unstable; the one implies the other.[2]

A monetarist cannot argue that the demand for money is unstable. For example, assume the economy is in long-run equilibrium, and that the money supply is growing at 3 percent per year, which is the same rate at which the economy is growing in real terms (which accounts for both changes in technology and increased quantities of factors of production). Under these conditions, no general rise in the price level should take place, although individual prices may be rising or falling. Further assume that a natural full-employment equilibrium exists in the labor market. Now assume that the money supply begins to grow at 5 percent per year. Because the price level does not change initially, individuals will find themselves with increased real money balances. What they do with these increased real money balances determines what effect they have. Monetarists argue that ultimately changes in the money

1. The second condition—that the variables defining the demand for money function be different from those defining the supply of money function—permits one to use the stable demand for money function to analyze the effects of changes in the money supply. If the variables defining the two functions were the same, then a stable demand for money function could not be used to analyze the effects of changes in the money supply. The third condition simply states that a monetarist must deny the existence of a liquidity trap, that is, a money demand function that is perfectly interest elastic at some low interest rate. (The liquidity trap is discussed in Chapter 20.) See Milton Friedman, "The Quantity Theory of Money—A Restatement," in *Studies in the Quantity Theory of Money* (Chicago: University of Chicago Press, 1956), p. 15.

2. Ibid., p. 16.

supply have a predictable effect on the level of economic activity. Since these predicted results will not occur if an unstable demand for money exists, the basis for the monetarist position would be destroyed.

In theoretically defining the demand for money, Friedman contends that people could choose to hold their wealth in any or all of several forms. They might choose to hold part of their wealth as money, bonds, or equities. Or they could hold part of their wealth in physical assets, such as a house or land, or in human wealth.[3] Human wealth is generally seen as investment by a person in himself or herself: for instance, getting an education or, for an actor, a "nose job."

Given these means for disposing of one's wealth, the amount of real money balances M/P that would be desired by any individual would be some function of the return on money r_m, the return on bonds r_b, the return on equities r_e, the expected or anticipated change in the price level over time $(1/P)(dP/dt)$, the total amount of one's wealth W, the ratio of human to nonhuman wealth n,[4] and one's tastes and preferences u.

For example, as the interest rate for lending money increases, people would be inclined to hold smaller money balances. If the price level began to increase (or began to increase at an increasing rate), people would hold smaller money balances to keep from absorbing a loss as the purchasing power of money declines. They would prefer to buy goods today as opposed to waiting until tomorrow, when prices will have risen. With a greater investment in human wealth relative to total wealth, people would hold greater money balances. If more of one's wealth were held in nonhuman form, it could be converted into money more readily than if a greater percentage of one's wealth were held as human wealth.

The functional relation may be written as follows:[5]

$$\frac{M}{P} = f\left(W, r_m, r_b, r_e, \frac{1}{P}\frac{dP}{dt}, n, u\right) \tag{19.1}$$

Note that this functional relation is similar to more recent theories in the

3. Ibid., p. 5.
4. Alternatively, n can be defined as the ratio of human to total wealth.
5. Milton Friedman, "A Theoretical Framework for Monetary Analysis," *Journal of Political Economy* (March-April 1970): 204.

Keynesian tradition.[6] Note also that with an increase in the money supply, the increase in money may or may not be held, depending on the rates of return for the alternatives where one's wealth could be held.

However, at this point Friedman says that while these alternative forms for holding one's wealth exist, some are empirically insignificant. For example, while the rate of interest has some effect on the demand for money, Friedman finds that it is insignificant; consequently, r_m, r_b, and r_e drop out of the demand function.[7] Tastes and preferences u are assumed to be constant over time, since no practical way exists at present to measure them. Similarly, because of difficulties in empirically verifying its influence, wealth itself W is replaced in the function by permanent income. Permanent income is the level of income derivable from total wealth year after year.

On the basis of empirical investigation, Friedman concludes that changes in the real stock of money per person M/NP are highly correlated with secular changes in real income per person Y_p/NP.[8] That is,

$$\frac{M}{NP} = \gamma\left(\frac{Y_p}{NP}\right)^{\delta} \tag{19.2}$$

Thus, according to Friedman, a causal relation between changes in the money supply and the income level exists.

Other economists have concluded that the demand for money function proposed by Friedman, based on statistical evidence, is not totally correct. Empirically investigating the demand for money, Karl Brunner and Allan Meltzer found that the inclusion of interest rates improved the results of their study on the demand for money.[9] David Laidler's studies verified the Brunner and Meltzer conclusion.[10]

6. This functional relation is similar to theories of the Keynesian tradition, since alternatives exist for holding money (that is, money may be held for other than transactions purposes). Not only may present-day monetarists be seen to have included variables that Keynesians felt were important, but it may work in the other direction: Keynesians are now including a wealth factor in their theories.

7. Milton Friedman, "The Demand for Money: Some Theoretical and Empirical Results," *Journal of Political Economy* 67 (August 1959): 329.

8. Ibid., p. 336. N stands for the population and P the price level. γ and δ are behavorial parameters.

9. Karl Brunner and Allan H. Meltzer, "Predicting Velocity: Implications for Theory and Policy," *Journal of Finance* 28 (October 1963): 339.

10. David Laidler, "The Rate of Interest and the Demand for Money—Some Empirical Evi-

Brunner and Meltzer also found that nonhuman wealth was a more accurate variable in the demand for money than Friedman's permanent income variable. They used nonhuman wealth in their study, but they could not test directly whether human or nonhuman wealth was the better variable because of the difficulty in measuring human wealth. However, permanent income is the income generated by one's total wealth on a sustainable basis. Since nonhuman wealth gave better empirical results than permanent income, Brunner and Meltzer concluded that human wealth was not as important as nonhuman wealth in determining the demand for money.[11] David Laidler in a later study found that permanent income was a better variable than nonhuman wealth.[12] Conflicting evidence exists, but most studies seem to indicate that some wealth variable, whether nonhuman wealth or permanent income (as an indirect measure of total wealth), is required in the demand for money function.

We have just seen how the monetarist demand for money function evolved from the classical quantity theory of money, modified somewhat by developments in the Keynesian liquidity preference theory.

With a stable demand for money function, monetarists can concentrate their attention on the money supply to discover the effects of changes in the money supply. These effects can now be illustrated by an examination of the natural rate of employment, the interest rate, and inflation. We shall deal with each of these issues separately for expositional purposes.

EMPLOYMENT

The first major issue we wish to consider in the general monetarist model is that of employment.[13] Monetarists believe that each economy has a *natural*

---

dence," *Journal of Political Economy* 74 (December 1966): 545–549. To an extent, all economists are Keynesians today. The reader will note that just as Keynes included the interest rate in the money demand function, Friedman also includes it when theoretically formulating the demand for money. He calls the interest rate insignificant on the basis of empirical evidence. Other monetarists, however, on the basis of empirical evidence, believe that the interest rate should be included.

11. Brunner and Meltzer, "Predicting Velocity," p. 339.

12. David Laidler, "Some Evidence on the Demand for Money," *Journal of Political Economy* 74 (February 1966): 55–68.

13. The present model follows that developed in a survey article by Milton Friedman. See Milton Friedman, "The Role of Monetary Policy," *American Economic Review* 58 (March 1968): 1–17.

full-employment level, which will contribute no inflationary or deflationary pressures. Furthermore, they believe that to try to modify that employment level through either monetary or fiscal policy (or some combination of the two) is to incur a real cost for society. Part of this real cost will be either increased unemployment (temporarily, as we shall see), if the direction is deflationary, or inflation, with only a temporary decrease in the degree of unemployment.[14]

This natural full-employment level is determined by factors in each society, only some of which are essentially economic. Noneconomic factors that would determine this natural employment level would be, for example, the value placed on work, the general level of education of the population and how that education is distributed throughout society, the mobility of the labor force, the homogeneity of the population, society's views on accepting welfare, and so on. One economic determinant would be the level of economic activity, which might influence the number looking for work. Should people view the current situation as unlikely to offer employment, they may not even look for work and thus would not be considered part of the labor force.[15] These basic determinants are likely to be different from one society to another, which would explain why unemployment in Sweden or the United Kingdom is generally lower than in the United States, whereas in other countries it is usually higher, given similar inflation rates.

The monetarist's concept of a natural full-employment level implies that there is a real wage rate that will equate the demand for, and supply of, labor. The *real wage rate w* is the *money* or *nominal wage rate W* adjusted for changes in the price level P; that is, $w = W/P$. As we saw in Chapter 16, the demand for labor is a function of the productivity of labor. Since the productivity of labor determines the real wage rate, the demand for labor is a function of the real

14. While it may be argued that deflation or inflation is essentially a monetary and not a real phenomenon, the costs clearly are real, especially for certain parts of society, as the effects of either will not be spread evenly through the population. Other effects of deflation or inflation may be reflected in a country's changing foreign trade balance, and so on. Moreover, changing rates of either inflation or deflation will also be a real cost to society because individuals must spend more time and effort trying to determine their overall effect in order to be able to make correct decisions. Finally, prolonged inflation or deflation in excess of what is considered normal may well result in a society beginning to disintegrate, as "correct" answers become ever more difficult if not impossible to an increasing number of individuals. As answers become more difficult, normal patterns become suspect, and the economic fabric of society is destroyed. For a further discussion of inflation, see Chapter 22.

15. See Chapter 22.

Figure 19.1 MONETARIST ANALYSIS OF LABOR SUPPLY AND DEMAND

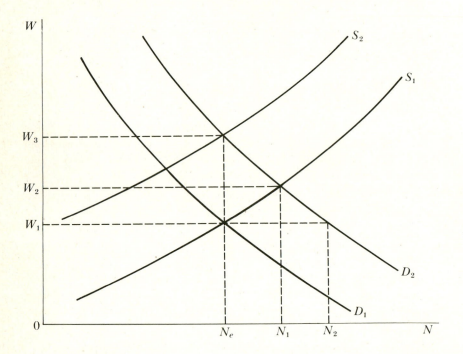

wage rate.[16] Likewise, the supply of labor is seen to be a function of the real wage rate also, in that while labor is sensitive to changes in the money or nominal wage rate, labor will not suffer illusions for very long as to the real purchasing power of that money wage rate.

To begin, let us assume that the supply of labor S_1 and the demand for labor D_1 are as shown in Figure 19.1. For expositional purposes, we will measure the money or nominal wage rate W instead of the real wage rate on the vertical axis, even though we are still assuming that the demand for labor is a function of the real wage rate, as is the supply of labor. On the horizontal axis we will measure the quantity of labor. Initially we find that the equilibrium money wage rate is W_1 and the equilibrium quantity of labor supplied and demanded is N_e. This implies a certain real wage rate.

16. See Chapter 16, Figure 16.1, and related discussion.

Now assume that society decides, democratically or otherwise, that the employment level indicated by N_e is unacceptable and that it would prefer a higher employment level. Assume further that society chooses to achieve this higher level of employment through an expansionary monetary policy; hence the growth rate of the money supply is increased. This higher growth rate brings about an increase in the effective demand for goods and services (although not immediately, as we shall see later in this chapter), resulting eventually in increased real output. Increased real output can come only from increased employment, which is the effect of an increase in the demand for labor, that is, a shift in the demand curve from D_1 to D_2. The increase in the demand for labor is caused by a decrease in the real wage rate, which is the result of a rise in the price level. The rise in the price level is caused by the increased demand, which in turn has been caused by the increased rate of growth in the money supply.[17] At nominal wage W_1, the quantity of labor demanded will be N_2. However, this cannot be the end of the process, according to the monetarists.

The increase in employment requires an increase in the quantity of labor supplied. Initially, any increase in the quantity of labor supplied comes about because labor does not realize that the real wage is falling even though the nominal wage is constant. Then, since employers cannot employ all the labor they want at nominal wage W_1, the nominal wage begins to rise (more slowly than the price level, however, because wages are assumed to be more rigid than other prices). Now this change in the quantity of labor supplied is the result of an increase in the nominal wage rate, not the real wage rate, and herein lies the problem. The quantity of labor supplied increases because labor anticipates and perceives an increase in the real wage rate, whereas what it receives is an increase in the money wage rate only. Hence the nominal wage rate tends toward W_2 and the employment level increases toward N_1.

As employment increases, the productivity of labor decreases because of the diminishing marginal product for labor. The decreased marginal product of

17. The demand curve for labor shifts because what is measured on the vertical axis is the money wage rate, not the real wage rate, and we assume the demand for labor is a function of the real wage rate. As a consequence, with a decrease in the real wage rate that applies to any given money wage rate, a greater demand for labor would exist. If the real wage rate were measured on the vertical axis instead of the money wage rate, a movement along the demand curve would result from a decrease in the real wage rate, not a shift.

labor implies an increased cost per unit of output; as a result, the price level will rise as prices are adjusted for these increased costs.

After some time, labor will perceive that its money wage rate may be increasing but the real wage rate has decreased. With a decrease in the real wage rate, the supply of labor must decrease, that is, shift back from S_1 until ultimately it reaches S_2.

The supply of labor will decrease because the real payment will be insufficient to overcome the opportunity cost for some units of labor. The supply curve will remain at S_1 only so long as labor suffers a money illusion; that is, so long as labor does not recognize that the purchasing power of the money wage is decreasing as the price level rises. While labor might suffer a money illusion for a while, it is unlikely that this situation would continue for very long. As labor correctly perceives the decrease in the real wage rate, causing the supply of labor to decrease from S_1 to S_2, the money wage rate will rise toward the new equilibrium money wage rate of W_3 (moving along D_2).

Equilibrium in the labor market will tend to decrease to the old equilibrium quantity of N_e. The money wage rate will have risen from W_1 to W_3, but this rise will be accompanied by an increase in the price level. The real wage rate will be the same, therefore, since we assume the productivity of labor does not change. Thus the money supply will determine what the money wage rate W will be: the greater the increase in the money supply, ceteris paribus, the higher the money wage rate—but also the higher the price level. Since there is a complementary rise in the price level for increases in the money wage rate, the real wage rate would remain the same.

Consequently, for employment to remain at a level higher than the natural full-employment level, the money supply would have to be increased continually, and probably the rate of increase, in an attempt to delude labor. As individuals began to perceive the movement in the price level arising from increases in the money supply, they would be less apt to suffer a money illusion. The only reason the employment level increases is because of the various lags—it takes time for the effects of an increased rate of growth in the money supply to work through the economy. If everyone anticipated these effects perfectly, employment would not increase.

Analogously, attempts to lower the level of employment below this natural full-employment level would also be temporary in nature. Intuitively, however, we feel that the adjustment in a deflationary direction might be less smooth and more protracted because people have learned to deal with inflationary situations better than deflationary ones, most likely because the former occur more frequently.

Generalizing, monetarists would see attempts to raise the employment level above (or lower it below) the natural full-employment level through the use of monetary and fiscal policy as futile in anything but the short run. Moreover, increasing real costs are incurred by society as attempts are prolonged. The monetarists would not ignore the unemployment problem, but would argue that it should be handled as a microeconomic problem.

THE INTEREST RATE

The monetarist position on the interest rate is, needless to say, different from that of the Keynesians. Monetarists believe that the *real interest rate* is determined by the marginal productivity of capital and society's rate of time preference. Given these determinants of the real rate of interest, it cannot be altered by changes in the money supply. Only the *nominal interest rate,* or money interest rate, may be influenced—and, as we shall see, at some cost, according to the monetarists.

It is critical that we recognize the crucial distinction between the *real* and the *nominal,* or money, rates of interest. While in the Keynesian system the interest rate is the price of money and is determined by the supply of, and demand for, money, the monetarist holds that the interest rate is the price of *credit.* Hence it is determined by the supply of, and demand for, credit, not money. For simplicity, assume an equilibrium situation exists, that is, there is no tendency for the interest rate to change, the money supply is growing at a constant rate, the labor market is in equilibrium at the natural full-employment level, and so on. Assume that the current per annum interest rate on a short-term Treasury bill is 8 percent. Assume further that the current rate of inflation is 5 percent per annum. For people to lend money to the government by buying a government debt instrument, they not only have to earn a rate of interest that will overcome their propensity to spend now as opposed to later, but they must earn enough so that when the bill matures they believe they will receive their principal in at least constant purchasing power.

For example, if an individual lends the government $100, one year later that individual would not want to get just $100 back when the inflation rate had caused 5 percent of its purchasing power to evaporate. Therefore, the interest rate would have to include a payment to compensate for the inflation rate. Hence if we add the inflation rate, $(1/P)(dP/dt)$, to the real interest rate r, we would have the nominal or money interest rate i:

$$i = r + \frac{1}{P} \cdot \frac{dP}{dt}$$

If we subtract the inflation rate from the nominal interest rate, we have the real interest rate. In this instance, the stated conditions would imply that the real interest rate was 3 percent per annum since prices are rising at 5 percent per year and the nominal interest rate is 8 percent.[18] As a consequence, the nominal rate of interest must reflect not only the real rate of interest but also the perceived and anticipated inflation rates.

Monetarists deny that the real interest rate can be influenced through monetary policy. As we have stated, they consider the real interest rate a function of society's rate of time preference and the marginal productivity of capital. Although they admit that the money rate of interest may be altered via monetary policy in the short run, they reject the idea that it can be either raised or lowered for long periods of time (unless it is toward the real rate of interest) without an ever-increasing real cost to society. In order to explain this real cost, we must discuss a phenomenon called Gibson's paradox.

Gibson's paradox is an empirical relationship between prices and interest rates that was observed in the early part of the twentieth century by an English economist named A.H. Gibson.[19] Gibson found that prices and interest rates tended to move in the same direction in the long run instead of in opposite directions as would normally be expected. The explanation for Gibson's

18. In order to find the real interest rate, it is necessary to know or be able to assume some very important data. Ordinarily, we would be unable to find the real interest rate by the simple method we have used. At any one time, we cannot assume correctly that the system is in long-run equilibrium, that the real inflation rate is accurately perceived by all individuals, that the money supply is growing at a constant rate, and that the underlying determinants of the supply of, and demand for, credit have remained unchanged, among other variables.

19. In the *Treatise on Money* (1930), Keynes discussed Gibson's work on the phenomenon that has come to bear his name as well as his own research in the area. See J.M. Keynes, *A Treatise on Money* (Vol. 2, *The Applied Theory of Money*); in *The Collected Writings of John Maynard Keynes*, Vol. VI (London: Macmillan, 1971), pp. 177–186, 346.

paradox had been offered earlier by Irving Fisher, who hypothesized that prices and interest rates would in fact display this behavior.[20]

The underlying feature of the direct relationship between changes in the price level and movements in interest rates lies in the phenomenon already discussed—that in formulating expectations about future inflation rates, based in part on their perception of the current inflation rate, people would refuse to lend (or would lend less) if the interest rate did not take account of this threat to the purchasing power of their principal. Monetarists do not claim to understand perfectly the exact process or mechanism by which this relationship occurs, nor do all monetarists agree on any specific postulated process. However, in very general and simple terms, it is seen to work something like the following.

Again assume the economy is in long-run equilibrium, and that the money supply is growing at 3 percent per year, which is the same rate at which the economy is growing in real terms. Under these conditions, no change in the price level should occur, although individual prices may be rising or falling. Further assume that a natural full-employment equilibrium exists in the labor market. Now assume that the money supply begins to grow at 5 percent per year. Individuals will find themselves with increased money balances because initially the price level does not change. As we saw in the last chapter, people have a desired level of real money balances for a given level of real income according to the demand for money function of the monetarists. Since they now find themselves with *actual* real money balances in excess of *desired* real money balances, they have an unbalanced asset portfolio given the implied rates of return on various assets. With an unbalanced asset portfolio, they begin to rid themselves of the excess real money balances. The first movement, according to the monetarists, would be out of money and into other assets like bonds, which are near substitutes for money or time deposits.

As a consequence, the prices of these financial assets would be bid up, causing the interest rate to fall. But notice that only the money or the nominal interest rate falls; nothing has happened to bring about a fall in the real interest rate. This fall in the money interest rate would be a short-run phenomenon. According to monetarists this initial movement in interest rates is

20. Irving Fisher, *The Purchasing Power of Money,* rev. ed. (New York: Macmillan, 1920), Chapter 4.

the change that Keynesians look for to signal a successful change in monetary policy—an increase (decrease) in money-supply growth rates leading to a decrease (increase) in interest rates.

The shift out of money balances and into these other assets would continue. Assuming that the economy is operating at the natural full-employment equilibrium, the increased demand for goods and services would tend to cause the level of money income to grow. Since more output cannot be forthcoming without an increase in the price level, inflation would appear. As inflation took hold, the nominal interest rate would begin to rise as more and more individuals became aware of the rise in the price level and began to anticipate its continued effects.

With the appearance of inflation, individuals would cease holding as much of their wealth in interest-earning assets as before because the return on these assets would no longer be sufficient to protect them against the general price rise. They would shift their wealth holdings to better hedges against inflation. Hence prices on interest-earning assets would fall as demand for these assets decreased, and the interest rate would rise. When the economy returned to long-run equilibrium, ceteris paribus, the nominal interest rate now would be 2 percent higher than it was because of the inflation rate (2 percent per year), whereas the real rate would be the same.

Empirical evidence suggests that this general pattern of interest rate movements in response to changes in the money supply involves a lag of several months, and that the process also includes lags that are not altogether regular. These two points will be significant when we discuss the usefulness of monetary policy as seen by the monetarists in Chapter 21.

INFLATION

Inflation is probably the single most important macroeconomic problem that most Western nations have faced in the past ten years, and it has the potential to become even more pressing over the next decade and perhaps longer. As a consequence, it is not surprising that the monetarist view on inflation and the inflationary process receives serious attention.

Monetarists believe that inflation is largely a monetary phenomenon in terms of its cause (generally), its continuation, and its cure, although they would not deny that nonmonetary factors might cause a temporary increase in the price level. (However, without an increase in the money supply, the price level would later have to fall to its earlier level, unless changes had occurred in the velocity of money.) What monetarists would deny is that the increase in the price level could continue without the proper monetary conditions; that is, a nonmonetary factor might explain a one-time rise in the price level, but not a continuing rise.

To construct a model of the inflation process, we must include the steps in the process, starting with the initial cause. The monetarists base their model of inflation on certain steps they consider critical in the reaction chain connecting the "cause" of the inflation with that which follows. Any simple monetarist model of inflation would probably contain the following points: (1) the concept of an equilibrium level of employment; (2) the role of the real stock of money; (3) the way in which prices are set by businesses, especially given anticipated changes in the general price level; and (4) the role of expectations in the inflation process and how expectations are formulated.[21]

To state the monetarist model of inflation somewhat more rigorously, we might develop it as follows. To begin, we assume that the labor market is operating at the natural full-employment equilibrium. Then we must have some concept of the role that changes in the money stock play in a monetarist model of inflation. In general, monetarists deal in real, as opposed to money, or nominal, terms. For example, they define the demand for money discussed earlier as the real money balances demanded in relation to different real income levels. Likewise, when discussing the money supply, monetarists are concerned primarily with the real money supply, that is, the money supply where changes in the price level are taken into account. In order for the equilibrium level of income in real terms to be disturbed, the real supply of money must be altered. An increase in real money balances will lead to an increase in real demand, the magnitude of the increase in real demand being a function of the magnitude of the increase in real money balances.

A third step in a model of the inflation process accounts for the way in which businesses are seen to set prices in terms of certain macroeconomic considerations, such as, among other things, increased costs and anticipated changes in the general price level. Increased costs arise when the economy

21. The inflationary model presented here is based largely on Thomas M. Humphrey, "A Monetarist Model of the Inflationary Process," Federal Reserve Bank of Richmond, *Economic Review* (November-December 1975): 13–23; and Denis S. Karnosky, "The Link Between Money and Prices, 1971–76," Federal Reserve Bank of St. Louis, *Review* (June 1976): 17–23.

operates at higher levels of real output than would result at the natural employment equilibrium. As real output increases, bottlenecks appear that raise real per-unit costs of production, which in turn create pressures for price rises. The greater the increase in real output, the greater the strain on the productive capacity of the economy and the more prices will be raised. Furthermore, the more prices are expected to rise in the next time period, the more prices will be raised over and above the actual cost increases to keep from losing ground. If prices are expected to rise at a 3 percent rate over the next time period, then prices will be raised an additional 3 percent.[22]

If expectations concerning inflation play a role in the way in which prices are adjusted, according to this simple monetarist model, a fourth point necessarily deals with the way in which these expectations are formed. The formation of expectations concerning inflation can be assumed to be a function of both the inflation that has occurred in the past and the difference between what the inflation actually was and the rate that had been expected. In both cases, the more recent time periods have greater significance. If inflation has been occurring at a 7 percent rate, for example, individuals are assumed to predict a 7 percent rate for the next time period, ceteris paribus. Moreover, if individuals had expected inflation to be 7 percent in the last period and it turned out to be 7 percent, then it is hypothesized that they would predict the same inflation rate in the present time period. They would not lift their expectations, because what they expected is what occurred. But if they had anticipated a 5 percent inflation rate and it actually turned out to be 7 percent, then individuals would be inclined to predict an inflation rate greater than 7 percent as they were wrong last time and do not want to be fooled again. How much greater than 7 percent they would predict for the next period would be a function of how they *read* market conditions.

Given these points, monetarists might well see the inflationary process working as follows. Assume once again that the economy is operating in a long-run equilibrium situation, that the money supply is growing at the same rate as the long-run rate of growth in real income (for example, 4 percent), that the nominal and real rates of interest are equal (for example, 3 percent), and that the labor market is operating at the natural full-employment level.

---

22. This part of the model clearly would not apply to perfectly competitive markets where the degree of market control exercised by an individual unit is so insignificant as to be nil. In such markets, individual units do not have the option to raise the price given their expectations concerning inflation.

Hence there should be no inflationary or deflationary pressures in the economomy.

Now assume that the money supply begins to grow at a faster rate than before, for example, 6 percent instead of 4 percent. After several time periods have passed, this increase in the rate of growth of the money supply will cause an increase in real demand because real money balances will be greater than desired real money balances. The increase in real demand will result in an increase in the rate of growth of the economy in real terms. Since we have assumed that the economy was operating at the natural employment level, an excess demand situation will appear, caused by the increase in the growth rate of the money supply. The increase in real output will mean greater strain on the economy; businesses will begin to raise their prices and inflation will appear. As individuals perceive this inflation, they will formulate certain expectations about inflation in the future. In an attempt to catch up in the time period when inflation was not expected but did occur, prices will be raised a "little extra." As a result, costs will rise by a greater amount and expectations about future price rises will be raised again. Each time period that inflation rises puts a new floor under the inflation expectations. When the economy returns to long-run equilibrium, the supply of, and demand for, labor will have returned to the natural equilibrium. Inflation will now be occurring at 2 percent per year and the nominal interest rate will now be 5 percent, 2 percent greater than the real interest rate.

In the example above, inflation started with an excess demand situation caused by an increase in the growth rate of the money supply. That increase in the growth rate of the money supply could have taken place for any number of reasons. Yet as we stated earlier, monetarists would not deny that the initial cause of an inflationary movement could be nonmonetary in nature. For example, the OPEC cartel, which has so effectively raised the price of petroleum at different times, caused the general price level in most countries to rise. To maintain the higher price level caused by each OPEC price rise and avoid the costs of adjustments during the resulting deflationary situation, a one-time rise in the money supply was required. However, monetarists would argue strenuously that after prices had initially risen once and for all due to a nonmonetary cause, the process would cease unless the money supply were increased at a greater rate. Inflation simply cannot continue without a continued increase in the money supply to support it. Thus the growth rate of the money supply is seen as the primary cause of continuing inflation.

KEY TERMS

Monetarism	Nominal wage rate
Monetarist demand for money	Nominal interest rate
Natural full-employment level	Real interest rate
Real wage rate	Gibson's paradox

REVIEW QUESTIONS

1. Explain the monetarist demand for money.

2. Does the monetarist demand for money appear to be a development more from the classical quantity theory or the Keynesian liquidity preference theory? Discuss.

3. Why are monetarists so careful to differentiate between the natural or real interest rate and the nominal interest rate?

4. Explain the natural rate of employment and its significance for the monetarist views on inflation.

5. Why do monetarists argue that inflation is generally a monetary phenomenon?

6. For a monetarist, the growth rate of the money supply is all important. Why?

SUGGESTED READINGS

Brunner, Karl, and Allan H. Meltzer. "Predicting Velocity: Implications for Theory and Policy." *Journal of Finance* 18 (May 1963): 319–354.

Friedman, Milton. "The Quantity Theory of Money—A Restatement." In Milton Friedman, ed., *Studies in the Quantity Theory of Money.* Chicago: University of Chicago Press, pp. 3–21.

Gibson, William E. "Interest Rates and Monetary Policy." *Journal of Political Economy* 78 (May-June 1970): 431–455.

Laidler, David. "The Rate of Interest and the Demand for Money—Some Empirical Evidence." *Journal of Political Economy* 74 (December 1966): 545–555.

———. "Some Evidence on the Demand for Money." *Journal of Political Economy* 74 (February 1966): 55–68.

Shiller, Robert J., and Jeremy J. Siegel. "The Gibson Paradox and Historical Movements in Real Interest Rates." *Journal of Political Economy* 85 (October 1977): 891–907.

Chapter Twenty

KEYNESIANS AND MONETARISTS

After developing the general Keynesian and monetarist models, we shall now compare some issues on which the Keynesians and monetarists disagree. We have already encountered certain differences between these two general views. For example, we have noted that Keynesians traditionally believe that the employment level is largely open to alteration given proper monetary or fiscal policy or some combination of the two. Monetarists, on the other hand, believe the employment level to be amenable to change through either monetary or fiscal policy only in the short run. Furthermore, any attempt to alter the employment level through monetary or fiscal policy implies distinct costs for society, according to the monetarists.

The first general topic we cover in this chapter is the difference in the relative importance of monetary and fiscal policy as seen by the Keynesians and monetarists. We utilize *IS-LM* analysis to examine this issue. In our examination we shall also note the differences in the Keynesian and monetarist views on the monetary transmission mechanism. This will permit us to point out the role of the interest rate in monetary policy for these two positions. Then we shall look at the crowding-out effect, an important and potentially lethal criticism of fiscal policy.

SLOPES OF *IS-LM* SCHEDULES

One of the major differences between the Keynesians and the monetarists as to short-run changes in real income and employment levels is in their views of the slope of the *IS* and *LM* schedules. It is significant whether the *IS* and *LM* schedules are relatively flat or steeply sloped, or which is more steeply sloped,

Figure 20.1   SPECULATIVE DEMAND FOR MONEY AND *LM*
SCHEDULE WITH LIQUIDITY TRAP

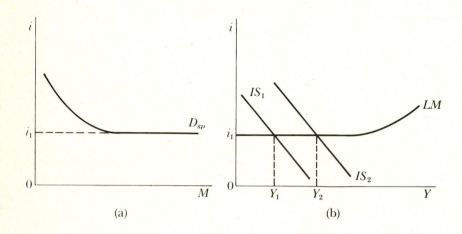

(a)   (b)

if we are to determine whether fiscal or monetary policy will be more effective. As we know, monetarists believe that in the long run employment is at the natural full-employment level; and as was argued in the preceding chapter this cannot be altered via monetary or fiscal policy. Thus monetarists conclude that increases in the money supply in the long run will result only in inflation if the money supply growth rate exceeds the real growth rate of the economy.

Figure 20.1b shows a perfectly flat *LM* schedule as well as two *IS* schedules. The perfectly flat *LM* schedule could result either from a liquidity trap or from a money supply function that is totally endogenously determined. A *liquidity trap,* as originally suggested by Keynes, was intended to describe a situation where the public preferred to be as liquid as possible; that is, the speculative demand for money would be perfectly interest elastic at some interest rate as in part (a) of Figure 20.1 because individuals believe the interest rate cannot fall any further. Under these conditions, any increases in the money supply would be immediately absorbed and held. Money balances would not be used to buy bonds or similar assets, because their prices would only fall or remain the same since individuals believe the interest rate can only increase or remain constant. Thus the cause of the liquidity trap was seen to be a *state of expectations* such that a person could only lose by buying an asset, that is, incur a capital loss. Money would be the only safe asset to hold.

A second explanation for the perfectly elastic segment of the *LM* schedule is the belief that the money supply is completely endogenously determined, that is, that the money supply will grow because of forces in the economy and not at the behest of the central bank. As we saw earlier, the money supply in the short run is probably at least partially a function of the interest rate; as the interest rate rises, the money supply increases.[1] As an extreme interpretation, some economists have suggested that when the central bank increases high-powered money, the money supply will grow only if the individuals and institutions in society wish it. If they do not wish it, the commercial banking system will be unable to increase the money supply through creation of demand deposits, either because the commercial banks will be unwilling to lend or because others will be unwilling to borrow. Analogously, if the individuals in the system want greater supplies of money and the central bank does not allow the orthodox money supply to increase, an extralegal money will be initiated.[2] A perfectly elastic money supply function with respect to the interest rate will result in a perfectly elastic *LM* schedule regardless of the elasticity of the demand for money.

Monetary policy would be totally ineffective if the *LM* schedule were perfectly flat because changes in the money supply would neither increase nor decrease the interest rate. Hence fiscal policy would be the means by which the income level could be altered. An expansionary fiscal policy, which would shift the *IS* schedule from IS_1 to IS_2, would increase the equilibrium income level from Y_1 to Y_2 while leaving the interest rate unaffected at i_1. However, after noting the possibility of a perfectly elastic *LM* schedule, we shall ignore it for two reasons. First, as Axel Leijonhufvud has noted, Keynes himself later stated that he knew of no time when a liquidity trap existed,[3] and most theories are not based on its existence anyway. Second, the assumption that the money supply is completely endogenously determined such that the central bank has no control over it seems rather unrealistic.

The other extreme in an *LM* schedule is one that is perfectly vertical, as shown in Figure 20.2. A perfectly vertical *LM* curve can result from the

1. See Chapter 17.
2. A situation suggestive of this possible interpretation was the so-called coin shortage of the early 1970s. Some communities that could not get the coinage required to carry on business began to make their own tokens as substitutes.
3. Axel Leijonhufvud, *On Keynesian Economics and the Economics of Keynes: A Study in Monetary Theory* (New York: Oxford University Press, 1968), p. 158.

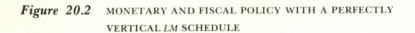

Figure 20.2   MONETARY AND FISCAL POLICY WITH A PERFECTLY
VERTICAL *LM* SCHEDULE

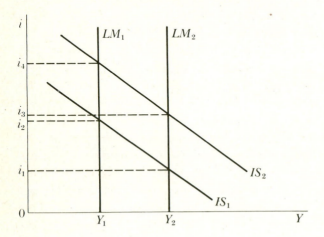

assumptions of the very basic and simple classical model.[4] For example, in the Fisher approach to the quantity theory of money, the demand for money was a transactions demand alone—there was no speculative demand for money.[5] Thus the demand for money was not a function of the interest rate. As a consequence, with a perfectly inelastic demand for money, the *LM* curve will show no response to changes in the interest rate and will be perfectly inelastic.

A second necessary assumption is that the money supply function be completely exogenously determined, that is, determined solely by forces outside the system or model. This necessarily means that the money supply cannot be a function of the interest rate.

If the *LM* schedule were perfectly vertical and descriptive of the actual working of the economy, fiscal policy would be of no avail. Shifts in the *IS* curve brought about by changes in taxes or government spending or some

4. If the assumptions of the simple classical model were followed completely, the entire *LM* schedule would be perfectly inelastic. Here, however, we are combining both possibilities—the Keynesian and classical interpretations—on the same *LM* schedule for efficiency in presentation.
5. The Cambridge approach also had no speculative demand for money. Another explanation for a perfectly inelastic *LM* schedule would be balances held for speculative purposes being drawn down to some irreducible minimum given a sufficiently high interest rate.

combination of the two would alter only the interest rate, the income level being fixed. If a fiscal policy designed to increase the income level were instituted, resulting in the *IS* curve shifting from IS_1 to IS_2, along LM_1, the interest rate would rise from i_2 to i_4. With an expansionary fiscal policy an increase in the income level would normally occur, but in this case it cannot. With no speculative balances to be drawn down to increase those available for transactions purposes to support a higher level of income, the interest rate would rise to eliminate as much demand as is necessary to make the net change in real demand zero. Thus for every dollar increase in demand through increased government spending or from the private sector due to decreased taxes, the interest rate would rise sufficiently to decrease investment or consumption by an equal amount.

The significance of assuming that the money supply is completely exogenously determined can be explained at this point. If the money supply were at least partially a function of the interest rate, an expansionary fiscal policy shifting the *IS* schedule outward would cause the interest rate to rise. This rise would bring about an increase in the money supply, which would then increase balances for transactions purposes, meaning that a higher income level could be supported. Thus a partially endogenously determined money supply necessarily implies that the *LM* schedule could not be perfectly vertical.

It follows that with a perfectly vertical *LM* curve, monetary policy would be the only effective alternative for changing the income level. A monetary policy causing a shift in the *LM* curve from LM_1 to LM_2 would result in an increased income level Y_2 assuming the *IS* curve did not shift (it remained at either IS_1 or IS_2). The interest rate would decrease whichever *IS* curve we were on.

Given the assumptions necessary for a perfectly vertical *LM* schedule, its likelihood of describing the actual economy is rather scant. That neither the demand for nor the supply of money will be a function of the interest rate seems very remote. Hence *LM* curves like those in Figure 20.2 seem about as realistic as one that is perfectly flat, and consequently we shall dwell on this possibility no longer.

LM schedules other than those that are perfectly flat or vertical are more likely to reflect the actual workings of the economy and thus cover most theories. We shall discuss the slopes of the *IS* and *LM* schedules first from the general view of most Keynesians and second from the general view of most monetarists.

GENERAL KEYNESIAN VIEW

If we look at the more traditional Keynesian position, we would probably find the following characteristics. First, in examining the *IS* curve the traditional Keynesian would hold that the *MEI* function is fairly inelastic with respect to changes in the interest rate. Thus a given percentage change in the interest rate will lead to a considerably smaller percentage change in investment, where it is an inverse relationship. In addition, the Keynesian postulates that savings is a function predominately of the income level and not the interest rate. Hence changes in the interest rate will not bring about significant changes in savings (or consumption, if looked at the other way around). Finally, the size of the multiplier is important—it determines the change in the income level given a change in investment, for example.[6] These factors together imply that the *IS* function will be relatively steeply sloped, as in Figure 20.3.

Second, in looking at the *LM* schedule, the traditional Keynesian would hold that the money supply is determined to a degree endogenously—that it is fairly elastic with respect to changes in the interest rate. The Keynesian would also hold that the demand for money tends to be relatively elastic, given changes in the interest rate, over the usual range of operations. These two factors combine to result in a relatively flat *LM* schedule such as described in Figure 20.3.

If we now examine the *IS* and *LM* curves in Figure 20.3, we find *IS* curves that are relatively steep and *LM* curves that are relatively flat, based on the immediately preceding arguments. The horizontal shifts in both functions are of equal dollar value, that is, $\Delta Y' = \Delta Y''$. Thus the shifts represented in the *IS* curve (from IS_1 to IS_2) and the *LM* curve (from LM_1 to LM_2) are of equal weight in one sense but will *not* be of equal importance because of the differences in slopes. The monetary policy that causes the shift in the *LM* curve along either of the two *IS* curves results in an increased income and a decreased interest rate: from Y_1 to Y_2 and from i_2 to i_1 along IS_1, or from Y_3 to Y_4 and from i_3 to i_2 along IS_2. At the same time an expansionary fiscal policy will increase the income level while raising the equilibrium interest rate. A fiscal policy that shifts the *IS* curve along LM_1 increases the income level from Y_1 to Y_3 and raises the interest rate from i_2 to i_3 (which will be equal to the

6. See Chapter 15 for discussions of multipliers.

Figure 20.3   COMPARISON OF MONETARY AND FISCAL POLICY
USING THE KEYNESIAN MODEL

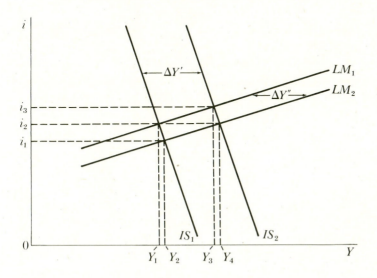

change in income Y_2 to Y_4, and interest rates i_1 to i_2 along LM_2). As a consequence, fiscal policy appears to be more effective than monetary policy in changing the income level given the general or typical Keynesian view.

We should pause for a moment to see why fiscal policy is more effective than monetary policy in the Keynesian model. Recall that the *LM* schedule is relatively flat because of the elastic nature of the money supply and money demand functions. Given changes in the supply of money (a shift from M_{s_1} to M_{s_2} in Figure 20.4), relatively small changes in the interest rate are sufficient to maintain equilibrium in the money market (that is, keep the demand for and supply of money balances in equilibrium). Since the Keynesian believes that investment and the purchase of consumer durables are fairly inelastic with respect to the interest rate, changes in the interest rate brought about by increases or decreases in the supply of money will result in relatively small changes in aggregate demand.

Keynesians, we should note, see the effects of monetary policy working through the interest rate, that is, indirectly. The reason for this view has to do with the assets that individuals are assumed to hold in their *asset portfolios*.

Figure 20.4   MONETARY SECTOR ADJUSTMENT IN THE KEYNESIAN
MODEL

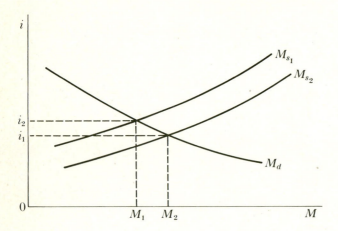

While businesses are assumed to hold all types of assets, households are assumed to hold only financial assets and one type of real asset—housing and related property—in their portfolios. Consequently, when increases in the money supply create excess money balances for households, the return on money is decreased and will be lower than on other assets. As households attempt to re-establish equilibrium in their asset portfolios, they utilize the excess money balances to buy substitute financial assets and housing. With increased demand, the prices for these goods are driven up and their rates of return down. Since these are the only assets households are assumed to place their wealth in, any effects monetary policy has on the real sector must be felt essentially through changes in the interest rate when changes in the interest rate affect the level of investment. Hence the interest rate becomes the most important criterion in the direction of monetary policy (easy or tight).

GENERAL MONETARIST VIEW

In general, the typical monetarist view is the opposite of the typical Keynesian view. To begin, the *IS* schedule is seen to be relatively flat given changes in the

---

Figure 20.5   COMPARISON OF MONETARY AND FISCAL POLICY
                     USING THE MONETARIST MODEL

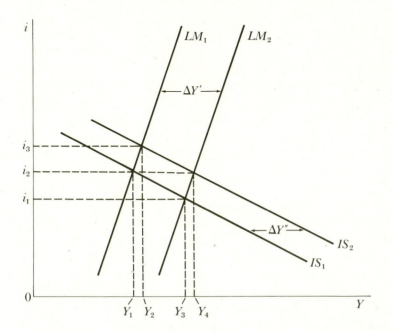

interest rate instead of more steeply sloped, as in the preceding Keynesian view. This decreased slope of the *IS* schedule is based on the belief that both investment and a large percentage of consumption expenditures—for example, automobiles, furniture, appliances, and so on—are responsive to interest rate changes. These consumer goods are not "used up" immediately, so the criteria used in their purchase are similar to the criteria used in business investment decisions. Consequently, the monetarist feels that the consumer durables are more responsive to changes in the interest rate than a Keynesian would. Therefore, the *IS* schedule is as depicted in Figure 20.5.

Whereas monetarists believe that the *IS* schedule is flatter with respect to interest rate changes than do Keynesians, they hold that the *LM* schedule is more steeply sloped. First, monetarists contend that the demand for real money balances is inelastic given changes in the interest rate. Second, they believe that by and large the money supply is exogenously determined and hence controllable by the central bank. As a result, the *LM* schedule under the general monetarist model looks like that in Figure 20.5.

In Figure 20.5 we have two *IS* and two *LM* schedules. The monetary and fiscal policies implied by the shifts in the functions are potentially of equal weight in bringing about an equal increase in income because the horizontal movement in each is equal ($\Delta Y' = \Delta Y''$). Assume that the current income level is Y_1 and that we would like to increase the income level. An expansionary monetary policy, which would cause a shift in the *LM* curve from LM_1 to LM_2, would increase income from Y_1 to Y_3 while decreasing the interest rate from i_2 to i_1, if we use IS_1. (The change in the income level and interest rate will be equal in amount if we use IS_2—from Y_2 to Y_4 and i_3 to i_2.)

If instead of an expansionary monetary policy we use fiscal policy, which shifts the *IS* curve, we find that the movement from IS_1 to IS_2 along LM_1 will increase the income level from Y_1 to Y_2 while raising the interest rate from i_2 to i_3. (Using LM_2, the shift from IS_1 to IS_2 results in an increase in income from Y_3 to Y_4 and an increase in interest from i_1 to i_2.)

Remember that for the monetarists any changes in the real income level obtained through either monetary or fiscal policy is of a short-run nature. In the long run, the real income level is determined by the natural full-employment level, which is not subject to change by monetary or fiscal policy.

The reason monetary policy is potentially more effective lies in the explanation for the differing slopes of the *IS* and *LM* schedules. First, the *LM* schedule is relatively inelastic because both the demand for and the supply of money are assumed to be inelastic. As a consequence, changes in the money supply result in fairly substantial changes in the interest rate. The monetarists argue that the *IS* curve is relatively flat because both investment and the purchase of consumer durables are more responsive to interest rate changes than the Keynesians believe. Hence changes in the interest rate resulting from changes in the money-supply growth rate imply significant changes in aggregate demand.

Whereas the Keynesians prefer to use the interest rate as the prime indicator of the ease or tightness of monetary policy, the monetarists argue for the use of growth rates of monetary aggregates like M_1, M_2, or the monetary base. The monetarists argue that interest rates are not necessarily a very adequate indicator of the current stance of monetary policy for two reasons.

First, higher interest rates can go hand in hand with increasing growth rates of the money supply due to the phenomenon referred to as Gibson's paradox.[7] In fact, increased growth rates of monetary aggregates alone may be sufficient to raise interest rates immediately. If increased growth rates of monetary aggregates are perceived as resulting in increased inflation, people and institutions may begin to rearrange their asset portfolios immediately, thus driving up interest rates. This adjustment in asset portfolios would occur only if individuals believe that these higher monetary aggregate growth rates are not a momentary phenomenon. Increased inflation will not appear for some time, but the expectation alone is sufficient to bring about a rise in interest rates. While the orthodox interpretation of rising interest rates is one of tighter monetary conditions, under these circumstances the opposite is occurring. Hence using interest rates as an indicator of monetary policy may give a false idea of what is actually occurring.

Second, the monetarist theorizes that the interest rate (rates of return on various assets) is the criterion by which households judge which purchases to make. However, because the monetarists open the asset choice facing households to almost all assets and do not restrict them as the Keynesians do, the monetarists argue that the interest rate is not as "knowable" as the Keynesians believe. As a consequence, they prefer to use growth rates of monetary aggregates instead.

If the results of monetary or fiscal policy are compared, it appears that, given the assumptions of the typical monetarist model, monetary policy is more effective. On this basis, monetarists might then conclude that monetary policy is a more powerful tool for regulating the income level. However, we find a rather pronounced reticence on their part to advocate the active use of monetary policy. Generally they prefer a more passive use. This reticence is based on two factors. First, the theoretical structure that monetarists feel best describes the actual operation of the economy argues against variable growth rates in the money supply. Second, the lags inherent in the use of monetary policy are felt to preclude its "correct" active use.[8] As we shall see, because of these reasons, monetarists want the money supply increased at some fairly constant rate.

It would seem logical that should monetarists not like an active monetary policy, they are left with an active fiscal policy by default. However, they are generally opposed to the use of fiscal policy. Part of the reason is explained by

7. See Chapter 19 for a discussion of Gibson's paradox.
8. See Chapter 21 for a discussion of lags.

the slopes of the *IS* and *LM* schedules as understood by the monetarists. And part of the reason lies in a phenomenon known as the crowding-out effect.

THE CROWDING-OUT EFFECT

While monetarists are more than a little worried about the efficacy of an active monetary policy, they are dubious about suggesting that fiscal policy should be actively used in its place. It is generally agreed that fiscal policy does not have many of the drawbacks of monetary policy in terms of either the lags involved[9] or the uneven impact, so-called secondary effects or equity issues.[10] Whereas the impact of fiscal policy may be uneven, it is determined "democratically" when the Congress approves government spending plans, and thus it is assumed that equity considerations have been duly noted and weighed. But despite these positive qualities of fiscal policy, it is still severely questioned by monetarists because of a phenomenon that has come to be known as the crowding-out effect.

In its most simple formulation, the *crowding-out effect* states that increases in government spending are unlikely to increase the income level because they tend to displace or "crowd out" other spending that would have taken place in the private sector. Depending on economic conditions or the nature of the functions being assumed by the individual arguing the point, increases in government spending may displace very little, an equal amount, or even a greater amount of private-sector spending.

As Spencer and Yohe point out in their article on the crowding-out effect,[11] the fear that the public sector could supplant other spending was of concern to economists from Adam Smith up through and including John Maynard Keynes himself. It is undeniable that Keynes seriously considered the subject and thought that it was an important criticism of fiscal policy. He offered two ways in which the crowding-out effect might be felt. In his *General Theory*, however, he dismissed this potentially devastating criticism of fiscal policy, apparently because he felt it to be inoperative given the economic conditions

---

9. See the section on "Lags in Monetary Policy," Chapter 21.

10. See the section on "Uneven Impact of Monetary Policy," Chapter 21.

11. Roger W. Spencer and William P. Yohe, "The 'Crowding-Out' of Private Expenditures by Fiscal Policy Actions," Federal Reserve Bank of St. Louis, *Review* 52 (October 1970): 12–24.

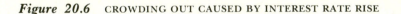

Figure 20.6 CROWDING OUT CAUSED BY INTEREST RATE RISE

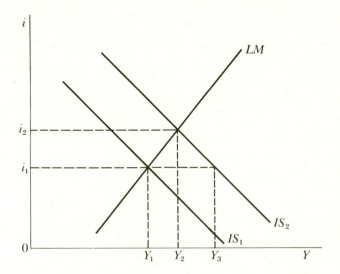

of the 1930s. Thus, since the publication of *The General Theory*, Keynesians have tended to deny either the validity or the importance of the crowding-out effect and find no difficulty in advocating the use of fiscal policy, ignoring or overlooking Keynes' earlier caveats concerning it. On the other hand, monetarists believe that the crowding-out effect offers grounds for generally rejecting an active fiscal policy, and they are usually the ones who broach the subject. Nevertheless, there is every reason to feel that it is a subject of concern to all, especially since it is a point of distinct contention.

We have already encountered the first way in which Keynes suggested that the crowding-out effect might occur, although we did not label it as such. The more steeply sloped the *LM* schedule is with respect to changes in the interest rate, the more increased spending by the government (where there is no accompanying increase in the money supply) results in significantly less of an increase in income than we would anticipate. Assume that the *IS* schedule is initially *IS*₁ as depicted in Figure 20.6. Now assume an increase in spending by the government such that the *IS* schedule shifts from *IS*₁ to *IS*₂ along the *LM* schedule. With no money market considerations to worry about, we would expect that the income level would increase as measured by the horizontal distance between IS_1 and IS_2. When the money market is taken into account, however, the expansionary fiscal policy causes the interest rate to rise, which chokes off varying amounts of aggregate demand from the private sector. The amount that is choked off depends on the slope of the *LM* schedule—the steeper it is, the greater the amount choked off. Thus we find that the income level increases from Y_1 to Y_2, which is considerably less than that initially indicated by the horizontal shift in the *IS* schedule alone (Y_1 to Y_3).

The most extreme case of the crowding-out effect of this type occurs under classical assumptions. In this model, the *LM* schedule is perfectly vertical for three reasons: a money supply function that is completely exogenously determined; an absence of speculative demand for money balances; and a transactions demand for money that is perfectly interest inelastic. Therefore, any fiscal policy, whether expansionary or contractionary, causes no change in the income level, only a change in the interest rate. In this instance, the crowding-out effect is 100 percent. For every dollar change in government spending, a dollar change of the opposite direction takes place in the private sector, the interest rate rising or falling sufficiently to accomplish this.[12]

Keynes also felt that the crowding-out effect might work through a psychological effect. Increased expenditures by the government might damage the expectations of those in business (for example, they might fear increased inflation) by increasing the degree of uncertainty, thus causing a shift to the left in the *IS* schedule that partially or totally offsets the shift in the opposite direction occasioned by the expansionary fiscal policy. In Figure 20.7 the *IS* curve has shifted from IS_1 to IS_3 along LM_1 because of increased government spending, which brings about an increased income level Y_4 from the original Y_1. But should an adverse psychological effect occur, the *IS* curve might, for example, shift only to IS_2 and the income level increase to Y_3 only.

James Tobin suggested that another way increased spending by the government might create an adverse psychological effect is to increase the degree of risk perceived by those holding assets. Increased risk could cause individuals to increase their demand for speculative balances; that is, the speculative demand for money balances would shift to the right. The increased demand for speculative balances would mean an increased aggregate demand for

12. Many of these models and more are included in an article by Keith M. Carlson and Roger W. Spencer, "Crowding Out and Its Critics," St. Louis Federal Reserve Bank, *Review* 57 (December 1975): 2–17.

Figure 20.7   CROWDING OUT ARISING PARTIALLY FROM
PSYCHOLOGICAL EFFECT

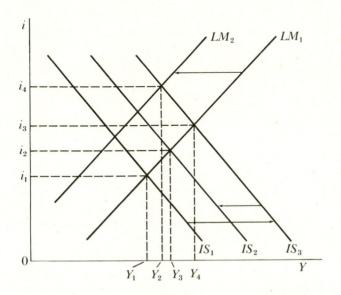

money balances at all interest rates, ceteris paribus, which would in turn imply
a shift to the left in the *LM* curve. The shift in the *LM* curve from LM_1 to LM_2,
for example, as depicted in Figure 20.7, would cause income to increase from
Y_1 to Y_2 along IS_3, after the initial shift from IS_1 to IS_3. Depending on the size
of the various effects, the net change in income could be positive, negative, or
zero.

As we noted earlier, Keynes dismissed the crowding-out effect in *The
General Theory* because it appeared to be unimportant given the economic
conditions during the Great Depression. Increased government spending
would not crowd out private-sector spending because it was not taking place
anyway. In Figure 20.8, an *IS* curve that is perfectly vertical over part of its
range reflects the disadvantageous expectations of entrepreneurs concerning investment opportunities during a severe recession. A perfectly inelastic
MEI function results in a perfectly vertical *IS* curve. An expansionary fiscal
policy shifts the *IS* curve to the right from IS_1 to IS_2 and raises the equilibrium
income level from Y_1 to Y_2. At the same time, the equilibrium interest rate rises

Figure 20.8   THE LACK OF CROWDING OUT WITH PERFECTLY
VERTICAL *IS* SCHEDULES

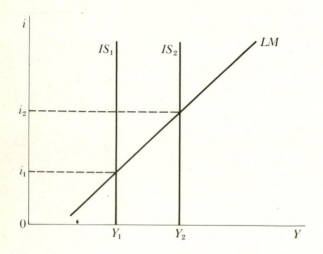

from i_1 to i_2. In this instance the rise in the interest rate causes no crowding out because the *MEI* function is perfectly inelastic with respect to the interest rate and hence the *IS* curve is perfectly vertical. Changes in the interest rate cause no change in investment, and the income level increases by the full horizontal shift in the *IS* curve.

Keynes could dismiss the crowding-out effect as irrelevant or insignificant during a severe recession, irrespective of the slope of the *LM* schedule (which a Keynesian would argue should tend to be fairly flat), because of the perception of deficient investment opportunities. Keynesians tend to feel that even though the crowding-out effect does exist, it is not as strong as the monetarists believe, and hence can generally be offset by an appropriate complementary monetary policy to keep interest rates from rising. Milton Friedman, on the other hand, argues in favor of the crowding-out effect, and feels that the slope of the *LM* schedule may not be all that crucial.

In the basic monetarist model, as we know already, the *LM* schedule is viewed as being relatively steeply sloped because the money supply function is largely exogenously determined and the money demand function relatively inelastic. The *IS* schedule is held to be flatter than in the Keynesian model because of the monetarist view that interest rate changes affect consumption and the investment function *MEI*. Furthermore, Friedman and most other monetarists deny that a situation of severe investment deficiency would ever exist[13] (which eliminates one escape from the crowding-out effect). Hence we would observe the crowding-out effect that arises from interest rate increases, which we have already discussed.

However, Friedman believes that this, in many respects, is beside the point. He argues that the effects of an expansionary fiscal policy are likely to be small for two reasons. Initially assume an expansionary fiscal policy, which shifts the *IS* curve from IS_1 to IS_2 in Figure 20.8; income should increase. However, Friedman believes that we are not going to see the anticipated increase in income. First, any wealth effects arising from increased public-sector bond issues to finance an expansionary fiscal policy will cause small, if any, increases in aggregate demand. Friedman believes that the potentially positive effects of increased aggregate demand will be offset by anticipated increases in taxes required to support these public-sector debt issues. Second, Friedman thinks that in the long run income will cease growing as rapidly as it might because of a deficient amount of private-sector investment. This deficiency of private-sector investment arises from increases in public-sector debt, which displaces that from the private sector. Hence less real capital will be accumulated as factors of production are bid away from the private sector into the public sector. Instead of increased capital acquisition by the private sector, the economy experiences capital absorption by the public sector. With less capital stock than would have existed without the competition for inputs from the public sector, a lower growth rate is possible. Thus the initial rightward shift in the *IS* curve is offset by leftward shifts that would tend in the long run to eliminate entirely any expansionary effects of fiscal policy.

After this description of the ways in which various economists see the crowding-out effect working, three questions seem to be important: (1) Does crowding out take place? (2) How strong is the effect? and (3) What is the time involved? We have no conclusive answers to these questions. The results of studies that test for the crowding-out effect using econometric models gener-

---

13. Monetarists hold that a general deficient level of investment at all interest rates is unrealistic. They believe that at very low interest rates investment projects requiring large amounts of funds become economically feasible, such as putting tunnels through mountains for automobiles and trains. For a further consideration of this point, see Martin J. Bailey, *National Income and the Price Level: A Study in Macro-economic Theory,* 2d ed. (New York: McGraw-Hill, 1971), pp. 140–151.

ally show that increases in government spending do crowd out private-sector spending, ceteris paribus. Some of the studies indicate that eventually crowding out is greater than 100 percent, but the time required is frequently very long, up to forty quarters. Only the St. Louis Federal Reserve Bank model showed a relatively short time necessary. The explanation for the differences between the St. Louis Federal Reserve Bank's results and others' lies in the model used: the St. Louis model is designed to show how monetarists believe the economy functions. However, the empirical results of the different studies as noted do not permit a general consensus and most economists agree that the testing is going to require considerably more work.[14]

KEY TERMS

Liquidity trap   Transmission mechanism
Asset portfolios   Crowding-out effect

REVIEW QUESTIONS

1. In general, the *LM* schedule is flatter in the Keynesian model than in the monetarist model. Explain why.

2. Explain why monetarists believe that fiscal policy is less effective than monetary policy in changing the income level if the factors explaining the slopes of the *IS* and *LM* schedules are the only consideration.

3. Show how a perfectly elastic speculative demand for money gives a perfectly flat *LM* schedule.

4. Define the crowding-out effect. Discuss factors that might cause crowding out to occur and explain how these factors would result in crowding out.

5. Show diagrammatically and explain how an expansionary fiscal policy might result in crowding out if the public perceives an increase in the degree of risk. (We suggest that you derive the *LM* schedule and show how an increase in risk would cause a movement in the *LM* schedule.)

14. For a recent article on the empirical investigation of the crowding-out effect, see Brian P. Sullivan, "Fiscal Policy—Crowding Out Estimated From Large Econometric Model," Federal Reserve Bank of Dallas, *Monthly Review* (June 1976): 1–10.

SUGGESTED READINGS

Anderson, Leonall C., and Denis S. Karnosky. "Some Considerations in the Use of Monetary Aggregates for the Implementation of Monetary Policy." Federal Reserve Bank of St. Louis, *Review* (September 1977): 2–7.

Dobson, Steven W., and Patrick J. Lawler. "Monetary and Fiscal Policies—Alternatives for 1977 and Beyond." Federal Reserve Bank of Dallas, *Review* (February 1977): 11–18.

Mishkin, Frederic S. "Liquidity and the Role of Monetary Policy in Consumer Durable Demand." Federal Reserve Bank of Boston, *New England Economic Review* (November-December 1976): 31–42.

Spencer, Roger W. "Channels of Monetary Influences: A Survey." Federal Reserve Bank of St. Louis, *Review* (November 1974): 8–26.

Part Six

THE MONETARY PROCESS AND STABILIZATION POLICY

Chapter Twenty-One

THE EFFECTIVENESS OF MONETARY POLICY

Monetary theory provides an analytical framework for understanding the monetary process within the economy. The essentials of monetary theory, as presented in Part Five, supplied a systematic approach to understanding money's role in the allocation of scarce resources and the determination of aggregate economic performance. In the conduct of monetary policy it is essential that actions be timely and reasonably well distributed in their impact on the economy. In terms of short-run objectives, monetary policy attempts to exert a moderating influence by providing stimulation when the economy is slack and by exerting restraint in times of overexpansion. However, monetary policy may have a delayed effect on economic conditions. In addition, even when monetary actions begin to take hold in the economy, disruptive effects can arise in various sectors. Thus the effectiveness of monetary policy is limited by the existence of various lags and by the unevenness with which its influence is felt in the economy. This chapter examines the nature of lags in monetary policy making and the unsettling effects of such policy. It concludes with a brief review and assessment of some proposals for improving the operating effectiveness of monetary policy.

LAGS IN MONETARY POLICY

Various lags occur in the conduct of discretionary monetary policy making, as illustrated in Figure 21.1. Initially, it takes time to recognize that the economy has reached a turning point requiring a change in monetary policy. If, for example, a business recession is under way, then easing actions are in order. Although the downturn emerges at point t_0 in Figure 21.1, time elapses

Figure 21.1 SCHEMATIC OF THE LAGS OF MONETARY AND FISCAL
POLICY

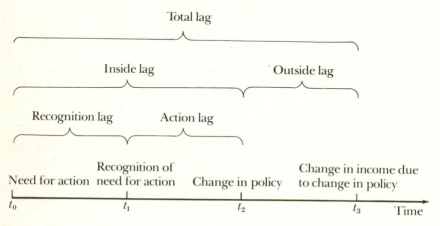

Source: Mark H. Willes, "Lags in Monetary and Fiscal Policy," Federal Reserve Bank of Philadelphia, *Business Review*, March 1968, p. 3.

before information detailing the decline reaches the monetary authorities. It then takes time to organize and analyze these economic intelligence data. Frequently, several economic series over a given time period are needed before a judgment is made that a distinct turning point has in fact occurred. The time between the onset of the downturn t_0 and when the decline is perceived t_1 comprises the *recognition lag*.

Once the need for stabilizing action is recognized, an *action lag* may occur before the orientation of monetary policy is changed, as shown in the period between t_1 and t_2 in Figure 21.1. This lag can arise from various factors. For example, action may be delayed before a firm consensus emerges among the authorities responsible for policy making. Time is also consumed in hammering out the details of the policy change and the subsequent administrative steps associated with implementing those details. Furthermore, political or other economic considerations may deter policy makers temporarily from making the policy change. As an illustration, a current or impending Treasury financing operation may impede an agreed-upon change in monetary policy. Or possibly, concern for the balance of payments may deter an expansive policy needed to stimulate the domestic economy.

The action lag need not always be lengthened because of the sensitivity of the monetary authorities to more than one objective. Such sensitivity may induce policy makers to change direction prior to their recognition of a general turning point in the economy. For example, an easier monetary policy might arise from a weakening employment picture or from a decline in the money growth rate at the same time that the economy shows no evidence of a general downturn.

Taken together, the recognition and action lags compose what is called the *inside lag* of monetary policy. This inside lag is not entirely a function of the monetary authorities' ability to perceive and react to some economic change. The extent of the inside lag is determined also by the base of reference for measuring the lag and by how this base is related to changes in other variables or conditions that impinge on policy decisions. The inside lag is affected not only by such technical factors as facility for data collection and analysis and administrative procedures but also, even more important, by priorities and tradeoffs among goals, economic and otherwise.

After a policy change is initiated, there is an *outside lag* before the change works its effects throughout the economy and finally alters spending. Referring to Figure 21.1, the outside lag is the time between points t_2 and t_3. Given the complex working of the economy, it is not surprising that economists offer various explanations of the outside lag in monetary policy. As compared with fiscal policy, the link between monetary policy changes and changes in spending is not as direct or clear-cut. Currently, research is varied and incomplete regarding the linkages or channels through which monetary policy works its effects in the economy.

Keynesians, we know, emphasize interest rates as the crucial means by which the effects of monetary policy are transmitted to the real sectors of the economy. In general terms, this view regards changes in interest rates as modifying investment and perhaps consumption, thereby causing a change in the rate of income growth.

Monetarists, on the other hand, stress the working of the monetary mechanism through the quantity of money rather than through its cost or availability. Stated simply, the monetarists regard the adjustments of economic decision-making units to changes in actual and desired holdings of money as underlying changes in aggregate income.

The continuing debate over the best application of monetary policy need not obscure one fact: the response of the commercial banking system to monetary policy changes is not necessarily uniform over time. Bank responsiveness to alterations in monetary policy will vary with a number of factors, including the bank's current reserve position, loan demand, interest rate expectations, and so on. The more these initial adjustments by banks are delayed, the longer will be the outside lag associated with monetary policy.

MEASUREMENT OF MONETARY LAGS

Although economists have long recognized the existence of lags affecting monetary policy, it has been only since 1960 that most quantitative estimates of monetary lags have been attempted. There had always been considerable debate about the effectiveness of monetary actions, but most analysts regarded monetary policy as a useful approach for economic stabilization purposes. This conventional view is strongly disputed by Milton Friedman. Essentially, he holds that discretionary monetary policy is subject to long and variable lags, making it a source of destabilization within the economy. Friedman's attempt in the early 1960s to measure the outside lag in monetary policy marked the first of numerous studies contributed by various researchers. This section summarizes the varied, and sometimes conflicting, results of these investigations into measuring monetary lags.

Recent investigations into the inside lag of monetary policy indicate that the monetary authorities generally have recognized cyclical turning points in the economy within three months (one calendar quarter) of their occurrence. For the post–World War II period, the lag associated with monetary actions indicates little or no delay as compared to cyclical turning points. In fact, there have been instances where the action lag was negative because the Federal Reserve reacted to changes that occurred prior to general downturns in the economy. This result is not too surprising, since the group making monetary policy is relatively small and homogeneous, and thus can act quickly once a policy change is deemed necessary. The favorable record on action lags in monetary policy suggests why many observers prefer monetary actions to fiscal policy for purposes of short-run economic stabilization.

The empirical measurement of outside lags affecting monetary policy is much more complicated and difficult, thus giving rise to varied estimates. A particular difficulty associated with the measurement of outside lags is that typically the effects of a given policy change will be distributed (or piled up) over a time span. A major part of these effects may or may not accumulate within a short time interval. Given this complication, the outside lag may be defined as the time required for a policy change to exert a *significant* effect on the economy, or the time required for a policy change to achieve its *peak* effect. Furthermore, as indicated earlier, estimates of outside lags are partly affected by the investigator's particular view of what constitutes the vital short-run link between monetary policy and the real economy.

Most theories of the linkages between monetary policy and economic activity start with the initial process of adjustment by banks to policy changes. Recent studies suggest that banks adjust relatively rapidly, within one or two months, to monetary actions. On the basis of this evidence, adherents of the availability doctrine stress that the effects of monetary policy changes are transmitted quickly to bank customers and that income is altered shortly thereafter.

Many monetarists start with a change in the rate of growth of the money supply (narrowly or broadly defined) to measure the major component of the outside lag of monetary policy. Friedman's ground-breaking study, for example, indicated that income changes followed changes in the money supply by an average of some fourteen months using one type of approach, and by five months using another analytical method.[1] Other researchers derived similar results.

Those studies using interest rate changes as a point of departure for measuring outside lags offered widely differing results. These estimates range from a minimum lag of three months up to a lag of eighteen months or more. Interestingly, there is little clustering of these estimates at any point within the three- to eighteen-month range. The variability of these and other estimates of outside lags emphasizes the need for additional work toward refining estimates of the distribution of the outside lag. Finally, the varied estimates of the lag structure offer no precise basis on which monetary authorities can reasonably justify large or frequent short-run adjustments in the growth rates of monetary aggregates.

Some studies offer evidence that the effects of monetary policy are felt rapidly enough that monetary policy does act in a countercyclical instead of a

---

1. See Milton Friedman, "The Lag in the Effect of Monetary Policy," *Journal of Political Economy* (October 1961): 447–466.

procyclical fashion, *procyclical* meaning to reinforce the cycle, and *coun-tercyclical* meaning to work against or dampen the cycle. William E. Gibson concluded an article on his empirical investigations of the lags encountered in monetary policy with a statement generally in favor of an active monetary policy.[2] Gene Uselton found a lag of six to eight months before the effects of monetary policy were felt and a period of six to ten months over which the effects lasted.[3] Other results disagree.[4] Generally, differences in results are explained by model specification and influences in the definition of money used (for example, M_1, M_2, or whatever). The question of the lags involved in monetary policy has led some economists to urge a rules approach to monetary policy. The rules approach is contrasted with a discretionary approach to monetary policy making later in this chapter.

MONETARY AND FISCAL POLICY
LAGS: A COMPARISON

The results of recent estimates of monetary lags provide useful data for comparison with lags encountered in fiscal policy. First, the estimates for monetary and fiscal lags show wide differences. These differences attest, at least partly, to the incomplete state of knowledge of the exact nature of lags as well as to the considerable methodological and statistical problems involved in empirical measurement of lags.

Second, monetary and fiscal authorities generally have been quick to recognize changes in the economy, on the average within one calendar quarter of their occurrence. This good record reflects the development and availability of timely statistical series for taking the pulse of the economy.

A third insight is that although monetary actions are taken promptly, their effects are not felt in the economy for considerable time. The underlying factors affecting these results were discussed previously, in the section dealing with the measurement of monetary lags.

2. William E. Gibson, "The Lag in Effect of Monetary Policy on Income and Interest Rates," *Quarterly Journal of Economics* 84 (May 1970): 288–300.

3. Gene C. Uselton, *Lags in the Effects of Monetary Policy: A Nonparametric Analysis* (New York: Marcel Dekker, 1974), p. 146; see especially Chapter 6 and the conclusion, pp. 103–148.

4. For a review article, see Michael J. Hamburger, "The Lag in the Effect of Monetary Policy: A Survey of Recent Literature," Federal Reserve Bank of New York, *Monthly Review* 53 (December 1971): 289–297.

A final observation is that generally fiscal actions are made slowly but their effects are felt usually within three months or less. The extended action lags affecting fiscal policy reflect the often dilatory decision making by the Congress and the president. The decision-making process in fiscal policy is slowed because of the diversity of opinion and objectives that may arise among the many groups involved as well as by the existence of complex administrative machinery in planning and legislating fiscal changes. Once fiscal action is taken, however, the effects are felt fairly quickly. Changes affecting personal income taxes, for example, generally achieve significant effects on disposable income and consumption spending within one or two months. Effects from corporate tax rate changes usually take longer, since corporate planning and spending are oriented more toward the long run.

The pace of economic activity generally responds quickly to changes in government spending plans. The placement or cancellation of government contracts may modify production and income prior to the time that an actual change in government spending occurs. Additional expenditures on ongoing projects frequently will have an immediately expansive effect on the spending stream, while contractive results occur more slowly when expenditures are reduced. Transfer payments afford another channel through which effects can be transmitted quickly to disposable income and spending. Alternatively, appreciably delayed effects on income may be associated with newly appropriated funds, because the projects require advance planning and organization. In the same vein, appropriation cuts need not induce an immediate reduction in government spending if a backlog of previous appropriations exists.

Given the existence of lags in monetary and fiscal policy, changes in policy may have their greatest impact only after the need has passed and the economy has once again changed direction. Here policy changes would destabilize the economy by producing adverse fluctuations in economic activity. Thus in certain instances policy changes might be initiated to lead or precede turning points in the economy, thus permitting the stabilizing effects to be felt at the appropriate time. These anticipatory actions would require effective economic forecasting that would detect general changes prior to their occurrence. Good forecasting would in effect produce a negative recognition lag and improve the timing of policy actions by allowing for the other lags. It is especially important for effective discretionary policy making if the outside or action lags are extensive.

**THE UNEVEN IMPACT OF
MONETARY POLICY**

The effectiveness of monetary policy is also influenced by the uneven impact of monetary actions on particular sectors of the economy. In recent years, much attention has been focused on the uneven, and allegedly unfavorable, allocation of credit among various economic sectors. These sectors include housing, state and local government, small business, low-income groups, and agriculture. The uneven impact of monetary policy not only entails questions of equity but can also create possible economic and political repercussions that complicate the task of the monetary authorities. If future monetary actions are to be fully effective, careful attention should be given to this uneven impact.

Three possible avenues are open in deciding what to do about the uneven impact of monetary policy: (1) simple acceptance or toleration of uneven impact as an unavoidable aspect of the free market's allocation of credit; (2) elimination of those market imperfections that contribute to uneven impact; (3) administrative and other direct attempts to deal selectively with this impact. The choice of any one of these policy approaches depends largely on one's philosophical view of the extent to which monetary actions should impinge on market forces in the allocation of scarce resources, including the credit resource.

Nonintervention Approach

The first approach mentioned involves a purely noninterventionist view of monetary policy based on an explicit estimate of economic costs and benefits. Here the uneven impact is traded off against the benefits derived from the free working of market forces. Although recognizing the desirability of a more even allocation of credit via the market, this view regards intervention as a disruptive force contributing to the misallocation of resources in the economy. Allowing for frictional elements and other impediments, the presumption is that the free market is the best available channel for allocating credit. This approach was well expressed in a speech by a Federal Reserve bank president:

I believe that the market system of credit allocation is superior to any other system. It provides greater economic welfare and more individual freedom of choice. Rather than attempting to improve welfare in specific sectors, the monetary authorities can make a greater contribution to overall welfare by concentrating on the maintenance of national economic stability. Given the appropriate actions for overall stability, market forces will assure that individual sectors are treated equitably in a competitive enterprise economy free from excessive restrictions. Consumer preferences as reflected by demands for goods and services will provide the incentive for producers in each sector to acquire necessary resources, including credit, for a level of output consistent with maximum satisfaction.[5]

Given increased public sentiment toward intervention in markets, proponents of the free market approach suggest use of direct subsidies rather than monetary policy for providing support to those specific sectors deemed important by society.

Reduction of Market Imperfections

Stressing the imperfect operation of market forces, a second option entails reduction, if not removal, of those imperfections that produce an uneven impact. Various examples arose in the late 1960s, particularly in markets for mortgages and savings. Proposed changes offered to enhance the competitiveness of mortgages within credit markets include modification of state usury laws, creation of a secondary market for conventional mortgages, and use of variable-rate mortgages.

Many observers regard interest rate ceilings imposed via Regulation Q as impairing the free flow of liquid savings in the economy. (You will recall that *Regulation Q* is the regulation that permits the Federal Reserve to change the maximum rates payable by member banks on time and savings deposits.) They contend that the abolition of these ceilings would promote the freer flow of funds among savings institutions, thus reducing the severe disruptions arising from wide disintermediation swings among financial institutions.

5. "Social Priorities and the Market Allocation of Credit." Speech by Darryl R. Francis, President, Federal Reserve Bank of St. Louis, to the College of Business and Industry, Mississippi State University, February 23, 1971, as quoted in Federal Reserve Bank of St. Louis, *Review* (May 1971): 8f.

Eliminating imperfections in credit markets is no simple or painless task. Frequently, the removal of market impediments to competition is more painful than simple immobilization of imperfections in order to maintain the status quo. A basic and unanswered question must be considered: What disruptive effects on existing institutional patterns would follow from removal of competitive obstacles in credit markets?

Selective Actions

The third approach suggests selective actions to lessen the uneven impact of monetary policy. Typically, the Federal Reserve has resorted to selective or direct actions whenever general monetary controls were shown to be limited in their effectiveness or under great pressure. Some prominent instances of dealing selectively are found in the history of the Federal Reserve:

1. In the latter 1920s direct action was aimed at moderating large flows of bank credit into the stock market.
2. In 1934 margin requirements were initiated in an attempt to dampen rising stock market speculation.
3. Moral suasion has been used at various times to modify credit flows in various sectors.
4. Selective credit controls in the form of Regulations W and X were directed toward restraining growth in consumer and real estate credit.
5. Operation Twist in the early 1960s attempted to change the interest rate structure for purposes of resolving conflicting domestic and international policy goals.
6. In September 1966 a direct letter from the Federal Reserve exhorted member banks to curtail business lending in return for more favorable accommodation at the discount window.[6]

Advocates of the selective approach for smoothing the uneven impact of monetary policy insist that general instruments of monetary policy have an unavoidably selective impact on different credit sectors. They therefore suggest the use of existing monetary controls, or even the creation of new devices, to influence credit selectively along socially desired lines. Questioning the

6. For further discussion, see Chapter 10, the section on "A Selective Approach to Monetary Control."

allocative results of free market operation, proponents of the direct approach contend that the market does not always allow for the community's social priorities. Furthermore, short-run imbalances sometimes occur within freely operating credit markets. For example, extremely easy availability of consumer credit may fuel a boom in the consumer durables sector. Given the fact that monetary policy is used for achieving overall economic stabilization by moderating extremes in the level of economic activity, it is quite reasonable to direct monetary actions to those crucial sectors that underlie these overall extremes. In effect, use of direct action is regarded as a logical extension in the conduct of monetary policy, especially as there is steady accretion in knowledge of how the economy and its constituent parts operate.

Finally, the question arises as to which of these particular approaches should be used in dealing with the problem of uneven impact. Experience suggests that the choice need not be exclusive and that the most effective solution involves some combination of the three approaches. Initially, reliance on free markets has the distinct advantage of enabling funds to be allocated according to intensity of demands. Thus the free market criterion provides a beginning point in fashioning policy dealing with uneven impact.

Adherence to the free market principle implies the elimination or reduction of barriers to the free flow of credit. How far correction of market imperfections could proceed without stirring a strong political backlash is open to question. Most likely, selective or direct actions will be required to complete the task of minimizing uneven impact. Effective use of the selective approach requires careful administrative preplanning to avoid hasty, ad hoc measures, with their usual shortcomings.

NONMEMBER BANKS AND THE EFFECTIVENESS OF MONETARY POLICY

In recent years, the growing importance of commercial banks not holding membership in the Federal Reserve System raises the possibility of their weakening the effectiveness of monetary policy. Generally small and holding relatively large excess reserves, nonmember banks respond more sluggishly to restrictive monetary policy than do member banks, taken as a group. However, both groups of banks react fairly promptly to monetary ease.

Compared to changes in the growth rate for member bank credit, non-member banks show smaller cyclical variations, and changes in nonmember bank credit growth rates exhibit a lag of some six months during periods of restrictive monetary policy. These results may reflect differences in size and location of nonmember banks, since studies indicate smaller banks located in nonmetropolitan areas generally are slow to respond to monetary restraint.

The impact of nonmember banks on the effectiveness of monetary policy is a debatable issue. Many analysts suggest that monetary policy is not retarded by the existence of nonmember banks because member banks control an overwhelming proportion of commercial banking assets. Other observers, minimizing the significance of asset and deposit concentrations within the member bank system, stress the importance of nonmember bank operating results. As a case in point, in 1969 restrictive monetary policy saw an appreciable spurt in nonmember bank deposits while member bank deposits declined. In the same year, the increase in total credit extended by nonmember banks was about 75 percent of the increase in member bank credit. These results occurred even though nonmember banks held less than one-fifth of total commercial bank deposits. Furthermore, in 1969 the two groups of banks had sharply diverging growth rates for earning assets: 3.6 percent for member banks compared with 11.7 percent for nonmember banks.

Additional contrasting results emerge when member and nonmember banks are grouped according to deposit size. During the credit crunch of 1969–1970, for example, nonmember banks in all size categories grew faster in total deposits, gross loans, and loans and investments than did member banks. Typically, the larger nonmember banks (with deposits exceeding $500 million) had the greatest differential growth rates.

Sensitive to these operating differences between member and nonmember banks, some observers suggest compulsory Federal Reserve membership for all institutions holding demand deposits.[7]

SOME REFORM PROPOSALS

The existence of lags and the uneven impact of monetary policy has elicited various proposals for improving the operating effectiveness of monetary

7. See Chapter 8, the section entitled "Suggested Changes in Federal Reserve Structure and Operations."

policy. A much debated approach that focuses on the role of monetary lags is the monetarist position already alluded to previously. Drawing on extensive empirical studies, monetarists contend that a long and variable lag exists between changes in monetary conditions and their effects on the economy. This finding suggests that current monetary changes be made for moderating future rather than present economic imbalances. However, monetary actions oriented toward anticipating expected changes in economic activity cannot provide satisfactory results, given the existing imperfect art of economic forecasting. Hence, to avoid the destabilizing effects associated with untimely discretionary monetary policy, the recommended strategy is to achieve a constant rate of growth in the money supply. Here the automatic rule of a fixed money supply growth rate is substituted for the monetary authority's discretionary approach. Proponents of the rules approach to monetary policy avoid any claims of a magical cure-all for their proposal. They do insist that the scheme would minimize destabilizing effects associated with discretionary monetary changes.

Sensitive to academic discussion of rules versus authority in monetary policy making, and after the credit crunch of late 1966 and the mini-recession of 1967, the Joint Economic Committee of Congress held hearings in May 1968 relating to appropriate guidelines for the conduct of monetary policy. These hearings, which reflected the diverse views of various monetary experts, provided the backdrop for the committee's subsequent report in which it proposed, among other things:

Congress should advise the Federal Reserve System that variations in the rate of increase of the money stock (currency plus demand deposits adjusted) ought not to be too great or sharp. In normal times, for the present, the desirable range of variation appears to be within the limits of 2 to 6 percent per annum, measured on a quarter-by-quarter basis—a range that centers on the rate of long-run increase in the potential gross national product in constant dollars, which is our sustainable real growth rate.[8]

This recommendation followed the spirit of earlier committee findings that Congress should carry more responsibility in guiding economic stabilization policy and that an experimental determination should be made of the aggregative economic effects associated with less variation in money supply growth.

8. *Standards for Guiding Monetary Action*, U. S. Congress, Joint Economic Committee, 90th Congress, 2d Session, 1968, p. 19.

In its report the committee took note of the variety of objectives for monetary policy and recommended that Congress make some priority ranking of these different objectives. The committee stressed the interconnections between monetary and fiscal policies and recognized that under certain conditions monetary actions necessarily must facilitate management of the federal debt. In this context, the committee acknowledged that the Federal Reserve cannot simultaneously stabilize the money stock and interest rates. Therefore, it urged congressional adoption of appropriate fiscal policies to avoid potential problems such as those arising from sharp disintermediation of funds from financial institutions, inflated mortgage interest rates, international capital flows, and other factors.

In answer to the committee's request, the Federal Reserve agreed to make annual projections of financial developments that would be consistent with the economic forecasts in the *Economic Report of the President.* To the committee's request for quarterly reports on money supply growth, the Federal Reserve proposed a more comprehensive analysis of significant financial developments following each calendar quarter.

Although the committee's recommendation for a formal congressional mandate specifying close control over growth in the money supply has not brought congressional action, its report spotlighted the monetarist view of monetary policy making. If nothing else, the report provided a channel for communicating to monetary authorities congressional sentiments on standards for monetary actions. Finally, it may be inferred that the Federal Reserve's increased attention to monetary aggregates in the early 1970s reflects at least partial adherence to the committee's recommendation for more disciplined control of the money supply growth. It is conceivable that in some future year Congress may amend the Federal Reserve Act to include a specific reference to an allowable range for adjusting growth in the money supply or in some other monetary aggregates.

Proposals aimed at smoothing the uneven impact of monetary policy generally entail revamping Federal Reserve operations to promote socially desirable flows of credit to particular sectors. One variant of this approach suggests widening the scope of Federal Reserve open market operations to include trading in securities issued by federally sponsored agencies directing credit into the housing and agricultural sectors. Interestingly, the Federal Reserve now conducts open market transactions in federal government agency securities under authority granted by the Congress in 1968.

Another proposal, as yet not formally enacted, for achieving a relatively more uniform impact of monetary policy involves the application of structured reserve requirements against bank assets rather than deposits and other liabilities. Considered initially by congressional committees in the early 1950s, asset reserve requirement proposals have attracted recent attention from observers sensitive to the uneven impact arising from monetary policy. As indicated in Chapter 10, setting required reserve ratios at different levels for different kinds of assets would tend to induce banks to extend credit to specified types of borrowers, because the level of reserve requirements is inversely related to bank profitability. Although many major foreign central banks frequently employ measures channeling credit into priority uses, traditionally the Federal Reserve regards market forces as superior to administrative or statutory discretion in allocating credit among various sectors. This view focuses on the central bank's task of affecting aggregate, rather than specific, credit flows. Thus the debate continues on the efficacy of direct allocation of credit. Indeed, future discussion of this policy issue should increase as the community's concern for social priorities increases.

KEY TERMS

Recognition lag	Procyclical
Action lag	Countercyclical
Inside lag	Regulation Q
Outside lag	

REVIEW QUESTIONS

1. Why is it important to distinguish among the recognition lag, the action lag, and the outside lag?
2. What do empirical investigations indicate about the time involved in monetary policy lags?
3. Discuss some of the possible remedies for improving the operating effectiveness of monetary policy.
4. One of the criticisms of an active use of monetary policy involves its so-called secondary effects or uneven impact. Discuss.

5. Discuss any lag arising from the use of fiscal policy and how it differs from monetary policy lags.

6. Reforms have been suggested to improve the operating efficiency of monetary policy. Discuss.

SUGGESTED READINGS

Cargill, Thomas F., and Robert A. Meyer. "The Time Varying Response of Income to Changes in Monetary and Fiscal Policy." *The Review of Economics and Statistics* 60 (February 1978): 1–7.

Harper, Charles P., and Clifford L. Fry. "Consistent Empirical Results with Almon's Method: Implications for the Monetary versus Fiscal Policy Debate." *The Journal of Finance* 33 (March 1978): 187–198.

Mason, John M. "Two Problems of Monetary Control Resulting from the Lag in Effect of Monetary Policy." *Southern Economic Journal* 42 (January 1976): 496–501.

Chapter Twenty-Two

STABILIZATION POLICY:
GOALS AND TRADE-OFFS

Because monetary policy is concerned with achieving economic stabilization, it is important to consider specifically the various goals toward which stabilization policy is directed. In this chapter, after discussing the definitions and measurement of different economic goals, we will analyze the trade-offs among individual goals, with particular reference to the Phillips curve approach. Finally, we will give an overview of the coordination of monetary actions with other types of stabilization policy, especially fiscal policy.

There are few, if any, hard answers provided in this chapter. Most of the major questions are continuously debated within the economics profession and in other public policy arenas. By the end of the chapter, readers will have to decide for themselves which camp they wish to belong to—Keynesian or monetarist, or something in between.

ECONOMIC STABILIZATION: GOALS AND OBJECTIVES

Monetary policy plays a major role in efforts to stabilize the economy. The concern for economic stability is reflected in various policy goals. In a modern society like the United States a regard for economic stability emerges in the establishment of specific economic goals, for example, as reflected in the passage of the Employment Act of 1946. These economic objectives, whose importance to society varies, generally include high-level employment, price-level stability, and maximum economic growth. We will examine certain definitional and measurement aspects relating to each of these goals.

High-Level Employment

Almost all people agree on the desirability of *high-level employment* within the economy, but they do not agree about its precise definition. At the extreme, it may be observed that high-level (or full) employment does not imply the complete absence of unemployed labor. In the actual economy, beset with frictional elements and other rigidities of labor markets, there is a certain irreducible amount of unemployment at any one time. The consensus among economic analysts, allowing for these frictional factors, was that high-level employment existed in the United States when unemployment was around 3 or 4 percent of the total civilian labor force. Now, with the recognition of changes in the labor force—like a higher labor-force participation rate by women and apparently increased numbers of individuals with deficient job skills—a strong movement has developed away from the definition of full employment as a given percentage of unemployment. As a consequence, presidents, whether Republican or Democrat, no longer commit themselves to a full-employment level of 4 percent.

Sources of Unemployment. In an economy as large and complex as that of the United States, many different sources of unemployment exist. We must briefly examine each of these sources before we can judge whether or not the unemployment each causes is amenable to change through monetary and fiscal policy.

One source of unemployment is individuals who are between jobs. They have quit one job and have not yet begun employment elsewhere. This form of unemployment is known as *frictional unemployment.*

A second source of unemployment is *seasonal* factors: labor demand varies with the weather and the calendar. For example, construction activity tends to decline in some regions in the winter. Localities catering to tourists experience predictable swings in employment rates. The heavy annual influx of students following the end of the school year is another major seasonal element in labor markets.

A third cause of unemployment is connected with *geographical* factors. The locations of job openings often differ from those of unemployed workers. There are several facets to the geographical immobility of labor, including lack of knowledge concerning available job vacancies and psychological and monetary costs involved in moving to new localities. This geographical immobility means that large concentrations of unemployed workers remain in certain localities despite the existence of job opportunities elsewhere. For example, unemployed aerospace workers continued to reside in such attractive regions as southern California and the Pacific Northwest around Seattle in the early 1970s.

Fourth, *structural* factors significantly affect unemployment, especially as skill requirements for job openings change rapidly. Specifically, structural unemployment originates when the experience or training of the unemployed workers does not match the jobs available. It takes time and resources to improve skills and relocate workers to take advantage of job opportunities. The hardcore unemployment found among teenagers, high-school dropouts, ghetto residents, the inhabitants of Appalachia, and women trying to re-enter the labor force after years away reflects mainly structural aspects.

Fifth, *cyclical* changes or fluctuations in the level of economic activity affect the level of employment.[1] As the economy goes into a recession, the level of unemployment increases; as the rate of economic growth increases, unemployment generally decreases.

The sixth and final cause of unemployment to be discussed here[2] is *discrimination* against certain groups in the labor force. Here job opportunities are restricted on the basis of various social criteria such as race, creed, color, national origin, political or religious affiliation, age, and sex. Social factors are a most insidious impediment to the effective working of labor markets.

Solutions. Examining the causes of unemployment, we can see that monetary and fiscal policy are not going to be equally effective in reducing the unemployment brought about by all of these causes. For example, unemployment resulting from adverse weather is not subject to change by monetary or fiscal policy. Moreover, unemployment or underemployment (the use of labor in positions of lower quality than the qualifications of the labor call for) arising from discrimination is based on ignorance and is probably handled best through educational and perhaps legal remedies. Consequently, monetary and fiscal policy are not very effective in dealing with this type of unemployment. However, this is not to say that economic conditions do not affect the

---

1. While *cyclical* connotes a predictable regularity, here it is used to imply *fluctuation* only.
2. Other causes of unemployment exist but are not discussed here. The interested reader should seek a reference in the area.

level of unemployment arising from discrimination. As an economy experiences a recession and someone has to be laid off, it will most likely be people who are objects of prejudice or the newest employees with the least seniority (who were probably the last to be hired). On the other hand, during times when economic conditions make it profitable to hire those who might ordinarily be discriminated against—during wartime, for example—patterns of discrimination may break down and not be re-erected later. Sometimes familiarity breeds understanding. Thus monetary and fiscal policy, to the degree that they affect the level of economic activity, may accentuate or diminish the level of unemployment arising from discrimination; they do not eliminate ignorance, however.

Similarly, unemployment arising from geographical factors is not directly affected by monetary and fiscal policy. Programs designed to inform individuals about job opportunities elsewhere and to help them move to new locations are probably more effective. Fiscal policy may be able to relieve unemployment in some regions if programs can be instituted in those regions. Frequently, however, either specially designed programs for a given area are not possible or skills are required that are not possessed by the unemployed in an area.

Structural sources of unemployment are not themselves directly affected by monetary and fiscal policy. To the extent that individuals without the required skills find jobs because of shortages in the labor market, increased costs in the production of products or services appear, either because these workers cannot do their jobs correctly or because businesses incur training costs, implicitly or explicitly. These costs will in turn add to pressures for price increases. Under more normal economic circumstances these people simply do not find jobs.

Frictional unemployment, in some ways, marks the irreducible minimum for unemployment. Most people have to be unemployed part of the time in order to be able to change jobs. The fact that individuals are changing jobs is an indication that the market place is working; inputs are being allocated where they are most needed. We might argue that it is possible to get individuals to change jobs more quickly, but except in unusual circumstances such as a major war, this is unlikely to happen.

As a consequence, cyclical unemployment caused by fluctuations in the level of economic activity appears to be the sole type of unemployment that monetary or fiscal policy might attack with any success. However, whether monetary or fiscal policy is successful or desirable depends on whether one is a Keynesian or a monetarist. As we have seen,[3] Keynesians believe that monetary policy is unlikely to be as effective as fiscal policy, and that fiscal policy can significantly influence the level of economic activity.

On the other hand, monetarists, because of the lags involved, generally prefer that monetary policy not be used as a stabilization tool. They feel that an easier monetary policy instituted to fight a recession usually makes its effects felt later during an upturn and hence results in inflation instead of lower unemployment. Similarly, a more restrictive monetary policy would probably increase unemployment later, rather than only act to curtail inflation, as it was designed to do. As far as fiscal policy is concerned, monetarists believe that any real effects from an expansionary fiscal policy are likely to be short term. More importantly, fiscal policy would probably result in crowding out.[4]

Hence to what degree monetary and fiscal policy can affect the unemployment level efficiently considering all the costs involved is a point of contention between monetarists and Keynesians. But what is important to note is that a statistic giving an unemployment rate of, say, 5.5 percent is not very informative. One would like to know if the unacceptable part of that unemployment rate (that is, the percentage above that measuring the frictional unemployment element) is the result of cyclical problems, structural factors, discrimination, or whatever. Not all have an equal potential for modification by monetary or fiscal policy.

Price-Level Stability

The economic and social costs associated with high unemployment give added importance to the goal of high-level employment for the community. The individual thrown out of work as a result of public policies aimed at moderating the rate of inflation probably gets little comfort from knowing that such painful effects are an unavoidable aspect of the pursuit of *price-level stability*. Quite likely, access to a job and the opportunity to stay ahead of the rate of price increases have strong appeal to many people. Many workers typically

3. See Chapter 20.
4. See Chapter 20.

regard inflationary effects generated within a high employment economy to be an inconvenient, but tolerable, cost of having access to jobs.

Nevertheless, price-level stability is an important goal of economic stabilization policy because price-level instability, especially in the form of inflation, can have widespread and adverse effects in the economy. The unfavorable side effects arising from inflation include a lessening of economic efficiency, an inequitable and capricious distortion of the distribution of income, and a weakened international economic position.

Price-Level Stability: Meaning and Measurement. Because a compelling case can be made for the high priority given price stability as a policy objective, we should examine its operational meaning and measurement. At the outset, we should note that the concept of price stability does not imply stable or unchanging prices. As an economic goal, emphasis is on stability in the average level of prices. The goal of a stable average level of prices allows for the many individual prices within that average to fluctuate in response to changing market forces. These market forces would reflect such underlying factors as changing patterns of taste or preference, changes in the level of demands, or modifications in the structure of costs. In this sense, then, recognition is given to the price mechanism's role in serving as a rationing or allocative device in guiding consumer choices and in organizing production. Changes in individual prices provide basic data for facilitating the allocation of resources among the many demands in the economy.

On an operational basis, relative price-level stability exists when the annual rate of increase of prices, measured by an appropriate price index, is less than 2 percent. The 2 percent benchmark reflects the allowance for certain technical problems encountered in the construction of price indexes. A particularly difficult problem involves adjusting the index's "market basket" of items to reflect technological change, which affects the quality of goods and services purchased, and to reflect variations in tastes and preferences. When price increases are linked to an upgrading of quality for specific items included in a given price index, it is not feasible to eliminate completely the qualitative improvement factor. Thus commonly used price indexes contain some upward or inflationary bias, which must be taken into account in judging results for price-level stability.

Three principal sources of data involving the measurement of price changes are the consumer price index, the producer price index, and the

GNP implicit price deflator, sometimes called the implicit price index. As outlined in Chapter 14, the suitability of these indexes as broad indicators of price changes is gauged by the purposes for which they were designed.

Inflation and Economic Efficiency. In a strong inflationary setting, economic inefficiency emerges fairly rapidly. In a situation in which rising aggregate demand propels the economy along a growth path that is incompatible with long-run real output capabilities, prices tend to increase along a broad front. Heightened business activity tends to tighten labor markets and to generate the employment of less productive workers, thus reducing the economy's productivity. Furthermore, overall productivity is dampened as productive capacity utilization rates exceed optimal levels and increasingly less efficient capital goods are utilized.

In this context, though output per man-hour declines, forceful wage demands emerge in lagged response to the previous rise in prices. Recent experience suggests that wage demands attempt to recoup the real income lost through prior price rises and also to anticipate expected price increases. Pressing wage demands, accompanied by lessened productivity gains, thrust unit costs of production upward. In turn, mounting costs induce firms to increase prices to protect profit margins, and thus the cost-price ratchet effect may generate a self-reinforcing inflationary process. The more this momentum grows the greater the likelihood that the inflationary psychology will persist, even in the face of faltering excess demand.

Inflation and Distribution of Income and Wealth. Beyond having adverse repercussions on economic efficiency, inflation has an arbitrary effect on the distribution of income and wealth. Although certain groups in the economy may find that their money incomes respond readily to rising prices, other groups on relatively fixed incomes are more vulnerable to inflation. Retired groups, for example, obtain income largely from pensions and other sources of retirement income connected with savings. These incomes derive partly from fixed money values in the form of saving deposits, insurance policies, and bonds. Even allowing for some appreciation in value for these assets—for example, increased interest rates paid on savings or legislated increases in social security benefits—retired people can suffer appreciable losses in real income as prices rise in the economy. Even though some workers and entrepreneurs may be able to improve their real income positions relative to others during inflationary periods, there is no compelling evidence that either business or labor, as a group, has extracted permanently larger gains in real income because of inflation. It is also doubtful whether inflation has altered significantly the long-run distribution of income between business and labor. Inflationary gains accruing to business and labor are more apparent than real, since advances made by specific business and labor sectors are usually offset by erosion in real income of less favorably situated workers or businesses.

Inflation and the International Sector. Inflation's adverse effects on the country's international economic position emphasizes the importance of price-level stability as a goal of economic stabilization policy. Appreciable inflation experienced by the United States after 1965 is a contributory factor in the steady decline of a once large merchandise-trade surplus. Reduced competitiveness stemming from inflation has a direct adverse effect on both export- and import-competing industries. Increased resort to protectionism by the United States would most likely stimulate retaliation by foreign nations, thus setting back the steady advance to freer trade in the world economy. Heightened tariff and nontariff barriers to trade would indeed reduce the allocative efficiency of a free market system.

Controlling Inflation. Both Keynesians and monetarists agree that inflation cannot continue without increases in the money supply to support it. However, they do not agree so readily on the means to eliminate or reduce inflation. Monetarists would prefer never to let the inflationary process begin (which is accomplished by limiting the growth rate of the money supply). Once it has begun, however, monetarists argue for a decrease in growth rates of the money supply. Whether a gradual or a sharp decrease is suggested depends on the individual making the case and the severity of the inflation. Monetarists contend that the sharper the decrease in money-supply growth rates, the more likely a recession will result. However, sometimes they argue that it is more efficient to pay the price for a current monetary policy that has gone out of control—in other words, suffer a recession now and get it over with.

At the same time, monetarists would generally contend that deficit spending has a tendency to cause inflation or increase it: deficit spending tends to drive up interest rates as the demand for funds increases when the government borrows to finance the deficit. Increased interest rates in turn decrease investment, ceteris paribus. To offset the higher interest rates, which are perceived by many as a threat to the continued health of the economy, strong pressures exist to increase the money supply. And increased money-supply growth rates, according to monetarists, necessarily imply increased inflationary pressures.

Keynesians do not see inflation as a necessary result of an easy monetary policy or a fiscal policy involving deficit spending. Keynesians are likely to emphasize the level of unemployment. The higher the unemployment rate, the more an expansionary monetary and fiscal policy will result in growth and not inflation. Because Keynesians see fiscal policy as being more effective than monetary policy, they generally advocate that monetary policy be used in a supporting role. Further, Keynesians are likely to stress that fighting inflation will necessarily result in increases in unemployment. They conclude that inflation may be a relatively lighter penalty to pay for lower levels of unemployment than vice versa.[5]

Economic Growth

Concern for economic growth is a vital aspect of economic stabilization policy in any modern economy. Economic growth considerations acquired additional significance for the United States in the post–World War II period. As the leading nation of the Western world, the United States took on added economic burdens in providing development aid and in countering various pressures arising from war—both "hot" and "cold." The USSR's launching of Sputnik in autumn of 1957 moved the question of economic growth to center stage. To this day, as well as for the future, sustained economic growth is a major objective of economic policy making in the United States.

Some Measures of Economic Growth. As a concept, economic growth has several facets, both quantitative and qualitative. Not surprisingly, there are several ways of measuring economic growth, since analysts are sensitive to the limitations inherent in using only one measure. The commonly used measures are all linked to output, or capability to produce output, of goods and services. One measure of economic growth for a particular country is the annual rate

---

5. The trade-off between unemployment and inflation is the basis of the Phillips curve, discussed later in this chapter.

of growth in total real output, that is, GNP adjusted for price change. However, the growth rate in real GNP must be contrasted with the population growth rate to determine the growth in average output available per individual. In this case, the specific measure consists of the annual rate of growth in real output (or real GNP) per capita. Furthermore, allowance should be made for the fact that not all improvements in productivity are reflected in the growth of real output per capita. Productivity gains may be taken via more leisure afforded by a shorter work week. Here the specific measure of economic growth is the annual rate of growth in real output (or real GNP) per man-hour. In operational terms, then, economic growth as an objective of economic stabilization policy involves sustained growth by one or more of the measures just described.

Growth Targets and Past Results. The record of the past provides background for gauging a specific target rate of growth for the economy. Since 1890 the average annual rate of growth in real GNP has been 3.4 percent, while that for output per man-hour has been 2.3 percent. Year-to-year growth rates are not uniform, and data taken over a long period indicate no tendency for long-term growth rates to diminish.

Since 1948 the average annual growth rate for real GNP in the United States has been closer to 4 percent than to 3 percent, while the growth rate for output per man-hour has been closer to 3 percent than to 2 percent. Annual changes have fluctuated widely within this period. From a more distant perspective, substantial variations have occurred not only from year to year but from decade to decade. Periodically, business recessions have dampened growth. Viewed conservatively, the postwar growth rates in the United States do not necessarily establish a trend. The postwar experience may constitute another instance in our economic history where growth rates have fluctuated, up or down, for short periods.

An example of the effect of these changes in growth rates and productivity can be seen in Figure 22.1. Figure 22.1 shows actual and potential *real* GNP from 1966 to 1979 and the output of goods and services lost during the 1973–1975 recession. Observe the two growth paths for potential GNP in constant dollars. The "new" growth path for potential GNP has been scaled down. The "old" growth path was based on an unemployment rate of 4 percent, which was assumed to be normal when the economy was operating at capacity. Due to increased participation in the labor force by younger workers and their

---

Figure 22.1 ACTUAL AND POTENTIAL GROSS NATIONAL
PRODUCT, 1966–1979

In billions of 1972 dollars; seasonally adjusted annual rates.

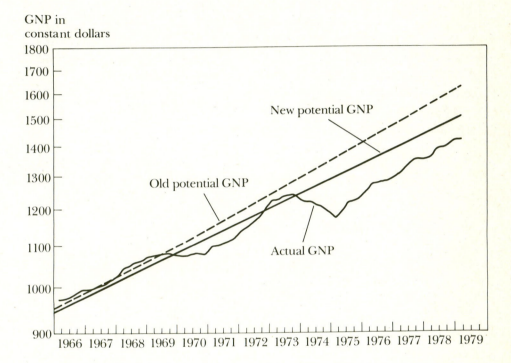

GNP in
constant dollars

Sources: *Economic Report of the President 1977*, p. 55; *Survey of Current Business.*

higher "normal" unemployment rates, the new growth path for potential GNP assumes an unemployment rate of 4.9 percent. Furthermore, the new growth path reflects the utilization level of fixed capital. The level of fixed capital utilization that is used as the full-employment level for capital is 86 percent. This percentage is based on years in which the economy was operating at what was seen to be capacity.

The new growth rate for potential GNP in constant dollars for the years from 1962 to 1976 gives an average annual growth rate of 3.6 percent, down from the previous estimate of 3.9 percent. The projected average annual growth rate for potential GNP is estimated to be 3.5 percent for the near future.

This reduction in the potential growth rate of GNP has meant a decrease of $58 billion in the estimate of potential GNP for 1976 (in 1972 dollars). Of that $58 billion gap between actual and potential GNP, $30 to $40 billion represents a lower growth in labor productivity and $5 to $10 billion the higher "normal" unemployment rate of 4.9 percent. The lower growth rate of potential GNP occurred despite above-normal increases in the labor force itself. Offsetting this above-normal growth in the labor force has been a decrease in the number of hours worked on average and changes in the age-sex composition of the labor force.

At this point, changes in labor productivity are difficult to estimate. The decrease that occurred during the recession ending in 1975 indicates that realistic productivity increases may now be at a lower level. On the other hand, over the next few years we may find that as the economic recovery continues, labor productivity increases will return to the 2 percent rate or even above it. Depending on what the data show, the average annual growth rate for potential GNP may have to be revised again shortly.[6]

If postwar trends in output per hours worked, labor force participation, and hours of work persist over the next twenty-five years, the private sector's productivity would increase by about 130 percent and per capita real GNP by about 80 percent.

Controlling Economic Growth. The use of monetary and fiscal policy to affect the rate of economic growth is debatable. Economic growth models show that, in the long run, the rate of economic growth is a function of real variables like the growth rate of technology, and of factors of production such as labor. In the long run, in fact, any increase in real *per capita* income is probably solely a function of improvements in technology, where technology is defined to include increased skill or educational levels of labor.[7] An increase in real per capita income is possible if individuals begin to work at the same intensity but for longer hours, if they work harder, or some combination of the two; however, changes like these are unlikely. An increase in the amount of capital

6. For a more complete discussion, see the *Economic Report of the President—1977*, pp. 52–57.

7. The reader should examine a book on growth models, especially the neoclassical growth model. For example, see Edward J. Shapiro, *Macroeconomic Analysis*, 4th ed. (New York: Harcourt Brace Jovanovich, 1978), pp. 413–422.

per worker—or *capital deepening*—could also increase per capita income. However, an increase in the capital stock per capita would require that the interest rate be lowered on average to make a higher level of investment economically feasible, and over the long run this seems highly improbable. Hence if monetary and fiscal policy are to enhance the rate of economic growth it must be in a short-run reference. More specifically, the best that can be hoped for is that the correct use of both monetary and fiscal policy will permit the economy to grow at its potential growth rate instead of below it. The fear is that the incorrect use of either or both will condemn the economy to grow at less than its potential.

As we saw in Chapter 19, monetarists claim that monetary policy cannot be used correctly in an active way to alter the employment level. They believe that the economy operates by and large at the natural rate of unemployment and that any use of monetary policy other than passive aggravates the situation more than ameliorates it. Except in the case of a depression (which the monetarist would see as probably the result of an active and generally inherent incorrect use of monetary policy), monetarists would argue against the ability of an active monetary policy to influence the unemployment rate and hence the rate of economic growth in a desirable way.

Monetarists contend, in fact, that economic fluctuations are generally explained by changes in growth rates of the money supply. They hold that economic recessions are generally caused by decreases in the money-supply growth rate and that severe recessions (depressions) are the result of absolute decreases in the money supply over a sufficient period. An absolute decrease in the money supply for three or four weeks would not be critical, nor might a gradual decrease over a long period like ten or twenty years if it were correctly perceived by the general public. On the other hand, monetarists believe that increases in the money-supply growth rates generally cause increased money income. Granting the monetarist assumption that the economy approximates the natural rate of unemployment, then increased money-supply growth rates imply that inflation (or less deflation) will result, depending on whether the growth rate exceeds or falls short of the natural growth rate of the economy. Hence for the monetarists, variable money-supply growth rates are more detrimental than beneficial to growth. Variable growth rates are held to be destabilizing.

Keynesians, on the other hand, might argue that economic growth can benefit in the short run by an active use of monetary policy. Keynes himself

Figure 22.2   FULL-EMPLOYMENT BALANCED-BUDGET CONCEPT

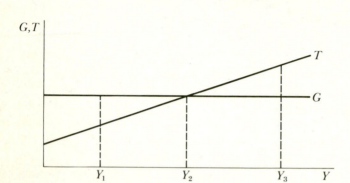

believed that it was important that the interest rate be kept low to encourage investment and therefore avoid a stationary or nongrowth economy. And in 1978 Keynesians believe in increased growth rates of the money supply to help decrease the rate of unemployment, thereby increasing the rate of economic growth. They would see monetary policy as a way to make economic downturns less severe (whereas monetarists would see any attempt to diminish the severity of recessions as implying an increased severity in the ensuing economic upturn's price problems).

However, as we saw in Chapter 20, Keynesians would generally prefer that the primary tool used in fighting economic downturns be fiscal policy. They feel that the effects are more direct and more predictable. The use of the full-employment balanced budget is intended to go a good part of the distance in seeing that fiscal policy is used correctly.

Full-Employment Balanced Budget. The objective of the *full-employment balanced budget* is that the federal budget not be balanced in any given year, but that expenditures and taxes be governed such that if the economy were operating at full employment, the budget would be balanced. Figure 22.2 shows a governmental expenditure function and tax function. Government expenditures G are assumed to be autonomous of the income level, which is measured on the horizontal axis, whereas taxes are assumed to be a function of income.[8]

8. In Chapter 15 we considered only an autonomous tax function, not one that is a function of income (that is, induced), which would be of the form $T = \bar{T} + tY$ where t is the marginal propensity to tax.

Balancing the budget at full employment instead of attempting to do so on an annual basis means that no fiscal drag would be created, so that the economy will approximate full employment more closely with minimal inflationary pressures. *Fiscal drag* exists whenever tax revenues generated exceed governmental expenditures. It is of concern because when tax revenues exceed governmental expenditures, the result is decreased aggregate demand, ceteris paribus. Hence one wants fiscal drag to minimize inflationary pressures but not impede the attainment of full employment.

For example, if the current income level were Y_2 and full employment were Y_3 in Figure 22.2, fiscal drag would work against any economic growth toward full employment. As the economy began to move to higher levels of employment than that represented by income level Y_2, the budget would go into surplus, which would tend to cut short any reductions in unemployment. Likewise, if the current income level were Y_2 and the full-employment level were Y_1, then the implied fiscal policy would be one of continued inflationary pressure and not one of moving in the direction of full employment. Hence the budget is to be balanced only if the economy is operating at full employment.

If income level Y_2 represented the full-employment income level, the budget would be balanced because taxes and expenditures are equal. Hence if the actual income level were Y_1, it would imply that the government should run a deficit; that is, expenditures would be greater than tax revenues generated, resulting in growth potential. If instead the current income level were Y_3, which implies that the economy is operating at a level in excess of full employment, the government should run a surplus, which, ceteris paribus, should put pressure on the economy for a slowdown in its growth rate.

Under the full-employment balanced-budget concept, it is up to the Congress and the administration to determine what combination of changes in expenditures and taxes are to be enacted to bring about an intersection of the two functions at the full-employment income level. This might involve changes in G or T alone, or some combination of the two. Thus if the current income level were Y_2 and full employment were Y_3, taxes could be decreased or governmental expenditures increased.

The current problem with the use of the full-employment balanced-budget concept is that there seems to be little difficulty running the deficit in the federal budget when the economy is operating at less than full employment. Every member of Congress and every senator has at least one project requiring increased governmental expenditures and/or would like to be identified with a tax cut. However, running a surplus in the budget when the economy is operating at employment levels exceeding full employment seems to be an impossibility. First, groups that are bearing a greater percentage of the existing unemployment than others begin to press for lower unemployment rates to define full employment. Second, as the unemployment level falls and the government receives increased tax revenues, those who have felt slighted under previous budgets begin to press for spending increases for themselves. Hence only a minority of those formulating fiscal policy argue for a surplus, whether brought about by expenditure reductions or by tax increases (and no one wants to be identified with the latter).

Note that adherence to a full-employment balanced-budget concept goes part way to making the use of fiscal policy a passive measure. Theoretically, the limits of the game are stated. The only active issues to be decided are about the specific alterations in tax and spending policies enacted to bring about their equality at full employment (however full employment is defined).

Monetarists are not nearly as willing to accept the concept of the full-employment balanced-budget concept as are Keynesians. As we saw in Chapter 20, monetarists believe that more spending by the government crowds out spending in the private sector. This crowding out, they fear, reduces the overall productive ability of the economy. Spending on courthouses, swimming pools, welfare, and so on does not automatically result in increased output of goods and services the way that increased spending by the private sector on plant and equipment would. Hence monetarists would be more inclined to argue for trying to balance the budget on a yearly basis and not on the full-employment basis.

Monetarists and Keynesians do not agree on the use of monetary and fiscal policy to make short-run conditions more amenable for growth. Monetarists would claim that the current use of monetary and fiscal policy does not enhance the opportunities for growth, whereas Keynesians would claim that it does (while not denying that it could be used better).

Trade-offs Among Goals: The Phillips Curve

In a world of scarcity, and in an economy beset with rigidities and factor immobilities, it is rarely possible to achieve fully, at one and the same time, all major economic goals and objectives. This has certainly been the United States experience in recent years. Incompatibility among basic economic goals gives rise to the pragmatic view of trade-offs among goals. A trade-off implies that additional progress toward one goal entails decreased achievement of another goal.

Analysis of trade-offs has focused particularly on the relation between the two goals of price stability and high-level employment. A pioneering study by Professor A. W. Phillips, a New Zealander, examined the relation between aggregate unemployment and aggregate money wage rates in Great Britain over the period from 1861 to 1957.[9] Phillips found a clear association between the two variables, with higher rates of money wage gains associated with lower rates of unemployment. The regression curve, or curve of "best fit," depicting the relation between the two variables is referred to as the *Phillips curve*. However, economists often use this same label to depict the relation between rates of unemployment and price, rather than wage, changes.

Following the work of Phillips, other economists have found that low rates of unemployment tend to be associated with substantial wage increases of inflationary proportions. Conversely, they have observed that the higher the rate of unemployment the lower the rate of inflation. The observable relation evidenced by the Phillips curve seems to indicate that as unemployment declines, prices rise as the economy nears full employment.

In Figure 22.3 a Phillips curve has been derived for the years from 1960 to 1969. The percentage change in prices for each year is measured on the vertical axis using the GNP implicit price deflator as a measure of price change; the unemployment rate is on the horizontal axis. As we can see, the curve or regression line fits the data points very nicely. This indicates that the Phillips curve seemingly reflects a real, inverse relation between percentage changes in the price level and changes in the unemployment rate.

However, it should be emphasized that a given Phillips curve shows past relations between annual price increases and unemployment rates. There is no assurance that such relations will persist into the future; the curve may shift. Furthermore, care must be exercised in using the Phillips curve as a guide to policy since not only can the relation between the two variables

9. A. W. Phillips, "The Relationship Between Unemployment and the Rate of Change of Money Wage Rates in the United Kingdom, 1861–1957," *Economica* (November 1958): 283–299.

Figure 22.3 PHILLIPS CURVE FOR UNITED STATES, ANNUAL DATA, 1960–1969

The line estimated for 1960–1969 is

$$\log y = 4.30081 - 2.26881 \log x; \ R^2 = 0.943$$

where y is the percentage change in the GNP implicit price deflator and x is the unemployment rate.

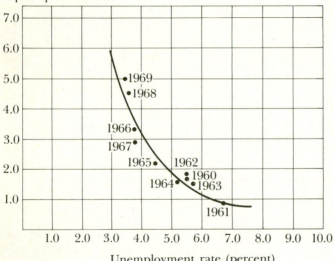

Percentage change in GNP implicit price deflator

Unemployment rate (percent)

change over a period, but also appreciable changes in some of the variables can occur within a calendar year, with such changes obscured by use of annual data.

To some analysts, the Phillips curve technique is an interesting, but fruitless, exercise. For example, Milton Friedman believes that the Phillips curve as presented in Figure 22.3 is a short-run phenomenon only and hence is of virtually no value as a policy tool for explaining trade-offs between unemployment and either price-level changes or changes in money wage rates. He claims that the trade-off exists only so long as labor suffers an illusion about real wages.

Figure 22.4 SHORT-RUN AND LONG-RUN PHILLIPS CURVE
ANALYSIS

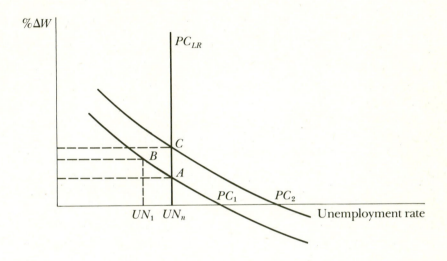

Recall from Chapter 19 that increases in employment required that the quantity of labor demanded increase where the demand for labor is assumed to be a function of the real wage rate (or that the demand for labor increase where money wages are measured on the vertical axis).[10] For the quantity of labor demanded to increase, the real wage rate has to fall. In turn, an increase in the quantity of labor supplied occurs because labor does not recognize that while money wages are rising, the price level is rising faster and hence real wages have fallen. When labor realizes that real wages have fallen, the supply of labor (with money wages on the vertical axis) decreases, that is, shifts to the left. The employment level returns to its original level, real wages are the same, and, although nominal wages are higher, so is the price level by a like percentage.

In Figure 22.4 we begin with a short-run Phillips curve, PC_1. Assume that the money supply is increasing at some rate such that nominal wages are rising at 3 percent annually. Assume further that productivity is increasing by 3 percent annually so that prices can remain constant on average. The

10. See Chapter 19, the section on "Employment."

unemployment rate is UN_n, or the natural rate of unemployment. Now assume that the growth rate of the money supply doubles.

As a result of the increased rate of growth in the money supply, the real wage rate decreases as the price level rises. The decrease in the real wage rate causes an increase in the demand for labor. Hence there is a movement from A to B on PC_1, showing a reduction in unemployment and an increase in prices. Unemployment decreases as long as labor does not recognize that prices are rising faster than money wages. As labor realizes that real wages have decreased, the supply of labor decreases and there is a movement back to the natural rate of unemployment, that is, from B to C. Thus the short-run Phillips curve has shifted up from PC_1 to PC_2. At C, the level of unemployment is the same as at A, but nominal wages have risen because of the increase in the money supply. For unemployment to decrease now, the wage rate has to increase at a faster rate; however, this will be successful only as long as labor again suffers an illusion about its real wage.

Friedman argues that the more correctly price level changes are anticipated, the more vertical the function showing the purported trade-off becomes; that is, if price level changes are perfectly anticipated, the function would be perfectly inelastic and there would be no trade-off. Hence Friedman's long-run Phillips curve is a vertical line. In the long run, the Phillips curve would then look like PC_{LR} in Figure 22.4.

Now let us see what happens when we lower inflation, that is, move from C to A. The economy will initially move down along PC_2, implying higher levels of unemployment but lower levels of nominal wage rate increases, which should mean lower rates of inflation. As expectations are changed to lower levels of inflation, the short-run Phillips curve will shift down. Clearly this is not a painless process. The real cost in eliminating inflation in the short run is increased unemployment and the decreased output of goods and services.

If the Phillips curve explains any trade-off, then it would seem that it must be in a situation where percentage changes in money wages and the price level are random, so that labor cannot anticipate changes correctly. If this is correct then the entire Phillips curve model becomes of rather dubious value as an analytical tool.

The conclusion that the Phillips curve model is of a short-run nature only and of exceedingly limited value may be indicated in Figure 22.5. Data for the years 1970–1978 are given, again comparing percentage changes in the price level and the unemployment rate. Here it is clear that there is no regression

Figure 22.5   ANNUAL DATA COMPARING PERCENTAGE CHANGE IN
GNP IMPLICIT PRICE DEFLATOR AND
UNEMPLOYMENT RATE, 1970–1978

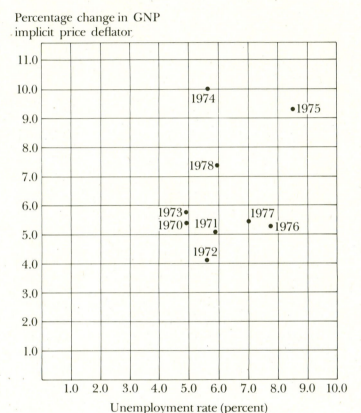

curve that fits the data very well. Hence the stability of the Phillips curve is open to question.

There are many economists who believe that the Phillips curve model shows a trade-off between employment levels and inflation rates. Whether or not the trade-off is in fact as short-run a phenomenon as Friedman and other monetarists believe has yet to be conclusively demonstrated. However, at a minimum, the model offers a chance to debate the point and allows everyone a chance to form an opinion.

Coordination of Stabilization Policies

Achieving the major economic goals of society requires a timely and balanced coordination of stabilization policies. In a democratic free-enterprise society such as the United States, monetary-fiscal policies, impersonal and indirect in their operation, are mainstays in stabilization efforts. Effective coordinated use and blending of fiscal and monetary actions are necessary in order that one does not tend to offset or neutralize the other.

Monetary policy has long been recognized for its flexibility in meeting changing economic conditions. Fiscal policy, on the other hand, is limited in its flexibility, and thus this potentially potent tool is utilized less frequently than is monetary policy. Enactment of various proposals to enhance the flexibility of fiscal policy would make it an even more important device for economic stabilization purposes. Improved flexibility for fiscal policy would facilitate its ready use in combatting inflationary pressures as well as in stimulating expansion in times of economic slack. In an inflationary setting, it is generally agreed, coordinated monetary-fiscal policies are more effective than one policy approach alone. Furthermore, a coordinated approach probably distributes more evenly the burden of restraint among sectors of the economy.

Interrelated, but different, features of monetary and fiscal policies lend themselves to altering the fiscal-monetary mix for meeting more effectively the needs of a particular situation. Some cases illustrating the latter point can be examined. During the credit crunches of 1966 and 1969–1970 monetary restraint in the face of surging credit demands contributed to an appreciable rise in interest rates. Certain sectors of the economy, housing for one, were hit especially hard by rising rates and reduced credit availability. Fiscal restraint linked with less monetary stringency would have eased pressure on these sectors and possibly would have evened the impact over the economy. Balanced monetary-fiscal policies provide a means for altering the distribution of expenditures and resources between consumption and investment. In an expansion fueled heavily by strong consumer demand and marked by sluggish investment activity, fiscal actions restricting consumer income and expenditures could be joined with a monetary policy oriented toward stimulating faster growth in investment and in productive capacity. On the other hand, in an investment boom posing a possible overexpansion in productive capacity, corporate tax changes could be coordinated with a tighter monetary policy to dampen the rise in investment spending.

In a time of economic downturn, the stabilization policy mix could lean more heavily on fiscal action to expand private disposable income. In turn, growth in consumer income and spending would absorb unemployed resources and contribute to a favorable setting for rising investment. Fiscal efforts can directly buoy up consumer disposable income by reducing personal taxes or selectively increasing government spending. The expansive effects generated are probably greater than those derived from an easing of credit. With the employment and profit outlook uncertain, consumers and business firms are hesitant to increase borrowing. As consumer expenditures pace a rise in business activity, excess productive capacity is absorbed. With rising profit expectations and a smaller pool of unutilized resources, policies aimed at fostering investment become more effective. Thus the policy mix could be oriented toward increasing investment as the economy shows stronger recovery.

In an economy experiencing both a recession and a balance-of-payments problem (when exchange rate fluctuations are deemed undesirable as the sole solution to balance-of-payments difficulties), stabilizing policies might rely more heavily on fiscal actions to stimulate consumption. These fiscal actions expanding disposable income would tend to put less downward pressure on short-term interest rates and thus probably lessen short-term capital outflows. In addition, Treasury financing of a fiscal deficit primarily through sale of short-term securities would buoy up short-term rates, with favorable effects for the balance of payments.

The different ways of combining monetary and fiscal policies provide various options for policy makers in achieving the major economic goals. However, it should be recognized that in the actual economy there are many operational elements that can thwart the delicate balancing of monetary and fiscal policies. Indeed, the complex and changing modern economy is not always responsive to the varied orchestration of stabilizing actions.

CONCLUSION

Much of the debate between the monetarists and the Keynesians might seem somewhat esoteric. However, whether or not a person recognizes the debate when it occurs in contemporary events, it exists in battle after not-so-minor battle. In any period, the day-to-day struggle to overcome current difficulties like inflation or what is felt to be excessive unemployment is always of prime concern. But over the past few years, a major change in the monetary-policy debate has been the use of announced target growth rates for monetary aggregates. The use of these target growth rates and the continuous examination of their "correctness" given current economic conditions emphasize the ever-increasing importance of monetary policy as society becomes more aware and curious about the effect of changes in the money supply.

The fact that target growth rates for monetary aggregates are announced is a change that monetarists have been advocating for years. The increased importance of the growth rate of monetary aggregates compared to the past, when the interest rate was almost the sole criterion of monetary policy, indicates the increased stature that the monetarist view has come to hold.

In 1977 the great debate was seen in whether or not Arthur Burns should be reappointed as chairman of the Board of Governors of the Federal Reserve System. In 1978 and 1979 the debate is seen in the "correctness" of money supply growth rates and the appropriate interest rate levels in light of current economic conditions. The economic conditions giving rise to serious questions are the employment level, the inflation rate, and the international position of the United States dollar.

In 1977 and 1978, the economy's bright spot was the reduced unemployment level. After reaching 8.9 percent in the bottom of the 1973–1975 recession (May 1975), unemployment in 1977 averaged 7.0 percent. It had declined to 6.4 percent by December of 1977 and averaged 6.0 percent in 1978. In comparison to previous recoveries, the economy has created jobs faster than usual. The unemployment rate would have fallen faster if the labor force had not been growing at unusually high rates compared to earlier periods. These higher rates reflect the increased participation rate of women and the young.

The dismal side of the picture is that inflation seems to be increasing. Prices rose by 6.8 percent on the consumer price index in 1977, measured from December 1976 to December 1977. Over the twelve months of 1978 prices increased by 9.0 percent (measured by the consumer price index), an increase instead of decrease from the 1977 rate as hoped for. By the end of 1978, inflation rates were approaching double-digit levels.

Finally, the United States dollar, as we know, was under serious pressure internationally, depreciating significantly against many other currencies. President Carter, in November 1978, made a commitment to help regain some of the lost value of the dollar and protect it in the future.

In early 1979 the Federal Reserve's goals were to restrict monetary-aggregate growth rates in order to maintain a generally higher interest rate level. The target interest rate level was a 9.875 percent federal funds rate. This higher interest rate level was intended to help strengthen the dollar internationally and to moderate inflationary pressures domestically by slowing the growth of aggregate demand. The growth rate in monetary aggregates being used to maintain a higher level of interest rates was 6 to 9.5 percent for M_2 as long as M_1 grew no faster than 5 percent annually.

In fact, M_2 in November and December of 1978 grew at 6.25 percent whereas M_1 grew at 0.25 percent. This represented a significant slowdown in growth rates. If these lower growth rates were maintained for approximately six months or longer, a business downturn would be reasonably likely; if they were continued for a shorter period, the chances of a recession would significantly decrease.

Many people feared that as the Federal Reserve became concerned with a growing potential for inflation and began to slow the growth rate of monetary aggregates, it increased (or guaranteed?) the likelihood of a recession in 1979. The question was what was the proper monetary stance for slowing the growth rate without tipping the economy into a recession. The problem was complicated by the OPEC oil price rise announced in late 1978, which was to average 10 percent in 1979. A strong tendency existed to create more money, which would allow prices to rise, thus eliminating the deflationary tendencies that would otherwise occur from this oil price rise. Higher energy prices, ceteris paribus, should mean that other prices would have to fall, and such a situation would generally lead to increased unemployment.

Monetarists would not wish to see monetary aggregates growing at rates that many Keynesians would think harmless in light of the threat to current employment levels. However, significantly decreased growth rates of monetary aggregates, if continued long enough, would most likely bring about a recession. Many Keynesians point out that many sectors of the United States have become relatively well adjusted to higher levels of inflation, and the return to prior levels of inflation would entail a painful and lengthy readjustment period. However, we should note that many of those who would like to see these monetary aggregates grow at a faster rate would be the same ones wanting to hold hearings eighteen to twenty-four months from now as to why prices are rising as rapidly as they are, blaming administered prices, greed, and the monopoly power of unions and business.

Many monetarists recommend "biting the bullet" by decreasing growth rates of monetary aggregates and taking the consequences, especially when they suspect it will be someone else who will be unemployed. At the same time, many Keynesians would seem to be satisfied with postponing the day when we come to terms with the inflation problem, looking at the probable increased unemployment rates that would result from an anti-inflation program.

In any event, three facts appear to be true: this is not the first time nor probably the last that the United States has had an unacceptably high rate of inflation; the problem is not amenable to a simple, painless solution; and there will be a solution of some type. The future promises to be interesting; stick around.

KEY TERMS

Frictional unemployment

Seasonal unemployment

Geographical unemployment

Structural unemployment

Cyclical unemployment

Discrimination unemployment

Price-level stability

Labor productivity

Capital deepening

Full-employment balanced budget

Fiscal drag

Phillips curve

Coordination of monetary
  and fiscal policy

High-level employment

REVIEW QUESTIONS

1. Discuss what the Phillips curve purportedly explains and its importance.

2. Explain whether or not monetary and fiscal policy can increase the rate of economic growth.

3. Does the source of unemployment have any bearing on the potential of either monetary or fiscal policy to change the unemployment rate?

4. Discuss the important considerations in reducing the inflation rate.

5. Using Figure 22.1 and data from a recent *Economic Report of the President* or

Survey of Current Business, find out how well the economy has been performing in comparison to the "new potential GNP" trend line. (The trend line may be extended linearly.)

6. Explain the significance of the full-employment balanced-budget concept.

SUGGESTED READINGS

Helbling, Hans S., and James E. Turley. "A Primer on Inflation: Its Conception, Its Costs, Its Consequences." Federal Reserve Bank of St. Louis, *Review* (February 1975): 2–8.

Karnosky, Denis. "The Link Between Money and Prices—1971–76." Federal Reserve Bank of St. Louis, *Review* (June 1976): 17–23.

Santomero, Anthony M., and John J. Seater. "The Inflation-Unemployment Trade-Off: A Critique of the Literature." *Journal of Economic Literature* XVI (June 1978): 499–544.

Schwab, Stewart, and John J. Seater. "The Unemployment Rate: Time to Give it a Rest?" Federal Reserve Bank of Philadelphia, *Business Review* (May-June 1977): 11–18.

Tatom, John A. "The Welfare Cost of Inflation." Federal Reserve Bank of St. Louis, *Review* (November 1976): 9–22.

INDEX